GENEALOGY
ONLINE

Genealogy Online
Millennium Edition

Elizabeth Powell Crowe

McGraw-Hill
New York · San Francisco · Washington, D.C.
Auckland · Bogotá · Caracas · Lisbon · London · Madrid
Mexico City · Milan · Montreal · New Delhi · San Juan
Singapore · Sydney · Tokyo · Toronto

Library of Congress Cataloging-in-Publication Data

Crowe, Elizabeth Powell.
    Genealogy online/Elizabeth Powell Crowe.—Millennium ed.
      p.   cm.
    Includes index.
    ISBN 0-07-135103-5 (acid-free paper)
    1. Genealogy—Data processing.   2. Internet (Computer network–
Handbooks, manuals, etc. I. Title
CS21.C67   1999
929'.1'0285—dc21   99-39910
                                                CIP

McGraw-Hill

A Division of The McGraw-Hill Companies

*The sponsoring editor for this book was Michael Sprague, the editing supervisor
was Penny Linskey, and the production supervisor was Clare Stanley. It was set
in Century Schoolbook by Don Feldman of McGraw-Hill's Professional Book
composition unit in cooperation with Spring Point Publishing Services.*

Printed and bound by Quebecor/Martinsburg.

Throughout this book, trademarked names are used. Rather than put a trademark symbol after every occurrence of a trademarked name, we used the
names in an editorial fashion only, and to the benefit of the trademark owner,
with no intention of infringement of the trademark. Where such designations
appear in this book, they have been printed with initial caps.

This book is printed on recycled, acid-free paper containing a minimum
of 50% recycled de-inked fiber.

To my mother, Frances Spencer Powell

CONTENTS

Introduction   xiii

 The Basics   1

Chapter 1   Getting Set Up: A Look at Hardware
                         and Connections   3

                       How to Select a Modem   4
                       ISDN and xDSL   7
                       ISDN   7
                       XDSL   9
                       Hold the Phone?   11
                       Web TV   11
                       Choosing an ISP   12
                       Go Shopping   13

Chapter 2   Software   17

                       Communications Software (The Engine)   18
                       Browser   19
                       How Browsers Work   19
                       Which Browser to Use   20
                       What It Looks Like   21
                       FTP   24
                       Mail-Reading Software   26
                       Filters   26
                       Spam Protection   26
                       File Attachments and Formats   32
                       Internet Mail Clients   34
                       Inoculations   36
                       Online-Ready Genealogy Programs   38
                       Ultimate Family Tree   38
                       Family Origins 7.0   38
                       Family Tree Maker   40
                       GedPage 2.0   41
                       The Master Genealogist 4.0   41
                       Generations Easy Tree   43
                       Shop Around   45

Chapter 3	Rules of the Road: How to Surf Happily	47
	Attitudes and Etiquette	47
	Answer, Please	49
	Cautions and Caveats	51
	Sources and Proof	52
Part 2	**The Internet**	**57**
Chapter 4	FTP	59
	Genealogy FTP Sites	61
	RootsWeb	61
	The Genealogy Anonymous FTP Site	63
	Genealogy Online FTP Archive	64
	The U.S. Government Census	65
Chapter 5	Usenet	67
	Complicated, but Useful	69
	Usenet History	70
	The Software	71
	Newsreaders	71
	Browsers	75
	Commercial Online Services	75
	Newsgroups of Interest to Online Genealogists	77
	Binary Files on Usenet	81
	Newsgroup FAQ Files	82
	Net Etiquette and Tips on Usenet	82
	Searching for Information within Newsgroups	85
	Beyond Usenet	86
Chapter 6	Genealogy Mailing Lists	87
	General Subscribing Tips	88
	An In-Depth Visit to ROOTS-L	88
	Some ROOTS-L Rules	90
	Communicating with People and Programs	91
	Available Files and Databases	91
	Putting ROOTS-L to Work	92
	Losing Contact with ROOTS-L	94
	Other Genealogy Mailing Lists	95
	General Genealogy Lists	96

Contents

	Ethnic Groups	99
	Family Name Lists	100
	Historical Groups	101
	Regional Groups	102
	Software Lists	103
	Email Newsletters	105
	Finding More Mailing Lists	107
Chapter 7	The World Wide Web	109
	What Does the World Wide Web Look Like?	110
	Browser Tips and Tricks	110
	Four Score and Seven Sites to See	112
	In-Depth Explorations of Some Major Genealogy Web Sites	128
	Genealogy Home Page (*http://genhomepage.com/*)	129
	AfriGeneas (*http://www.afrigeneas.com*)	131
	DearMYRTLE'S Place (*http://members.aol.com/dearmyrtle/*)	134
	USGenWeb (*http://www.usgenweb.org/*)	137
	Library of Congress (*http://www.loc.gov/*)	140
	Find Your Own Favorites	144
	AOL NetFind	146
	Lycos	148
	Excite	148
	General Directories	149
	People Search Engines	152
	File Search Sites	153
	Searching for Information in Newsgroups	154
	Moving On	154
Chapter 8	Chat: Hail Thy Fellow on the Net!	155
	How It Works	158
	Chat Flavors	160
	AOL Instant Messenger	160
	Ding 2.5	162
	ICQ	164
	Microsoft Chat	166
	mIRC	167
	How to Chat	167

Where to Chat	170
Chat Etiquette	173

Part 3   Specific Online Resources | **177** |

Chapter 9	RootsWeb	179
	RSL—RootsWeb Surname List	180
	Other Search Engines	180
	Automatic Surname Notification Program	182
	GenConnect	183
	Web Sites	183
	ROOTS-L and State Resource Pages	184
	The HelpDesk	185
	RootsWeb Review	186
	Mailing Lists	186
	How RootsWeb Is Different	187

Chapter 10	Online Library Card Catalogs	189
	Connecting to Card Catalogs by Web Browser	191
	Connecting to Card Catalogs by Telnet	194
	Where to Find More Online Card Catalogs	197

Chapter 11	The Church of Jesus Christ of Latter-day Saints	201
	FamilySearch Internet	202
	A Run-Through	203
	Alternative Methods	205
	Other Cool Stuff	205
	How to Use Information from LDS	210
	Some Background	212
	A Visit to an FHC	214
	The Future	216

Chapter 12	Commercial Web Sites	217
	Everton's (*www.everton.com*)	220
	Kindred Konnections (*www.kindredkonnections.com*)	221
	Genealogy.com (*www.genealogy.com*)	223
	Yourfamily.com	224

Contents

Part 4 **Commercial Online Services** **227**

Chapter 13 America Online's Golden Gate Genealogy
Forum 231

Member Welcome Center 234
Beginners' Center 235
FAQ/Ask the Staff 235
The 5-Step Research Process 236
DearMYRTLE's Beginner Lessons 237
Beginners' Tool Kit 238
For Starters Conference Room 239
Other Resources 239
Quick Start Guide 240
Message Boards 242
Genealogy Chat Center 246
File Libraries Center 248
Resource Center 248
Internet Center 248
Surnames Center 250
Search the Forum 250
Other Resources 250
Genealogy Forum News 251
DearMYRTLE Daily Column 251
Telephone Search Facilities 252
Software Search 253
Golden Gate Store 253
Ancestral Seasonings Cookbook 253
The Staff of the Genealogy Forum 255

Chapter 14 CompuServe's Genealogy Forums 259

Forum Decorum 262
Advertising on the Forums 263
Sysops: The Forum Managers 264
A Tour 264
The Genealogy Vendors' Support Forum 271
Genealogy Sysop Dick Eastman 272

Appendix A The Genserv Project 275
Appendix B Online Genealogy Books 291

Appendix C   Forms of Genealogical Data   293
Appendix D   Internet Error Messages   301

Glossary   307

Index   323

INTRODUCTION

"I've gotten more genealogy done in 1 year on Prodigy than I did in 20 years on my own!" my mother exclaimed. This quote, from a 30-year genealogy veteran, shows how technology has changed even this popular hobby. The mind-boggling deluge of data needed to trace one's family tree has finally found a knife to whittle it down to size: the computer.

This book will help you understand that there's a rich community of information out there—information that can help you find where those missing ancestors are lurking. Some of the sources are free, some cheap, some dear. However, until you know about them, they're worthless to you. Once you know, you can decide for yourself whether to use them.

Genealogy Online does not intend to teach you how to do genealogy, but how to use the tools of the online world to help you do it better. Still, I feel I should at least touch on how and why we do genealogy.

FOR THOSE NEW TO GENEALOGY

Royalty has always made great use of genealogy; knowing who is related to whom has shaped the history of nations. Figure I-1 shows how modern European monarchs are related. You can find this at http://www.royal.gov.uk/history/graphics/europe.pdf.

When you study your own genealogy, you trace your place in history. Your results can be shown in charts, trees, circles, quilts, scrapbooks, or even a published hardback book. In the process, you are bound to learn about history, law, sociology, and eugenics. Most amateur genealogists find that history is much more exciting when they see exactly how it affected and shaped their own families.

Another major appeal of genealogy is that it provides people with a sense of continuity and of belonging. This sense of belonging extends to other genealogists, for it is almost impossible to research any family line by yourself.

It's not as hard to find some information as you might think. Almost any self-respecting public library, no matter how small, has a local history and genealogy section. Some libraries have entire floors dedicated to those subjects.

In addition, the Church of Jesus Christ of Latter-day Saints (the Mormons) has collected an extensive bank of genealogical data (official

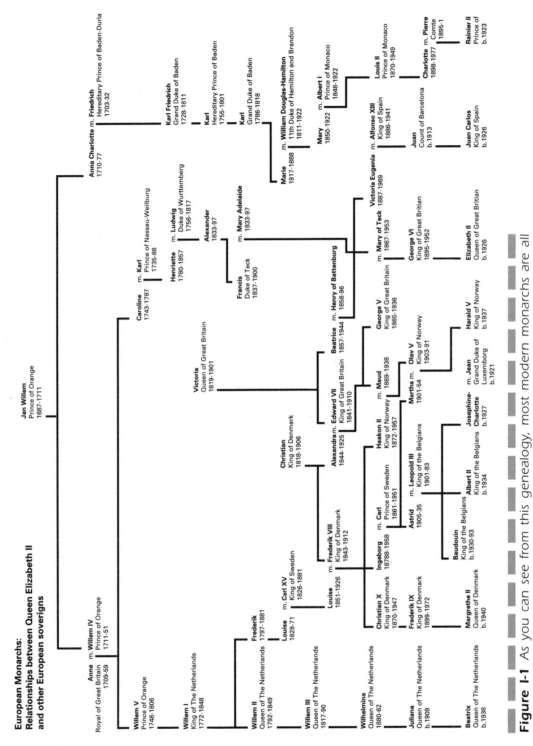

Figure 1-1 As you can see from this genealogy, most modern monarchs are all descended from the same person.

registers of births, marriages, and deaths, and related documents), probably the greatest such collection in existence. Church members use these records in order to bring their ancestors posthumously into the church. As I was writing this book, the Mormons began experimenting with putting indexes to this information on the Internet.

The federal government has recently started to put much of its data, such as death records, veterans' records, and so on, in machine-readable databases, which could then be accessible via an internet.

Genealogy can be used to research medical histories, to confirm your rights to an inheritance, or to qualify for certain scholarships. Overall, however, genealogy for most people is just a fascinating hobby. The U.S. alone, for example, has numerous genealogical societies that trace people's descent. Some of these are national, but many more are local or regional, such as the Tennessee Valley Genealogical Society or the New England Historical Society. Others are specific to certain names. Many patriotic organizations, such as the Daughters of the Confederacy, limit membership to descendants of a particular historical group.

A recent cover article in *CompuServe* magazine highlighted the uses of their online forum for genealogy. "We get several thousand users per week on this forum," says forum leader Dick Eastman. The article then proceeded to describe how the forum helped one woman find her natural father, how stories about ancestors are swapped, and the sort of informational files uploaded to the library.

WHERE COMPUTERS COME IN

Databases, online services, online card catalogs, and bulletin boards are changing the "brick wall syndrome"—that frustrating phase of any lineage search where the information needed seems unavailable. Genealogists who have faced the challenges and triumphed are online helping others.

There's no denying that the computer has changed just about everything in our lives, and the avocation and vocation of genealogical research is no exception. Further, a wonderful new resource for computers, the Internet, has come into being and is still developing at a pace that's dizzying. This book will explore many different networks, services, and Web sites that can help you in your pursuit of your ancestry.

Stories about how online communities have helped people in their genealogical research abound. Following are some examples.

DearMYRTLE Finds a Patriot

DearMYRTLE, a daily genealogy columnist on the Internet (see Chapter 7 or http://members.aol.com/dearmyrtle/), was helping a friend move files, data, and programs from an old computer to a new one. In the course of the conversation, DearMYRTLE's friend wondered aloud what online genealogy could do for him but expressed doubt anything useful could turn up online.

Then the conversation turned to the first of the new U.S. quarters, the one with the Delaware patriot Cesar Rodney on the reverse.

"Who was he?" asked DearMYRTLE's friend.

"All right," she replied, "let's run a test. Your wife here will look him up in the Encyclopaedia Britannica. You look him up on your old computer using Microsoft Encarta 97. I'll look him up on the Internet with your new computer."

The friend and his wife both found short text mentions that Rodney had signed the Declaration of Independence and led the Delaware Militia (the wife slightly tore a page in the book in the process). In the same amount of time, DearMYRTLE had found the Web site of the Historical Society of Delaware (http://hsd.org/george.htm) with a short biography on him, and a copy of a letter from George Washington to Rodney discussing troop movements, along with two others written by Delaware patriots Caesar Rodney and Jacob Broom!

Now *that's* how online research can help you (Fig I-2).

Nancy's Story

Nancy is a friend of mine from high school who knows more about computers and the Internet than I do, but not quite so much about genealogy. When her stepmother died recently, Nancy got a large box of her father's memorabilia and photos. In August 1998, we spent some time at the beach together, and I showed her some good genealogy sites on the Internet on her laptop computer.

I didn't think much more about it until she called me in early 1999 in considerable excitement. She had not only found the USGENWEB (see Chapter 7 or http://www.usgenweb.org) site for her father's home county in Texas but also that the moderator of the site had known both her father and her grandfather. She was scanning in the old photos and emailing them to the fellow, and he was identifying people in them left and right. One was of Nancy's grandfather as a child. Another showed

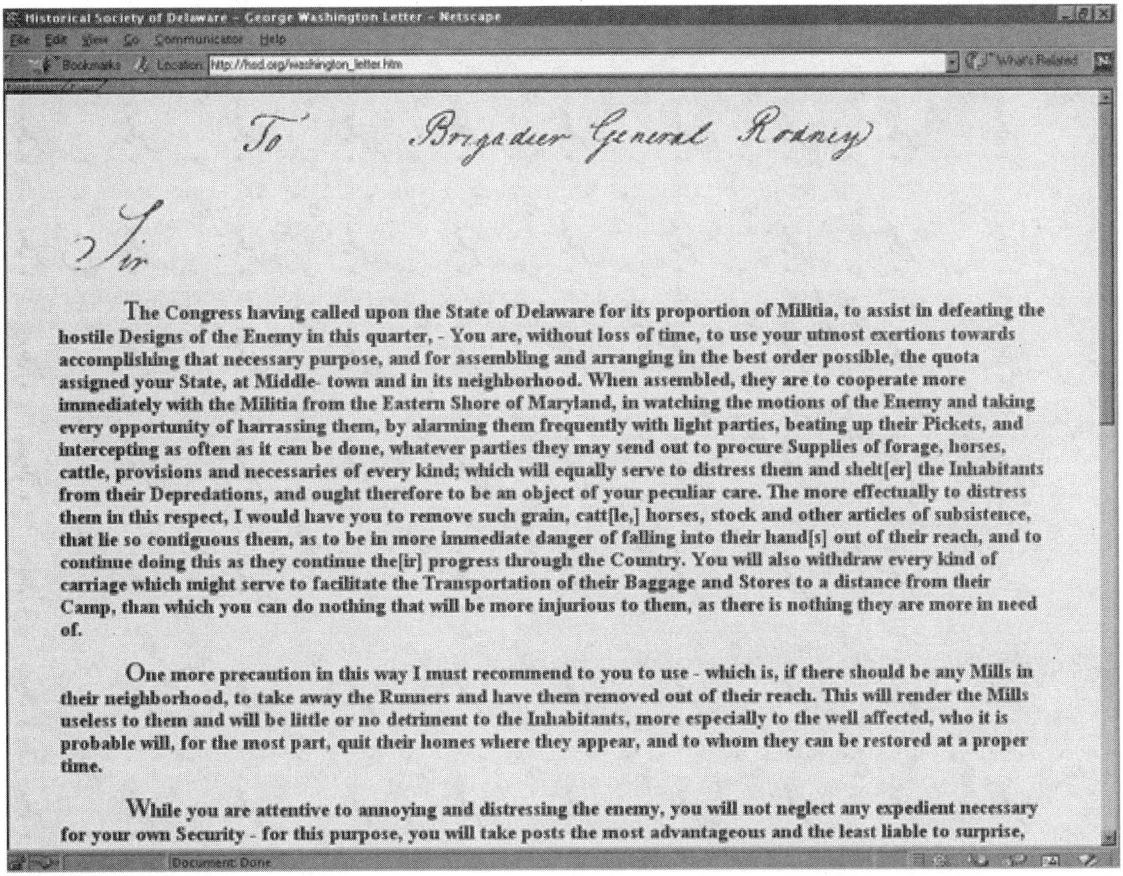

To Brigadier General Rodney

Sir

The Congress having called upon the State of Delaware for its proportion of Militia, to assist in defeating the hostile Designs of the Enemy in this quarter, - You are, without loss of time, to use your utmost exertions towards accomplishing that necessary purpose, and for assembling and arranging in the best order possible, the quota assigned your State, at Middle- town and in its neighborhood. When assembled, they are to cooperate more immediately with the Militia from the Eastern Shore of Maryland, in watching the motions of the Enemy and taking every opportunity of harrassing them, by alarming them frequently with light parties, beating up their Pickets, and intercepting as often as it can be done, whatever parties they may send out to procure Supplies of forage, horses, cattle, provisions and necessaries of every kind; which will equally serve to distress them and shelt[er] the Inhabitants from their Depredations, and ought therefore to be an object of your peculiar care. The more effectually to distress them in this respect, I would have you to remove such grain, catt[le,] horses, stock and other articles of subsistence, that lie so contiguous them, as to be in more immediate danger of falling into their hand[s] out of their reach, and to continue doing this as they continue the[ir] progress through the Country. You will also withdraw every kind of carriage which might serve to facilitate the Transportation of their Baggage and Stores to a distance from their Camp, than which you can do nothing that will be more injurious to them, as there is nothing they are more in need of.

One more precaution in this way I must recommend to you to use - which is, if there should be any Mills in their neighborhood, to take away the Runners and have them removed out of their reach. This will render the Mills useless to them and will be little or no detriment to the Inhabitants, more especially to the well affected, who it is probable will, for the most part, quit their homes where they appear, and to whom they can be restored at a proper time.

While you are attentive to annoying and distressing the enemy, you will not neglect any expedient necessary for your own Security - for this purpose, you will take posts the most advantageous and the least liable to surprise,

Figure I-2 Online research leads to treasures such as this letter from George Washington to Cesar Rodney.

her father as a teenager. Every day, the USGENWEB sysop was helping her fill in more holes in her family history.

What's a Hoosier? Genealogy Has the Answer

Randy Hooser of Huntsville, Alabama, has been working on his genealogy for years. One result has been his work with a University of Indiana professor to publish a white paper in February 1999 to prove his family is the origin of the nickname "Hoosier." A fascinating story, the migration of Randy's family involves religious and political movements of this nation's history. You can see the results of his research on his Web site, http://www.geocities.com/Heartland/Flats/7822/. In it he postulates that his pioneer ancestors, being usually the farthest west of civilization, were the origin of the nickname "Hoosier" (Fig I-3).

However, that's not the only use for Randy's Web site. Randy is using it to plan a big family reunion in the year 2000, to exchange genealogical data among the cousins, and to publish a newsletter. An email list with all his known relatives keeps everyone up-to-date on births, marriages, and deaths among those living and similar data on ancestors as the family historians find them.

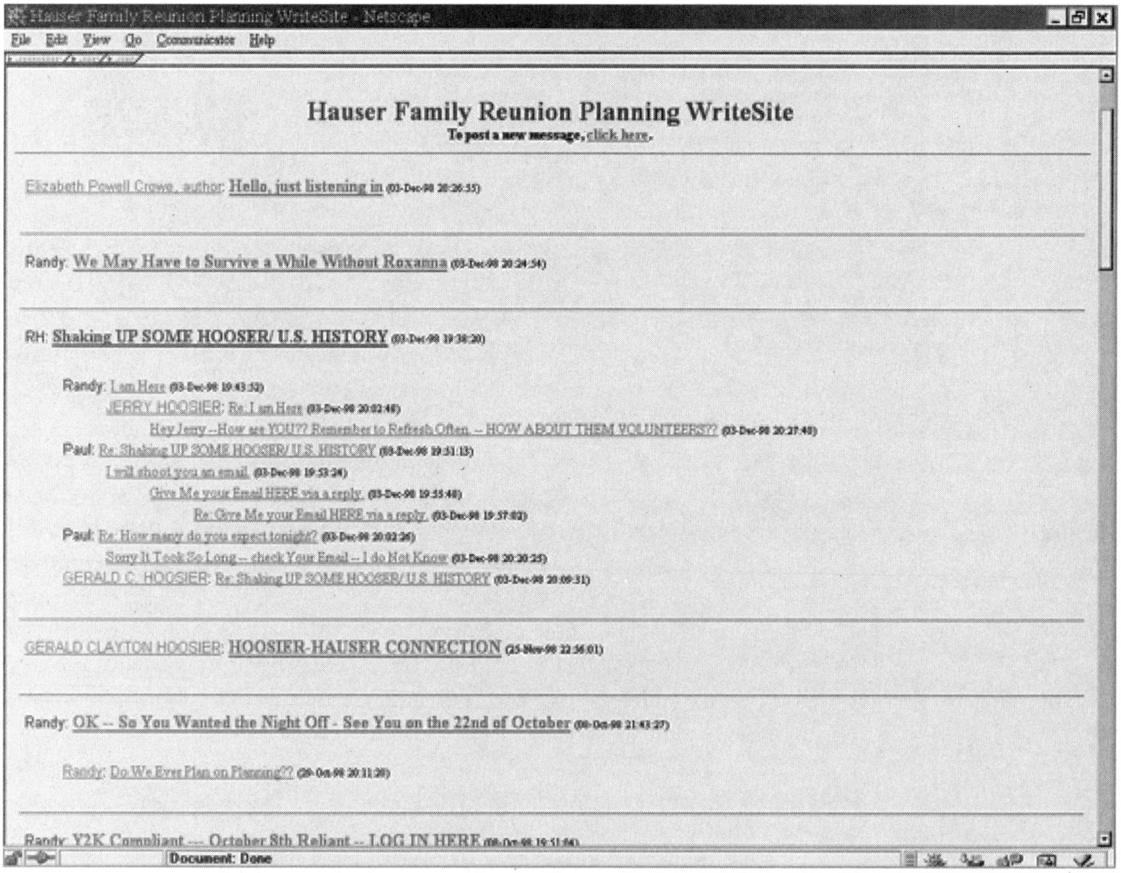

Figure I-3 Genealogy has convinced Randy Hooser that his family is the origin of the nickname "Hoosier."

Regular family meetings take place on Randy's Hooser message board. Not exactly like chat (see Chapter 8), the family post messages to the site's message board. They put the "body" of the message in the "subject" line and leave the message blank. It runs faster than a normal message board, but unlike chat, it is not as vulnerable to spammers. Refreshing the page to get new message subject lines is almost like reading the message itself this way. Longer points, of course, must be made in the body of the message.

In this way, Randy is using the Internet for past, present, and future generations of his family.

SOME CONCEPTUAL BACKGROUND ABOUT ONLINE GENEALOGY

Genealogists have had publications to turn to for many years. From local/regional publications such as the Tennessee Valley Genealogical Society's *Valley Leaves* to the venerated *Genealogical Helper,* a wealth of information has been printed to help genealogists find others working on the same ancestral lines, publish interesting tidbits, and help each other with vexing research problems.

For not quite so long but for some time now, they have also had computers and genealogical database programs to help them track, organize, analyze, and share their genealogical information. For a while there was a dearth of such programs, then a widening choice of formats, and then, finally, a standard in the GEDCOM. (See Appendix C for a discussion on GEDCOM.) Everyone was plugging away, gathering and storing information. They all had more information than they could use—some of it germane to their own lineages, some of it not, but surely useful to someone, so why throw it away?

So, here were all these collections of data, and all these users wanting to share that data. Soon a problem arose: how to transfer data, for example, from a CP/M (for "Control Program for Microprocessors," an early operating system) to Windows-based machine or to a Mac? In other fields, people were faced with the same problems. Astronomers, teachers, and the military were all doing the same thing genealogists were on different subjects.

The answer was to create new ways to communicate. Electronic mail systems (email), bulletin board systems (BBS), and the Internet all came into being to solve the problem of getting data from one place to another. By using phone lines and protocols (or a way of transmitting data), regardless of the machinery and proprietary software involved, people could exchange data.

ELECTRONIC MAIL

Electronic mail systems are simply a way to send text from one place to another, just as regular mail does. Through a variety of different programs, that text can be private messages, public postings of articles, text files, graphics, even sounds.

However, please take that "private messages" phrase with a grain of salt. I'll make this point several times in this book: Posting something to a list, echo, or board means that many, many people will read it. Posting something to a certain person at his or her email address means you and that person will read it, but so will the people who run the system to which you posted the text. As of this writing, no law or court case has established that electronic mail is as private as first-class mail. One or two court cases, indeed, have held the opposite: When something is posted to a company-owned, company-run electronic mail system, the text is considered the property of the company.

An email system might be a part of an internet, a bulletin board, or a pay-per-use commercial service; it might even be part of a combination of these. Alternatively, it might stand alone, as a company-run email service does. You need to check out any email service you use, including its costs and distribution, carefully.

BULLETIN BOARDS

In previous editions, I spent many words on bulletin board systems (BBSs), which were dial-up services for exchanging files, messages, and real-time comments. They were usually hosted in someone's home. Dial-up BBSs still exist, but for this edition I have eliminated them from the text in favor of Usenet, email, and online forums. Many of these BBSs have folded, others have become Internet service providers, others are still running but are not nearly as popular as they used to be.

NETWORKS AND ECHOES

Connections of computers are called *networks*. The connection may be constant or intermittent, but the point is that computers that are in different places can share information. Although BBS networks still exist, this edition will be concerned more with the Internet.

These networks are not unlike the Internet in purpose. However, when you get to the Internet, the functions and services are expanded to the extreme and are ever-changing.

THE INTERNET

The Internet, with a capital "I," is more of a concept than an entity. The concept is, hook up lots of computers running the same protocol (a way of communicating digital data) and let people communicate over their computers with pictures, words, sounds, and whatever else they can digitize. The Internet is a network of networks to implement that idea. There are several smaller "internets" with government, educational, or research purposes that connect to the Internet at certain points.

A network is a group of computers working together through some connection, either intermittent or continuous. The connection can be phone wires (most common) but also can be cables or radio, satellite, or other wireless connections. The Internet is a set of computers connected all the time (the "backbone"), to which your computer can connect any time and through which your data can travel. The data is sent with a protocol called *TCP/IP* (Transmission Control Protocol/Internet Protocol). It makes sure the data goes in the most efficient (not necessarily the shortest) route available at the moment.

The backbone consists of companies such as America Online (often referred to as AOL), MCI, and AT&T, along with universities, research institutions, and government organizations, all running computers connected with the Internet protocols. In other words, every facet of the communications industry gives some support to the Internet.

At first, you couldn't use the Internet unless you were an employee or student at one of the above places, and your connection was probably free, supported by tax and research dollars. There were a few exceptions to this. Some entrepreneurs paid for an Internet connection at one of those places and then sold access: These are known as *Internet service providers* (ISPs). Then the government decided it had done enough to get the Information Superhighway paved and bowed out. The infrastructure was opened to commercial use, and the number of Internet service providers went from a few dozen to about a thousand.

Today, a great deal of scientific, educational, and technical research still goes on over the Internet, but entertainment and hobby use has grown phenomenally. The Internet is a resource, a method of research, and a "place" called cyberspace, all at the same time.

Much more is involved in how the Internet developed and works today than this book can cover. For the genealogy hobbyist, it's enough to understand that the Internet is a worldwide connection of computers; you can connect to it, and it has a wealth of information and many people willing to share on it.

HOW TO USE THE INTERNET

To use the Internet, you use different services. All of these services started out as text-based programs. Most of them are now available in some Windows or Macintosh graphical user interface. The main Internet services are as follows:

- *Chat.* Typing conversations in real time over a network with someone. If you liked CB radio, you'll like online chat. Though it's popular, I haven't found much use for it in genealogy, except on the commercial online services. The chapters dealing with CompuServ and America Online, note the genealogy chat services (sometimes called "conference") they offer. Chapter 8 deals with Internet chat.

- *Email.* Sending and receiving messages at your individual Internet account's address.

- *Finger.* Sending a test signal to a person's email address. If that person has written a text file to respond to a finger command, the file will be returned to you. Some systems will also tell you if that person is logged on to the Internet right now or the last time that person logged on to the system.

- *FTP.* The File Transfer Protocol is how you get files, programs, pictures, and other data from another site to yours, and how you send those items to another site. Anonymous FTP is a system where a lot of files are stored at a certain computer, and anyone is welcome to download them. You simply log in as "anonymous" or "ftp" and give your email address as the password.

■ *Ping.*   Sending a test signal to a specific computer on the Internet. Useful for when you cannot connect to a World Wide Web (WWW), Telnet, or other Internet site; ping will tell you if the computer is down, or running but busy. Windows 95 comes with a ping program, but you have to drop to the MS-DOS prompt to use it.

■ *Telnet.*   A text-based system of running a distant computer from your own. Once you log in, you must know and use the commands at that remote computer, but you can run programs and services such as FTP from Telnet connections. The most common use for genealogists is to look at library card catalogs. Windows 95 comes with a Telnet program, but there are graphical user interface ones that are better.

■ *Usenet.*   Also called "Internet bulletin boards," Usenet newsgroups number in the thousands. They are organized by topic, and when you post a message to one, you are talking to the whole world, usually. Usenet is not email; it's many-to-many or one-to-many communication.

■ *World Wide Web.*   An interface called a *browser* ties together all these services except ping and finger. It's the easiest way to use the Internet.

A QUICK LOOK AT THIS BOOK

This book will give you a basic education in the online world. Nevertheless, please be aware that what is written here was current as of early 1999. Since that time, commercial online services and the Internet will have added, expanded, revised, and changed what they offer, as well as how and when they offer it. The only constant in the online world for the last five years has been change, and at an exponential rate. So, be prepared for adventures!

Part I   The Basics

Chapter 1   Getting Set Up: A Look at Hardware and Connections

Here we'll look at what it takes to make the connection: computer, hardware, and Internet service providers.

Chapter 2   Software

This chapter contains a brief overview of Internet clients and how to use them, plus we'll take a quick look at some prominent genealogy programs that are online-ready, allowing you to perform searches on the Internet and publish to the Internet.

Chapter 3   Rules of the Road: How to Surf Happily

If cyberspace is uncharted territory for you, be sure to read these cautions and caveats. Learn to speak the lingo, from *online etiquette* to *smileys*. In addition, this chapter includes a little discussion of sources and proof as they relate to online resources.

Part 2   The Internet

Like a physical city or state, the Internet has certain services for its citizens. Among these are chat, email, FTP, Usenet, and the World Wide Web. We looked at the client programs in Chapter 2. These used to be all separate; now they often overlap: A Web site may offer FTP files, chat rooms, and discussion forums. In this section, you'll see how to use them to do genealogical research.

Chapter 4   FTP

FTP sites with files and programs for genealogists can be a real time-saver.

Chapter 5   Usenet

We will have discussed newsreaders in Chapter 2. This chapter discusses newsgroups and online forums, as well as Usenet search engines.

Chapter 6   Genealogy Mailing Lists

Learn how to have genealogical information and discussions delivered to your virtual mailbox! This chapter has an updated list of genealogy mail lists.

Chapter 7   The World Wide Web

The Web is the main place Internet things are happening. I have collected a set of great genealogy sites to get you going.

Chapter 8   Chat: Hail Thy Fellow on the Net!

You can learn a lot in live online discussions with genealogists from around the world. I'll show you the best genealogy chat rooms.

Part 3   Specific Online Resources

Chapter 9   RootsWeb: The Hub of What's Happening in Online Genealogy

This site has it all: Data files, mailing lists, chat rooms, and a Dear MYRTLE link.

Chapter 10   Online Library Card Catalogs

This chapter shows you how to find books through the Internet—before you leave home.

Chapter 11   The Church of Jesus Christ of Latter-day Saints

Ancestral File, the results of research by Mormons around the world, and the International Genealogical Index (IGI), a CD-ROM set of original documents, can be searched from the LDS site. I'll show you how the site looked in the beta test and how to use a Family History Center.

Chapter 12   Commercial Web Sites

Popular genealogy publishers such as Everton and Ancestry offer many services on their subscription sites. We'll also look at other commercial sites, including Kindred Konnections, Genealogy.com (from the publishers of the Family Tree Maker genealogy software package), and Yourfamily.com.

Part 4   Commercial Online Services

Chapter 13   America Online's Golden Gate Genealogy Forum

Chapter 14   CompuServe's Genealogy Support Forums

Appendix A   The Genserv Project

Appendix B   Books about Online Genealogy

Appendix C   Forms of Genealogical Data

Appendix D   Internet Error Messages

Glossary

—ELIZABETH POWELL CROWE

ACKNOWLEDGMENTS

As with any book, this one was made possible by the efforts of many people besides the authors. First, I would like to thank every person mentioned and quoted in this edition of the book. Obviously, without all your help, the book would still just be a dream.

Very special thanks to Cliff Manis, Terry Morgan, and DearMYRTLE for helping me out of many a dead end. Gratitude is also due to Michael Sprague and the folks at McGraw-Hill.

To my family and friends, who patiently waited for me to emerge from the writing frenzy, and especially Marianne, Matthew, and Mark, who were the best support a writing mom and wife ever had, a big thank you.

But most of all I want to thank my mother, Frances Spencer Powell, who urged and encouraged me, baby-sat and researched for me, and traveled and travailed with me ever since I first got the idea to write a book about online genealogy.

GENEALOGY
ONLINE

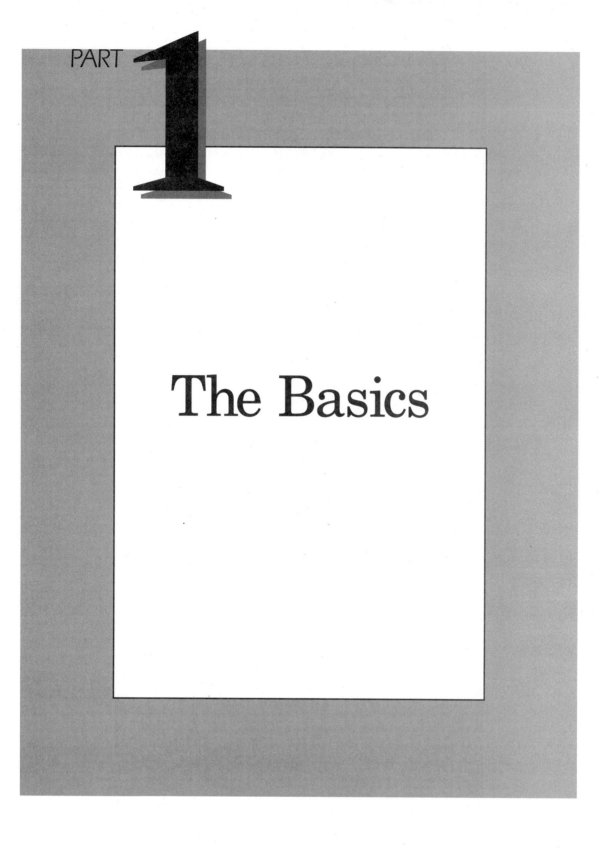

PART

1

The Basics

Online genealogy is only different from the old-fashioned kind in the tools you use. Instead of using a photocopier, you'll get copies by FTP. Instead of sending queries in an envelope, you'll send them by email. Instead of reading an article in a magazine, you'll read it in a browser. And instead of going to the library in a car, you might visit it by modem.

You will have to learn the ins and outs of hardware, software, and techniques for online information exchange in order to get the most out of the experience. In this section, the chapters will cover hardware considerations, software you might want to use, and online techniques and tips you should know.

I don't mean to imply that you will never do things the old-fashioned way again. Of course you will. You'll just find yourself using these online techniques, sometimes, before you try to do research the traditional way.

1

Getting Set Up

A Look at Hardware and Connections

In this chapter, you will learn what you need to get connected to the Internet. People speak of online services and the Internet (often called "the Net") as a place—cyberspace or the Information Superhighway. If you like to envision it that way, think of the modem as your car and the software you use as the engine. You need the software to make the modem go.

How to Select a Modem

To use the Internet, you need a way to connect your computer to the wires. You can do this through a modem or through a digital data service such as an Integrated Services Digital Network (ISDN) or a digital subscriber line (DSL), which require different equipment.

NOTE *Telephone lines have very little electrical resistance. If lightning strikes a telephone wire outside near your home, the electricity can travel right into your home's phone lines. The stories you've heard about people who are killed while talking on the phone in a thunderstorm are true. Therefore, if you have a modem or other phone connection device attached to your computer, you should always disconnect it from the wall during a thunderstorm. If you don't, your modem, computer, and even printer could be irreparably damaged by a lightning strike. The added measure of installing a surge protector on your phone lines wouldn't hurt, but it's no substitute for unplugging during electrical storms.*

So what are these doodads?

A *modem* is a gadget that converts the data of your computer system into sounds, which are sent out on a phone line (or a cable physically connecting two computers) to another computer. That process is called *modulation*. The other computer, with its modem, translates these sounds back into computer-readable signals. That's *demodulation*. The modulator/demodulator, or modem, makes it possible for computers to "talk to each other."

NOTE *A modem, incidentally, changes the data from digital to analog to digital. That's important later on when we discuss ISDN and xDSL.*

Most modems on the market today are capable of receiving information at up to 56,000 bits of data per second (referred to as 56 Kbps, or kilobits per second) and sending out at up to about 36 Kbps. The reason it's faster coming in than going out is that the wiring in your house ends and begins with analog transmission. Once it gets to your phone company's equipment, it is going all digital.

The modems compress the data according to a protocol. The protocol used must be the same for both the devices sending and receiving the data. When such protocols are grouped together and approved by the

International Telecommunications Union (ITU), they become a "standard." When you buy a modem, be sure it meets the V.90 ITU standard. This is the latest technology, and it includes past technologies in it. So, a V.90 modem will be able to talk to other V.90 modems, as well as to older modems that don't have the standard yet.

NOTE: *A protocol is a standard set of formats and procedures for the exchange of information between systems. There have been many modem protocols in the past. The latest one in 1999 is V.90.*

You will find hundreds of makes and models of modems, ranging in price from under $100 to more than $1000. Some are "internal"—that is, they fit into a slot inside your computer. Others are "external"—that is, they are in a case, sit on your desk, and have lights on the front to show you the status of various functions. External modems must have their own power supply and case, so they are slightly more expensive. An external modem also requires a high-quality cable to connect it to the communications port on your computer. Be sure to ask if one is included when you purchase an external modem. If not, don't go home without buying one.

Other important features to consider when selecting a modem include:

- *Fax capabilities, fax speed, and fax software.* Being able to send and receive faxes can be a convenience, if the software is user-friendly. Many modems have this built in and include software to run it. Also, Windows 95 and 98 can be installed with Windows Fax functions. Unless you have a scanner as well, you won't be able to fax anything that you didn't create on your computer, but even without a scanner, you can use your fax modem as a printer and send anything you create on your computer as a fax. This can be a real convenience.

- *Flash upgrade programs.* Modem technology is changing and developing all the time and has been for over 15 years. But customers got pretty tired of being told every 18 months or so that their modem was obsolete, and the only solution was to shell out another $200 for a new one. So flash upgrades were developed. This is a special program that rewrites the chip in the modem called read-only memory (ROM). The ROM holds permanent information for the modem, such as the V.90 standard. Someday that standard will be replaced by a newer one, and if your modem has flash upgrade capability, then you can upgrade without getting a new modem. This is definitely much more expedient.

■ *Software and hardware extras.*   Extras such as software or hardware allow you to have two computers that use one modem or to connect two computers together to share data. One such gizmo is the OfficeConnect 56K LAN modem from 3Com. At about $200, it's pricey for a modem, but a bargain for a Local Area Network (LAN). Right this minute, my tower Gateway and my Gateway Solo laptop are both on the Internet. I'm typing this and answering email while my laptop is searching for mentions of "genealogy" with "online" on the Internet. It works great on my Gateways (although *PC Magazine*'s labs found other brands where it didn't work so well). My main problem has been Windows 98 wanting to dial with the old modem instead of using the LAN. It seems to be something America Online (AOL) resets every time you use it. Other that than, I'm doing back flips over this thing. When I take my laptop somewhere for research, I simply bring it home, plug it into the LAN, and boot it up. Then, transferring work and files from one computer to another is as simple as drag and drop.

■ *Wherefore UART?*   If your computer is older, the UART is a consideration. The UART (Universal Asynchronous Transmitter and Receiver) is the part of the computer that sends the data out the wire. Internal modems have their own built-in UARTs. External modems, however, use the UART in your computer. If you are using an external modem, therefore, it is crucial that you understand what type of UART your COM port is using. An internal modem probably will be equipped with a suitable UART, but checking it out wouldn't hurt. And if your computer is more than five years old, you may have to replace the UART to make your modern modem work its best.

How Do You Find Out What Kind of Modem You Have?

Run a program on your Windows computer called MSD.EXE (Microsoft System Diagnostics). Search your computer for it; it's probably in the DOS directory, if your computer is more than three years old. Run the program in DOS, not Windows. (It can produce incorrect results if run from Windows or in a DOS session under

Windows.) Select the PORTS option. If MSD reports a 16550x-type UART (where x is one or more letters), chances are, you are fine. However, if MSD reports an 8250- or 16450-type UART, the UART is an older model. All is not lost. If you have a serial card (or motherboard) with a socket for the 8250 or 16450 UART, you can replace the chip with a 16550A. Add-on high-speed data communications cards with 16550A (or equivalent) UARTs are also available at your local computer store at prices ranging from $20 to $75, depending upon the number of ports and other features.

ISDN and xDSL

ISDN

The modem isn't the only way to connect to Internet services, nor is it the fastest. The alternatives, ISDN and xDSL, are so innovative and expensive I hesitate to mention them, but in the interests of completeness, I feel I must. This will be a very short introduction; if you want to try to jump into ISDN, you'll have to read much more than this brief description before you're ready.

The phone companies currently marketing ISDN to their customers would like you to believe that faster is better and that's all there is to it. ISDN is a new kind of connection that has three channels, A, B, and Data, to carry your signals. Phone companies have been promising for years that ISDN would replace our old (and reliable) analog phone lines. With an ISDN line hooked up to your PC, phone, fax, and what-have-you, you can send and receive just about any kind of data—voice, documents, graphics, sound, the full-motion video necessary for movies or teleconferencing—over the line at speeds up to 64,000 bits per second (bps).

Another selling point is versatility. With the right equipment and software on your end, a single ISDN line can support two phone numbers. In effect, you could get a video phone call from Grandma on one line while transmitting a report to your company on the other. ISDN also lets your phone be a little smarter, because the "ring" sent down an ISDN line could tell your phone who's calling, the type of call (data or speech), the number dialed, and so on. Your intelligent phone could analyze this information and act appropriately. For example, your phone could be programmed to answer calls from certain numbers only, or to answer specific calls on specific lines, such as all fax calls, on line two.

Unfortunately, ISDN isn't cheap, although prices are falling each month. Although you'd treat an ISDN line like your old analog phone line—you would be billed for long-distance charges, you could have Call Waiting features, and so on—it comes with a passel of complications. Cost, for one thing.

Although an ISDN line costs as little as $20 a month in California, it's considerably more expensive in the East. Moreover, installation runs about $200. An ISDN line would eliminate the need for a modem—after all, a MODulator-DEModulator is designed to turn digital data into analog and back again, and ISDN is all-digital. Yet hooking up your PC to an ISDN line will require a special adapter that can cost up to $1000 or more, depending on the application. Moreover, using your existing fax machine, telephone, and so on requires buying bridging devices and still more software. The alternative is to buy all new, ISDN-smart equipment. 3Com, ADTRAN, and many other companies are starting to offer consumer-priced equipment like this, so if you shop hard enough, you may find something in your price range.

Another consideration: The ISDN system is powered by your household current, not the phone company's. If the power to your ISDN system goes out, you're unreachable. This is why many businesses that have jumped on the ISDN bandwagon also buy a separate power source for their ISDN system—and keep an old analog line around, just in case of thunderstorms, brownouts, and earthquakes.

The price tag for your local telephone company is also steep, and no doubt some of that cost will find its way onto your monthly bill. For starters, all the switches in your phone company's central office have to be replaced with digital switches that can recognize ISDN. The new switches also have to be within 3½ miles of your house. Therefore, the cost on both sides of the ISDN connection is high.

Consequently, communities that have adopted ISDN have found themselves isolated digital islands in an analog sea. But the Baby Bells have been selling ISDN hard over the last year or two, so many major cities in the U.S. have it, as well as smaller communities, such as Chapel Hill, North Carolina, and Huntsville, Alabama. The web of ISDN communities is growing, so that sending and receiving data at blinding speeds from point A to point B across country may be possible fairly soon. But not just yet.

Criticizing ISDN is easy—after all, adopting it involves more than a few leaps of faith. Many companies that you'd expect to be taking the

ISDN leap—such as commercial online services—are moving very slowly to implement ISDN. You're lucky if you can find an Internet service provider who has an ISDN link. Nevertheless, ISDN may be coming to a town near you.

The idea of high-speed, multichannel phone lines is appealing. But like most cutting-edge technologies that don't offer immediate, quantum gains in productivity, ISDN won't make serious inroads until it's as ubiquitous, invisible, and cheap as cable TV—when ISDN support is built into PCs, phones, and faxes, and can be accessed via a plug in the wall. Personally, I'm waiting until then.

xDSL

Then there's xDSL, or "digital subscriber line," with the *x* being a letter that designates a type. There's asymmetric, rate adaptive, very high, single line, and all sorts of flavors. There are those who will tell you, "Dump your modem. Forget ISDN. Leave the cable attached to your TV." If you believe the boosters, we could all be surfing the Net merrily at megabits per second using some form of DSL.

I can't really pass judgment on these claims, but at least I can give you an overview of the claims. What all the various DSL versions have in common is they're much faster than modems. They use plain old telephone lines to carry data at up to 51 megabits per second (Mbps), and they're not cheap (yet).

How does DSL do its magic? Naturally, you need DSL modems at both ends of the connection. Using everything from digital signal processing to fancy compression algorithms, DSL shoots data over your phone line at a much different frequency than that used by voices and standard modems. And while DSL is using your existing phone line to transmit data, it also lets you talk over it, because your voice is traveling at different frequencies than the data.

As you might suspect, getting on the DSL track requires new hardware and services from your local phone company. Although you don't have to order a new physical line, you do have to order DSL service from your local telephone company (assuming it offers it; many don't). You also need to buy a DSL modem and, in some cases, a splitter, which lets the phone line carry both DSL data transmissions and your voice. For Internet access, you'll need to order a DSL account from your local Internet service provider (America Online, for example, offers DSL access).

Chapter 1

DSL: Not Quite 31 Flavors

Which DSL may be right for you? Here's a quick look.

ADSL. Asymmetric DSL, as the name implies, downloads data faster (from 1.5 Mbps to 9 Mbps, depending on the provider) than it sends them (about 640 Kbps). That rate is slow compared to some DSL methods, but downloading is still 20 times faster than with a 56-Kbps modem. Chances are the DSL your local phone company installs will be ADSL. There are two catches: You'll need a splitter, and ADSL signals can only travel about 3.4 miles. That means every 3 miles or so your phone company must install a repeater to push the signal along. Given the costs, your phone company may opt to provide ADSL only in limited areas.

UDSL or UADSL. Universal DSL is ADSL without splitters, but it limits download/upload speeds to 1.5 Mbps and 640 Kbps, respectively. Some people call this service "ADSL light."

RADSL. Rate-adaptive DSL allows two DSL modems connected to one another to adjust their speed-to-line conditions. The connection is typically 600 Kbps to 7 Mbps in the download direction and 128 Kbps to 1 Mbps in the upload direction, but there's no distance limitation.

VDSL. Very high bit rate DSL is the Godzilla of DSL technologies. It can download data at up to 52 Mbps and upload them at speeds approaching 2.3 Mbps. The only problem is it's limited to about 4500 feet. That makes it a good solution for moving data in-house or, perhaps, bringing HDTV signals from the curb to your house.

HDSL. High bit rate DSL uses two twisted pairs of copper wire (instead of ADSL's single twisted pair, the configuration found in most homes) to send and receive data at 1.544 Mbps or 2.048 Mbps. The distance limit is about 2½ miles. Because of the wiring requirements, HDSL is best suited to office connections, such as linking Internet servers and linking LANs in different buildings.

SDSL. Single-line DSL is as fast as HDSL, but it uses one twisted pair of copper wires. Its distance limit is about 10,000 feet, which makes it a good solution for local area networking.

Hold the Phone?

Chances are, consumers will be using UDSL and businesses will opt for ADSL. But when will DSL become more widely available and affordable? At the moment, various Bells around the country are doing trials. For example, BellSouth has been offering ADSL in limited areas of Birmingham, Alabama, for about six months now and has declared the experiment a success. (For information, see www.bellsouth.com/fastaccess/adsl/.)

But don't rush out and sign up just yet. For starters, make sure your Bell even offers DSL. Second, make sure your ISP offers matching service (I suspect most will go the ADSL or ADSL light route). Third, make sure the DSL modem you buy is appropriate to the service you're getting: Different flavors of DSL require different modems.

Don't forget that DSL speeds can vary wildly, due to local conditions. That 52-Mbps line may actually only deliver 13 Mbps. Remember, too, that various standards have yet to be ironed out. Most versions of DSL are incompatible with each other. Also, no doubt there will be bugs in the DSL hardware and in Windows' attempts to work with DSL. Besides, it won't be cheap.

Consider U.S. West's (www.uswestcom.com) ADSL offerings. The company's MegaHome residential service, limited to 256 Kbps, costs $40 per month. The MegaBit 7-Mbps download/1-Mbps upload service costs $840 per month, not counting installation or the cost of hardware.

In short, DSL isn't likely to displace ISDN, T1, or Ethernet connections just yet. But it does offer the promise to bring multimedia/full-motion video, high-definition TV, and more into homes and businesses. Whether that promise will be fulfilled is still unknown.

NOTE *To learn more about DSL, check out the ADSL Forum at www.adsl.com and TeleChoice at www.telechoice.com.*

Web TV

Many cable companies are offering Internet access via cable to your television. I won't say much about it except this: Saving and printing information from your television set is problematic. I don't think this option is much use to the online genealogist just yet.

Choosing an ISP

Like choosing a mate, you should know what you want before you start looking. Your choice isn't final, of course, but you don't want to hop-scotch from one email address to another. So, go into this knowing that Internet providers are as different as dog breeds. All of them will get you onto the Net, but access speeds, services, software, and other goodies will vary. Before you lay down any cash, ask yourself some basic questions:

- What services do I need?
- How often do I need them?
- How fast do I need them?
- How many hassles am I willing to put up with to save money?
- How much am I willing to pay?

Just keep in mind that there are trade-offs no matter what provider you finally choose. For example, you may find there is a price break for slower and less-direct connections, or a premium to be able to dial into your account from various places in the country. In addition, you may find that companies consider support extremely expensive to provide, so if you sign up with a full-service provider, it will cost a bit more.

You may save money by choosing only what you need. However, in the end you will find you need the whole shebang: While some users are happy with just electronic mail, to find all the genealogical treasures out there, you will need more features, such as a WWW browser to fetch sound, pictures, and animation. You will also need a provider who can offer a high-speed connection.

When it comes to services, you should insist on the whole range: email, Telnet, Usenet newsgroups, FTP, Gopher, and more—in short, everything that the Internet has to offer. Even if the ISP service is austere, you should get at least a little support with that too.

Baby Steps

As mentioned, the commercial online services now offer Internet access; and for your first online forays, they are probably your best bet. Once you are online with CompuServe, America Online (AOL), or a similar service, you'll learn the ropes and get familiar with what's out there. Then, you may decide you want an Internet service provider (ISP) instead. To find a local Internet service provider, look in your Yellow Pages. Or use AOL, CompuServe, or Prodigy to find one of the several sites that let you search for an Internet service provider by area code, cost, or other factors. Two such sites are as follows:

http://www.isps.com   From a publisher called CMP Net, this one lets you search by area code, name, and price. It also lets you look for national and toll-free ISPs.

http://www.thelist.internet.com   From a publisher called Meckler Media, this is a buyer's guide to ISPs.

Go Shopping

Make a list of two or three Internet service providers and contact them. Ask these questions and listen for these answers:

- *Do you offer 56-kbps and faster access?*   The answer should be yes. The faster the better, because the genealogical information out there is immense.

- *Will I get busy signals if I call during prime time in the evening?*   In other words, how many high-speed lines does the provider have? How many customers log in on average during prime time? (And test them on their answer: Dial them up just after supper!) The answer should be that you can get on any time you want; they have enough lines or enough ISDN capability to handle their current customer base.

- *Do you offer anything else besides Internet access, such as BBS echoes and file collections?*   The answer should be yes; this is part of support.

- *Can I use a graphical third-party front end like Netscape to access your system? Do you provide this software?*   Both answers should be yes. If the first answer is no, then you have to deal with a text-oriented UNIX system, and the provider should supply a written manual. If there's no manual or menu system, this should be a really cheap service.

- *Which message readers can I use with Usenet newsgroups?* The answer should be a client that runs on your machine that they can provide you. If the answer is "rn" or "nn," beware! These are arcane UNIX newsreaders that are text-based and a real pain to use. Windows and Mac-based user-friendly readers like Free Agent are better; new browsers such as Microsoft Internet Explorer and Netscape Navigator include newsreaders as part of the program.

- *What's the capacity of private email boxes?* Here, the answer should be at least 100 KB of space. Bigger is better. If you subscribe to even a few genealogical mail lists and newsgroups, your mailbox could be stuffed quickly. If your mailbox is limited to 100 messages, you might miss important mail.

- *Will my connection be SLIP (Serial Line Internet Protocol) or PPP (Point-to-Point Protocol)?* PPP is better: It's newer, faster, and more reliable than SLIP, but if SLIP is all you can get, take it.

- *Do you provide access to all Usenet newsgroups or just a selection?* The answer should be all. This is very important for some of the more arcane genealogical newsgroups.

- *When do you schedule downtime for maintenance? How heavily loaded is the system?* Good luck getting straight answers to either question, but they should at least reassure you that downtimes will be announced in advance somehow. For the real answer, nose around Internet discussion areas and ask users of the service for the real poop.

- *Do you have points of presence (POPs) across the country, so if I'm on the road, I can still reach you with a local (or toll-free) call?* You hope the answer is yes. But reality may dictate that you get Internet accounts from two different providers—one for home and one for the road.

- *How do you charge?* A flat monthly fee for unlimited connect time is the ideal answer. Second best is a flat fee with a generous allotment of online time and a low hourly fee ($1 to $3) for use beyond that allotment. Beware of hourly based connect charges, which can add up in a hurry.

In addition, really smart Internet service providers offer a complete manual, training classes, and online news featuring phone number changes, service enhancements, and other information of interest to users.

With prices ranging from $10 a month for Telnet access to $260 a month for an always-open direct line, there's something out there for everyone. The trick is knowing what you want, asking tough questions of prospective Internet providers, and finding a company that will give you what you need. Don't forget to compare the answers to these questions with the national Internet service providers and to check up on how prices have changed every few months.

2

Software

Once you have your hardware in place and you know how you are going to connect, you need to look at your software. As noted before, many Internet service providers (ISPs) include software as part of the package. AOL, CompuServe, Prodigy, MindSpring, Netcom, and most other national Internet service providers have front-end software that includes the communications software, browser, FTP, mail, and other programs you need.

Communications Software (The Engine)

What makes a modem work is your communications software, which can be likened to the engine in a car (your modem is the car). There are two basic types: serial communications programs and TCP/IP stacks. The first is older technology that was used for dialing into bulletin board systems and some commercial online services. You can still find it, and it works very well for direct linking with another computer, if, for instance, you want to send your data files to your cousin directly, not over the Internet.

TCP/IP (Transmission Control Protocol/Internet Protocol) is the standard communications format for the Internet. It has become the standard way to connect to other computers. Windows 95 with the Plus! package has a TCP/IP stack built into it; Windows 98 has it without the Plus! package (Fig 2-1). There are versions for DOS, Macintosh, and many other platforms too.

In many cases you won't have to worry about finding communications software for your modem; it will find you. Most of the commercial services have front-end software to connect to their service. America Online, CompuServe Information Service (CIS), Prodigy Internet, and other ISPs will usually supply you with the software you need.

In addition, in many bookstores you can now find Internet connection packages. These run from $19 to over $100, depending on how much soft-

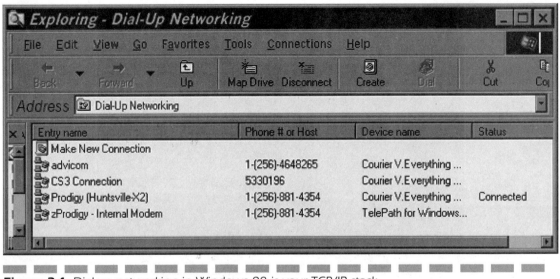

Figure 2-1 Dial-up networking in Windows 98 is your TCP/IP stack.

ware and documentation is included. Netscape Navigator, for about $30 for PC and Macs, is an excellent package that gives you not only the TCP/IP but also several programs you need to use the Internet effectively. Many times such packages come with a trial subscription to an ISP.

Find a good ISP, as outlined in the previous chapter. The best ones will include a package of software, manuals, and hand-holding to get you started.

Browser

At the beginning of this decade, the Internet was a lot harder to use. For each function (or "Internet service"), you needed to be familiar with a different program, with a different set of arcane commands. Once you got the hang of it, it wasn't hard to use the Internet; however, switching from one program to another was clumsy.

To transfer a file, you used File Transfer Protocol, or FTP. To search for a file that you wanted to get by FTP, you might use a search program called Archie. To run a computer on the Internet by remote control, you used Telnet. To look at documents on a system, say, a university's information system, you might use a menu-based display system called a Gopher. To search the Gophers for a specific document, you might use a program called Veronica to search all the Gophers in the world, or Jughead to search just one Gopher.

Finally, a Swiss research group, CERN, decided to try to pull all these different services into one interface, with a single protocol. At first, their new program, called a "browser," was text-based, too, just as the entire Internet was. Very soon, however, graphic interfaces were added, making the browsers even easier to use. This set of interlinked documents from around the world eventually became known as "the World Wide Web," or WWW.

So now, for most people "the Internet" is the World Wide Web, which can be thought of as an attempt to link information all over the world on the Internet. Of course, genealogists are involved in this too!

How Browsers Work

The World Wide Web (or "the Web," as it is often called) has its own lexicon of terminology. These terms can be confusing. Here are a few you should know before you get going:

- *HTML* (Hypertext Markup Language) is the language that turns a text document into a WWW-browsable one. Many shareware, as well as commercial, products have popped up in the past year to help you create HTML documents, but if you get a good book on the subject, you can create HTML code in any word or text processor.

- *URL* (Uniform Resource Locator) is an address in the WWW. The format of a URL is *accessmethod://machine.name/directory/file*. The *access method* can be FTP, HTTP, Gopher, or any other Internet service. The *machine name* is the computer that holds what you are after. The *directory* and *file* indicate where on that computer the object is. You type the URL in your browser's address box to get there.

- *Page* is a file presented to you in the browser. The file will be simple ASCII text, with embedded commands to tell the browser how things should look to you. Some text will be designated a "headline"; other text might tell the browser to show a picture in a certain place. The most important part of this coding scheme, called *HTTP* for Hypertext Transfer Protocol, is the *link*.

- *Link* is a pointer to another file. The term for linking files is *hypertext*. Hypertext is a system whereby pointers are embedded in text, presented to you usually as underlined colored words or a picture, that will have the browser display another file, either on that same site or somewhere else on the Internet. When the cursor changes from an arrow to a hand, you are pointing your mouse at a link.

- If you click on a link, you will be taken to another document, perhaps at another site, that has information on your choice. You might also be taken to a sound bite, if you have a sound card, or to a picture, if you have VGA graphics.

WARNING   *Sound and pictures across the Internet are still very slow at this writing.*

What we love about browsers is that they combine many Internet services: sending and receiving email, reading and posting to Usenet, transferring files with FTP and Gopher.

Which Browser to Use?

I'm often asked, "Which is the best browser?" I can only reply that this is like asking, "Which is the best car?" It all depends on your taste, habits, and budget.

The current leaders in the browser wars are Netscape Navigator and Microsoft Internet Explorer, and entire books are devoted to helping you get the most out of them. The major online services and Internet service providers have lined up with one or the other for their customers to use.

Microsoft Internet Explorer is free, but it makes major changes to your operating system and, therefore, sometimes causes trouble with other programs. Netscape Navigator is not free (about $40 as of this writing), but it has a nice user interface, is easy to use, and is the most popular. Others such as Opera, Mosaic, and Ariadne are less feature-packed, but they are free and very easy to use, and sometimes much faster.

Netscape Navigator and Microsoft Internet Explorer are chock-full of features, but they are also what I call "hardware hogs": They need super-duper hardware and lots of disk space to run. If you have an older or smaller machine (in terms of RAM and hard disk drive size), check out some other browsers too. They have fewer features but take up much less room on your hard disk and in your RAM (random access memory; see Glossary). For a good list of them, visit http://www.tucows.com and search for "browser."

My advice is to try a few of them (most of them allow you to try before you buy) and see which one suits you best.

What It Looks Like

The Genealogy Home Page, in Netscape Navigator Version 4.5, is shown in Figure 2-2. To see this page in your browser, type this in the address box:

http://www.genhomepage.com/

You can also use the menu option File | Open, and type the URL in the dialog box.

In the figure you can see the browser's title bar at the top of the screen. This tells you the title of the Web page you're viewing. The title is often the same as the page's first headline, but it can be different. When you save a Web page's address (URL) in your bookmark file, the name associated with the URL is usually taken from the title. Sadly, many Web developers don't realize this and name their pages something uninformative, such as "My Page" or "Link."

Next is the browser's menu bar. Most browsers will have File, Edit, View, Go, Bookmarks (or Hotlist or Favorites), Options, and maybe a few others. Usually, under File you can save or open a page, among other commands. Edit allows you to search for a word or save something to the clipboard; generally the same sort of commands in any Edit menu

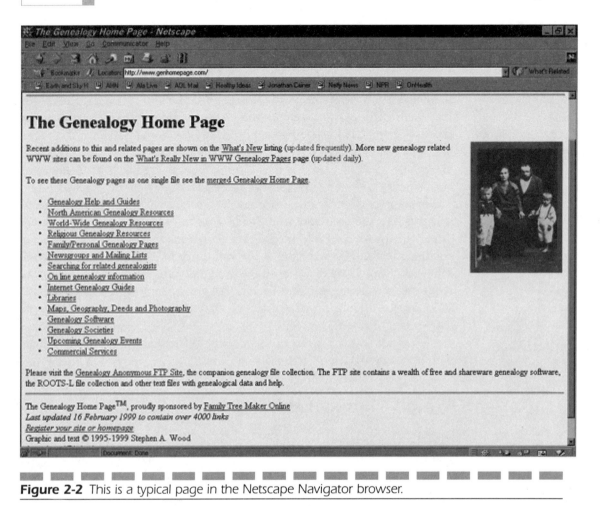

Figure 2-2 This is a typical page in the Netscape Navigator browser.

in Windows. `View` will often let you reload the page or see details of the HTML. `Go` is the navigation command; clicking it will give you a list of the sites you've visited today. `Bookmark` is for remembering the URL of good sites. `Options` lets you decide things such as the typeface shown in the window.

Below the menu bar is the toolbar. Most browser toolbars let you move backward and forward through Web pages, reload a page, travel to a home page, print a page, stop the current load action, and so on. They are simply one-click shortcuts to the commands in the menu bar.

At the end of this toolbar is the Netscape icon. Whenever you're loading a page, you'll see an animation of comets raining down on the poor little Netscape planet. If you double-click the N, you'll be taken immediately to Netscape's home page at http://home.netscape.com.

Underneath the toolbar is the URL bar. At the far left is the bookmarks icon. Click this and a menu will pop up, allowing you to save the location's address so you can come back later. You can create different folders to sort your bookmarks into so that you can organize them. Next to it is a small bookmark icon. Click and drag this to your desktop and a bookmark is created on the spot where you let go of the mouse button; in Windows 95 and 98, this is called a "shortcut" to that site. Double-click that shortcut, and your browser starts and takes you to the page. Microsoft Internet Explorer has a similar icon that does the same thing.

Of course, what dominates this line is the Location box, where you actually enter a Web site's address. If you need to copy a URL to your clipboard, you can just select it, press Ctrl-C, and it's ready to be pasted elsewhere. Are your fingers tired of typing "http://www"? Just type the unique part of the URL (such as genealogy.com), and the browser will fill in the first part. Type in an FTP site like "ftp.symantec.com", and the browser will insert the necessary "ftp://". If you click the down arrow on the right side of the Location box, you'll see a list of the last 15 or so URLs typed in this way. This feature is handy if you can't remember that neat place you visited yesterday. Place the pointer in the Location box, and press the down arrow key. You'll hop to the next URL in the list.

The next toolbar is your Personal toolbar. You can click and drag bookmarks to it for ready reference. It comes to you with pages that Netscape thinks are cool, worthwhile sites. For example, NetSearch takes you to a page of Web search engines. The People button jumps you to a form for searching online white pages, while Software takes you to the Navigator software site where a new version of the program is posted almost weekly. (Microsoft Internet Explorer has similar buttons.) But you can delete the ones that came with the program and add your own. The area below, taking up most of the screen, is Netscape's active window, where the current Web page is displayed.

Finally, let's go to the bottom of the screen. At flush left is a little open lock icon. In Navigator, this means the page you're viewing has no built-in security. That's not a problem in this case, because you're not filling out a form or providing any information. If the page had a form, the little open lock would indicate that someone else could see your answers. When a secure site is being viewed, you'll see a solid blue line at the top of the screen and a closed lock icon. Every browser notes security in different ways. Get to know yours well.

Below the display part, you'll find the status line. This line tells you how much of a page the browser has loaded. Move your mouse pointer over links on a page, and you'll see the associated URLs displayed here too. If the site's developer is versed in Java, a message can scroll across this box like a ticker tape. Next to the status line is a "thermometer" bar, another visual cue that shows how long you have to wait for an operation to finish. Over to the far right at the bottom of the screen are icons that take you to other parts of Netscape Communicator: the mail program, the HTML editor, and so on.

FTP

File Transfer Protocol (FTP) is how files are sent and received from many places on the Internet. When receiving a file, say, a photograph or a program, your browser handles that just fine. No worries. However, if you want to upload (send) a file, you should use an FTP program. Some browsers can handle sending, but an FTP program does it faster and more easily.

Programs for FTP abound on the Internet. Some of the more popular ones include CuteFTP, ActifFTP, and LeechFTP. But my favorite has always been WS_FTP. You can try the limited edition for free if it's for home, educational, or nonprofit use.

I love WS_FTP because it makes downloading files from an Internet FTP server or maintaining your Web site easy. You can select multiple files and/or directories and transfer them with a single click. WS_FTP lets you tell it what local directory and remote directory to log in to for each connection by default. It automatically keeps a log that you can save and view to see if there was a problem during a transfer, or just to remind yourself what you sent and what you got. Many of the display features can be personalized, such as directory sorting and window layout. It comes with a ready-to-use list of popular public FTP sites, and adding new ones is as simple as filling out a form. The Limited Edition version doesn't offer some advanced features (e.g., resuming interrupted downloads), but it's free to qualifying users, easy to use, and well documented. It's what I use every day.

Figure 2-3 shows how WS_FTP looks. I set up this connection myself by clicking the button on the bottom left that says "Open" before you connect to an FTP site and "Close" while you are connected.

I input the address of the site, ftp.cac.psu.edu, and the opening direc-

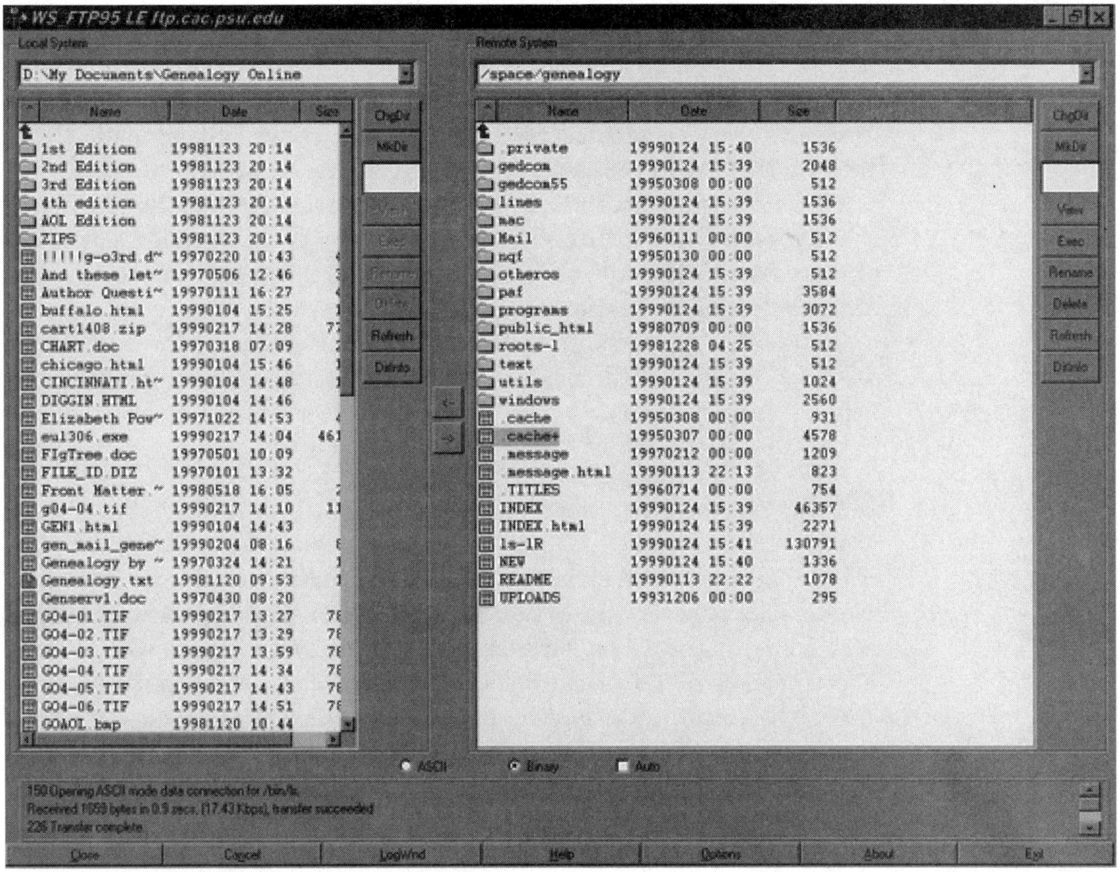

Figure 2-3 WS_FTP is an easy-to-use program for sending and receiving files from Internet sites.

tory, space/genealogy/ftp/. Then I entered my Genealogy Online directory on my machine for the default on the left side. This is an anonymous FTP site, so my email address was automatically entered as the password. Now all I have to do is highlight any files or folders and click the arrow to show which direction for them to go: left to bring them to my machine, right to send mine there. I've taught people to use WS_FTP in less than 15 minutes.

Mail-Reading Software

Reading mail is the biggest part of online life. Some of the best information, and even friendships, come through electronic mail, or email. If you sign up with AOL, you don't have much choice about how you read your mail, but I'll give you some tips to make it easier later in the chapter. If you are on any other Internet service provider, a mail reader makes life much easier. The mail readers in browsers tend to have fewer features than the stand-alone clients.

In order to get the most out of email, you need to get a few techniques under your belt. In the next sections, we'll go over filters, dealing with "spam," file attachments and formats, and Internet mail clients.

Filters

The programs I review below all have the ability to let you filter your email. This is a very important feature. Email filtering software allows you to specify the action you want the mail program to take when a message matches certain conditions. You can have an email program copy, move, or destroy a message based on such things as the sender, the subject line, or words found in the text. You can have the email program do all that before you read your mail, or even before the email gets downloaded from the Internet service provider's mail server.

If you have never dealt with email, this may seem like merely bells and whistles. However, believe me, when you get involved in really active mail lists (see Chapter 6), you're going to want to be able to sort your mail by geography, surname, and time period, at least. Furthermore, there will be some people you just don't want to hear from. You can have your mail filters set up to simply delete mail from those people.

This brings us to the next important topic: spammers.

Spam Protection

The old netheads were right. Once the Internet was opened to the public, they warned, the demons of advertising would hound us. They would flood our mailboxes, clog the bandwidth with their shilling and hawking, and make the Internet much less useful and fun. Well, we opened Pandora's box anyway and got junk email. Now the spammers are loose.

"Spammers" get their name from an old Monty Python skit where people are prevented from having a normal conversation because some other folks insist on loudly praising Spam. The email advertisements you receive uninvited are often called "spam," because like the skit, they interrupt you rudely. They are also called "UBE" for "unsolicited bulk email," and they are sent by folks who claim it's their First Amendment right to use a service you paid for to sell their stuff to you.

These twerps are everywhere. They send message after message about get-rich-quick schemes, pyramid schemes, vitamins—you name it. Sometimes the pitch is disguised as a newsletter, and they include some bogus return address if you want to be removed from their list. But whatever the pitch, the purpose is the same: They are using your paid online account for their advertising.

Why You Get It   Anytime you post a message to a Usenet newsgroup, use a chat room on America Online, CompuServe, or the Internet, or supply an online service with your profile, the spammers are there collecting your email address and any other information they can find. Then they sort the addresses and sell them, and then you get junk email.

Naturally, spammers know that not everyone will be pleased to hear from them. They disguise themselves with bogus "From:" and "Reply to:" lines. You can try to reply and "remove" or "unsubscribe" from their lists, but it seldom works. The return addresses either don't exist or aren't designed to receive mail. To reach the spammers and get off their lists, you have to do some detective work.

What to Do   Frankly, I'm intensely opposed to this noxious form of telemarketing (can you tell?). The first step is for all netizens to write to Congress and have this practice stopped. If Washington can pass a law controlling junk faxes, why can't it do the same for junk email?

Second, learn to protect yourself. One harsh measure would be to never use chat, post to Usenet, use a forum on AOL or CompuServe or a bulletin board on Prodigy, or post your member profile online. But then online life would be pretty dull, wouldn't it?

A less harsh solution is to create two email accounts: one public and one private. You use the public one for Usenet, chat, anonymous FTP, and so on. The other is like an unlisted phone number; you only give it out to people you really want to hear from. Only check your private email box, and ask your Internet service provider to delete any mail that comes to the public one.

If you use an email program like Eudora or Pegasus (discussed later in the chapter), you can also filter out the junk. Both programs can, based on a message's address, subject line, or body text, drop email into specific folders. Whenever I get junk email, I copy the address, header, and any catchphrase like "money-making opportunity" to a filter. The next time I get a message from the spammer, it's dumped into my Trash folder and deleted. (In Eudora, for example, select `Tools|Filters`, enter the email address, check the `Transfer to` box, and select `Trash`.) For some suggestions of who to add to your twit filter, see the sidebar "Libbi's All-Time Spammer Parade." Another good source for names and strategies (some of which I suspect aren't quite legal) is the Internet Black List at www-math.uni-paderborn.de/~axel/BL/#spam.

And what about America Online and CompuServe users? AOL can now automatically intercept incoming email from known spammers, thanks to a recent court decision. The controls are set by default. To turn them off, use the keyword PREFERRED MAIL. Of course, AOL's action keeps out only so much spam. If you get junk email from an AOL account, forward it to TOSSPAM. AOL's staff will tell that person to stop sending you email. You can also control what you get by entering the keyword MAIL CONTROLS. The only drawback is it can only filter out email based on the From: field, which spammers frequently change.

CompuServe (often referred to as "CIS" for "CompuServe Information Service") doesn't offer as many options for blocking spam, but it's always been against the rules for CIS members to send advertising to other CIS members. If you do, CIS can terminate your account. As for non-CIS mail, you can set your email preference to never receive or send any Internet mail, but that's hardly a solution.

Desperate Measures   Is junk email still deluging you? You can try to track down the spammers, even though they try to disguise their true whereabouts. Don't look at the From or even the Reply-to lines. Look at the lines that say "Comments: Authenticated sender is:" or "Received." These lines will tell you the route of the message from your mailbox back to its origin. Once you have a domain name (like yxt2@srdinc.com), you at least know which ISP the spammer uses. See Figure 2-4.

Send a message to the ISP using the format postmaster@*provider*.com. Politely explain that you don't want to receive any more messages from the spammer. Do this consistently, and the UBE sender's privileges might be revoked.

```
Headers ---------------------------------
Return-Path: <yxt2@srdinc.com>
Received: from  rly-yc04.mx.aol.com (rly-yc04.mail.aol.com [172.18.149.36])
by air-yc05.mail.aol.com (v56.24) with SMTP; Sat, 06 Feb 1999 18:40:50 -0500
Received: from ntserver1.agency1 ([204.95.231.66])
by rly-yc04.mx.aol.com (8.8.8/8.8.5/AOL-4.0.0)
with ESMTP id QAA04730;  Sat, 6 Feb 1999 16:59:33 -0500 (EST)
Date: Sat, 6 Feb 1999 16:59:33 -0500 (EST)
From: yxt2@srdinc.com
Message-Id: 199902062159.QAA04730@rly-yc04.mx.aol.com
Received: from 501 (hil-qbu-ppv-vty33.as.wcom.NET
[209.154.56.33]) by ntserver1.agency1 with SMTP
(Microsoft Exchange Internet Mail Service Version 5.5.1960.3)
id 1K1TF9GW; Sat, 6 Feb 1999 16:58:27 -0500
To: ntnalv3s@aol.comSubject: Out to lunch
```

Figure 2-4 Look carefully at email headers to track down a spammer. Then complain to the Internet service provider that sent it on.

Note Do not insult or scold the Internet service provider. It may not know the client is using the account this way. Assume the spammer's Internet service provider is on your side when you write.

At the moment, there is no surefire, legal way to shut spammers up as they fill our email boxes, clog the already crowded Internet, and cost us extra toll charges. Although recent court decisions indicate more controls are coming, you never know. Be prepared. Use the strategies outlined above, and your email box should have less digital clutter.

Libbi's Spammer Twit List

Which junk emailers should you filter out? Well, each time you get a piece of unsolicited bulk email, add that sender's entire domain (what's after the @) to your filter list. Also, here's a starter list:

1Cust40.tnt2.sdg1.da.uu.net

202.188.95.1

194.202.128.76

205.176.181.63

212.250.196.101

aaaflyhi@aol.com

advanix.net

aravinthan.force9.co.uk

a-z-marketing.com

bball@exchangecom.net

brichards@mailexcite.com

cb-s.co.uk

chinachannel.net

cn.net

cuffs.com

cyberemag.com

cyberfiber.net

cyberpr0m0.com

cyberpr0m0ti0ns.com

cyberprom0.com

cyberpromo.com

cyberpromotions.com

dial-access.att.net

dialup-171.apc.net

emailers1@juno.com

foticomm.com

Friendsnnn@aol.com

globalfn.com

gothere.net

hosted2u.net

inetsvs.com

inter.net.il

jeffg@crushnet.com

keyholding.co.uk

legend.co.uk

listnet.net

m-22569@mailbox.swip.net

metronet.de

mike1@est1-rave.co.uk

netseek@dial.pipex.com

news.newswire.microsoft.com

nnn@nnn.com

online.sh.cn

p4a@juno.com

pacificcoasts.net

postnet.com

progress.com

propertyworld.co.uk

renee358@hotmail.com

rhaney19@ally.ios.com

rsdesigns.force9.co.uk

save-net.com

SIMPLE1GIL@aol.com 550

smartwall.taldem.com

sosglb.com

srdinc.com

stlnet.com

sub-mit-it.com

tankards.com

tas74883@yahoo.com

tech-center.com

telcom.co.nz

telintar.net.ar

top-10.com

UCanDoItac@aol.com

userk663.uk.uudial.com

usr11-dialup6.mta.198.3.99.199.excite.com

web-style.com

xlg02@dial.pipex.com

yougotmail.com

youvegotmail.com

zeus.scolo.net

File Attachments and Formats

Judging from the comments of my readers, nothing causes more gnashing of teeth to new Internet users than file attachments. You get a message that looks like gobbledygook, or has some filename like foobar.mim, and you don't know what to do with it.

The Internet is so big and powerful that we sometimes lose sight of its limitations. For example, email—the Net's original reason for being—is limited to transmitting the 128 alphanumeric characters (the ones on your keyboard) of the basic ASCII set. Just about every computer, large and small, uses ASCII (American Standard Code for Information Interchange), which is why email (and Usenet newsgroups) are limited to these characters.

Yet how does NASA send Hubble telescope pictures over Usenet? The secret is the processes of encoding and decoding. Like Little Orphan Annie's Secret Decoder Ring, encoding schemes turn binary files (such as .EXE files, graphics, spreadsheets, and formatted documents) into strings of text that, when properly decoded on the other end, resume their original form. The downside is that an encoded file can be 25 to 100 percent larger than the original file.

There are many different encoding schemes used on the Internet. As with File Transfer Protocols, you must know which scheme your correspondent used so you can properly decode the file you've received. The key schemes and their file extensions are as follows:

■ *UUENCODE (.UUE, .UU)* Its name comes from "UNIX-to-UNIX encoding," and it's a very common, very old method. UUencoded files are deciphered with UUDECODE.

■ *XXENCODE (.XXE)* This is a slightly different version of UUENCODE, for later versions of UNIX.

■ *BINHEX (.HQX, .HEX)* This scheme originated on the Mac, but you can now find BinHex encoders and decoders for the PC.

■ *MIME (.MME, .MM)* The Multipurpose Internet Mail Extensions scheme is the new kid on the block, and unlike its peers, it specifies the kind of file being sent. This allows many email and Web browser programs to recognize what's in that MIME file and to display its contents with the appropriate helper application.

When you receive a coded file, how do you translate it? If you're using a fairly decent email program like Pegasus or Eudora and you get a MIME or BinHex file, you don't have to do anything—the software's built-in decoders will do the job for you. However, if you get a file that's been coded with another format, you'll need a third-party program to do the dirty work for you. I've noted some sources below.

"But wait," says a reader. "I sometimes get a coded file that has another coded file within in it. In my email program, I see this huge ream of nonsense text. What do I do?" Look closely and you'll see instructions in this mess of text: probably the words "copy below this line" and "copy above this line." Select the text between these lines, and paste it into a word processor. Save the file as text only, with the .UUE file extension (because this is a uuencoded file). Then run a UUDECODE program, and the hidden file will emerge.

NOTE *Sometimes a large UUencoded file is split into a number of email messages, usually labeled FILE1.UUE, FILE2.UUE, and so on. Carefully cut and paste the contents of these files, from the first message to the last, into a single file. Then follow the steps in the text.*

Which programs decode (and encode) attached files? My favorite one is WinCode 2.7.3c, available at www.members.global2000.net/snappy. This free Windows program is as simple as such utilities ever get, and it supports seven different coding schemes. It can even install itself within Netscape, AOL, and WinCIM (2.0.1). The full manual costs $10, but I never needed it.

Another superior decoder (though it cannot encode) is Decode Windows 95 Shell Extension, available at ftp://ftp.funduc.com/decext.zip. It can handle multiple attachments and multipart files, as well as XXENCODE and UUENCODE, MIME, and BinHex files. It can embed itself right into Windows Explorer, so when you right-click a file, Decode is one of your choices. There are many other decoders for DOS, Windows, and the Mac. Search www.shareware.com for the latest releases. For more information on this gripping topic, check out "Binaries for Beginners" at www.agbamu.demon.co.uk/binbeg.htm and the Binary Info-Page FAQ (frequently asked questions) at shell.ihug.co.nz/~ijh.

Internet Mail Clients

Mail reading programs (also known as "clients") are everywhere, and some do quite a bit of fancy stuff. But to get you started, I recommend Eudora Light, Pegasus Mail, or Microsoft Outlook 98.

Eudora Light (http://eudora.qualcomm.com/eudoralight/)
Eudora is a mail program named for author Eudora Welty, and it's as simple and powerful as her stories. If all you need is simple mail management, Eudora Pro, or its free version called Eudora Light, will take care of it with ease. If you do have a provider, you simply enter the mail server's address (a painless task) and log on. See Figure 2-5.

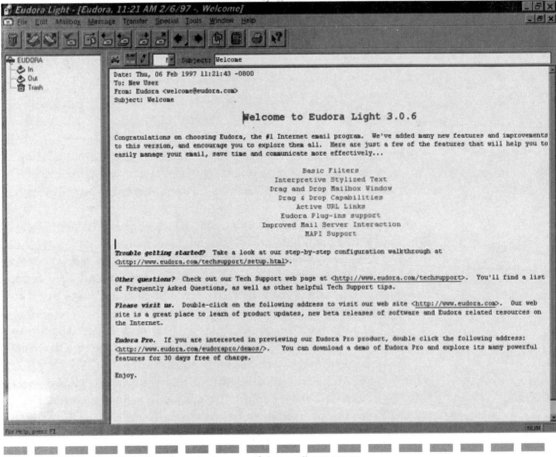

Figure 2-5 Eudora Light is a free, but powerful, email program.

After you've logged on to your mail server, sending and receiving messages are done with one click. You can log off to read the mail, then log on to post your replies, using Eudora Pro's spelling checker to help prevent embarrassing mistakes. Eudora also lets you set up a timer for retrieves—anywhere from every few seconds to once a day. Eudora Pro and Eudora Light both offer configuration options stored in one easy-to-navigate Settings window; for example, you can set the program so it won't retrieve messages larger than, say, 20 KB.

Eudora Light puts all received mail in the New box and lets you sort the messages into others by hand, but Eudora Pro lets you filter messages as they come in, route them to specific mailboxes, and sort messages by various criteria. You can also search all message headers and bodies for text strings in both versions. The Macintosh and Windows versions of Eudora Pro are nearly identical in capabilities, except that the Mac version lacks support for multiple mailboxes. Eudora Light works perfectly under Windows 95 as well. On either platform, Eudora is so simple to install and configure that you'll be sending and collecting email less than 30 minutes after opening the box.

To get Eudora Pro, call Qualcomm Inc. at 800-238-3672 or 619-658-1292. The list price is $89. To get the slightly less functional version called Eudora Light, check you local BBS or log on to http://cwsapps.texas.net/smail.html#eudora to download it. The price of Eudora Light is to send the author a postcard!

Pegasus (http://www.pegasus.usa.com/)   Pegasus Mail has all the features of Eudora Light and more. Because it has so many more features, it's a little harder to learn at first, but once you get the hang of it, Pegasus Mail is just wonderful. It is an extremely intuitive, great-looking mail program with integrated address books and mailing lists. The program itself is free, but if you want a printed manual to help you learn all the features, that costs $40.

Extensive drag-and-drop capabilities also help to make Pegasus Mail easy to use. You can attach or include a file in a message with Pegasus Mail, but there are so many wonderful options for how to do that, you may have to do it a few times to get the hang of it.

Pegasus also includes a spelling checker, advanced filtering controls for incoming messages, and a feature that lets you minimize Pegasus and have it check the mail at regular intervals and play a sound file when it finds new mail. Most functions are one click off the menu bar, and you can change your setting easily from the Configuration menu. One of the best features of Pegasus Mail is how wonderful it is to use offline: You only have to connect to post and retrieve. In addition, in sending or replying to a message, you have the option of sending a copy to both the recipient and yourself or just to the recipient, and you can review or delete queued mail. The price is nice too...it's free!

To download Pegasus Mail, go to the Pegasus home page at http://www.pegasus.usa.com/.

Microsoft Outlook 98 If you are a registered Microsoft Office user, Microsoft Outlook 98 can be downloaded from http://www.microsoft.com/office/outlook/ for free. This program not only reads email but also Usenet (see Chapter 5). It can keep track of email addresses, just like Pegasus and Eudora, but it's also a full-fledged contact manager. See Figure 2-6.

When I first used Outlook 98, I kept thinking about those old late-night ads for the Vegematic: "It slices, it dices!" It's not perfect, but Outlook 98 is a vast improvement over the bloated, buggy, and benighted Outlook that shipped on the Office 97 Professional Edition CD-ROM. That program crashed at every opportunity, couldn't import or export contacts worth a farthing, and was impossible to figure out.

But Outlook 98, with its two-click filter creation (while reading a message, click on `Actions|Create Rule` and it leads you through it) and the ability to color-code as well as file, save, delete, copy, or forward messages with the filters really impressed me. You can flag items for follow-up, put someone in the address book by right-clicking on the email address, and do lots of other cool things. If you are already using Microsoft Office, give Outlook 98 a try.

Inoculations

No journey is without risk. Whenever you enter the realm of file transfer, the dreaded microorganism, the computer virus, might be lurking. A *virus* is a program hidden on a disk or within a file that can damage your data or your computer in some way. Some simply display a message. Others will wipe out your entire hard drive. I strongly recommend that you inoculate your computer before using this mode of electronic travel. Programs to detect and remove viruses are available on BBS, in your local computer store, and on various online services. Some are shareware, others more costly, but if the program ever deletes a virus before it harms your system, it's worth the price.

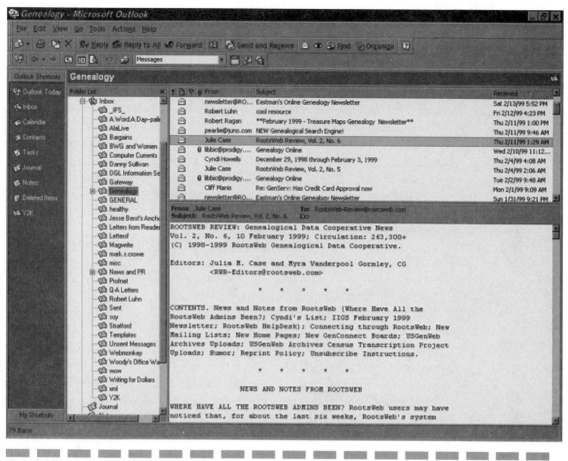

Figure 2-6 Microsoft Outlook 98 is part of the Microsoft Office suite. It does a lot more than just email.

Generally, before you download, look for an indication that the files have been checked for viruses. If not, reconsider downloading from that site. If someone sends an attachment or hands you a diskette with data, always run a virus checker on the disk before you do anything else. Once a virus is copied onto your hard disk, getting it off of there is a headache. In addition, run the virus checker on your hard drive at least twice a month, just to be certain. This should be part of your regular tune-up and maintenance.

Online-Ready Genealogy Programs

Many genealogy database programs will translate your genealogy data into HTML format, so that you can publish them on the World Wide Web. A few words of caution here, however. Some people are upset to find so much as their names published online without their written permission. Some genealogists consider anything published online or in hard copy to be false unless documentation proving it is also published. Still others feel that sharing their hard work without getting data and/or payment in return is a bad idea. For these and other reasons, you may want to: (a) publish data only on deceased people, (b) publish only enough data to encourage people to write you with their data; and (c) use a program that can cite your sources as well as your data.

Nevertheless, if you want to create a Web site with your genealogy on it, you have lots of choices. Following are a few of these.

Ultimate Family Tree

Ultimate Family Tree is available from http://www.uftree.com/ and has versions costing from $40 to $75, depending on features. Creating a Web page with this program takes several steps, but happily, they are all out-lined in the program's help file. The results are several pages; the "home" page of the set of files is as you see in Figure 2-7. From the main page there are links to each surname as well as descendants, a drop chart, and an index of all names. Although the program includes space for your sources, the Web output does not include them.

A nice feature is that if you check the correct box in the process, living persons' names, but not their data, can be included. The notation "(still alive)" prints below the name.

Family Origins 7.0

Family Origins for Windows, available for $30 at http://www.parsonstech.com/software/fowin7.html, generates the HTML files automatically, from the `Create Web Site` option under the Tools menu. Although it has a number of options for whom to include, you have to accept its choice of filenames of the Web pages themselves. To each page, you can add pictures, if you have scanned in images of your ancestors.

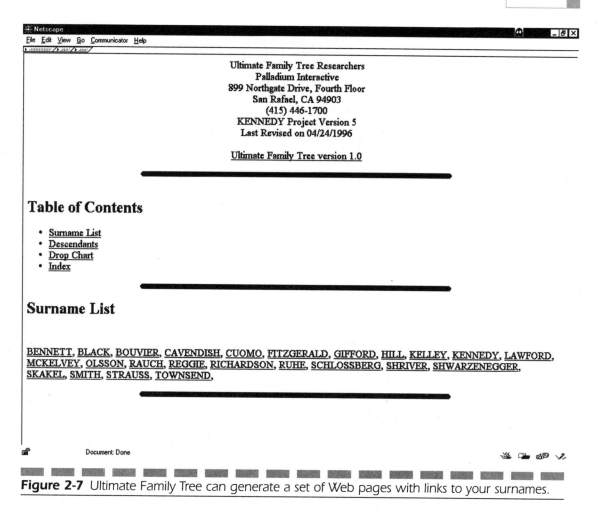

Figure 2-7 Ultimate Family Tree can generate a set of Web pages with links to your surnames.

The program's routine creates a surname list with links to each page that mentions that surname, an index of names (first and last) with links to pages that mention them, and a page of sources. If you choose to include your sources, then each source is a link that appears as a footnote number in the text of the other pages. Clicking on the footnote number takes you to the footnote page. Figure 2-8 shows the Sources page. The result is pretty, easy to navigate, and with the sources, quite respectable.

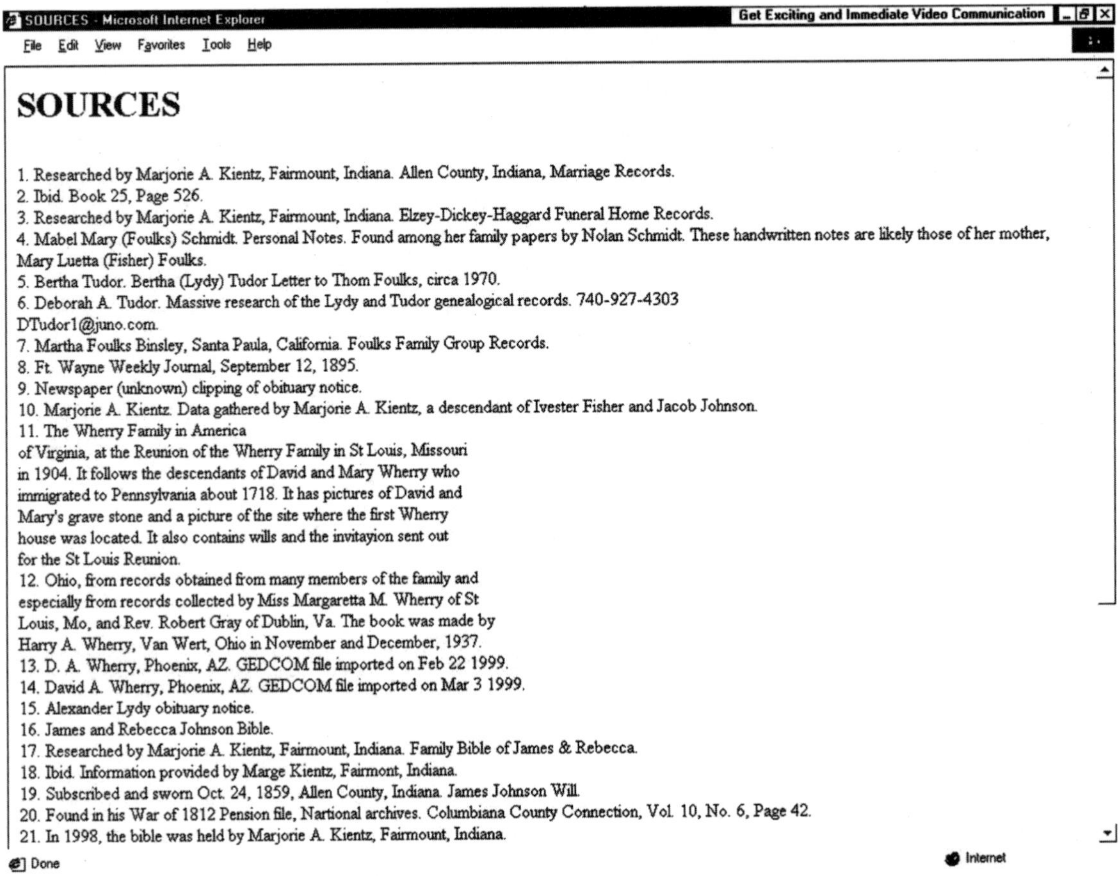

SOURCES - Microsoft Internet Explorer   Get Exciting and Immediate Video Communication

File   Edit   View   Favorites   Tools   Help

SOURCES

1. Researched by Marjorie A. Kientz, Fairmount, Indiana. Allen County, Indiana, Marriage Records.
2. Ibid. Book 25, Page 526.
3. Researched by Marjorie A. Kientz, Fairmount, Indiana. Elzey-Dickey-Haggard Funeral Home Records.
4. Mabel Mary (Foulks) Schmidt. Personal Notes. Found among her family papers by Nolan Schmidt. These handwritten notes are likely those of her mother, Mary Luetta (Fisher) Foulks.
5. Bertha Tudor. Bertha (Lydy) Tudor Letter to Thom Foulks, circa 1970.
6. Deborah A. Tudor. Massive research of the Lydy and Tudor genealogical records. 740-927-4303 DTudor1@juno.com.
7. Martha Foulks Binsley, Santa Paula, California. Foulks Family Group Records.
8. Ft. Wayne Weekly Journal, September 12, 1895.
9. Newspaper (unknown) clipping of obituary notice.
10. Marjorie A. Kientz. Data gathered by Marjorie A. Kientz, a descendant of Ivester Fisher and Jacob Johnson.
11. The Wherry Family in America
of Virginia, at the Reunion of the Wherry Family in St Louis, Missouri
in 1904. It follows the descendants of David and Mary Wherry who
immigrated to Pennsylvania about 1718. It has pictures of David and
Mary's grave stone and a picture of the site where the first Wherry
house was located. It also contains wills and the invitayion sent out
for the St Louis Reunion.
12. Ohio, from records obtained from many members of the family and
especially from records collected by Miss Margaretta M. Wherry of St
Louis, Mo, and Rev. Robert Gray of Dublin, Va. The book was made by
Harry A. Wherry, Van Wert, Ohio in November and December, 1937.
13. D. A. Wherry, Phoenix, AZ. GEDCOM file imported on Feb 22 1999.
14. David A. Wherry, Phoenix, AZ. GEDCOM file imported on Mar 3 1999.
15. Alexander Lydy obituary notice.
16. James and Rebecca Johnson Bible.
17. Researched by Marjorie A. Kientz, Fairmount, Indiana. Family Bible of James & Rebecca.
18. Ibid. Information provided by Marge Kientz, Fairmont, Indiana.
19. Subscribed and sworn Oct. 24, 1859, Allen County, Indiana. James Johnson Will.
20. Found in his War of 1812 Pension file, Nartional archives. Columbiana County Connection, Vol. 10, No. 6, Page 42.
21. In 1998, the bible was held by Marjorie A. Kientz, Fairmount, Indiana.

Done   Internet

Figure 2-8 Family Origins for Windows allows you to publish your notes on sources as well as your data.

Family Tree Maker

Family Tree Maker (FTM) is available for $30 to $100, depending on how many CD-ROMs are included with the version you choose from http://www.familytreemaker.com/ftmvers.html. Family Tree Maker will not create stand-alone HTML pages. To create the Web page, you must upload your GEDCOM (see Appendix C) to the FTM web site, where a program on their server will translate it into HTML and place it on the Internet for you.

If you would like to use the Family Tree Maker program, but would like to make your own pages, you can get a program that coverts GEDCOMs to HTML, such as GedPage 2.0, below.

GedPage 2.0

GedPage 2.0 has a unregistered version at http://www.frontiernet.net/~rjacob/gedpage.htm. It is currently available for Windows and Macintosh. This is a limited version that has all the features of the $10 registered version, such as adding backgrounds and pictures. In this trial version, you can use any color for your background, but not a graphic background; an "UNREGISTERED" message will appear at the top of every generated page, and a "nag" screen will appear when you exit GedPage. Also, in the trial version, the Notes, Soundex Codes, and Sources features will be disabled. In the $10 version, all this is included. The sources are all on one page, with a numbered link from each datum to the source.

You run the program, pointing it to the GEDCOM you have exported from your genealogy program. When you start, a pop-up window lets you to change the color of the background, the text, the link, and the visited link. You can also add your home page URL, a nice advantage if you create different pages for other names.

GedPage uses a Family Group Sheet format, as shown in Figure 2-9. This is a nice program that gets your files into HTML using half as much disk space as some others I've tried. It supports GENDEX, optional notes, sources, and Soundex codes, all as links in your pages.

The Master Genealogist 4.0

You can order The Master Genealogist (TMG) from www.whollygenes.com in one of two versions: Gold Edition ($99) and Silver Edition ($59). The Gold Edition is the one that can convert your data directly to a Web page. TMG allows you unlimited entries for people, events per person, names per person, relationships, user-defined events, sources, citations, graphics, and more. Most data entry fields have unlimited length, so you don't have to abbreviate.

Another advantage of TMG is that you can import your data directly (i.e., without GEDCOM) from a long list of other genealogy programs,

```
Fredrick Leopold Jacob/Emma Marie Gross - Netscape                    _ ☐ ☒
File  Edit  View  Go  Communicator  Help
```

Husband: **Fredrick Leopold Jacob**   (J210)

```
   Born: 5 Feb 1889      at: Kurtovian, Russia, Lithuania 1
Married: 21 Jul 1921     at: Ev. Luth. Church, New Kensington, Westmoreland, PA  2
   Died: 25 Jun 1962     at: Brushton, Allegheny, PA 3
Father:Robert Ephram Jacob
Mother:Marie Freiman
        Other Spouses:
NOTES
```

Wife: **Emma Marie Gross**   (G620)

```
   Born: 27 Sep 1898     at: Tauroggen, Russia, Lithuania 4
   Died: 25 May 1976     at: Wilkinsburg, Allegheny, PA 4
Father:Alexander Gross
Mother:Dorthea Leitke
        Other Spouses:
NOTES
```

CHILDREN

```
   Name: Emma Johanna Jacob
   Born: 7 May 1922       at: Pittsburgh, Allegheny, PA 5
Married:                  at:
   Died:                  at:
Spouses: Frank MacNeil
NOTES
```

```
   Name: Walter Leopold Jacob
   Born: 29 Jul 1923      at: Pittsburgh, Allegheny, PA 6
Married: 19 Mar 1956      at: Pittsburgh, Allegheny, PA 6
   Died:                  at:
Spouses: Margarete Kraus
```

```
Document: Done
```

Figure 2-9 GedPage creates an HTML page from a GEDCOM.

including Brother's Keeper, Ancestral Quest, Family Origins, Family Tree Maker, Ultimate Family Tree, and others. You can export to all those and to many word-processing and database programs, as well as to HTML. (See Figure 2-10.)

TMG Gold Edition can generate its reports directly to your word processor's format, and because some word processors can save to HTML, this gives you lots of flexibility in your final product. TMG Gold Edition produces most reports in more than 50 native file formats. The Silver Edition supports RTF and ASCII only.

TMG can create your site to include a table of contents, endnotes, multiple indexes, and bibliography. Most people I have talked to find TMG's

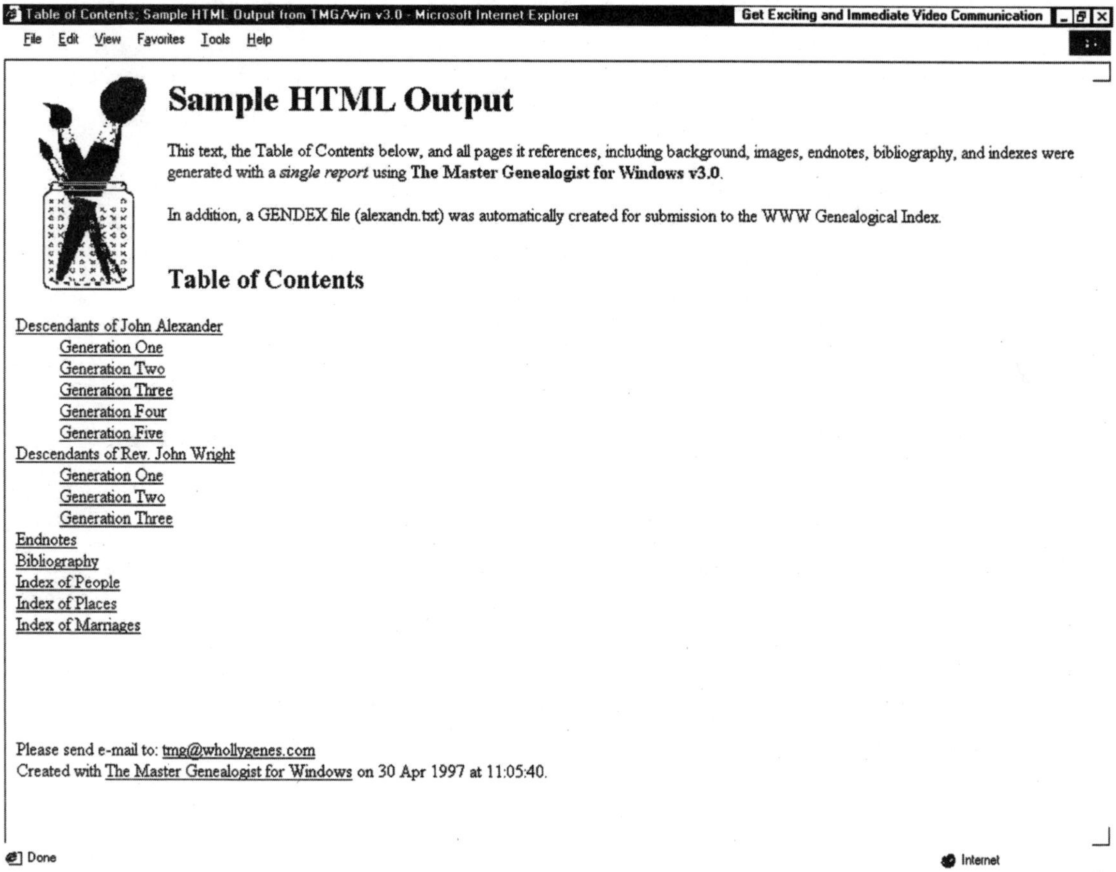

Table of Contents; Sample HTML Output from TMG/Win v3.0 - Microsoft Internet Explorer   Get Exciting and Immediate Video Communication

File   Edit   View   Favorites   Tools   Help

Sample HTML Output

This text, the Table of Contents below, and all pages it references, including background, images, endnotes, bibliography, and indexes were generated with a *single report* using **The Master Genealogist for Windows v3.0**.

In addition, a GENDEX file (alexandn.txt) was automatically created for submission to the WWW Genealogical Index.

Table of Contents

Descendants of John Alexander
    Generation One
    Generation Two
    Generation Three
    Generation Four
    Generation Five
Descendants of Rev. John Wright
    Generation One
    Generation Two
    Generation Three
Endnotes
Bibliography
Index of People
Index of Places
Index of Marriages

Please send e-mail to: tmg@whollygenes.com
Created with The Master Genealogist for Windows on 30 Apr 1997 at 11:05:40.

Done   Internet

Figure 2-10 The Master Genealogist is a favorite among genealogists for its many features; HTML publishing is just one of them.

source citation unequaled by any other genealogy program. Sources are not required, but you'll find yourself recording them because it is so easy.

Generations Easy Tree

Generations Easy Tree (GET) is only one part, though it is the lead component, of Generations Grande Suite, a 12-CD-ROM package of software and research files from Sierra Online that is available at www.sierra.com for $80. In addition to Easy Tree and a snapshot graphics application, the package also includes a cookbook/recipe package.

Easy Tree can generate any of its reports in HTML—almost anything you can send to the printer. I was surprised to find it lacks a quick way of excluding personal information about living people. (Its help file suggests you cut off such data at about 1900 but gives you no tips on how to do this easily.)

For each of the differing styles of Web reports, Easy Tree creates a similar, linked, multipage directory structure. You transfer the entire structure to your Web site. The linked HTML pointers are accurate and easy to follow online. Figure 2-11 shows an Ahnentafel Web page created with this program (see Appendix C for a discussion of the Ahnentafel standard).

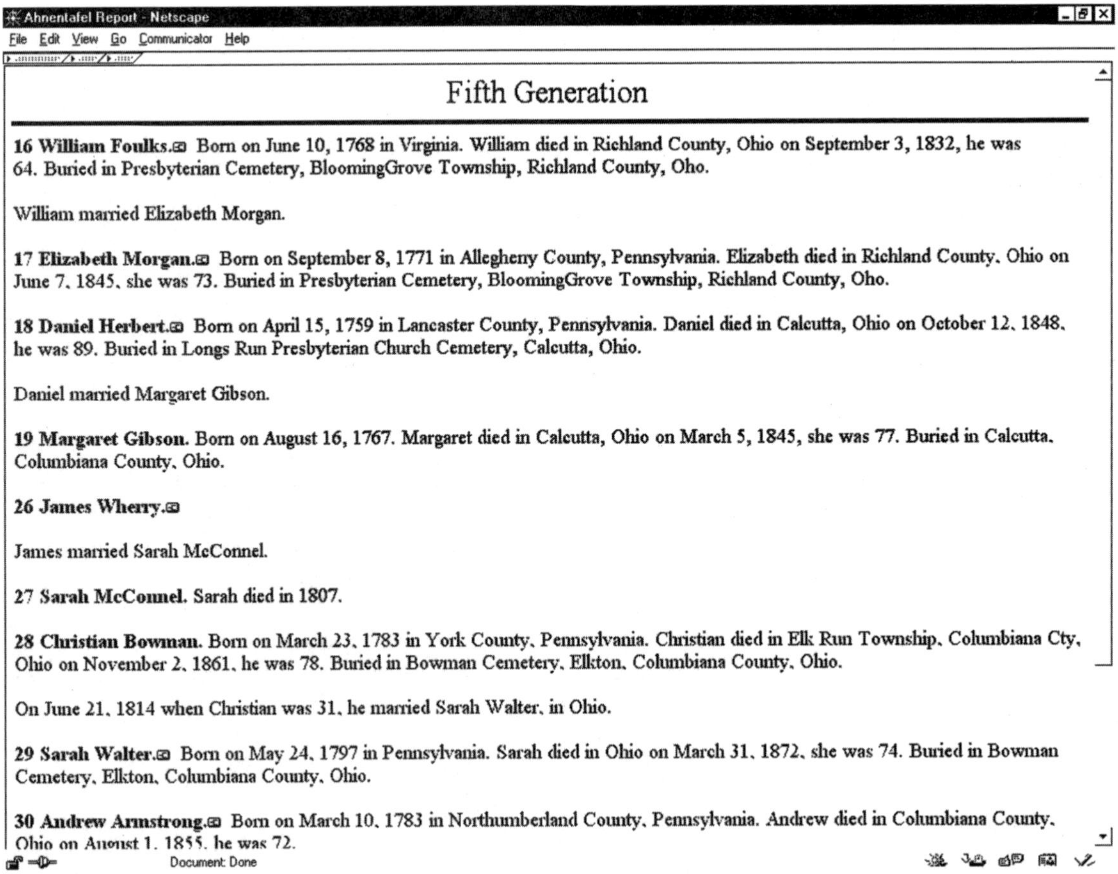

Ahnentafel Report - Netscape

File Edit View Go Communicator Help

Fifth Generation

16 William Foulks. Born on June 10, 1768 in Virginia. William died in Richland County, Ohio on September 3, 1832, he was 64. Buried in Presbyterian Cemetery, BloomingGrove Township, Richland County, Oho.

William married Elizabeth Morgan.

17 Elizabeth Morgan. Born on September 8, 1771 in Allegheny County, Pennsylvania. Elizabeth died in Richland County, Ohio on June 7, 1845, she was 73. Buried in Presbyterian Cemetery, BloomingGrove Township, Richland County, Oho.

18 Daniel Herbert. Born on April 15, 1759 in Lancaster County, Pennsylvania. Daniel died in Calcutta, Ohio on October 12, 1848, he was 89. Buried in Longs Run Presbyterian Church Cemetery, Calcutta, Ohio.

Daniel married Margaret Gibson.

19 Margaret Gibson. Born on August 16, 1767. Margaret died in Calcutta, Ohio on March 5, 1845, she was 77. Buried in Calcutta, Columbiana County, Ohio.

26 James Wherry.

James married Sarah McConnel.

27 Sarah McConnel. Sarah died in 1807.

28 Christian Bowman. Born on March 23, 1783 in York County, Pennsylvania. Christian died in Elk Run Township, Columbiana Cty, Ohio on November 2, 1861, he was 78. Buried in Bowman Cemetery, Elkton, Columbiana County, Ohio.

On June 21, 1814 when Christian was 31, he married Sarah Walter, in Ohio.

29 Sarah Walter. Born on May 24, 1797 in Pennsylvania. Sarah died in Ohio on March 31, 1872, she was 74. Buried in Bowman Cemetery, Elkton, Columbiana County, Ohio.

30 Andrew Armstrong. Born on March 10, 1783 in Northumberland County, Pennsylvania. Andrew died in Columbiana County, Ohio on August 1, 1855, he was 72.

Document Done

Figure 2-11 Almost any report in Generations Easy Tree can be saved in HTML format, including Ahnentafel.

Shop Around

This is just a small sampling of programs that can help you collect and then publish your genealogical research. Most of the major programs have some sort of demonstration program you can download and try. So shop around, find one that suits you, and share your data!

3

Rules of the Road

How to Surf Happily

Attitudes and Etiquette

I've already noted that the online world has definite communities, and none is friendlier and more helpful than the genealogical ones. Nevertheless, as with any community, there are customs and etiquette you're expected to follow. Some of these you should know before you sign on.

One good idea is to "lurk" first, which is to say, read a list without posting messages yourself. It's sort of like sitting in the corner at a party without introducing yourself, except it's not considered rude online; in some places you're expected to lurk until you get the feel of the place. Read the messages for a while, and find out who's interested in what. If the board or service has a help or information file, read it well, understand what's allowed and not allowed with this particular group, then introduce yourself with your first message.

When you post a query, which should be your second message, never make the subject line (called the "title" in some places) something vague and general such as "query" or "searching my family." Some people choose what messages to download based on the subject line; if yours isn't specific enough, it might not get read at all. Your subject line should have the surnames mentioned in the messages, such as "SPENCER, POWELL, CRIPPEN, BEEMAN." If it's a general-information request, don't use "General information" as your subject line, but rather, "Is the IGI on CD-ROM?" or similar specific phrase. Respect people's time (and lack thereof) by being quite clear about the subject matter in your title.

Flames

Be warned, you might get "flamed." This is when someone sends an insulting or offensive message. Flames are usually personal attacks in response to an opinion on an issue. When the insults start getting tossed back and forth in the mail list or Usenet group, it's called a "flame war."

If you're flamed, the best, easiest, and safest thing to do is ignore the flaming message. Forget it. Put the sender on your "twit" filter and go on. The optimum course of action is never start or get involved in a flame war.

Another commonly accepted practice is to target your messages. When posting a message, you have a choice of how wide the distribution will be on most systems; sometimes you can flag it to a subcategory, as on CompuServe and AOL.

Choose wisely, for the same reasons you want to use descriptive titles. It's considered bad form to post a message to the wrong subject heading; certain groups have rules about what can be posted and how it must be worded. You may inadvertently break some rules by posting it to the wrong heading. In addition, post a message only once, especially to groups where all the messages are stored somewhere. This doesn't mean you can't repeat a query once in a while; just don't do it so often that you become annoying. This is an obvious courtesy to those trying to control the traffic.

Many people store a signature, which serves the same purpose as a return address label. This should be a pure ASCII file with the details of how to reach you, inserted at the end of a message. Try not to make yours overly long and complicated, but do try to update it often, since it helps someone contacting you directly. (Surnames in the signature are discouraged on the Internet due to the archiving of the messages.) In addition, sometimes a "tag line" is added, some pithy or humorous statement of 10 words or less. Following are some examples:

I'm in shape…round's a shape isn't it?

If this were an actual tag line, it would be funny.

It's only a hobby…only a hobby…

Libbi's Law: You cannot do just one thing…

Again, they're fine if not overdone. Lurk a while to see whether tag lines are accepted before using them in a certain group.

> **NOTE**   *Don't take seriously or execute any code mentioned in a tag line like "<Ctrl><Alt><Del> to read the next message." On the Internet a most vicious code has appeared in tag lines, for example one that a certain program would eventually interpret as RM * (a command to remove all files on the current disk, like DEL.), and there are no recovery tools like Norton on UNIX. Sadly, vandalism has followed us into the virtual world.*

Answer, Please

Eventually, you'll see a message you want to answer. Great! However, remember that there are customs to be followed in this case too. First, look at the top of the message. Several lines will tell you who posted the message, from where and when, and how it traveled. This is the header. Use it to direct your answer.

Be as brief as possible. Everyone is busy. Postings on some networks are huge in number. With so many going so far, only the most important bytes of information should be included. Also, remember that, somewhere, someone down the line is paying a long-distance charge to send your postings on. The briefer the article, the more likely it is that people will take the time to read it.

When you see something you want to answer, comment on, or discuss, it's traditional to summarize the message in the following format:

```
Joe Usenetter said in the title or subject line:
>what he said, with one arrow for each quoted line.
>>two arrows for information Joe quoted.
My answer to this is:
```

and so on. Some mail readers will take care of this, quoting the original for you. This way, if someone didn't see the beginning of the message, he or she can take the time to look up the original or take your word for the direct quote. However, don't directly quote the whole article. Only truly pertinent parts, at most four or five lines, should be repeated.

Use a direct response to the sender to answer a question posted at large. Instead of posting an article that everyone reads, post a mail response only to the person who asked the question. Also, check to be sure no follow-ups have already been posted; someone might have already given "your" answer. The questioner is then expected to post all the answers received in an edited, summarized form. Editing means stripping the headers and signatures, combining duplicate responses, and briefly quoting only the original question.

NOTE   *Rule #1, indeed, could be stated as "Never forget that the person on the other side is human." You're using machines to upload and download, so your interaction with the online world at first might seem pretty dry and impersonal. But the whole point of the Net is to connect people. Don't treat the people out there as machines. Remember, they have feelings.*

Smileys (Emoticons)

Humor and sarcasm are best used cautiously. Subtle humor, especially satire, is hard to get across with no facial expressions, body language, or hand signals. Well-done sarcasm so closely resembles the attitude it belittles that it's sometimes taken for a genuine attitude when delivered only in written form. Therefore, it's polite to clearly label all humor. How? Well, smileys (also called emoticons) are used. Here are some examples (tilt your head to the left):

:-) or :-]   A smiley face

:-D or HAHAHA   A laugh

;-)   A wink

| LOL | laughing out loud |
| ROTF | Rolling on the floor |

Other expressions besides humor are as follows:

IMHO	In my humble opinion
TAFN	That's all for now
TTYL	Talk to you later

There are more smileys in the Smiley (Emoticon) Glossary at the end of the book.

It might seem silly, but these symbols can help prevent misunderstandings. Moreover, should you be tempted to become incensed over something you've read, remember that some people on the Net consider themselves above using these silly symbols. Don't "flame" the author unless you're sure he or she was serious.

Cautions and Caveats

If you can avoid it, don't ask over the Net what can be more easily, efficiently, and quickly answered over the phone or at your own library. Sometimes your local sources don't have an answer that to others seems simple; in that case, ask. Nevertheless, you might get flamed (see sidebar earlier in the chapter).

Be aware of how your postings reflect on you. Never write anything you wouldn't say at a party or in a crowded room. Those postings are all many, many people will know about you, and you never know who's out there reading. The world is in constant motion today; no matter where they are right now, people online now might someday be clients or work with you or meet you in other circumstances, and they could remember your postings. In the end, you can't really hide behind the modem.

In many cases, a mailing list or Usenet group stretches across oceans and borders. Don't criticize someone's spelling or grammar; that person might be using English as a second language.

Unless you use an encryption program, email is not private, necessarily. It all depends on your system administrator and the other person's. Generally, yes, something you sent to someone's email box will be seen only by you two. However, system operators *have* been held responsible for what goes over their boards and nets, so they have good reason to spot-check messages. Be aware of that.

Be careful about copyrights and licenses, and cite original authors properly. Copyright law is complicated, and no clear-cut case has defined the use of copyright in electronic versions of text. Further, no one "owns" some of these networks. You could be personally guilty of plagiarism unless copyright laws and rules are carefully followed. Posting licensed software anywhere is another good way to get flamed, if not sued.

It's also important to cite references. If you give statistics, quotes, or a legal citation to support your position, you'll be much more believable if you give full credit to the source.

Finally, on the subject of rights, be aware that because of the powerful editing programs that come with mail readers, it's possible to post a message from one network to another, either in its original form or altered in some way. For this reason, some networks have a rule against posting something from another network; it's very possible to misquote a message, accidentally or deliberately, with the originator's signature still attached. Be sure you're quoting accurately and that the forum or net you're using allows quotes from other sources.

NOTE   *The same scammers who peddle useless "coats of arms" and "genealogies" that are little more than phone books have found the Internet too. These scams are usually quickly exposed on the discussion groups and in the frequently asked questions (FAQ) files.*

Sources and Proof

Most serious genealogists who discuss online sources want to know if you can "trust" what you find on the Internet. Many professional genealogists I know simply do not, period. Their attitude is that a source is not a primary source unless you have held the original document in your hand, and it is not proof unless supported by at least one other original document that you have held in your hand. To them, seeing a picture of a scanned original will on the Internet is not "proof." (See Figure 3-1.)

Others are even angry with those who publish their genealogy data on the Internet without citing each source in detail. "Lies!" one respected genealogist told me at a genealogy conference, where I was teaching a

Figure 3-1 The *Mayflower* passenger list has been scanned in at Caleb Johnson's site, Mayflower Passenger List, at http://members.aol.com/calebj/passenger.html Do you consider this a "primary source"?

class on how to publish on the Internet. "You're telling people to publish lies, because if it's not proven, it might not be true!"

I have to admit that I don't quite see it that way. In my opinion, you must evaluate what you find on the Internet just as you evaluate what you find in a library, courthouse, or archive. Many a genealogy book has been published with errors; so will online genealogies. On the World Wide Web, there are no real editors. You will find all kinds of information and sources on the Internet, from casual references in messages to documented genealogy to original records transcribed into HTML. The range is astounding.

You *will* be able to find some limited primary materials online. People are scanning and transcribing original documents onto the Internet, such as the Library of Virginia and the National Park Service.

Secondary materials, however, are much more common. The main value of the resources on the Internet will be, first of all, finding other genealogists searching the same lines, second finding leads to primary and secondary sources offline, and very rarely, glancing at an actual data source, perhaps a primary source. Yet, often, simply knowing a source exists can be a breakthrough.

Others are putting their family trees online, and while it is true many of them don't sacrifice the disk space to include the complete documentation, most who do so are willing to provide that to anyone who has data to exchange with them. Therefore, I still believe in publishing and exchanging data over the Internet. However, you must use good judgment.

The criteria for the evaluation of resources on the Web must be the same as you would use for any other source of information. Be aware that just because something is on a computer that does not mean it is infallible. As the saying goes, garbage in, garbage out. With that in mind, ask yourself some questions in evaluating online genealogy sites:

■ *Who created it?* You will find resources on the Internet from libraries, research institutions, and organizations such as the National Genealogical Society, as well as from the government and universities. These would give you more confidence than resources from a hobbyist, for example. Publications and software companies also publish genealogical information, but you must read carefully at the site to determine whether they've actually researched this information or simply accepted anything their customers threw at them. Finally, you will find tons of "family tradition," and while tradition usually has the grain of truth, it's usually not unvarnished.

■ *How long ago?* The more often a page is updated, the better you can feel about the data there. Of course, a page listing the census for a certain county in 1850 need not be updated every week, but a pedigree put online should be updated periodically as the author finds more data.

■ *Where does the information come from?* If the page in question doesn't give any sources, you will want to contact the page author to determine this. If there are sources, of course, you must decide if you trust those: Many a genealogical error has been printed in books, magazines, and online.

■ *In what form?* A simple GEDCOM published as a Web page can be useful for the beginner, but ideally, one wants an index to any genealogical resource, regardless of form. If a site has no search function, no table of contents, and no document map (a graphic leading you to different parts of the site), it's much less useful than it could be.

■ *How well does the author use and define genealogical terms?* Is it clear the author knows the difference between a yeoman farmer and a yeoman sailor? Does the author seem to be knowledgeable about genealogy? Another problem with online pages is whether the page author understands the problems of dates—both badly recorded dates and the 1752 calendar change. There are certain sites that can help you with calendar problems.

■ *Does the information make sense compared to what you already know?* If you have documentary evidence that contradicts what you see on a Web page, treat it as you would a mistake in a printed genealogy or magazine: Tell the author about your data and see whether the versions can be reconciled. That sort of exchange, after all, is what online genealogy is all about.

PART

2

The Internet

As noted in the Introduction, the Internet is a lot of computers connected together in a series of networks, which in turn are connected to the "backbone" of the system. That's the concept. The practice is that the Internet is a way to access computers all over the world, to get files full of text, pictures and records. The Internet is used in several different ways. This section will tell you how to use the Internet "services", as the different functions are called. You will learn how to transfer files, send messages in various ways, and read documents over the Internet. The most famous Internet service is the World Wide Web, which ties together most of the services of the Internet. Note: There are few editors on the Internet. The information you find there may be carefully researched or simply slapped together. Approach information on the Internet as you would any self-published book in the library: as a very good clue, but only rarely as conclusive proof.

FTP

File Transfer Protocol, or FTP, is a way of getting files from here to there—from another computer to yours or from yours to another computer—via the Internet. Browsers can receive files with FTP, and in versions 5 of Microsoft Internet Explorer and Netscape Navigator, they can send files as well. However, sending and receiving FTP files with a browser is like planting flowers with a steak knife. Sure, you will get the job done eventually, but it's best to use a tool designed for the job.

NOTE   Throughout this chapter you'll find references to newsgroups and Web sites. This is only to illustrate how interconnected the genealogy resources on the Internet can be. You will learn everything you need to know about newsgroups and Web sites in other chapters.

When you have a Web page to publish, FTP is the best way to get files to the server that will be on the Internet so that people can see your work. If you want to retrieve a shareware program or large text file, FTP is the best choice.

WS_FTP for PCs (see Chapter 2) and Fetch for Macintosh are good choices, and they are relatively cheap. They both have features that I enjoy: the ability to read text files, to save the addresses of FTP sites you visit, and to batch send and receive. Every FTP program is different, so when you get one, poke around its help file or manual to discover its particular tricks. Some let you store the settings for getting to several different FTP sites, or let you set default FTP sites. Many that store sites also let you set the initial directory to search, such as /PUB.

To use FTP, you simply give the program an address, probably your address at your Internet service provider, and a password. (If you are using FTP to get files from a public site, you log in as "anonymous" and give your email address as a password. If "anonymous" doesn't work as a login name, try "ftp".)

Using the CD command to change directories and LIST to look at filenames, you can send and receive files, usually by clicking an arrow (as in WS_FTP), but if you have a text-based client, you simply use GET and SEND.

In FTP, casing, spelling, and punctuation count. If you try to get to FOOBAR.some.edu by typing foobar.some.edu, it probably won't work. If you try to get a file called FAMILY.LOCLIST.README.html, you must follow that punctuation and capitalization exactly, or you'll get a File Not Found error message.

NOTE   Many of the remote computers you're FTPing to are big machines running UNIX and DOS that have more or less adopted UNIX's subdirectory structure. Therefore, if you know DOS, you can wend your way through a remote computer's subdirectories.

If the server you want to access is always busy, one way to get in is to repeatedly try until you hit that moment when someone has just logged off. Another trick: Determine which time zone the remote site is in and access it during local mealtimes or rush hours. A server in the UK, for instance, will be easier to access at 4 P.M. UK time when everyone is at tea. Granted, the Internet is international in nature, but a computer tied to a given university or organization will have peak usage at predictable times. Use that to your advantage.

Many Web browsers have an FTP program built in. If you want to jump to an FTP site, just enter the address by prefacing it with FTP://. Be prepared for some unsuccessful attempts to connect to an FTP site. FTP site addresses are always changing. The Internet is dynamic, so expect a few detours along the way.

Any time you are using FTP, you need to know some conventions. Files that end in .zip, .lzh, .exe, .arj, .arc, and .com are binary and should be transferred in binary mode. Files that end in anything else are probably text files and should be transferred in ASCII mode. If you are transferring files to a UNIX system, binary mode is generally the best mode to use for all transfers. The programs for uncompressing files are available at several software sites, such as www.shareware.com and www.tucows.com, as well as at ftp://ftp.cac.psu.edu/pub/genealogy/INDEX.html.

Binaries will usually be in ZIP format with a file extension of .zip. A self-extracting copy of PKWARE's shareware programs is in the DOS file pkz204g.exe. ZIP files can also be read with the DOS program unz50p1.exe.

Some files are also compressed with a program called lharc having the extension .lzh. The software to unpack those files can be found in the self-extracting DOS archive lha213.exe. Files that end with .arj may be uncompressed with unarj.exe, which is in the ZIP file unarj230.zip. .arc files may be decompressed with a program in pk361.exe. There are also several files that end with .exe. These are generally either self-extracting DOS archives or DOS programs.

Files ending in .Z have been compressed with the UNIX compress command. Files ending in .gz have been compressed with gzip.

Genealogy FTP Sites

RootsWeb

RootsWeb ftp.rootsweb.com

RootsWeb, as you'd expect, has many files for the beginning and experienced genealogist. These range from transcribed census records to the text of the messages on the ROOTS-L mailing list stretching back to 1989. (See Figure 4-1.)

Files on RootsWeb are either "virus-checked" or "uninspected." The page http://www.rootsweb.com/rootsweb/files.html lists which are which.

The virus-checked files are either plain ASCII text with no escape sequences for a virus to hide in, files the RootsWeb staff have virus-scanned, or files that have been virus-scanned by a RootsWeb user. While they are not guaranteed to be safe, at least someone has tried to detect whether they are dangerous.

Uninspected files have not been specifically checked for viruses. RootsWeb accepts files only from known sources, so even these files are probably safe. Still, in case someone unknowingly uploaded a virus, you

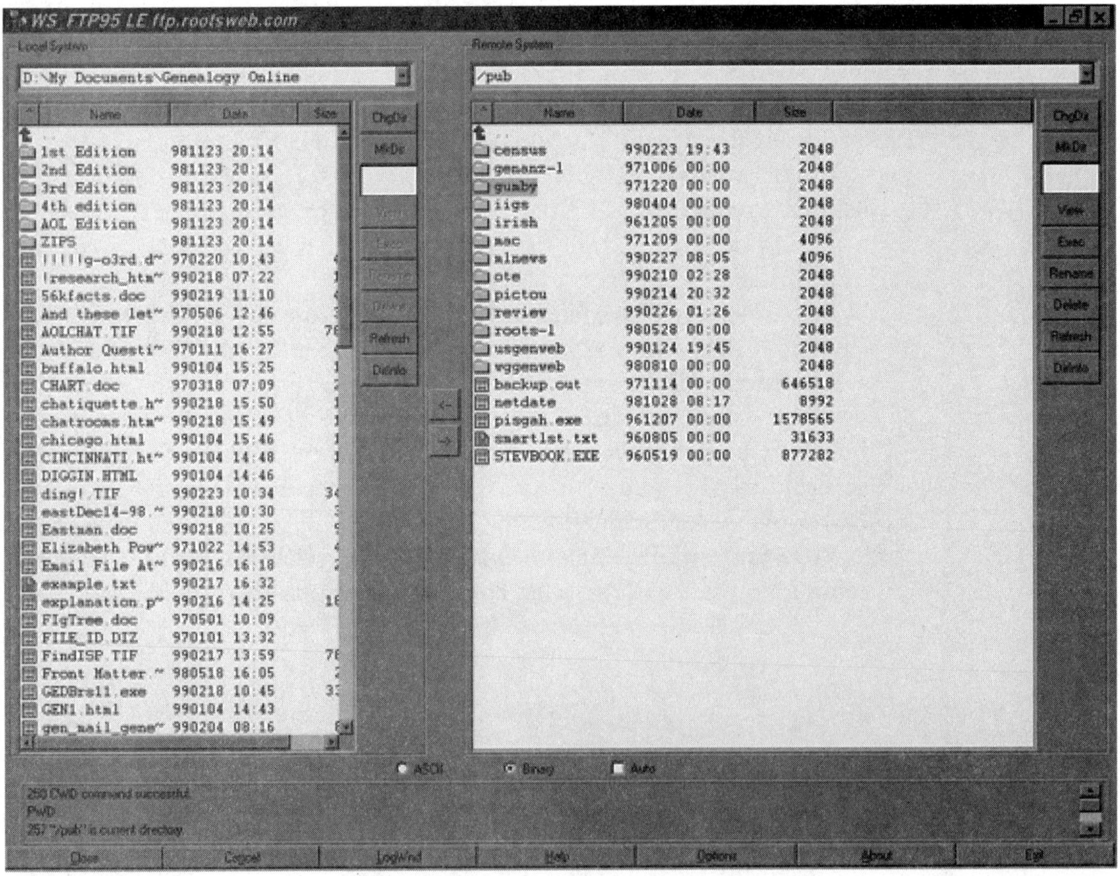

Figure 4-1 The RootsWeb FTP server has several directories full of goodies.

should run a virus checker on any uninspected file if you download it. If you download and virus-scan an uninspected file, email the RootsWeb folks at helpdesk@rootsweb.com about the results. Then they can move the file to "virus-checked" status or remove it from the server if you find it to be infected.

RootsWeb has more files than I can cover here, and besides, there will be even more on the system by the time you read this. Still, I'd like to point out how to find what's there. Point your FTP client (or browser, if you prefer) to ftp.rootsweb.com/pub/. As of this writing, you'll find several "folders" (called "directories" in FTP-speak), such as:

census

iigs

irish

mac

review

roots-l

usgenweb

wggenweb

and more. Under the census directory, you'll find subdirectories for each of the 50 states. Under the Alabama (al) subdirectory, you'll find that about 10 counties have directories. Keep clicking down and eventually, in /pub/census/al/madison/1850, you'll find two dozen text files with the index and some actual pages of the 1850 census that have been transcribed. These can be quickly transferred to your computer for later research.

Similar treasures are buried in the usgenweb and wggenweb directories; log files of important chats (see Chapter 8) are in the iigs directory; the roots-l directory has messages of the mail list; and the review directory has copies of the RootsWeb electronic newsletter.

The Genealogy Anonymous FTP Site

ftp.cac.psu.edu/genealogy/ftp/

This is a venerable site, one of the first on the Internet to start storing files of interest to the genealogist. Figure 4-2 shows you the directories in Netscape Navigator. Here you'll find shareware programs, text files, and

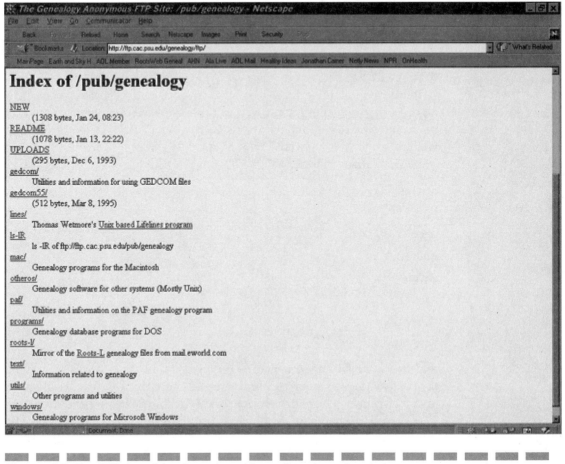

Figure 4-2 The FTP site of the Genealogy Home Page is updated about once a month.

general-purpose utilities such as programs to read compressed files. While it is one of the oldest, it is not updated very often these days—usually about once a month. Still, here you will find lots of genealogy programs for DOS, Mac, and other non-Windows operating systems.

Genealogy Online FTP Archive

ftp.genealogy.org/genealogy

Here you'll find a small library of GEDCOM and PAF files (see Appendix C), a mirror of the Roots Surname List through December 1996, and a few utilities. Michael Cooley's Genealogy Online site, though it has the same name, is not associated with this book.

The U.S. Government Census

ftp://148.129.129.31/pub/genealogy/

Names, pictures, FAQ files for searching government records—there's just a little at the federal government's census FTP site; much more can be found on the NARA Web site (see Chapter 7).

It looks to me as if someone started this FTP site with enthusiasm the in the mid-90s, then either lost interest or got laid off. What little was put up may be of help to you, but you'll find fresher information on the Library of Congress Web site. (This Web site is discussed at length in Chapter 7.)

Usenet

Usenet has been called "Internet bulletin boards," "Internet news," and many other names over the years. My definition of Usenet is this: an Internet service where messages to the world are posted. Email might be where messages to a specific person or group could be posted; forums and bulletin boards as well. When you post to Usenet, however, you are posting to the whole world.

Usenet isn't an organization per se, nor is it in any one place. Lots of machines carry the messages, receiving them and sending the on down the line. Your Usenet feed comes from your Internet service provider.

> **NOTE** *Throughout this chapter you'll find references to mailing lists and Web sites. This is just to illustrate how interconnected the genealogy resources on the Internet can be. You will learn everything you need to know about mailing lists and Web sites in other chapters.*

Like so many things, Usenet has its own frequently asked questions (FAQ) file. It is updated about once a month and posted every month to the news.announce.newusers, news.admin.misc, and news.answers newsgroups, and on the Web at http://www.faqs.org/faqs/ (see Figure 5-1). Much of what it says is in this chapter, but reading it won't hurt!

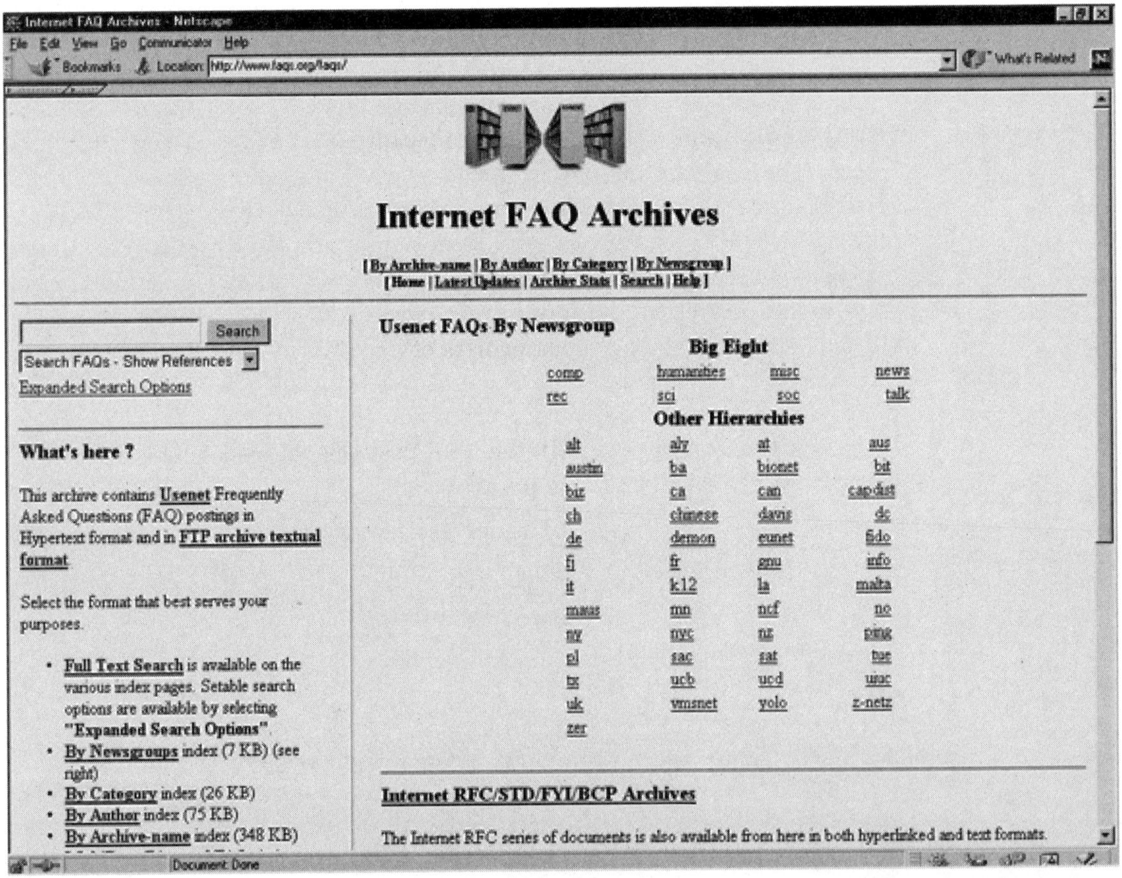

Figure 5-1 Frequently asked questions and answers are at http://www.faqs.org/faqs.

Complicated, but Useful

The first thing to understand about Usenet is that it's hard to understand. Don't be discouraged about that. It has been said that many Usenet flame wars arise because the users themselves don't comprehend the nature of the network. And these flames, of necessity, come from people who are actually using Usenet. Imagine, then, how hard it is for those unfamiliar with Usenet to understand it! On the other hand, it should be comforting to the novice that so many people are successfully using Usenet without fully understanding it.

One reason for the confusion is that Usenet is a part of the Internet, and for some people, it's the only part they use. Yet, it isn't the Internet, any more than Boston is Massachusetts. Usenet's messages are sorted into thousands of *newsgroups*, which are sort of like magazines (you subscribe to them), sort of like late-night dorm discussions, and sort of like a symposium. A newsgroup is supposed to be a set of messages on a certain subject, although abuses abound. Usenet's flavor depends on the newsgroups you subscribe to. Some newsgroups are wild, some very dull, most are in-between.

A *moderated* newsgroup has a referee, who decides what messages get to go on that newsgroup. An *unmoderated* one isn't edited in any way, except you'll get flamed (insulted) if you post a message off the proper topic. Most Usenet newsgroups are unmoderated.

There are eight major categories of newsgroups:

- COMP for computer-science related topics
- HUMANITIES for discussion of philosophy and the classics
- MISC for miscellaneous items.
- NEWS for topics about Usenet itself
- REC for recreation, hobbies, and interests.
- SCI for science not related to computers
- SOC for social interaction and hobbies. Most genealogy topics are in SOC.
- TALK for general conversation, usually for no purpose at all

Often the terms "Internet" and "Usenet" are confused. Tom Czarnik, who is a Usenet guru from way back, says, "Let's make a distinction between the Internet and Usenet. The Internet has come to mean the sum of the regional nets, while Usenet is a system for the exchange of newsgroups." Despite this clear separation, you'll often hear of "pictures sent over the Internet" or "messages on the Internet," when Usenet, a particular part of the Internet, is meant.

No person or group has control of Usenet as a whole. No one person authorizes who gets news feeds, which articles are propagated where, who can post articles, or anything else. These things are handled one newsgroup at a time. You won't find a Usenet Incorporated or even a Usenet Users Group. This means that, although the freedoms of expression and association are almost absolute, Usenet is not a democracy. It's anarchy—that is, something with little or no control except as exerted by the social pressures of those participating.

Therefore, sometimes Usenet is not fair—in part because it's hard to get everyone to agree on what's fair and in part because it's hard to stop people from proving themselves foolish.

Usenet History

Usenet got started, according to legend, in 1979, when a group at Duke University in North Carolina wanted to exchange data on research with some other universities. This group was in on the ground floor of the development of UNIX, an operating system. Soon they had written programs in UNIX to allow them to exchange data and analysis back and forth to other universities running the same programs. The neat part was that they could send programs that had been changed into plain text (encoded) and could be changed back into their digital form (decoded) so that they could send anything without using up the very limited bandwidth of the time.

They then began to use the program to send each other messages to discuss hardware, problems, industry gossip, and how to fix certain bugs. Then messages started about current events. And jokes. And dreams. And chatting about their hobbies.

Soon they began routing the more interesting stuff through an automated program. This program's duty was calling other UNIX sites while people slept, leaving off packets of data and programs and messages, picking up others destined for other places, and calling another site. As the amount of information increased (more than 500,000 articles a day are routed this way today), some sort of categorizing became necessary. So messages were labeled according to their "newsgroup," and people signed up for them the same way you subscribe to a newspaper. Your subscribed newsgroups are presented to you in your "newsreader." I'll show you more about that later.

Because all of this happens largely on a volunteer basis, you must understand that access to Usenet is not a right. Usenet is not a public utility, at least not yet; there's no government monopoly and little or no government control, so far. Some Usenet sites are publicly funded or subsidized, but most of them aren't. Lots of universities are connected, and often the hard work of keeping Usenet going is done on campus, but it's not an academic network.

Moreover, although many people are connected through and because of their work, Usenet is not to be used for advertising. Commercials are tolerated only when they're infrequent, informative, low-key, and preferably in direct response to a specific question. The only exception is the .biz groups, where advertisements are accepted.

In addition, the Usenet is not restricted to the U.S. Many, many correspondents are from around the globe, so be polite about grammar and spelling. The heaviest concentrations of Usenet sites outside the U.S. are in Canada, Europe, Australia, and Japan.

The Software

To read any Usenet newsgroup, you need some sort of newsreader. Many mail readers, such as Microsoft Outlook, include a newsreader.

America Online, Netcom, CompuServe, Delphi, Microsoft Network, Portal, PSI, The Well, and many other commercial services offer Usenet connections. You can also read Usenet on the Web at Deja (www.deja.com, shown in Figure 5-2).

In the "old days" (the first edition of this book!) we had to learn disagreeable, arcane UNIX commands and use unfriendly UNIX newsreaders to access the wonders of the Usenet. You may still have to do that, and text-based newsreaders are explained below. But, happily, times have changed. We now have a plethora of graphical newsreaders for any platform, be it Windows, Mac, UNIX, the X Window System, or whatever. The online commercial services have all integrated newsreaders into their front-end software too.

Newsreaders

You may prefer to use a dedicated newsreader. Figure 5-3 shows Free Agent, a free Windows newsreader from Forte software. You can download it from their site at http://www.forteinc.com/getfa/download.htm.

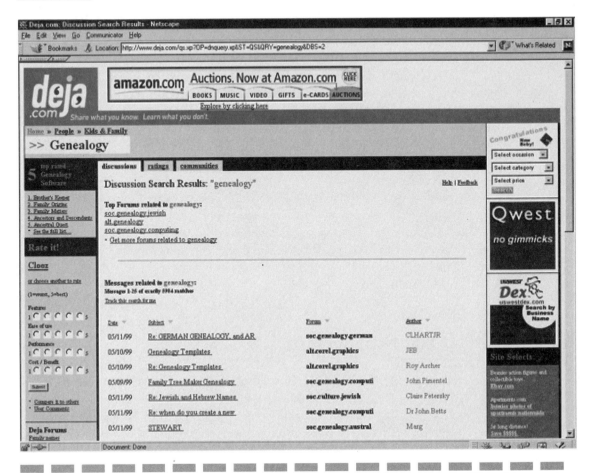

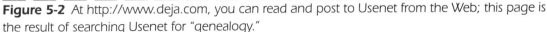

Figure 5-2 At http://www.deja.com, you can read and post to Usenet from the Web; this page is the result of searching Usenet for "genealogy."

Alternatively, you can try the full-fledged $29 Forte Agent reader with more features. However, Free Agent does quite well for a free program, so let's look at it.

After the program is installed in Windows, you have to tell the newsreader your news server. Your Internet service provider tech support people should tell you what it is; it will be something like news.*yourISP*.com. For example, the news server at CompuServe is news.compuserve.com. Generally, you have to be a signed-in customer to use a system's news server: You can't get into CompuServe's server if you are logged into another Internet service provider, for example.

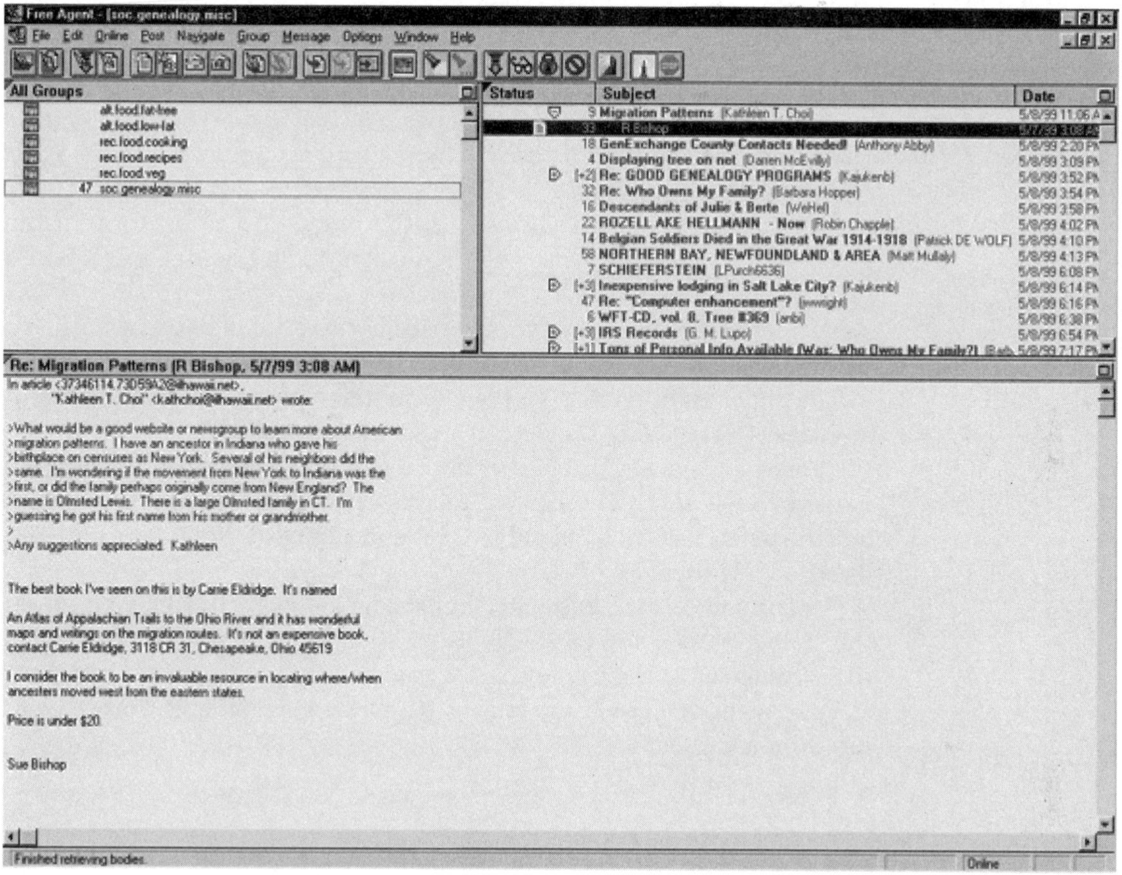

Figure 5-3 Free Agent presents you with subscribed groups, message headers, and the message body.

Agent's layout is very typical. The default is for three panes of the window to show you information from your Usenet site: The upper left pane shows the names of the newsgroups. The upper right pane shows the message headers of a selected newsgroup. The lower pane shows the body of the message. If you don't like this particular layout, use the menu item `Options|Window Layout`, and choose another one. The Newsgroups pane can be set to show you all newsgroups or only the ones to which you have "subscribed" (that is, told the program that you want to read this one regularly).

A nice feature of this reader is the search feature. Under `Edit|Search` on the menu, or the flashlight icon on the toolbar, you can search this list of all newsgroups for genealogy. When you have clicked in the pane showing the list of message subject lines, you can use the same tool to search them, say, for a surname or a state. In addition, when your cursor is in the body of a message itself, you can search that message as well. A newsreader with a search function can save you tons of time and online charges.

A simple click in the box next to the name of a newsgroup in the group's pane subscribes you. Then you can click on the All Groups bar to turn it into Subscribed Groups in order to view only the names of the newsgroups to which you have subscribed; the rest don't appear until you decide to look at the whole list again.

The upper right pane is where information appears about the current messages ("articles" in Usenet parlance) in the newsgroup highlighted in the upper left pane. Double-clicking on one of these lines brings up the message itself in the lower pane. You can choose what colors mean what, but the default is that red subject lines are unread, and black ones are ones you have seen.

Replying and posting are accomplished by simply clicking on icons on the toolbar at top. You can reply by email to just the person who posted the message or to the whole Usenet group.

Free Agent is a good newsreader. It's commercial sibling, Forte Agent, has even more features, including:

- Filters for subjects and senders you do or don't want to be sure to see
- Sorting by thread, subject, author, date, or size
- Launching your browser when you click on URLs; integration with other Internet applications
- Customizable toolbar
- Folders for mail and news
- Address book
- Email as well as Usenet send and receive
- Ability to skip or sample long email messages
- Automatic filing of email messages in folders by rules you decide
- Ability to import email messages from Pegasus and Eudora
- Spellchecker

Any newsreader you buy should have these features; however, for a free one, Free Agent is very good.

Although I don't own a Mac and so couldn't test it, three different sites on the Web recommended John Norstad's NewsWatcher for the Mac-connected. NewsWatcher does everything you'd want a newsreader to do, except filtering by keywords; however, there's an add-on called Value Added NewsWatcher if you need filtering. It gets updated and improved so often that you'll sometimes find a new version every week. You can find it at http://src.doc.ic.ac.uk/public/packages/mac/newswatcher/, and ftp://ftp.tidbits.com/pub/tidbits/select/newswatcher.hqx.

Browsers

Reading newsgroups with a Web browser (see Chapter 2) is another way to go. Microsoft Internet Explorer and Netscape Navigator 5 both come with a newsreader window. In addition, you can set Microsoft Internet Explorer 5 to use any newsreader program registered with the Windows system.

In Netscape Navigator 4.6, this means choosing Edit|Options|Mail News Preferences, and choosing Newsgroup Servers in the left pane, as in Figure 5-4. Then, in the right pane, click the Add button and put in information for your news server (for example news.prodigy.net). Now Netscape Navigator is ready to read news for you.

In Microsoft Internet Explorer, select Tools|Internet Options, and choose the Programs tab, as in Figure 5-5. If you have installed Microsoft Internet News, Forte Agent, or some other Windows newsreader, you can use the drop-down box to choose one of those to be the default newsreader.

In some other browsers, you may have to find the "helper programs" dialog window and put in the news server and newsreader information.

Commercial Online Services

Microsoft Network, CompuServe, America Online, and the other major online services also have ways for you to read Usenet. Most of them involve reading online, while the meter is ticking.

AOL, however, has an option to let you retrieve newsgroup articles when you retrieve email for offline reading. First, you use the keyword USENET to go choose your newsgroups. Simply click on the Search Newsgroup button, search for genealogy groups you want, and then close the window. Back at the AOL Usenet window, click on the Read Offline button. Those that you would like to read offline, put in the right-hand pane of the window (see Figure 5-6).

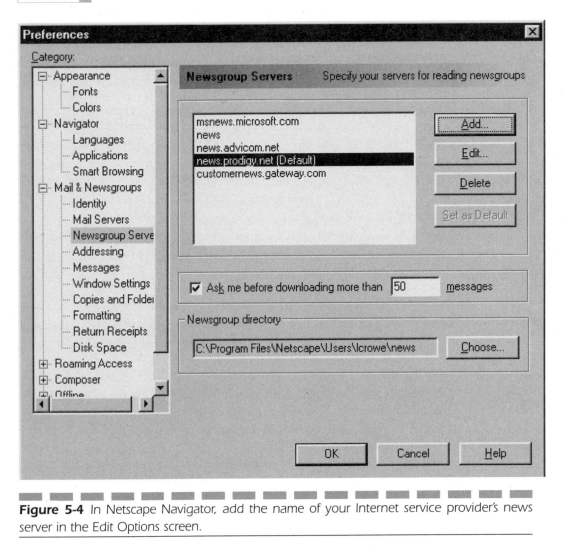

Figure 5-4 In Netscape Navigator, add the name of your Internet service provider's news server in the Edit Options screen.

Close that window, and click `Mail Center|Set Up Automatic AOL`. Put checkmarks in the boxes about sending and receiving newsgroup messages. Now whenever you run Automatic AOL (also known as "Flashsessions") to retrieve your AOL mail, you'll get the genealogy newsgroups you chose too. This will make the sessions longer, but it will involve less online time than reading the newsgroups "live."

On CompuServe and MSN, you have to read Usenet online as of this writing.

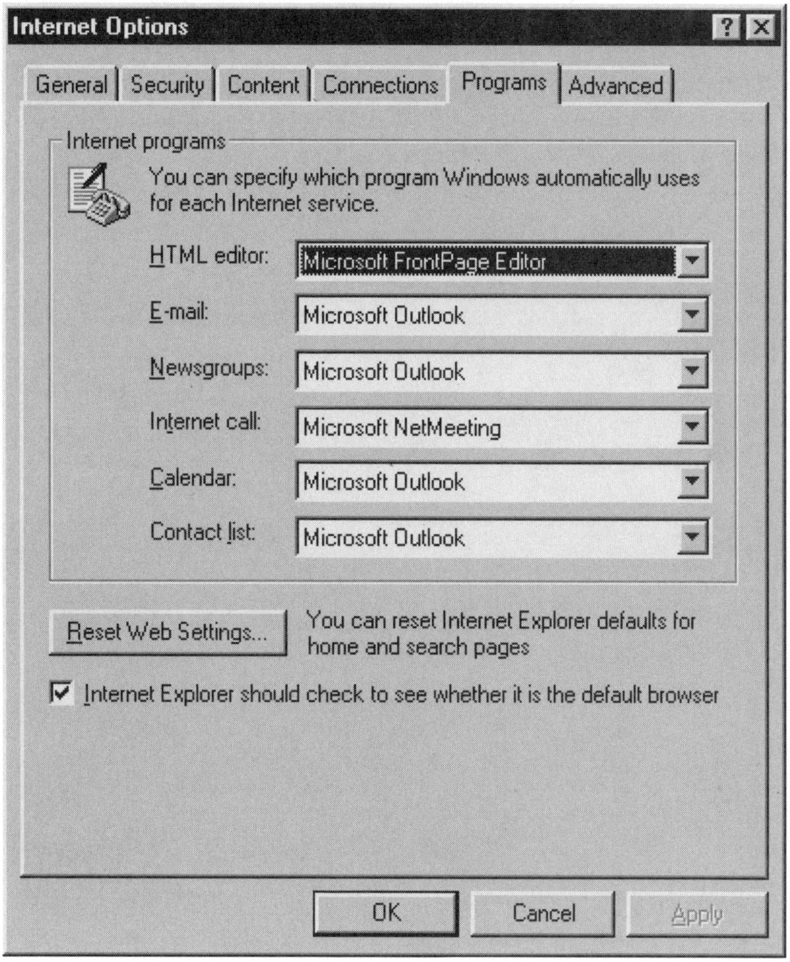

Figure 5-5
Microsoft
Internet Explorer
lets you choose
your
newsreader.

Newsgroups of Interest to Online Genealogists

Once upon a time, there was one online genealogy Usenet newsgroup for genealogy: soc.roots. But it became unwieldy to try to discuss beginners' questions, software, history, specific regions, specific family name queries, and the joy we get from our hobby all in one newsgroup. After much discussion, soul-searching, argument, pleading, and finally, reconciliation, we now have an embarrassment of riches in genealogical newsgroups, including:

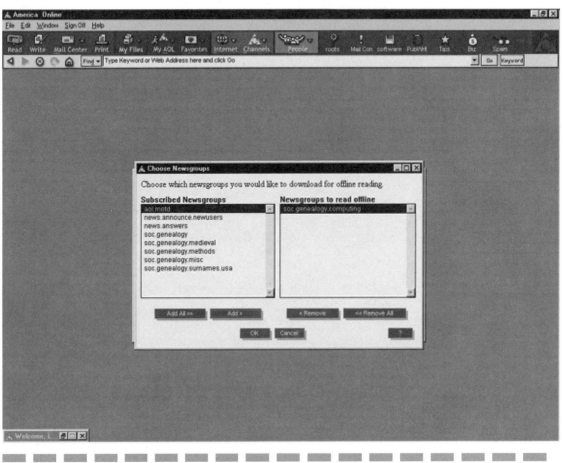

Figure 5-6 You can choose to read Usenet messages offline in AOL.

alt.adoption—A newsgroup that discusses adoption issues, including the search for birth parents.

alt.genealogy—An older genealogy group, very general, and mostly people who don't want to use soc.genealogy.misc for some reason. Gatewayed with the ALT-GENEALOGY mailing list.

alt.culture.cajun—A discussion of Cajun history, genealogy, culture, and events.

fido.eur.genealogy—A FidoNet echo copied to Usenet and meant for those researching European genealogy. FidoNet is a message network for dial-up bulletin board systems.

fido.ger.genealogy—As above, but for German genealogy research, with most messages in German.

fr.rec.genealogie—Gatewayed with the GEN-FF-L mailing list for the discussion of Francophone genealogy—the genealogy of French-speaking people. The primary language here is French.

no.slekt—General genealogy topics, with most of the messages in Norwegian. Gatewayed with the NO.SLEKT mailing list.

no.slekt.programmer—Discussions of genealogy computer software, with most messages in Norwegian. Gatewayed with the NO.SLEKT.PRO-GRAMMER mailing list.

soc.genealogy.african—For the study of genealogy in Africa and for the African diaspora.

soc.genealogy.australia+nz—For genealogical research into Australia, New Zealand, and their territories.

soc.genealogy.benelux—For genealogical discussions of Luxembourg, Belgium, and the Netherlands

soc.genealogy.computing—For genealogical programs, bugs, and how-to instructions. Mostly about software, with some hardware discussions. Gatewayed with the SOFTWARE.GENCMP-L mailing list.

soc.genealogy.french—Genealogy of French-speaking peoples, with most messages in French. Gatewayed with the GEN-FR-L mailing list.

soc.genealogy.german—Discussions of family history for anyone with a German background. Messages are mainly in German. Gatewayed with the GEN-DE-L mailing list.

soc.genealogy.hispanic—Genealogy discussions as related to Hispanics, including Central and South America, with many messages in Spanish.

soc.genealogy.jewish—A moderated discussion of Judaic genealogy. Gatewayed with the JEWISHGEN mailing list.

soc.genealogy.marketplace—For buying, selling, and trading books, and to read about programs, seminars, and so on related to genealogy.

soc.genealogy.medieval—Gatewayed with the GEN-MEDIEVAL mailing list for genealogy and family history discussions among people researching individuals living during medieval times. "Medieval times" are loosely defined as the period from the breakup of the Western Roman Empire until the time public records relating to the general population began to be kept, and extending roughly from A.D. 500 to A.D. 1600.

soc.genealogy.methods—A general discussion of genealogy and methods of genealogical research. Gatewayed to the GENMTD-L mailing list.

soc.genealogy.misc—This is what became of soc.roots. It is a general discussion of genealogy. Gatewayed into the GENMSC-L mailing list, it is a list for topics that don't fit into other soc.genealogy.* categories. This newsgroup is shown in Figure 5.7.

soc.genealogy.nordic—Genealogical products and services for Northern Europe.

soc.genealogy.slavic—Slavic genealogy. Some messages in Slavic languages.

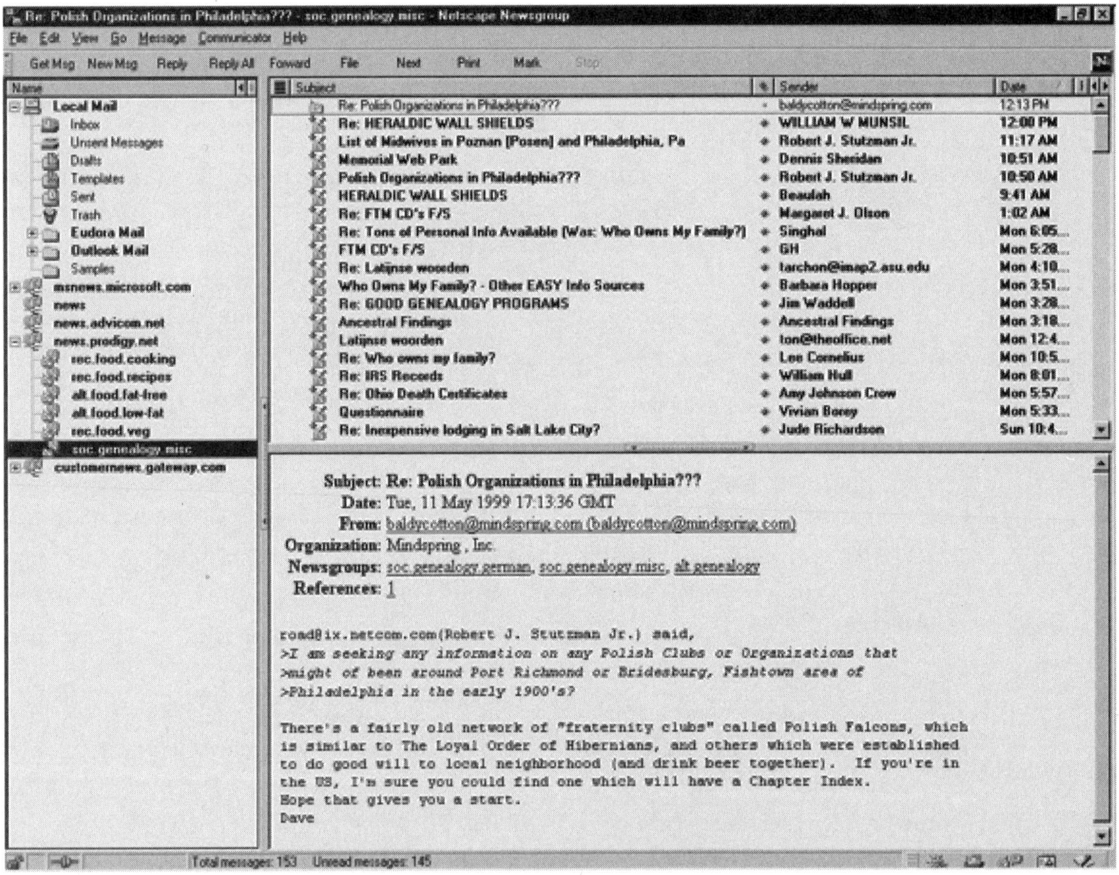

Figure 5-7 The newsgroup soc.genealogy.misc is for general genealogy discussions.

soc.genealogy.surnames.global—A central database for sending queries about surnames from around the world. This newsgroup is moderated.

soc.genealogy.uk+ireland—Gatewayed with the GENUKI-L mailing list for the discussion of genealogy and family history. Also for discussions among people researching ancestors, family members, or others who have a genealogical connection to any people in any part of the British Isles (England, Wales, Ireland, Scotland, the Channel Isles, and the Isle of Man).

soc.genealogy.west-indies—For Caribbean genealogy; most but not all of the messages are in English.

In addition, are several groups in the soc.history.* hierarchy that discuss areas touching on issues genealogists face: records, sources, and so on.

Binary Files on Usenet

Some newsgroups carry binary files; they have the word "binaries" in their names. This isn't seen so much on Usenet anymore because the World Wide Web is far superior for trading sounds, pictures, and programs. Still sometimes people do encode a binary file, which has nontext characters, into ASCII codes that can transfer on Usenet. This is called *uuencoding* or *binary encoding*. Readers such as Agent, discussed earlier in the chapter, automatically take care of this for you. On AOL, you have to jump through a few hoops, however.

When you first join AOL, your account is set to the default to block all binary files in Usenet, because most of the groups that send binaries are pornographic. To turn this off, go to the keyword PARENTAL CONTROLS, click on Set Parental Controls Now, click on Custom Controls, and click on Newsgroups. Click on Newsgroups Controls and Edit. Choose the screen name. Uncheck the Block Binary Downloads box.

Encoded binary files are often broken up across several different messages. Gathering up the pieces, putting them together, and converting them back to original form used to be a real hassle. America Online's FileGrabber utility makes it very simple.

To get the most out of it, set the Complete Binaries Only preference. In the Usenet window, click Read My Newsgroups. Click on a newsgroup name in your list that contains the word *binary* or *binaries* to select it. Click the Preferences button and select Complete Binaries Only.

Note: You have to do this newsgroup-by-newsgroup; this setting is not available in the Global Newsgroups Preferences window.

AOL's newsreader alerts you when you are viewing encoded data and gives you three choices: Download the file (and the AOL software will automatically decode it for you), download the article that contains the code or a piece of it (and you decode the pieces yourself), or Cancel.

Newsgroup FAQ Files

Many newsgroups post files of information called *frequently asked questions* (FAQs). About once a month, these get posted to their own newsgroup and to the soc.answers newsgroup. Look for a message called the Meta Genealogy FAQ, posted about the 22nd of each month to most of the soc.genealogy newsgroups; this message will show you how to get the FAQ files for the individual genealogy newsgroups.

Net Etiquette and Tips on Usenet

Try to stay on topic in a newsgroup, or you might receive insulting messages, called "flames." In general, the following topics are welcomed in the genealogy newsgroups:

- Your own family history information and requests for others to help you find information. Tiny tafels (see Appendix C) are often posted for this purpose.

- Information on upcoming genealogical meetings, workshops, symposiums, reunions, and so forth.

- Reviews, criticisms, and comments for software or hardware you've used about genealogy/family history.

- Telling others about bookshops around the world that contain books or information about this subject.

- Almost any message about genealogy in general.

Remember that what you send is posted as you sent it, unless it is to a moderated group such as soc.genealogy.surnames, where all messages must pass the moderator's muster.

The basics of etiquette in this group aren't very different from general online etiquette discussed in the Introduction. The participants in this forum want the topics of discussion to relate to genealogy or family history, however, and it's held that anything a subscriber thinks is appropriate is, if it relates to genealogy.

Assume an attitude of courtesy among subscribers and readers. Keep in mind that your postings and comments might be seen by as many as 20,000 readers on different networks in many different countries throughout the world. Remember the rules I mentioned earlier and:

- Read carefully what you receive to be certain that you understand the message before you reply.

- Read carefully what you send to ensure your message won't be misunderstood. As a matter of fact, routinely let a reply sit overnight, then read it again before sending. It prevents that sinking feeling of regret when you realize what you posted is not what you meant.

- Avoid sarcasm. If humor seems appropriate, clearly label it as such. Use smileys (emoticons; see Smiley (Emoticon) Glossary) to indicate humor. It's easy to misunderstand what's being said when there's no tone of voice, facial expressions, or body language to go by.

- Know your audience and double-check addresses. Make sure that the person or list of people to whom you're sending your message are the appropriate one(s) with whom to communicate.

- Be tolerant of newcomers, as you expect others to be tolerant of you. None of us were born knowing all about the Internet or Usenet. Do not abuse new users of computer networks for their lack of knowledge. As you become more expert, be patient as others first learn to paddle, then swim, then surf the Net. And be an active participant in teaching them.

- Avoid cluttering your messages with excessive emphasis (**, !!, >, and so on). It can make the message hard to follow.

- When you respond to a message, either include the relevant part of the original message or explicitly refer to the original's contents. People will commonly read your reply to the message before they read the original. (Remember the convention outline in Chapter 3 to precede each quoted line of the original message you include with the > character.) Do not quote more than necessary to make your point clear, and please don't quote the entire message. Learn what happens on your particular system when you reply to messages. Is the message sent to the originator of the message or to the list, and when is it sent? When responding to another message, your subject line should be the same, with "RE" at the beginning.

- Always include a precise subject line in your message. It should get attention, and the only way to do that is to make sure it describes the main point of your message.

- If you're seeking information about a family, include the surname in uppercase in the message subject. Many readers don't have time to read the contents of all messages.

  Bad sample subject line

  Wondering if anyone is looking for JONES?

  Good samples:

  Researching surname JONES

  SPENCER: England>MA>NY>OH>IN>MS

  Delaware BLIZZARDs pre-1845

  ? Civil War Records

  - In the good samples, note these conventions: Surnames are in all caps, but nothing else. An "arrow" (angled bracket) is used to denote migration from one place to another. A date is always helpful. If your message is a question, indicate that in the subject line. Although passages in all uppercase are considered shouting, the exception to this rule in the case of genealogy echoes is that surnames should be in uppercase, just as in any query.

- Keep messages to only one subject. This allows readers to quickly decide whether they need to read the message in full. Second subjects within a single message are often missed. Questions are often the exception to this rule. When you ask a question, end it with a question mark (?) and press the Enter key. That should be the end of that line. This makes it much easier for people to reply, because most newsreaders will quote the original message line by line.

- Be specific, especially when asking questions. If you ask about a person, identify when and where the person might have lived. In questions concerning specific genealogical software, make it clear what sort of computer (PC/MS-DOS, PC/Windows, Apple Macintosh, etc.) is involved. The folks reading these newsgroups are very helpful but very busy, and they are more likely to answer if they don't have to ask what you mean.

- Always, always put your name in the text of your message, along with your best email address for a reply. The end of the message is a good place for your name and email address. Furthermore, this newsgroup is read by many people who have read-only privileges; they cannot reply by email. So it's a good idea to also put your postal address in your messages so anyone can reply to you.

■ Whenever any newsgroup posts an FAQ, *read it*. If you can't find an FAQ message or file, make one of your first questions on the group, "Where and when can I get the frequently asked questions for this group?"

In addition, sometimes (as when, in early 1994, rotten weather, an earthquake, and a national holiday all converged on a certain Monday) you'll find the Usenet newsfeed absolutely clogged with messages, because so many people found themselves unable or not required to go to work. In that case, you must choose what to read based on subject line or sender, because it's impossible to read everything posted to the group that day. This is when a newsreader that lets you search the subject headings is invaluable.

Searching for Information within Newsgroups

You don't always have to read the whole newsgroup to find the information you need. There are several places where you can search newsgroups, one or several, or all at a time. You can use several different search sites to search newsgroups, either the messages (sometimes called "articles") or the newsgroup descriptions. Good sites for searching for specific information within newsgroups are AOL's NetFind, Infoseek, and DejaNews (now called simply "Deja").

Infoseek has the last two weeks of all Usenet newsgroups in a searchable database. Using a Web browser (see Chapter 4), go to http://www.infoseek.com. Use the drop-down box on the page to choose `Usenet Newsgroups`, and type in the surnames you want and `+genealogy`. Infoseek Guide will return a list of the messages. Each message title is a link; click on it to read it. AOL's NetFind (www.aol.com) works in much the same manner. However, keep in mind that these sites won't let you choose which groups to search.

That's why Deja is my favorite way to search newsgroups. Deja has more like a month's worth of messages. Using a Web browser (see Chapter 4), go to http://www.deja.com. At the top of the page there's a graphic called Power Search. Click on that, then choose `Create a Query Filter`. Type in `soc.genealogy.*` for all the groups, or just the full name of the one you want. Click on `Create filter`, and you're back to the search page. Now type in the surnames you're looking for, and within seconds, Deja will return a list of messages that match the search. Other search engines such as http://www.lycos.com have similar features, but Deja is my favorite.

Beyond Usenet

There's more to communicating with others on the Internet than Usenet, of course. In addition, some people find delivery to their own mailbox more convenient than Usenet. For that, we have mailing lists, the subject of the next chapter.

6

Genealogy Mailing Lists

Electronic mailing lists are electronic discussion groups based on email messages. All subscribers can send email to the list and receive email from the list. Messages sent to the mailing list get forwarded to everyone who subscribes to the list. Replies to messages from the list get sent to the list, where they get forwarded to all participants. And so it goes.

Mailing lists can be completely automated, with a program taking care of subscribing people to the list, forwarding messages, and removing people from the list. Or humans can get into the loop, handling any and all of the mailing list functions that programs can do. Such *moderated* mailing lists could have restricted membership (only adoptees, for example), or the humans could review each incoming message before it gets distributed, preventing inappropriate material from making it onto the list.

There are plenty of mailing lists that focus specifically on genealogy. In addition, there are many more lists that, while not specifically for genealogists, cover topics of interest to genealogists, such as ethnic groups or historic events. With a decent mail program (see Chapter 2), it's easy to participate in mailing lists.

NOTE *Throughout this chapter you'll find references to newsgroups and Web sites. This is just to illustrate how interconnected the genealogy resources on the Internet can be. You will learn everything you need to know about newsgroups and Web sites in other chapters.*

Each mailing list uses more than one email address. You use one to subscribe or to change how you use the mailing list, and you can use a different one to actually post messages to the other people on the mailing list. Some other mailing lists might have a third address to use for certain administrative chores, such as reporting to the moderator some violation of the list's rules. Later in this chapter, you will find plenty of mailing lists to send to; the next few paragraphs will tell you how to do it.

General Subscribing Tips

Say you want to subscribe to the ROOTS-L genealogy mailing list, and you know that you need to send email to roots-l-request@rootsweb.com, with the message "SUBSCRIBE," to join the list. Here is how you do it:

1. Click the Compose Mail icon in the your mail program.
2. In the To: box, type `roots-l-request@rootsweb.com`
3. In the Message box, type `subscribe`. For some lists you might also have to add your full real name; for other lists you might have to add the actual name of the list here. For Roots-L all you need is "subscribe." Do not put any signature at the bottom.
4. Click the `Spell Check` button to be sure there are no typos, then click the `Send` button.

An In-Depth Visit to ROOTS-L

Imagine a worldwide, never-ending conversation about genealogy, where novices and experts exchange help, information, ideas, and gossip. Now imagine that this conversation is conducted by electronic mail (email), so you don't have to worry about missing anything. You've just imagined ROOTS-L, the grandparent of genealogy mailing lists on the Internet.

ROOTS-L has spawned entire generations of newer genealogy mailing lists—some large, some small—but this is the original. The home page at http://www.rootsweb.com/roots-l hosts thousands of mailing lists about genealogy and history (see Figure 6-1).

The volunteers who bring ROOTS-L to the world include:

- Alf Christophersen, the fearless leader (http://www.uio.no/~achristo/)
- Dan Chase (http://pobox.com/~danimal/)
- Karen Isaacson
- Sandy Myers

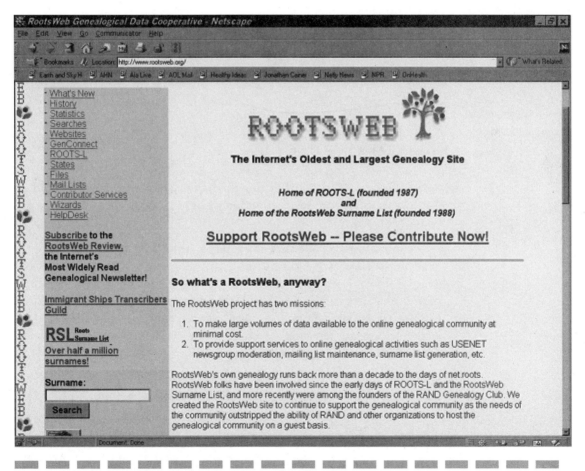

Figure 6-1 The RootsWeb site has hundreds of mailing lists.

- Vicki Lindsay

- John Salter

- Rick Carpenter

- Cliff Manis (http://soback.kornet.nm.kr/~cmanis/gecscli1.htm)

In 1999, over 9000 people were subscribed to ROOTS-L. To subscribe, you need two things:

1. You need a large email box to hold the volume of messages that you'll get

2. You need to send an email to roots-l-request@rootsweb.com, with the message SUBSCRIBE. Don't include anything else in the message—no signature block, no name or address—just the word subscribe.

NOTE   *If you ever decide to leave the list, you unsubscribe by sending email to roots-l-request@rootsweb.com, with the message UNSUB-SCRIBE. Don't include anything else in the message—no signature block, no name or address—just the word UNSUBSCRIBE.*

Some ROOTS-L Rules

Roots-L clearly states all its rules in the welcome message. It would be wise to apply them to all mailing lists you join, whether or not they are explicitly stated.

- You must memorize this rule: Messages to people go to roots-l@rootsweb.com; commands to programs go to roots-l-request@rootsweb.com. One of my tricks to do this: I save the "request" address in my email's address book under the name ROOTS-L REQUEST and the posting address under ROOTS-L POST. When I'm ready to send a message to one or the other, I choose it from the address list just as I would a person's.

- The list is not a place to refight old wars or discuss religion or politics.

- Advertising or selling a product is not, in general, acceptable. You can, however, post a new-product announcement.

- Make sure you spell the word *genealogy* correctly in all your messages.

- Don't post messages longer than about 150 lines unless you are sure they will be of very general interest.

- Don't include a "surname signature" in your messages. These are lists of surnames that appear at the end of every message some people send. The surnames play havoc with the lists archive searches, so don't use them.

- Don't post copyrighted material like newspaper articles or email messages sent to you by other people.

Communicating with People and Programs

We covered this rule earlier in the chapter, but people tend to get confused about this, so here are more details. If you're already sure you know where to send messages to people subscribed to ROOTS-L, as opposed to sending commands to the software at ROOTS-L, you can skip the rest of this section.

It can be hard to keep in mind the distinction between the list server that runs a mailing list and the list itself. This problem is common to most mailing lists. The list server gets all the commands: subscribe, unsubscribe, send me digests, and so forth. The list gets messages you want to send to other people. For ROOTS-L, messages addressed to roots-l@roots web.com go to the mailing list. Messages addressed to roots-l-request@rootsweb.com get posted on the list for all to see.

So if you wanted to request help finding information about your Aunt Tilly, you would send your message to roots-l@rootsweb.com. If you wanted to request a copy of the Roots Surname List (described in the next section), you would send your message to roots-l-request@rootsweb.com. If you need an index of all the files you can get by email from RootsWeb, you send the command list to roots-I-request@rootsweb.com).

Available Files and Databases

ROOTS-L has tons of files and databases, and you can get these by emailing the appropriate commands to the list server that runs ROOTS-L. You can search the ROOTS-L Library for everything from a fabulous collection devoted to obtaining vital records, to useful tips for beginners, to book lists from the Library of Congress, and more. Some of the available files are as follows:

- *The Roots Surname List (RSL).* A list of over 350,000 surnames and contact information for the 50,000 people researching those surnames

- *The Roots Location List (RLL).*   A list of locations of special interest to individual researchers, along with contact information for those researchers
- *U.S. Civil War Units.*   A file containing information about the military units that served in the United States Civil War.
- *The Irish-Canadian List.*   A list of Irish immigrants who settled in Canada, including (where available) dates and locations.
- *Books We Own.*   Books and other genealogical resources owned by Internet genealogists, in which, under certain conditions, the owners are willing to look up information.

When you subscribe to ROOTS-L, you receive a long welcome message that tells you everything you need to know to get started, including how to ask the list server to email files to you.

NOTE   *You can also retrieve files yourself by going to the RootsWeb site and browsing for them.*

Putting ROOTS-L to Work

Now that you are subscribed to ROOTS-L and know all the rules, it is time to learn how to put the list server to work. You can control your subscription from your email program. But you must remember that you can only control your subscription from the same email account with which you subscribed in the first place. The commands you send will be processed automatically by the list processor—if you remember to send them to roots-l-request@rootsweb.com. If you send your commands to roots-l@rootsweb.com, you'll just succeed in irritating the people running the list.

When you first subscribe to ROOTS-L, you are subscribed in *digest mode*. That means once or twice a day you will receive a large message from ROOTS-L containing a list of all the messages that have been posted to the list since the last digest message. For each topic, there is a topic number, a subject, and who posted it. Figure 6-2 shows a piece of a typical digest message.

Digests from ROOTS-L tend to be larger than many email programs can view. Instead of showing the whole message, you might get a display of only the first part of the message, or even a blank message with an icon noting an attachment. A copy of the entire message is converted into

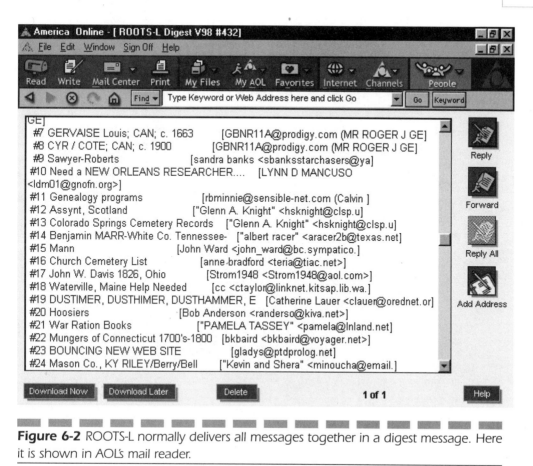

Figure 6-2 ROOTS-L normally delivers all messages together in a digest message. Here it is shown in AOL's mail reader.

a text file and stored as an attachment. From there, it's up to you to open the file with a word processor or text editor and read the messages.

You can get around this by telling the list server to give you each message separately by switching to *mail mode* or *index mode*. Instructions on how to switch modes are included in the welcome messages you receive when you join ROOTS-L.

In index mode, all you'll get will be message subject lines, with associated message numbers. If you see a message that interests you, send email to roots-l-request@rootsweb.com. In this message, the subject should be ARCHIVE. In the body of the message, you list the numbers of the messages you want to read, say, messages numbered 103608 and 103609. The body of your message would look like this:

```
get messages/103608
get messages/103609
```

The commands must be in lowercase, you must use the forward slash (/), not the backward slash (\), and there is no space after the slash. You can only include one request per line. So a complete message to the list server asking for the full text of messages 103608 and 103609 would look like Figure 6-3.

Losing Contact with ROOTS-L

It's possible that you'll stop receiving messages from a mail list even though you didn't unsubscribe. There are two likely causes for this problem:

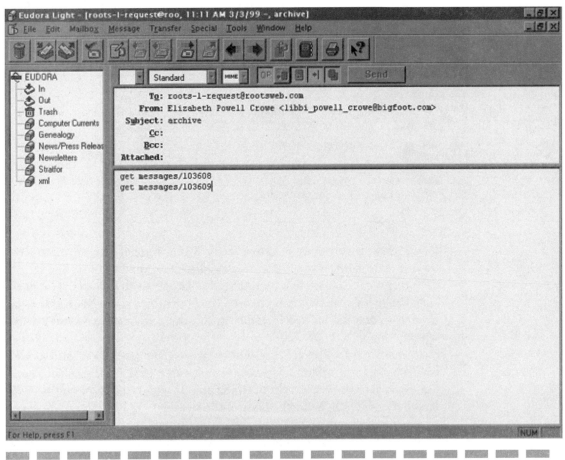

Figure 6-3 An email message (in Eudora Light) requesting the full text of two messages posted to ROOTS-L.

1. Your Internet service provider could be having troubles with its email service. Any service can have intermittent service problems; sometimes a whole section of the Internet might be out of order for a few minutes or hours. And, in fact, AOL has had such problems in the past. If all your email has stopped coming, not just mail from ROOTS-L, this could be the cause.

2. You are using a different email address than the one you used to subscribe to ROOTS-L. ROOTS-L will only send to the return address of the subscribe message.

If all else fails, just subscribe to ROOTS-L again. That should get the messages flowing for you.

Other Genealogy Mailing Lists

Once you've mastered how ROOTS-L works, you're ready to sample other mailing lists. Over the next several pages, I've listed just a sampling of mailing lists related to genealogy that you can join. Where noted, the messages are copied (gatewayed) to the specified newsgroup.

Not all mailing lists run on a list server. Some are managed "by hand," so to speak. This means there is some person out there who receives all the messages, then forwards them to all the list subscribers. You subscribe to such lists by sending a politely worded message to an address such as afrigeneas-request@drum.ncsc.org. The message will go to the list owner, who will read it when he or she has the time, then add you to the list as soon as possible (assuming the list owner decides he or she wants to add you to their list).

When you see the word *request* in the subscription information for one of the following mailing lists, assume your message is going to a real live person, not a machine. Complete sentences, proper English, and a polite approach are appropriate. When the subscription information says *list-serv*, assume you are talking to a machine and use the commands described earlier in the chapter.

You'll generally get a welcome message when you subscribe to a list. This message tells you the purpose of the list and other useful information.

NOTE *I make it a practice to save the welcome message as a text or word-processing file for future reference. It saves a lot of confusion and frustration later.*

Sometimes a list is aimed at particular countries or regions. While these lists are not focused on genealogy, the list owners have indicated that genealogy is an acceptable, although in some cases unusual, subject for the list.

The mailing lists included below address many subjects, some only tangentially touching genealogy. Some touch on heritage, culture, and the genealogy of particular ethnic groups. Some concentrate on specific family names, some on specific historical periods. Some address software and computer-related topics that may be of interest to online genealogists. The list here will get you started. Be on the lookout for messages that contain the names of other lists and things could snowball. Just remember to come up for air once in a while!

General Genealogy Lists

These lists are concerned with general genealogy, apart from any specific ethnic group, surname, region, or historical period. Beginners should explore these mailing lists first.

- *Adoptees* To share information, experiences, and feelings as related to adoption search, reunion, and many other adoption-related issues. Membership is restricted to adoptees and adoptee-lites, who are people who were raised without one or both birth parents, but who were never legally adopted. This list has an associated Web site, the Adoptees Internet Mailing List Web site at http://www.webreflection.com/aiml/ (see Figure 6-4). To subscribe, send email to listserv@maelstrom.stjohns.edu with the message: *SUBSCRIBE ADOPTEES <firstname lastname>*. The address for posting is adoptees@maelstrom.stjohns.edu.

- *Adoption* Discussions of anything and everything connected with adoption. To subscribe, send email to adoption-request@think.com with the message: *SUBSCRIBE ADOPTION <firstname lastname>*. The address for posting is adoption@think.com.

- *Elijah-L* A list for believing members of the Church of Jesus Christ of Latter-day Saints to discuss their ideas and experiences relating to genealogy in the LDS Church. Individuals not of the LDS faith are welcome to join as long as they respect the beliefs of the LDS faith and do not deliberately offend these beliefs. To subscribe, write to byrondh@juno.com. This list is to be used specifically for sharing LDS-related genealogy ideas, tools, and approaches; sharing LDS-related

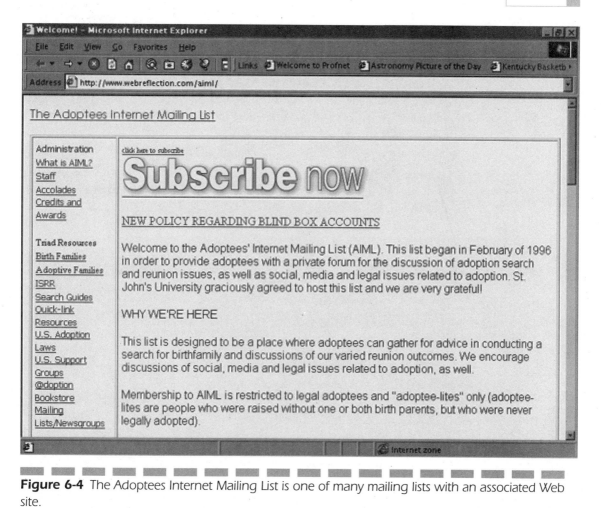

Figure 6-4 The Adoptees Internet Mailing List is one of many mailing lists with an associated Web site.

genealogy experiences and testimonies; and discussing answers to LDS-related genealogy questions and scriptures relating to genealogy. Members share LDS-related genealogy news from throughout the world, as well as other LDS-related genealogical topics.

- *GENMSC-L* This group's messages also appear in the soc.genealogy.misc newsgroup for miscellaneous genealogical discussions that don't fit in one of the other soc.genealogy.* newsgroups. To post, send messages to GENMSC-L@rootsweb.com. To subscribe, send a message that says only *subscribe* in the text to genmsc-l-request@rootsweb.com (mail mode), genmsc-d-request@rootsweb.com (digest mode), or genmsc-i-request@rootsweb.com (index mode).

- *GENMTD* This group's messages also appear in the soc.genealogy.methods newsgroup. It discusses general genealogy research techniques and resources. To post a message, send it to genmtd-l-request@rootsweb.com. Send a message that says only *subscribe* in the text to genmtd-l-request@rootsweb.com (mail mode), genmtd-d-request@rootsweb.com (digest mode), or genmtd-i-request@rootsweb.com (index mode).

- *GEN-NEWBIE-L* A message exchange mailing list for the beginner, where the most basic genealogy questions are answered. This mailing list has an associated Web page at http://www.rootsweb.com/~newbie/, show in Figure 6-5. To subscribe, send email to gen-newbie-l-request@rootsweb.com with the message SUBSCRIBE.

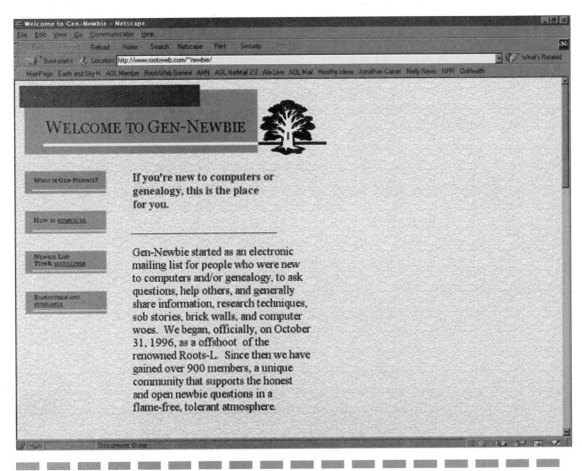

Figure 6-5 If you are new to genealogy, or new to computers, this is a great Web site to visit.

■ *Roots-L* This is probably the best-known genealogy mailing list in the world, with thousands of subscribers. We discussed ROOTS-L in detail earlier in this chapter. To subscribe, send email to roots-l-request@rootsweb.com with the message SUBSCRIBE.

Ethnic Groups

These lists aren't specifically about genealogy but cover the culture, history, and current events of particular ethnic groups. Most of them will accept the occasional genealogy query, and they're great places to lurk if you want to learn a little bit about other people.

■ *AFRIGENEAS* A private mailing list created as a place to discuss and promote family history research. There is an associated Web site at http://members.aol.com/gfsclint/Afrihome.html. Archives of past messages are at http://www.msstate.edu/listarchives/afrigeneas/. This list will discuss African ancestors, as well as genealogical interests, history, culture, and resources. Discussion areas include, but are not limited to, queries on surnames, records/events, getting started, census, locations, people and places, and resources. Messages about research, queries, and resources go to afrigeneas@msstate.edu. Request to be added to the list by sending a message that says *subscribe afrigeneas <first name last name>* to majordomo@msstate.edu.

■ *AFROAM-L* A discussion group focusing on the pivotal issues that confront African-Americans in everyday life. This is an extremely busy list, with rates of 25 messages an hour possible. Posting specific genealogy questions is not considered appropriate, but postings that address broader areas of interest to genealogists are acceptable. To subscribe to this list, send the text *subscribe AFROAM-L* with your name in the body of the message to listserv%harvarda.bitnet@ listserv.net. To unsubscribe from this list, send the text *unsubscribe AFROAM-L* in the body of the message to listserv% harvarda.bitnet@listserv.net. Human administrator: AFROAM-L-request@HARVARDA.

■ *Brazil* A mailing list for anyone with genealogical interest in Brazil; most of the messages are in Portuguese. The mailing address for postings is brazil-l@rootsweb.com. To subscribe, send the word *subscribe* as the only text in the body of a message to brazil-l-request@rootsweb.com (mail mode) or brazil-d-request@rootsweb.com (digest mode).

- *SURNAMES-CANADA-L*   To subscribe, send a "Subscribe" message to SURNAMES-CANADA-L-request@rootsweb.com. This list is an echo of the soc.genealogy.surnames.canada newsgroup.

- *GEN-DE-L*   Mirrored in soc.genealogy.german newsgroup for the discussion of German genealogy; you subscribe by sending an email to gen-de-l-request@rootsweb.com with the text *subscribe*. The address for posting is gen-de-l@rootsweb.com.

- *GEN-FF-L*   Messages from the fr.rec.genealogie newsgroup are mirrored here. It discusses, in French, the genealogy of French-speaking people. To subscribe, send the word *subscribe* as the only text in the body of a message to gen-fr-l-request@rootsweb.com (mail mode), gen-fr-d-request@rootsweb.com (digest mode), or gen-fr-i-request@rootsweb.com (index mode). The posting address is gen-fr-l@rootsweb.com.

- *INDIAN-ROOTS-L*   Features discussions of Native American genealogical and historical research. To subscribe, send email to listserv@listserv.indiana.edu with the message *SUB INDIAN-ROOTS-L <firstname lastname>*.

- *JEWISHGEN*   Features discussions of Jewish genealogy and is mirrored with the soc.genealogy.jewish newsgroup (JEWGEN is a synonym for JEWISH-GEN, and postings to both will just give subscribers two copies of the same message). The Web site is at www.jewishgen.org; you'll find there are logs of special subgroups. To subscribe, send email to listserv@lyris.jewishgen.org that says *subscribe jewishgen <firstname lastname>*.

- *PIE*   Italian genealogy is the emphasis of this list and its companion Web site (http://www.cimorelli.com/pie/piehome.htm). PIE stands for Pursuing (Our Italian Names Together) In Email. The easiest way to subscribe is to go http://www.cimorelli.com/pie/cfopie/subpie.htm and fill out the form.

Family Name Lists

The best place to find a mail list based on surnames of interest to you is to go to RootsWeb (http://www.rootsweb.com) and click on the Mail Lists link from the home page (see Figure 6-1). You usually have to request permission to join one of these lists. There are now literally thousands of them.

There are other name-specific lists all over the Net. I suggest you check out these sites to search for the surnames you are interested in.

Genealogy Resources on the Internet: Surnames

http://members.aol.com/gresinet/gen_mail_surnames-gen.html
This page is a list of general surname search/query mailing lists. Some
are regional, such as SURNAMES-IRELAND. Others are very general,
such as the Roots Surname List. Instructions for subscribing are
included in each list.

Genealogy Resources on the Internet: Mailing Lists

http://members.aol.com/johnf14246/gen_mail.html
Scroll down this page to the fifth entry. Click on a letter of the alphabet
and search for your surnames.

The Internet Sleuth: Surnames

http://isleuth.com/surnames.html
This is a Web search catalog, with a genealogy category and a surnames
subcategory. You'll find not only mailing lists but also other Internet
resources (databases, Web pages, etc.) here.

Genealogy Listservers, Newsgroups, and Special Home Pages

http://www.eskimo.com/~chance/lists.html
This is a searchable list of resources on surnames and localities. You can
either click on a letter for an alphabetized table of contents or enter a
name in the Search box. It's not as complete as the Genealogy Resources
on the Internet pages, mentioned above, but it seems to be updated often.

Historical Groups

These lists focus on historical events or groups that could be invaluable
to you in your genealogy research.

- *CIVIL-WAR*   Discusses the American Civil war, its history, and its
  issues, including genealogy. Subscribe by sending the word *subscribe*
  as a message to civil-war-request@rootsweb.com (mail mode) or civil-
  war-d-request@rootsweb.com (digest mode). Post messages to civil-
  war@rootsweb.com.

- *GEN-MEDIEVAL-L*   These messages also appear in
  soc.genealogy.medieval for genealogy and family history discussions
  among people researching individuals living during medieval times.
  "Medieval times" are loosely defined as the period from the breakup of

the Western Roman Empire until the time public records relating to the general population began to be kept, and extending roughly from A.D. 500 to A.D. 1600. To subscribe, send an email message with the word *subscribe* to gen-medieval-l-request@rootsweb.com (mail mode), gen-medieval-d-request@rootsweb.com (digest mode), or gen-medieval-i-request@rootsweb.com (index mode). Post messages to gen-medieval-l@rootsweb.com.

■ *MAYFLOWER*   This is for all Mayflower descendents, any time, any place. The mailing address for postings is mayflower-l@rootsweb.com. To subscribe, send the word *subscribe* as the only text in the body of a message to mayflower-l-request@rootsweb.com (mail mode) or mayflower-d-request@rootsweb.com (digest mode).

■ *OVERLAND-TRAILS*   Devoted to discussions concerning the history, preservation, and promotion of the Oregon, California, Santa Fe, and other historic trails in the western United States. One project of particular interest to genealogists is a database containing all the names inscribed as graffiti on the various rocks along the trails. If one of your ancestors is rumored to have traveled one of these trails, you may be able to confirm that by consulting this database. To subscribe, send an email to listserv@calcite.rocky.edu with the following message: *SUBSCRIBE OVERLAND-TRAILS <firstname lastname>*. The address for posting is overland-trails@calcite.rocky.edu. You must be subscribed to post messages.

Regional Groups

RootsWeb has many mailing lists for specific geographical locations; there's a separate list for almost every county in Ohio! Check out the RootsWeb mailing list page (http://www.rootsweb.com/~maillist/) for names and instructions.

The following mailing lists focus on specific geographic areas:

■ *LISTSERV at Indiana University*.   This server has several different genealogy discussion lists, listed at http://listserv.indiana.edu/archives/index.html. Many of them have searchable archives of old messages reaching back years. For each list, send a message to listerv@listserv.indiana.edu with the following message: SUB *nameoflist your name*. Some of these lists include:

   ▪ *Arkansas-Roots-L*—Has about 800 subscribers

- *Deep-South-Roots-L*—Discusses Alabama, Georgia, Florida, and Mississippi; has about 1100 subscribers
- *IA-NEB-Roots-L*—Discusses Iowa and Nebraska; has about 600 subscribers
- *IN-Roots-L*—Discusses Indiana; has about 800 subscribers
- *Inscriptions-L*—Discusses tombstones; has about 200 subscribers
- *Louisiana-Roots-L*—Has about 400 subscribers
- *Mid-Atlantic-Roots-L*—Discusses Delaware, Maryland, DC, and New Jersey; has about 500 subscribers
- *Missouri-Roots-L*—Has about 800 subscribers
- *NC-SC-Roots-L*—Has about 1400 subscribers
- *NewYork-Roots-L*—Has about 500 subscribers
- *Northeast-Roots-L*—Covers New England; has about 1100 subscribers
- *Ohio-Roots-L*—Has about 1000 subscribers
- *Pennsylvania-Roots-L*—Has about 1000 subscribers
- *Texahoma-Roots-L*—Discusses Texas and Oklahoma; has about 600 subscribers
- *TN-Roots-L*—Discusses genealogy in Tennessee; has about 1200 subscribers
- *VA-WVA-Roots-L*—Discusses the Virginias; has about 850 subscribers
- *Western-Roots-L*—Discusses Hawaii, Alaska, Washington, Oregon, California, Nevada, Arizona, Utah, New Mexico, Idaho, Montana, and Wyoming; has about 400 subscribers

- *Maggie_Ohio.* This list is designed to provide a discussion forum for anyone who has an interest in genealogy in the state of Ohio. Send the word *subscribe* as the only text in a message to Maggie_Ohio-D-request@rootsweb.com.

- *KYRoots.* Discusses Kentucky genealogy and historical research. To subscribe, send an email to listserv@lsv.uky.edu with the message, *SUBSCRIBE KYROOTS <firstname lastname>*.

- *VA-Roots.* Discusses Virginia genealogy. To subscribe, send an email to listserver@leo.vsla.edu with the following message: *subscribe VA-ROOTS <firstname lastname>*.

Software Lists

These lists have information about genealogical software and computer standards (like GEDCOM) of interest to genealogists.

■ *GENCMP-L.* A general discussion of genealogy and its relation to computers and computing. To subscribe, send an email to listserv@apple.ease.lsoft.com with the message *SUB GENCMP-L <firstname lastname>*.

NOTE *This list usually subscribes you in digest mode. If you want mail mode, you must send a second message to the list server* SET GENCMP-L MAIL.

■ *BK-L.* The discussion list for Brother's Keeper is currently being hosted by RootsWeb. To join the list, send an email message with only the word *SUBSCRIBE* in both the subject and the body of the message to BK-L-request@rootsweb.com (for mail mode) or to BK-D-request@rootsweb.com (for digest mode). After you subscribe, you will then get messages from everyone who sends messages to the list, and you may then send messages to the list by sending them to BK-L@rootsweb.com. If you only subscribe to digest mode, you will only get one message each day instead of possibly several messages each day.

■ *Family-Origins-Users.* If you use the Family Origins genealogy software program, this list is to interact with other users, seek help in using the program, and exchange ideas and solutions regarding problem areas. To subscribe, send the word *subscribe* as the only text in the body of a message to family-origins-users-l-request@rootsweb.com (mail mode) or family-origins-users-d-request@rootsweb.com (digest mode). Post messages to family-origins-users-l@rootsweb.com.

■ *GEDCOM-L.* A technical mailing list to discuss the GEDCOM specifications. If you aren't a computer programmer, a serious genealogical computer user, or haven't read the GEDCOM specification, this list is definitely not for you. To subscribe, send an email to listserv@listserv.nodak.edu with the message *SUB GEDCOM-L <firstname lastname>*. The address for posting is gedcom-l@listserv.nodak.edu.

■ *PAF.* A mailing list for discussion of issues relating to the Personal Ancestral File genealogy program. To subscribe, send an email to majordomo@rehtori.kasanen.fi with the message *SUBSCRIBE PAF*. The address for posting is paf@rehtori.kasanen.fi.

■ *GENWEB.* A discussion list for ROOTSBOOK, a project to link genealogy trees on a mass basis. To subscribe, send an email to listserv@ucsd.edu with the message *SUB GENWEB*.

Email Newsletters

Another email resource is the newsletter. Unlike interactive mailing lists, newsletters are not interactive; they are meant to be read like a magazine. You can write letters to the editor if you like, but you won't often see them in the newsletters. Some email newsletters are worthy of note.

- *Eastman's Genealogy Index (http://www.ancestry.com/home/ times.htm).* This is a weekly all-text newsletter on genealogy topics. A typical issue covers reviews of genealogy computer programs; news items of note to genealogists; a list of Web sites to visit; book, CD-ROM, and TV reviews; and more. The reviews in this newsletter are specific without being verbose, and they are honest. Each issue is posted at the site listed above, as well as emailed to subscribers. You can also find back issues here. To subscribe, send an email to subscribe@rootscomputing.com with the subject. *SUBSCRIBE*

- *Treasure Maps Newsletter (http://www.firstct.com/fv/sub.html).* Treasure Maps (Figure 6-6) is one of the best sites on the Web for novices. It is aimed at hands-on, how-to information to help you actually do research online. To keep track of the latest news on Treasure Maps, you might want to subscribe to their monthly newsletter. The newsletter also has genealogy information that hasn't been released yet. To subscribe, send an email message to ragan@southeast.net with the subject *SUBSCRIBE TM*. Within 24 hours, you should receive your first issue, as well as a help file telling you how to make the program work best.

- *Genealogy Today Newsletter (http://www.enoch.com/genealogy/ newslet.htm).* This monthly newsletter has tips, information, meetings and seminar announcements, and queries. To subscribe, just send an email with only the word *subscribe* to GenToday-L-request@rootsweb.com. You may also submit a query by emailing it to tfarris268@aol.com with *Query* in the subject line.

- *RootsWeb Newsletter (http://www.rootsweb.com/~review/ index.htm).* This newsletter keeps you up-to-date on the RootsWeb site, genealogy news, and success stories. Send a message with only the word SUBSCRIBE to ROOTSWEB-REVIEW-request@rootsweb.com.

- *DearMYRTLE Newsletter (http://members.col.com/dearmyrtle/ index.htm).* DearMYTLE has a daily column, tips and online courses,

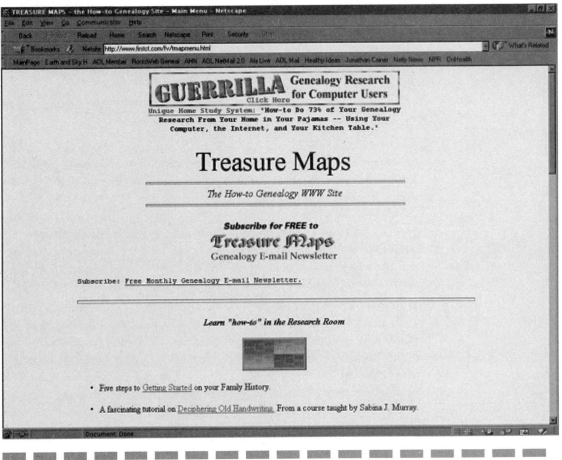

Figure 6-6 The Treasure Maps site is a great tool for learning how to learn about our ancestors.

and much more. Her columns can be emailed to you. Go to http://members.aol.com/dearmyrtle/subscribe.htm, and follow the instructions.

- *JOG (http://www/onlinegeneology.com).* The Journal of Online Genealogy is a monthly ezine (electronic magazine) on techniques, trends, and reviews of books, programs, and other materials for the genealogist. Log on to it on the 15th of each month for a new issue.

- *Missing Links (http://www.rootsweb.com/~mlnews/ index.htm).* This is a weekly online newsletter for the genealogist by Myra Vanderpool Gormley and Julia M. Case. To subscribe, send an email message with only the word *SUBSCRIBE* to MISSING-LINKS-L-request.rootsweb.com.

Finding More Mailing Lists

Even if the above seems like plenty of mailing lists, you may want more. If so, you don't need to dig them up yourself; the folks at the RootsWeb site have done much of the work for you. If you point your Web browser to http://www.rootsweb.com/~maillist/, you'll have access to the hundreds of mailing lists hosted by RootsWeb.

Another good site to keep up on the latest in mail lists and newsletters is Cyndi's List, at http://www.CyndisList.com/magazine.htm. There's a link to have a program send you an email message every time that page changes. (See Figure 6-7.)

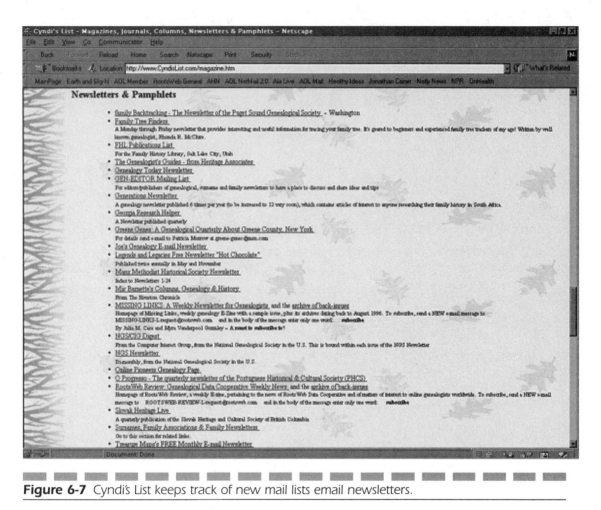

Figure 6-7 Cyndi's List keeps track of new mail lists email newsletters.

The World Wide Web

The World Wide Web (or "the Web," as it is known, or WWW) is also a great resource for online genealogists. Much of the growth of the Internet over the last few years has been on the Web. Thousands of Web sites spring up every month. Many people, particularly newcomers to the Internet, don't even use any other part of the Internet.

As you might imagine, any place on the Internet that combines ease of use, lots of excitement, and lots of new people is a place genealogists will want to be. You can find hundreds of Web sites of interest to genealogists. In this chapter you'll find short profiles of 50 good ones for you to start with; some of the major sites have their own chapters later in the book.

NOTE *America Online's software comes with a version of Microsoft Internet Explorer as its Web browser, as does CompuServe and Prodigy. Other Internet service providers may provide you with Netscape Navigator, Opera, or some other browser.*

What Does the World Wide Web Look Like?

You may not realize it, but you've almost certainly seen the Web before. With all the hype and excitement about the Internet, the Web, and the material available through them, pictures from the Web are constantly showing up on TV and in newspapers, magazines, and books. Plus, if you've been reading this book from cover to cover, you've already seen several figures showing Web pages and may already have ventured out onto the Web. But just so everyone is clear on this, Figure 7-1 shows a Web page, the Genealogy Home Page, in Netscape Navigator. The URL (see Chapter 2) for this page is http://www.genhomepage.com/.

Browser Tips and Tricks

There are ways to use your browser to better surf the World Wide Web. This list contains some of the most valuable tips available:

- Versions of Microsoft Internet Explorer (IE) and Netscape Navigator above 3.0 will input the http:// for you if you type in the unique part of the address. For example, type `www.genhomepage.com`, and the browser will automatically add `http://` at the beginning of the address.

- Microsoft Internet Explorer and Netscape Navigator versions 4 and above will also search for you. Put a question mark and your search terms in the address box, and the program will try to find related pages for you.

- Type in an address that begins with the letters *ftp* (`ftp.symantec.com`, for example), and the browser will insert the necessary `ftp://`. (An *FTP site* is a collection of files for public download, see Chapter 4.)

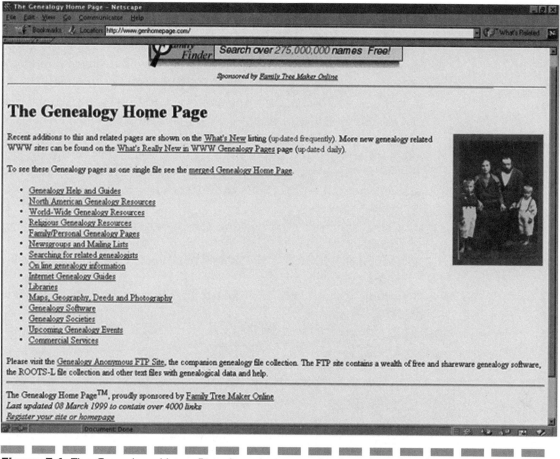

Figure 7-1 The Genealogy Home Page is a nicely organized starting place for beginners.

- If you need to copy a URL to your clipboard, you can just click in the Address box, press Ctrl+C, and you have a copy of the URL that's ready to be pasted elsewhere. This can be useful if you want to make reference to it in another program.

- You can change your browser's opening page. To do this in Microsoft Internet Explorer, select View|Internet Options. On the General tab, in the Home Page section of the tab, click on Use Current. This will make IE treat the page you are viewing at the time as your home page. You can click on Use Default on the same tabbed sheet to restore Microsoft's home page as your browser home page. In Netscape Navigator, select Edit|Preferences, and click on Use Current to set it to the current page. In both browsers, you can browse your disk and set your bookmark.htm file as your home page.

- Click on the down arrow in the Address box to see a list of the URLs you've visited recently. This comes in very handy if you can't remember how to get back to a particularly neat site you visited recently.

- If you forgot to bookmark a site, and the URL list in the Address box doesn't help, you can take a look in your History folder. Netscape Navigator and Microsoft Internet Explorer both keep a history of all the sites and pages you've visited recently. You can go to the History folder and rummage around if you think seeing the name of the Web site will get you on the right track. Here's how you do it in Microsoft Internet Explorer.

   1. Using Windows Explorer, find the History folder in the Windows directory.
   2. Double-click the `History` folder. You'll see a collection of Calendar folders.
   3. Double-click a `Calendar` folder. Inside the folder you'll see Site folders.
   4. Double-click a `Site` folder to see links to all the pages you've visited recently at that Web site.
   5. Double-click a link to go to that Web page.

   In Netscape Navigator, it's much easier. With Netscape Navigator running, press `Ctrl-H`. You can search that list with `Ctrl-F`. See Figure 7-2.

- All browsers save copies of the text, pictures, and other files you see in your Web browser window. They use these stored files the next time you visit the site, loading the ones on your disk if they are the same as the ones at the remote site, for faster display. If you are running low on disk space on your PC, you can delete these files. Web pages may take a little longer to load, but you'll free a ton of space on your hard drive. On Microsoft Internet Explorer, choose `View|Internet Options`, then on the General (first) tab, click on `Delete Files`. In Netscape Navigator, choose `Edit|Preferences`, then under Advances, click on `Clear Disk Cache`.

Four Score and Seven Sites to See

Since the first publication of this book, the number of genealogy-related Web pages has gone from a handful to literally thousands. And with the

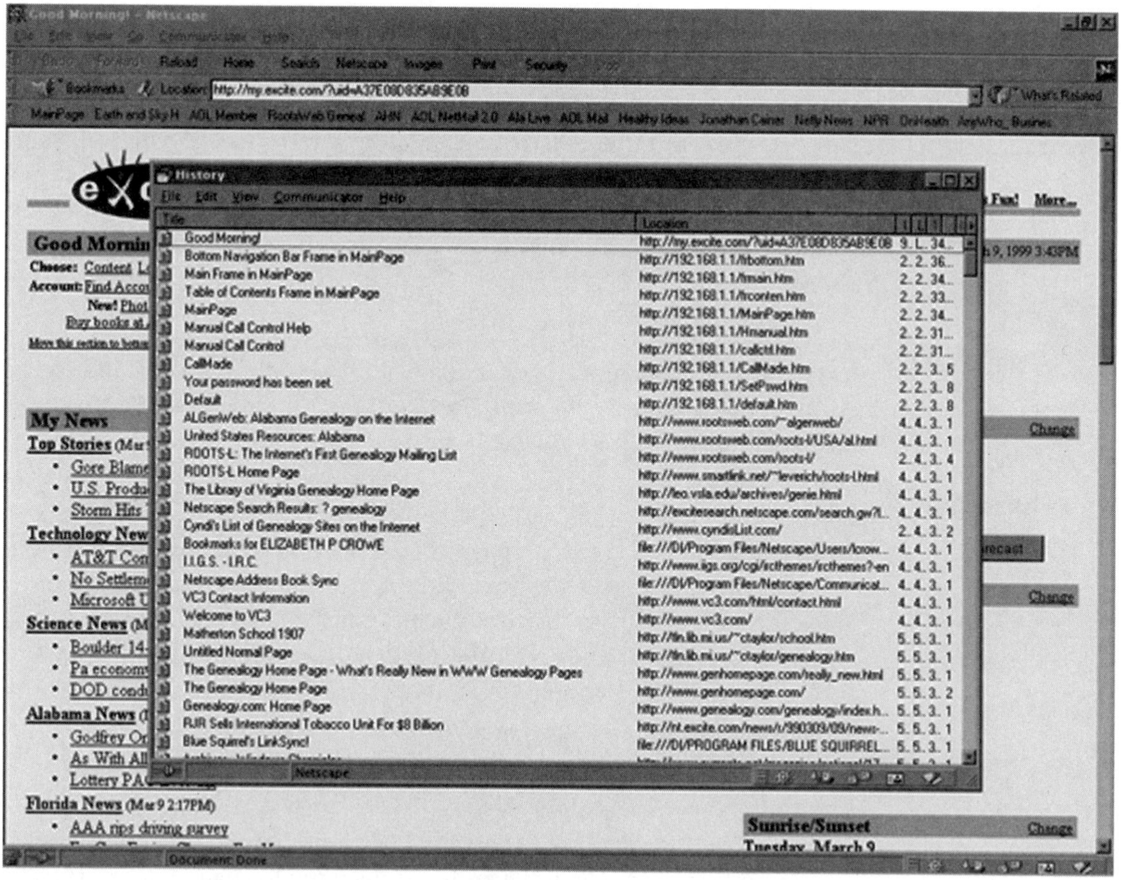

Figure 7-2 Your browsing history can be recorded and searched in Netscape Navigator.

rate at which things appear, disappear, and change location on the Internet, you'll never be able to see them all. So how do you find genealogy sites that are worth seeing? To make things easier for you, here is a list of 87 Web sites that are good starting places for online genealogists. Not all of these sites address genealogy specifically, but they can all be of use in your research.

The criteria for including the sites are as follows:

■ *Timeliness.*   How often it is updated and kept accurate

■ *Usefulness.*   How well it matches the needs of genealogists

■ *Uniqueness.*   Information not found elsewhere, or presented in a unique manner

■ *Organization.* How easy it is to find and retrieve the information there

In the manner of Web sites everywhere, these sites will all lead you to other sites, eventually, it is hoped, leading you to exactly the information you need. Realize that this isn't even close to an exhaustive list; for that, see Cyndi's List and Genealogy Resources on the Internet, listed below. In the list that follows, the sites are listed alphabetically, not ranked.

NOTE   All of these links were active when I wrote this. With the rate at which things change on the Web, it's likely that at least some links you find here will be gone by the time you read this. That's just the way things go on the Web.

1. Acadian Genealogy Homepage (http://www.acadian.org/) contains information about French Acadian and French Canadian genealogy, and includes ordering information for a CD-ROM covering over half a million people of almost exclusively French Acadian/French Canadian ancestry.

2. AfriGeneas Home Page (http://www.afrigeneas.com) is the starting place for African-American family history. Don't miss the in-depth profile of this site later in the chapter.

3. Allen County (Indiana) Public Library Historical Genealogy Department (http://www.acpl.lib.in.us/genealogy/genealogy.html) has over 220,000 printed volumes, 251,000 microfilms and microfiches, and 38,000 volumes of compiled genealogies in their collection. They also have census data going back to the 1700s, city directories, passenger lists, military records, Native American records, African-American records, and many other sets of records. If you ever want to do a genealogy road trip, consider putting this library on your itinerary.

4. American Civil War Home Page (http://sunsite.utk.edu/civil-war/) has links to fantastic online documents from all sort of sources, including two academics who have made the Civil War their career.

5. Ancestry Inc.'s Discovering Your Heritage (http://www.ancestry.com/dyh/intro2.html) is a basic beginner's how-to information source on genealogy.

6. AOL Hispanic Genealogy Special Interest Group (http://users.aol.com/mrosado007/) is the gathering place for a group of Hispanic genealogists on America Online. Links include a newsletter, heraldry information, a surname list, and more.

7. Archaic Words & Phrases (http://home.sprynet.com/sprynet/lgk71/2archaic.htm) is a list of some words and phrases that once had meanings different than those used today.

8. A Thousand Genealogy Links (http://members.tripod.com/surnames) actually has over 2000 links, most of them to online searchable databases, such as ships passenger lists, church records, cemetery transcriptions, and censuses for England, Scotland, Wales, Ireland, Europe, U.S., Canada, Australia, and New Zealand.

9. Branching Out Online (http://www.geocities.com/Heartland/Lane/5256/branch/index.html) is a tutorial on learning about online techniques and genealogy sites. Many other sites use "Branching Out" in their title, but this one is special.

10. The British Heraldic Archive (http://www.kwtelecom.com/heraldry/) is dedicated to increasing interest in heraldry, genealogy, chivalry, and related topics.

11. Calendars (http://home.sprynet.com/sprynet/lgk71/2calenda.htm) is an explanation of the transition from the Julian to the Gregorian calendar, which occurred in 1752.

12. Canadian Genealogy Made Easy! (http://www.geocities.com/Heartland/4051/) will get you started in Canadian genealogical research. It has links to different provinces, native information, and more.

13. Canadian Heritage Information Network (http://www.chin.gc.ca/) is a bilingual (French or English) guide to museums, galleries, and other heritage-oriented resources in Canada. Figure 7-3 shows the home page of this site.

14. Carrie's Adoptee & Genealogy Page (http://www.mtjeff.com/~bodenst/page3.html) offers links to resources for adoptees, as well as for German heritage and general genealogy.

15. Census Bureau Home Page (http://www.census.gov/) has a list of frequently occurring names in the U.S. for 1990, Spanish surname list for 1990, an age search service, and a frequently asked questions file on genealogy.

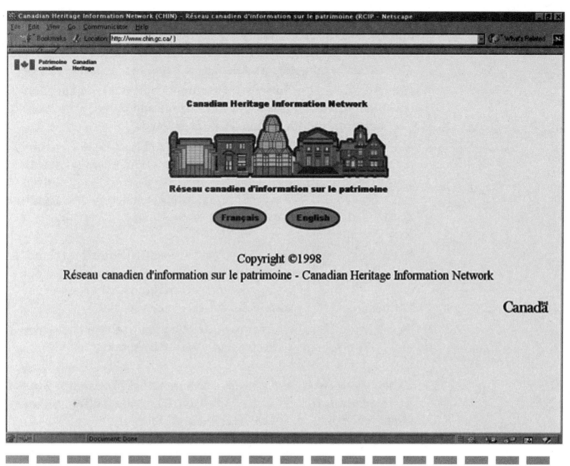

Figure 7-3 The home page of the Canadian Heritage Information Network.

16. Corporate Investigative Services Searchable Databases on the Internet (http://www.hsv.tis.net/~pvteye/search.html) has links to over 200 places where you can search for people, places, and definitions on the Internet.

17. CLIO-The National Archives Information Server-Genealogy (http://www.nara.gov/genealogy/genindex.html) lists genealogy holdings of the United States National Archives. You can find information on their Quick Guides to genealogy topics, and browse a catalog of aids for genealogical research. You can also look at the NARA Bookstore, use the Soundex machine to find the Soundex code for your surnames, and much more.

18. Cyndi's List of Genealogy Sites on the Internet (http://www.cyndislist.com/) is the best-organized and annotated list of WWW genealogy sites. A must-see!

19. David Eppstein's home page (http://www.ics.uci.edu/~eppstein/gene/) has information on his shareware program, called Gene, for the Macintosh.

20. Dead Person's Society, Melbourne, Victoria, Australia (http://avoca.vicnet.net.au/~dpsoc/) contains valuable information for people researching Australia and New Zealand. Includes old place names, wills, diaries, and more. (Gotta love those dancing skeletons!)

21. Dear MYRTLE (http://members.aol.com/dearmyrtle) is indispensable for the beginner. See in-depth profile later in this chapter.

22. Directory of Royal Genealogical Data (http://www.dcs.hull.ac.uk/public/genealogy/royal/catalog.html) is a database containing the genealogy of the British Royal family, along with many other ruling families of the Western world (they seem to have all been interrelated somehow). Contains over 18,000 names.

23. Eastman's Online Genealogy Newsletter (http://ww.ancestry.com/home/eastarch.htm) is a weekly all-text newsletter on genealogy topics. A typical issue will cover reviews of genealogy computer programs; news items of note to genealogists; a list of Web sites to visit; book, CD-ROM, and TV reviews; and more.

24. Everton's Guide to Genealogy on the World Wide Web (http://www.everton.com/) includes an online version of the venerable Helper, as well as links to online resources and a tutorial for genealogy beginners. Test-drive their genealogical database, On-Line Search.

25. Family Chronicle (http://www.familychronicle.com/) is the Web site for this magazine, which is dedicated to families researching their roots. Check out their offerings and request a free sample of the magazine.

26. Family History—How Do I Begin? (http://www.lds.org/en/2_How_Do_I_Begin/0-How_Do_I_Begin.html) is the Church of Jesus Christ of Latter-day Saints' basic tutorial.

27. Family Tree Maker Online (http://www.familytreemaker.com/) boasts the FamilyFinder Index, which has genealogy data from users of their programs, as well as 153 million names you can

search, the Internet FamilyFinder, and *Genealogy How-To*, a 1200-page guide to genealogy. This site is by Borderland Software, the publishers of Family Tree Maker.

28. FreeBMD (http://test.rootsweb.com/FreeBMD) FreeBMD stands for Free Births, Marriages, and Deaths. The FreeBMD Project is made up of volunteers transcribing the Civil Registration index information for England and Wales onto the Internet. The FreeBMD Project will place Civil Registration index information that is greater than 100 years old on the Internet, from 1837 to 1898. Progress is sporadic; volunteer if you can.

29. Gathering of the Clans Home Page (http://www.tartans.com/) is described as a reference for people researching the Scottish clans.

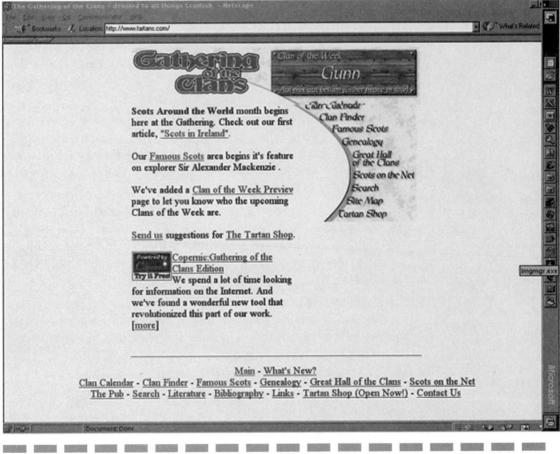

Figure 7-4 If you are of Scottish descent, you should check this site out.

This site includes information on 65 clans, as well as specifically Scottish genealogical resources. See Figure 7-4.

30. GENDEX (http://www.gendex.com/) is the home site of the GENDES and GED2HTML software. When you use GED2HTML to post your genealogy on the Web, you can register to be part of the worldwide GENDEX, a search engine for all such genealogy sites.

31. Genealogical Dictionaries (http://home.navisoft.com/scrolls/dict-inry.htm) is actually, despite the name, a pair of dictionaries that give the English translation of old German terms for occupations and causes of death.

32. Genealogy for Teachers (http://www.execpc.com/~dboals/geneo.html) lists resources, organizations, guides, and tutorials. Aimed at educators, it would help any beginner.

33. Genealogy Gateway to the Web (http://www.polaris.net/~legend/genalogy.htm) is a collection of links to free genealogical services, as well as over 29,000 online resources. The site is sponsored by the Family Tree Maker Online.

34. Genealogy Home Page (http://www.genhomepage.com/) is a wide-ranging index of genealogy resources on the Internet. It includes links to maps, libraries, software, and societies. This site, which is sponsored by Family Tree Maker Online, is examined in detail later in this chapter.

35. Genealogy of the Royal Family of the Netherlands (http://www.xs4all.nl/~kvenjb/gennl.htm) is a detailed genealogical history of the House of Orange-Nassau. Covers from Heinrich the Rich of Nassau (born 1180) to Juliana Guillermo (born 1981).

36. Genealogy on the Web Ring (http://www.geocities.com/Heartland/Plains/5270/webring.html) is a group of genealogy Web pages and sites, all connected one to the other in a giant ring. From this page, you can explore the ring's sites in sequence or select random jumps to put some serendipity into your research.

37. Genealogy Online (http://genealogy.emcee.com/) is a site that provides many resources for online genealogists, including an online copy of the 1880 U.S. census, links to other resources, and Web site hosting.

38. Genealogy Resources on the Internet (http://members.aol.com/johnf14246/internet.html) is an AOL member's site that provides you with a quality sorted list for finding just the genealogical information you are looking for.

39. Genealogy Today (www.genealogytoday.com) announces and rates genealogy sites, has news updates, allows readers to vote for their favorite sites, contains links to databases, and so on.

40. GenServ-Genealogical Server Information (http://www.genserv.com) is the GenServ's home page and includes general information and how to register. GenServ is covered in detail in Appendix A.

41. GENUKI (http://midas.ac.uk/genuki/) contains genealogy information for the UK and Ireland.

42. GenWeb Database Index (http://www.gentree.com/) has links to all known genealogical databases searchable through the Web. Now includes GenDex, an index of name databases with over two million entries.

43. German Genealogy Home Page (http://german.genealogy.net/gene) features all German genealogy, all the time. Includes links to regional research sites, German immigration info, and more.

44. Global: Everything for the Family Historian (http://www.globalgenealogy.com/) is the Global Genealogy Supply Web site. Shop online for genealogy supplies (maps, forms, software, etc.) and subscribe to the Global Gazette, a free email newsletter covering Canadian genealogy and heritage.

45. Internet Tourbus (http://www.tourbus.com/) is Patrick Douglas Crispen's email course on how to use every part of the Internet. It taught my mom everything she knows about the Net.

46. Hauser-Hooser-Hoosier Theory: The Truth about Hoosier (http://www.geocities.com/Heartland/Flats/7822/) shows how genealogy may have solved the mystery of "What is a Hoosier?".

47. HIR—Hungarian Information Resources Genealogy Page (http://mineral.umd.edu/HyperNews/get/hungarian-american-genealogy.html) is a good place to start if your research leads you to Hungary. Primarily links to other sites with Hungary-specific genealogical information.

48. How to Get Past Genealogy Road Blocks (http://www.firstct.com/fv/stone.html) is a quick refresher on what to do when you are just plain stuck and can't get past, over, around, or through that brick wall.

49. IIGS—The International Internet Genealogy Society (http://www.iigs.org) is a newsletter, chat site, and more about

cooperation in finding, storing, and making available genealogical information.

50. International Research (http://www.intl-research.com/) is an association of accredited genealogists who will, for a fee, do your genealogical research for you. A place to go if you are really stuck.

51. ISleuth-Arts & Humanities-Genealogy (http://www.isleuth.com/gene.html) is a place to search for genealogical resources. ISleuth (Figure 7-5) connects to lots of online databases for you: selected

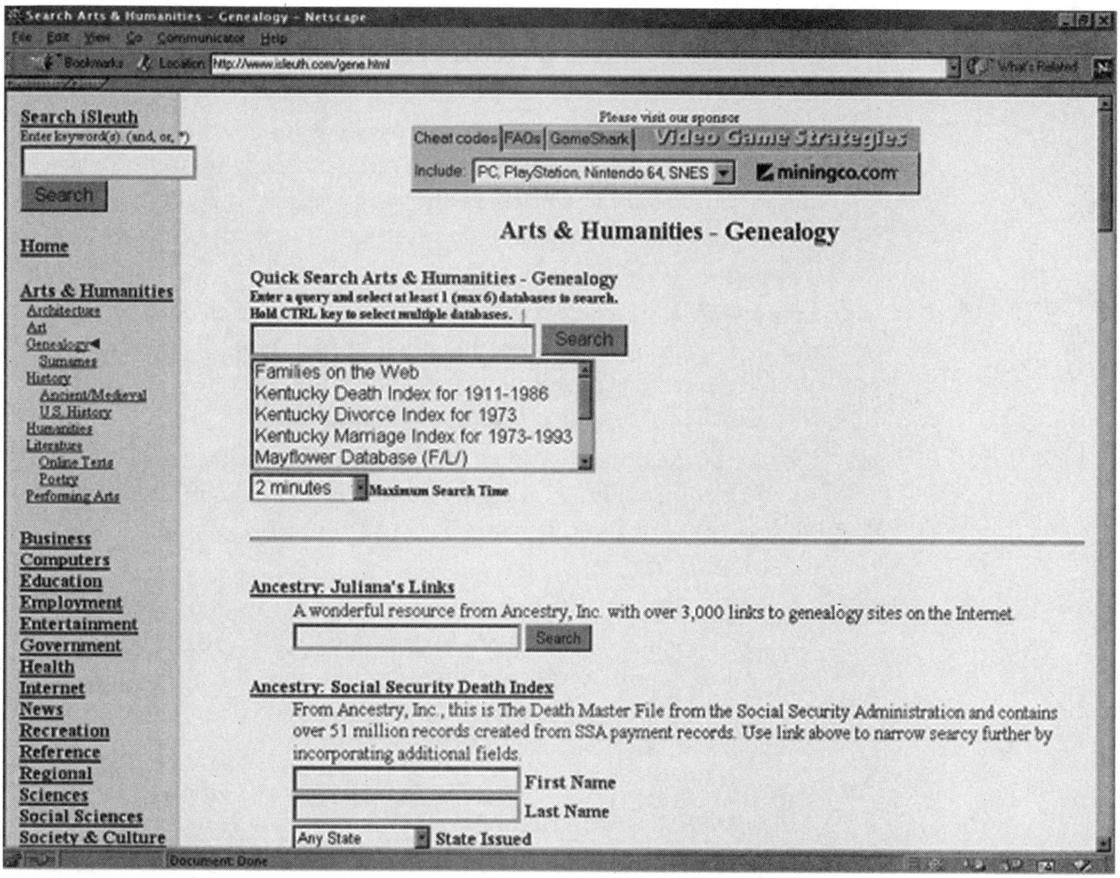

Figure 7-5 ISleuth gives you one-site searching of many databases.

census records, Social Security Death Index, British Columbia cemeteries, and more.

52. Italian Genealogy Home Page (http://www.italgen.com/) has chat forums, databases, tips, and a toolbox for researching Italian family names.

53. Janyce's Root Digging' Dept. (http://www.janyce.com/gene/root-dig.html) is yet another good place for beginners to start their online genealogical research.

54. JewishGen (http://www1.jewishgen.org/) is a comprehensive resource for researchers of Jewish genealogy worldwide. Among other things, it includes the JewishGen Family Finder, a database of towns and surnames being researched by Jewish genealogists worldwide, and it can be searched on the WWW or via email (email commands to the server, and results are emailed back to you).

55. Journal of Online Genealogy (http://www.onlinegenealogy.com/) is a monthly Web-based newsletter about genealogy, including news, techniques, advances in technology, and more. If you use Microsoft Internet Explorer, make this a "subscription" channel. See Figure 7-6.

56. Library of Congress (http://www.loc.gov/) is the Web connection to the U.S. government's vast collection of historical documents and other resources. There's plenty of information on how to tap into this monstrous resource later in the chapter.

57. Library of Virginia Digital Collections (http://image.vtls.com/) is a starting point where you can search Virginia colonial records, as well as bible records, newspapers, court records, and state documents.

58. Lineages, Inc. (http://www.lineages.com/default.asp) is the Web site for a group of professional genealogical researchers who'll help you find your roots, for a fee. In addition, their site includes some free information, such as "First Steps for Beginners," a free genealogical queries page, and more.

59. Marston Manor (http://www.geocities.com/Heartland/Plains/1638/) is a site that offers numerous useful items for online genealogists, including a chart for calculating family relationships and a detailed discussion of the terms "proof" and "evidence" as they relate to genealogy.

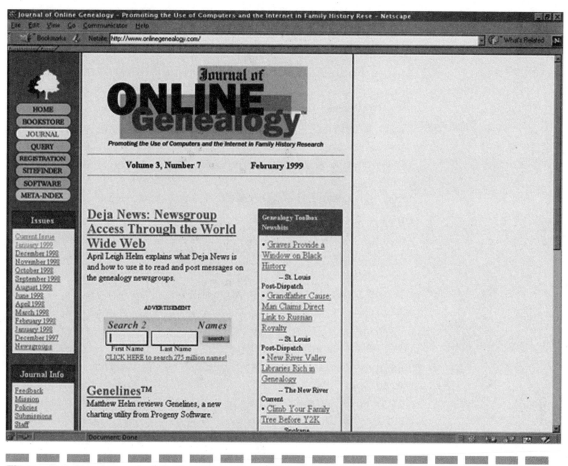

Figure 7-6 The Journal of Online Genealogy will help you keep up with advances in the field.

60. Mayflower Web Pages (http://users.aol.com/calebj/mayflower.html) contain the passenger lists of the *Mayflower*, *Fortune*, and *Anne*, plus many related documents.

61. Medal of Honor Citations (http://www.army.mil/cmh-pg/moh1.htm) contains the names and text of the citations for the more than 3400 people who have been awarded the Congressional Medal of Honor since 1861.

62. National Genealogical Society (http://www.ngsgenealogy.org) is the granddaddy of all genealogical societies. Here you'll find announcements of NGS seminars, workshops, and programs;

information on their home study course; youth resources; and other NGS activities. This is an excellent site for learning genealogy standards and methods.

63. Native American Genealogy (http://members.aol.com/bbbenge/front.html) is an AOL-based site that tries to keep up with the latest in sites and resources for Native Americans.

64. New England Historic Genealogical Society (http://www.nehgs.org/) is designed to be a center for family and local history research in New England. The Society owns 200,000 genealogy books and documents. If you are a New England genealogist, you should check them out.

65. Online Genealogy Classes (http://asc.csc.cc.il.us/mneill/csc/index.html) at Carl Sandburg College cost $35 per class and include topics such as Beginning Genealogy, Land Records, and Using Online Genealogical Databases.

66. Oregon History & Genealogy Resources (http://www.rootsweb.com/~genepool/oregon.htm) is a collection of genealogy information for Oregon, with links to the wider world of genealogy sites as well.

67. Our Spanish Heritage: History and Genealogy of South Texas and Northeast Mexico (http://www.geocities.com/Heartland/Ranch/5442/) is an interesting source if you're looking for relatives from the South Texas/Northeast Mexico area. The database has over 11,000 names, all interrelated as lineages.

68. Pitcairn Island Web Site (http://www.wavefront.com/~pjlareau/bounty1.html) is the place to find information about the current inhabitants of Pitcairn Island. But more importantly for genealogists, this is the place to go to get information on over 7500 descendants of the crew of the HMS *Bounty*, of *Mutiny on the Bounty* fame. See Figure 7-7.

69. Poland Worldgenweb (http://www.rootsweb.com/~polwgw/poland-gen.html) has maps and other information on Polish provinces, as well as a surname search. You can also adopt a province, becoming the provider of information about it.

70. Quick Guide to Genealogy in Ireland (http://www.bess.tcd.ie/roots/prototyp/qguide.htm) is a beginner's guide to Irish genealogical resources.

71. Repositories of Primary Sources (http://www.uidaho.edu/special-collections/Other.Repositories.html) is a listing of over 2500 Web

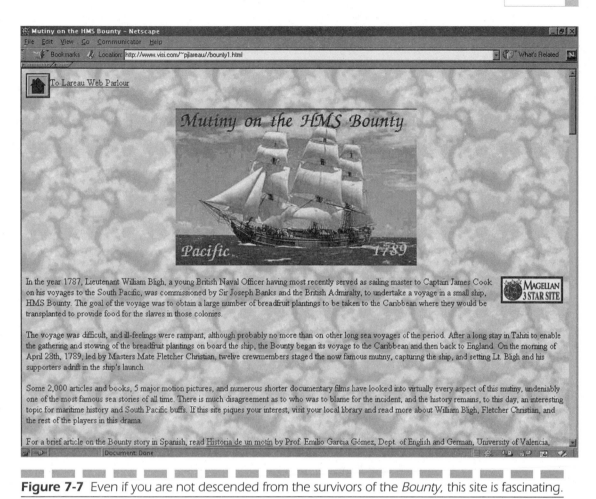

Figure 7-7 Even if you are not descended from the survivors of the *Bounty,* this site is fascinating.

sites describing holdings of manuscripts, archives, rare books, historical photographs, and other primary sources. It's worth a look.

72. ROOTS-L Page (http://www.rootsweb.com/roots-l) is the home page of the ROOTS-L mailing list.

73. RootsComputing (http://www.rootscomputing.com/) is a categorized guide to genealogy on the WWW. It's CompuServe's genealogy forum's presence on the Web and worth a look.

74. Social Security Death Index (http://www.ancestry.com/ssdi/advanced.htm) is a tool that allows you to search the Social Security Administration's record for birth and death dates of deceased Americans. Other information includes social security number, last known residence, and more.

75. South Carolina Library (http://www.sc.edu/library/socar/
books.html) is an online card catalog for the South Carolina
Library, which houses an extensive collection of genealogy
holdings.

76. Spanish Heritage home page (http://members.aol.com/shhar/) an
AOL-based site, is the home of the Society of Hispanic Historical
and Ancestral Research.

77. Surnames.com (http://www.surnames.com/) has genealogy in general, Arizona in particular. It includes a surname search and a
map of genealogical organizations in the United States. The site
also has a useful beginner's section.

78. Surnames: What's in a Name? (http://clanhuston.com/name/
name.htm) is a large collection of surnames and their meanings.
(The site describes the list as "fairly extensive—but it certainly
isn't all-inclusive.") There is also a brief history of surnames, with
references. See Figure 7-8.

79. Swiss Genealogy Project (http://www.mindspring.com/
~philipp/che.html) is a set of pages for researching Swiss genealogy, maintained by a group of volunteers. It includes several maps
with detailed information on each district.

80. Tracking Your Roots (http://members.aol.com/GenWebLisa/) is an
AOL-based gold mine of Alabama genealogy information, county
by county. The Tennessee River, which flows through North
Alabama, was a major Westward immigration route from
Tennessee, Virginia, and the Carolinas. We'll give you the full low-
down on this site later in the chapter.

81. Traveller Southern Families (http://www.traveller.com/geneal-
ogy/) is dedicated to the genealogy of Southern Families, contains
Civil War pages, government Web servers, genealogy software
companies, family societies and/or associations pages, books for
sale, and genealogy newsgroups. See Figure 7-9.

82. Treasure Maps: The How-To Genealogy Site (http://
www.firstct.com/fv/tmapmenu.html) is one of the best sites on the
Web for novices. It is aimed at hands-on, how-to information to
help you actually do research online: tutorials on writing queries,
using the U.S. census, and more. To keep track of the latest news
on Treasure Maps, you might want to subscribe to their monthly
newsletter.

83. U.S. Gazetteer (http://www.census.gov/cgi-bin/gazetteer) is a site
where you can just type in a city and/or state, and a map will

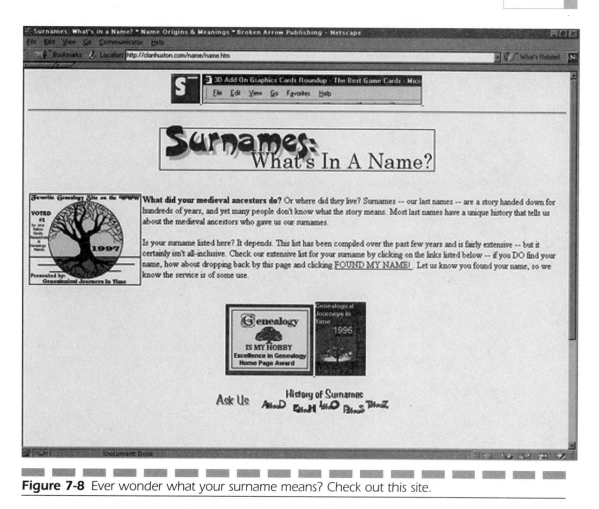

Figure 7-8 Ever wonder what your surname means? Check out this site.

appear showing the location. This service is run by the U.S. Census Bureau, and it uses information from the 1990 Census.

84. USGenWeb Project (http://www.usgenweb.org) is a noncommercial project with the goal of providing Web sites for genealogical research in every county and every state of the United States. There is much more information on this project later in the chapter.

85. Utah State Archives (http://www.archives.state.ut.us/) is a site where you can click on the research center for the archives' public services, which include research, answering questions, and sending you records. Not everything here is free, but it's very convenient!

86. Xerox Map Server (http://pubweb.parc.xerox.com/map) offers interactive maps for finding anyplace in the world.

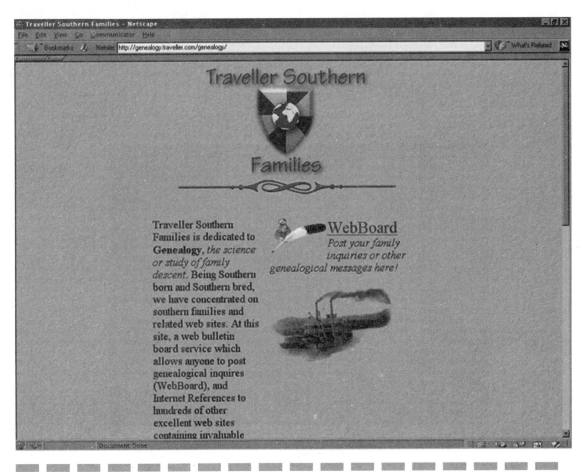

Figure 7-9 If you are researching the American South, you'll want to visit Traveller Southern Families.

87. Yahoo Genealogy Page (http://www.yahoo.com/Arts/Humanities/ History/Genealogy/) is a huge collection of links to guides, resources, and personal genealogies on Web sites. It includes links to related resources as well.

In-Depth Explorations of Some Major Genealogy Web Sites

While one of the common joys of genealogy and Web browsing is the joy of discovery, some sites deserve a guided tour. These sites are particularly interesting or useful to online genealogists, and each one has something in particular I want to be sure you'll know about. However, if you want to discover everything yourself, you have more than enough information to spend years researching online. Just skip past the rest of this section and be on your way.

Genealogy Home Page (http://genhomepage.com/)

The Genealogy Home Page is a wide-ranging index of genealogy resources on the Internet. It includes links to maps, libraries, software, and societies. Right from the start, you can see that this site is more of a guide to the genealogy resources available on the Web than a direct source of genealogical information. The home page (shown in Figure 7-1) starts off with two links to new, or newly discovered, genealogy sites. The URL Suggestion Form at http://www.genhomepage.com/mail.html (Figure 7-10) allows you to submit a URL for inclusion on the Genealogy Home Page. If you decide to create your own genealogy Web site, this is one way you can announce it to the world.

One of the most useful sections of the Genealogy Home Page is its collection of links under the heading Genealogy Help and Guides, at http://www.genhomepage.com/help.html. As I was writing this, there were 11 specific resources listed. Here are some of them:

- The ROOTS-L Library link takes you to documents from the famous ROOTS-L mailing list. From the beginner to the grizzled genealogy veteran, this library has information you need.

- Getting Started in Genealogy and Family History is another useful beginner's guide. If you are into printed documents as well as the computer screen, this guide includes an annotated bibliography of print references.

- Serendipity, a collection of stories describing serendipitous genealogical discoveries others have made, will give you a lift when the amount of work involved in researching your roots seems overwhelming.

- Another set of useful links from the Genealogy Home Page is on the Genealogy Societies page at http://www.genhomepage.com/societies.html. Here you'll find direct links to more than 30 genealogical societies, divided into three categories:
    - *Umbrella Organizations* are groups like the Federation of Genealogical Societies.

- *Geographic, National, Ethnic,...based Societies* covers groups like the American-French Genealogical Society and The Computer Genealogy Society of San Diego.
- *Family-based Societies* are organizations dedicated to research on specific surnames, like the Brown Family Genealogical Society or the Pelletier Family Association.

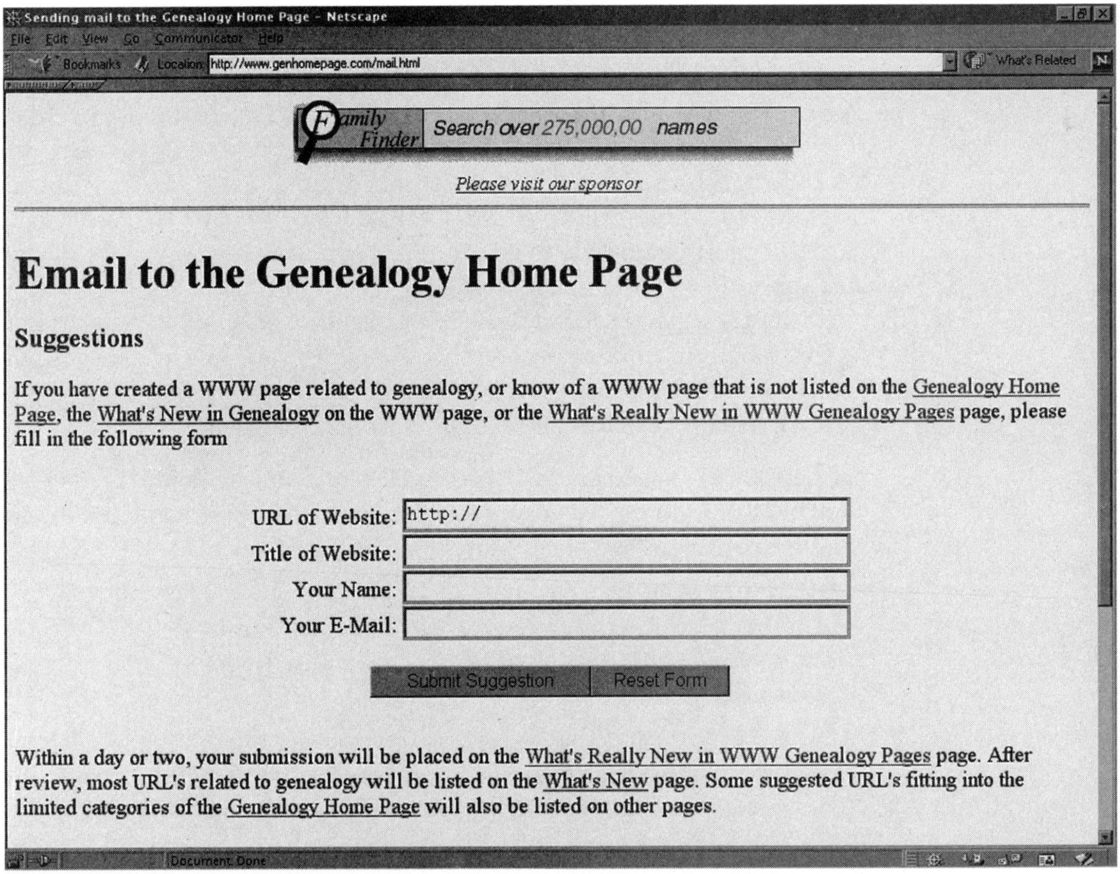

Figure 7-10 Anyone can use this form to submit new, or newly discovered, genealogy Web sites to the Genealogy Home Page.

AfriGeneas (http://www.afrigeneas.com)

AfriGeneas began as a mailing list for African ancestry and genealogical research into families of African ancestry and has developed into a multimedia online resource, including this lively mailing list. The AfriGeneas Web site (Figure 7-11) gathers and presents information about families of African ancestry, and is a central location for pointers to genealogical resources around the world. Members of the mailing list are invited to contribute information and resources, perhaps going as far as taking responsibility for information for a certain area; many others are now contributing, as well.

Generally, when a Web site supplies an About or FAQ (Frequently Asked Questions) page, that's the place to start learning about the site. And AfriGeneas is no exception. The AfriGeneas FAQ (http:// www. afrigeneas.com/mail-list.html#faqs) gives you background information on the mailing list.

Next, check out the newsletter at http://www.afrigeneas.com/ news.html, and the forum at http://www.afrigeneas.com/www.board/ shtml. This will give you a feel for the community this Web site serves. Now you should be ready to start making use of the resources available at AfriGeneas.

One of the valuable tools you'll find here is the Surname Database (http://www.afrigeneas.com/surnames.html), Figure 7-12. This database is a collection of surnames of people of African ancestry. What's most interesting about this database is that it isn't really a database of genealogical information. Instead, it is a database of contacts.

To use the database, you click on the first letter of the surname you are interested in. This takes you to a list of surnames that begin with that letter. Now click on a particular surname. You don't get a collection of genealogical information about that surname. Instead, you get a Compose Message window from your default mail program. On the To: line of that window, the AfriGeneas Database inserts the email address of the person who has information about the surname you clicked. You can then enter the surname in question on the Subject: line and send a message directly to a person who can help you find information about that surname. This person-to-person approach helps build connections between researchers and fits well with the philosophy "Each One Teach One" that is stated in the AfriGeneas FAQ.

The AfriGeneas list of links is worth a look too. Links such as African American Military History And Muster Rolls and African American

Figure 7-11 The AfriGeneas Web site.

Studies And History may have exactly the information you need. And don't miss the collection of wills, diaries, Bible records and slave manifests at the Slave Data Collection (http://www.afrigeneas.com/slavedata/). This data base is still growing as volunteers transcribe their finds and submit them to the site.

The AfriGeneas Web site also provides plenty of links to other genealogy resources on the Web and Net, oriented both toward general genealogy and genealogy of people of African ancestry. Two of the resources I found particularly interesting are:

- National Park Service Database on African-American Soldiers in the Civil War (http://www.itd.nps.gov/cwss/usct.html) contains the names

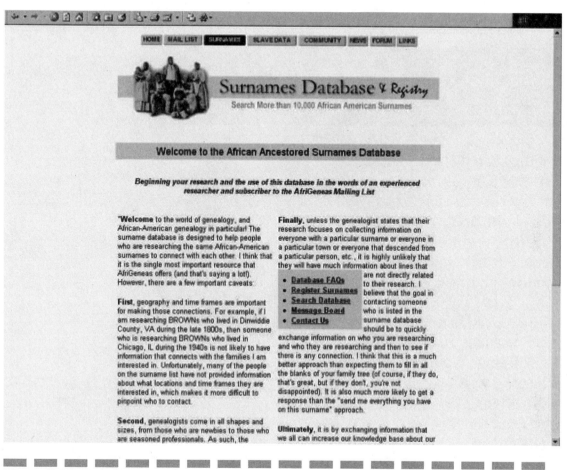

Figure 7-12 The AfriGeneas Surnames Database is a database of surnames for people of African ancestry.

of over 230,000 people who served in the United States Colored Troops during the war. See Figure 7-13.

■ The list of African American Genealogy resources, state by state.

DearMYRTLE'S Place (http://members.aol.com/dearmyrtle/)

For the beginning to intermediate genealogist, there is no better spot than DearMYRTLE's Place. DearMYRTLE has helped hundreds of

A database of over 230,000 names of the United States Colored Troops (USCT) has been developed by the NPS and its partners in the Civil War Soldiers and Sailors (CWSS) project. It has been made available in conjunction with the dedication of the African American Civil War Memorial. In addition to the 235,000 names, the current data includes 180 histories of USCT units/regiments and links to the most significant battles they fought in. Click here for help using the database of soldiers, regiments (units), battles, and NPS civil war

Figure 7-13 This database of information about African-American soldiers who fought in the Civil War is only one of the useful links from the AfriGeneas Web site.

genealogists with her daily columns, weekly chats, newsletters, and online courses. Her site will help you learn and grow as a genealogist; it got over 70,000 hits in its first three months!

NOTE *AOL Members, keep in mind that DearMYRTLE has her own keyword: MYRTLE, and that her columns are archived on AOL back to 1995. The web site has her columns beginning in 1999.*

The first page of DearMYRTLE's site (see Figure 7-14) will have announcements, links to features on the site, and often a seasonal greeting. There are two sets of links worth following here. The first set is shown in Figure 7-14, the buttons leading to Chat, Contact, Digest, Lessons, List, and Topics. The second set is near the bottom of the page. Here is a short list of links to her daily columns, sorted for you by topic (when you click on the DearMYRTLE graphic in Figure 7-14, you get the columns sorted by date, most recent first). The topics are Books, Lessons, Heirlooms, Index of All Articles (alphabetical), Internet Sites, and Sites for AOL Members.

One of the exciting things going on at DearMYRTLE's site is her Family Heirlooms Archive Project (see Figure 7-15). It began as the result of a DearMYRTLE column that described a photo quilt made for her father's 80th birthday in August 1998. In response, readers started to send her photos or scanned images of their quilts. Other readers wrote asking to open this up to other artifacts, and so the Family Heirlooms Archive Project was born. If you would like to participate, email to DearMYRTLE@aol.com a scanned image of your ancestor's quilt, watch, rocking chair, writing table, bible, reading lenses, dinner plate, hair comb, and so on for this special memorial collection. Be sure to include the name of your ancestor and the time period he or she lived.

Here's a quick look at other parts of DearMYRTLE's site:

■ *Chat* leads you to Myrtle's scheduled chats. You need an IRC program such as mIRC or Microsoft Chat (see Chapter 8) to connect. Set your IRC chat software to: Description: rootsweb; Server: irc.rootsweb.com; Port: 6667; Channel: #DearMYRTLE. Her regular Monday-night chats have scheduled topics (see Figure 7-16). Topics have included getting organized, using LDS resources, using land records, and finding things on the Internet.

■ *Contact* has the ways you can reach DearMYRTLE with questions and comments, or with books, maps, and programs for possible review.

■ *Digest* is the page that describes how you can get each DearMYRTLE daily column by email, once a week in digest form. *List* will show you how to subscribe to get each column individually, each day.

■ *Lessons* are DearMYRTLE's free tutorials on how to do genealogy. If you subscribe to the List or Digest, you will get the lessons by email. You can read past lessons online and look at the topics coming up. The text of a new lesson is added each week.

■ *Topics* is a collection of links to all her past columns, sorted by topic. Let the whole page load, then use your browser's "search" or "find" function to look for your topic on the page, for example, "France" or "Internet Resources."

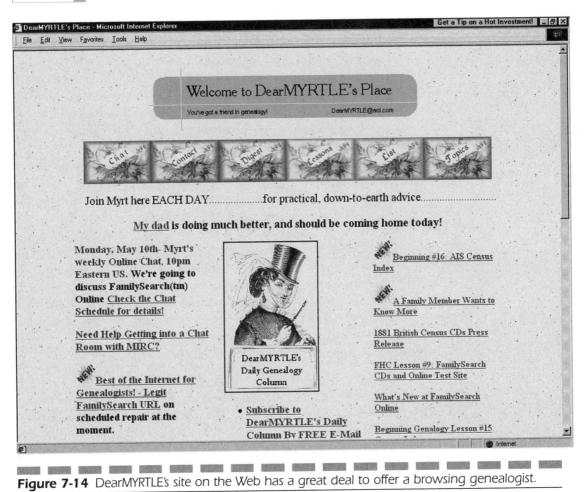

Figure 7-14 DearMYRTLE's site on the Web has a great deal to offer a browsing genealogist.

Bookmark DearMYRTLE's site. You'll be coming back often!

USGenWeb (http://www.usgenweb.org/)

The USGenWeb Project is a group of volunteers working to provide non-commercial genealogy Web sites in every county of every state in the United States. These sites are freely accessible to anyone—no memberships or fees are required. The online center of this effort is the USGenWeb Project Home Page at http://www.usgenweb.com (Figure 7-17).

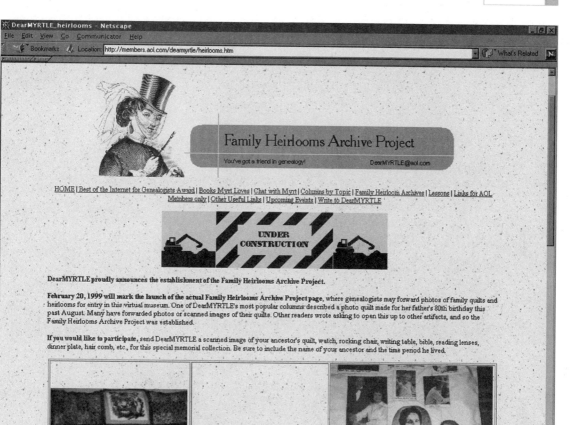

Figure 7-15 DearMYRTLE is collecting images of heirloom quilts and other items on her site.

Originally, GenWeb was a single entry point for all counties in Kentucky, where collected databases would be stored. In addition, the databases would be indexed and cross-linked, so even if an individual were found in more than one county, he or she could be located in the index. The idea quickly caught on and has been taken far beyond Kentucky. Today (mid-1999) there are links to every state, plus the District of Columbia. Each state site is unique, with its own look and feel. The state-level sites serve as your gateways to the counties within the states. State sites are also the best place for certain activities, like unknown county queries, family reunion bulletins, state history, and county maps. Some state sites are working on special projects such as transcribing Civil War troop records or reuniting families.

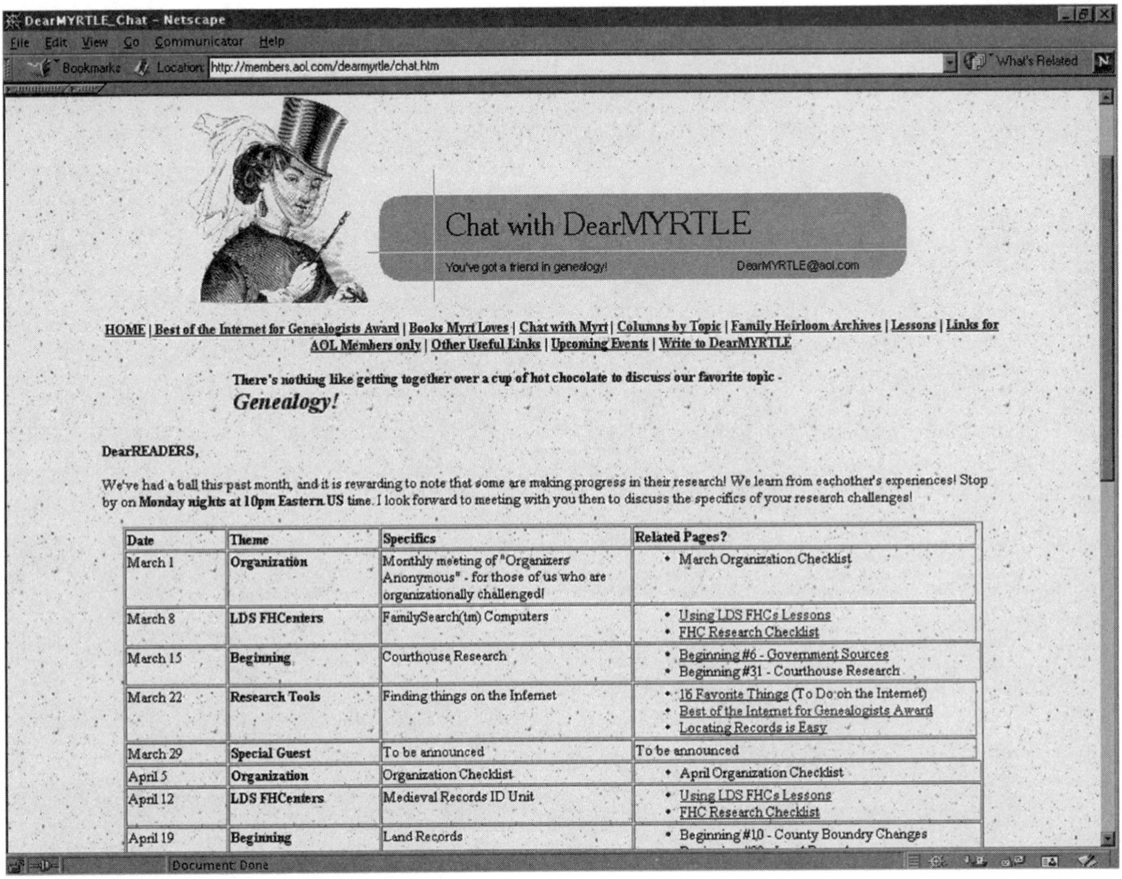

Figure 7-16 DearMYRTLE schedules topics for her moderated Monday-night chats.

You'll see lots of variety at the county level. Every page or database is created by a volunteer, and the resources they provide can be as individualistic as the people themselves. But at a minimum, each county site provides links to post queries, get back to the state's home page, and access state archives. USGenWeb is an impressive accomplishment, and the volunteers who do the work deserve the thanks of everyone doing genealogical research in the United States.

NOTE *If you have a lot of genealogical information about a particular county, check the listing on that county in the USGenWeb Project. Maybe you should join the volunteers who make this project possible. If you're interested, click the Information for Current and Prospective Volunteers*

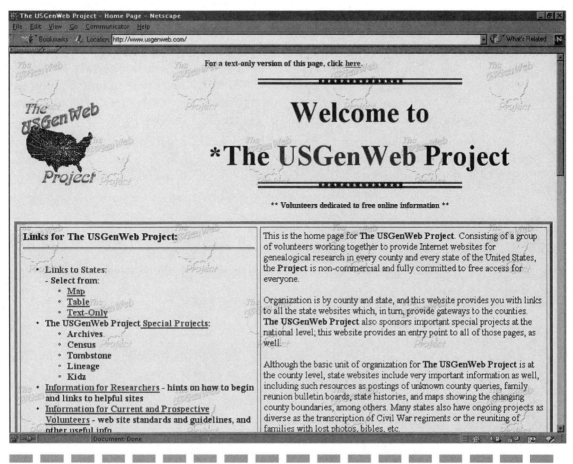

For a text-only version of this page, click here.

Welcome to
*The USGenWeb Project

** Volunteers dedicated to free online information **

Links for The USGenWeb Project:

- Links to States:
  - Select from:
    - Map
    - Table
    - Text-Only
- The USGenWeb Project Special Projects:
  - Archives
  - Census
  - Tombstone
  - Lineage
  - Kidz
- Information for Researchers - hints on how to begin and links to helpful sites
- Information for Current and Prospective Volunteers - web site standards and guidelines, and other useful info

This is the home page for **The USGenWeb Project**. Consisting of a group of volunteers working together to provide Internet websites for genealogical research in every county and every state of the United States, the **Project** is non-commercial and fully committed to free access for everyone.

Organization is by county and state, and this website provides you with links to all the state websites which, in turn, provide gateways to the counties. **The USGenWeb Project** also sponsors important special projects at the national level; this website provides an entry point to all of those pages, as well.

Although the basic unit of organization for **The USGenWeb Project** is at the county level, state websites include very important information as well, including such resources as postings of unknown county queries, family reunion bulletin boards, state histories, and maps showing the changing county boundaries, among others. Many states also have ongoing projects as diverse as the transcription of Civil War regiments or the reuniting of families with lost photos, bibles, etc.

Figure 7-17 The USGenWeb Project Home Page is the place to start for county-by-county genealogical information.

link. This takes you to the Volunteers page (http://www.usgenweb.org/ volunteers/volunteers.html), where you can learn about being a volunteer.

While the main objective for USGenWeb is the creation of the county-by-county sites, there are also several special projects under way. You can find out about them on the USGenWeb Special Projects page (http://www.usgenweb.org/projects/projects.html). Some of the special projects under way at this writing are as follows:

■ *Archives Project.* USGenWeb was originally designed to provide information county by county, but there is plenty of genealogical information that can't be organized this way. The Archives Project aims to put noncounty public domain information onto the Web. This project has several subprojects, including the Tombstone Project (http://www.rootsweb.com/~cemetery/), shown in Figure 7-18. In this subproject, volunteers are traveling to cemeteries around the country and transcribing the inscriptions on the tombstones. These inscriptions are then made accessible through this Web page.

■ *Lineage Project.* For people who want track down a particular ancestor, this project provides a place to list information about the ancestor, along with contact information (an email address or Web page) for the researcher.

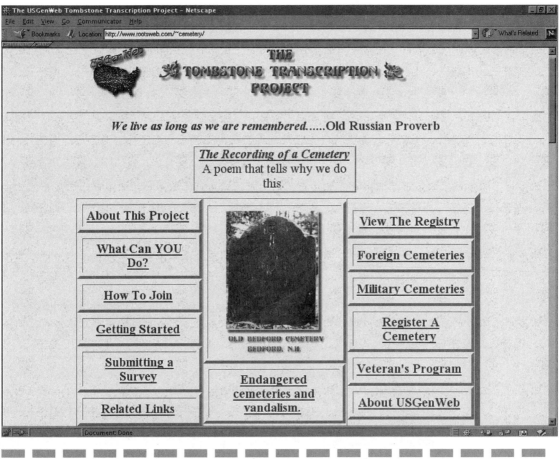

Figure 7-18 The Tombstone Project is just one piece of USGenWeb's Archive Project.

■ *National and International Links Project.* This is a collection of links from USGenWeb to sites of general genealogical interest around the world.

Going back to the USGenWeb home page, another link you should check out is Information for Researchers (http://www.usgenweb.org/researchers/researcher.html). This takes you to a page full of helpful research tips, plus to an interesting section on taking care of old documents. As a genealogist, you probably have some old books, photos, and newspaper articles you would like to preserve. Visit the Information for Researchers page and learn how to preserve these precious pieces of family history.

USGenWeb is one of the most important online genealogy sites, in my opinion. I hope you agree.

Library of Congress (http://www.loc.gov/)

The mission of the Library of Congress is to "make its resources available and useful to the Congress and the American people and to sustain and preserve a universal collection of knowledge and creativity for future generations." To that end, the Library of Congress has, since its founding in 1800, amassed more than 100 million items and has become one of the world's leading cultural institutions. The Library of Congress Web site (Figure 7-19) makes a small portion of the Library's contents available to the world through the Internet.

Three sections of the Web site are of particular use to genealogists. The American Memory section contains documents, photographs, movies, and sound recordings that tell some of the U.S.'s story. The Research Tools section of the site offers many online databases, along with connections to resources at other sites. The American Treasures section of the site is of interest more for the wonderful historical artifacts found there than for any specific genealogy information.

Click the American Memory link to begin your exploration of the Library of Congress site. The subtitle for this page is "Historical Collections for the National Digital Library." This project is a public/private partnership that is designed to create a digital library of reproductions of primary source material that will support research into the history and culture of the United States. Since this is an ongoing project, you can expect that the resources here will continue to grow for the foreseeable future.

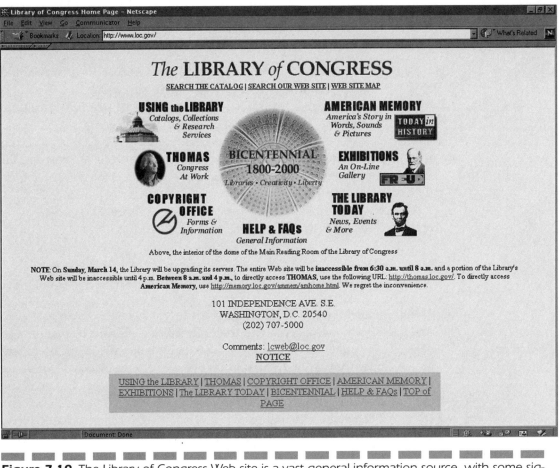

Figure 7-19 The Library of Congress Web site is a vast general-information source, with some significant genealogical resources.

If you are researching African-American roots, you'll want to click the African-American Odyssey link. This exhibition examines the African-American quest for full citizenship and contains primary source material, as well as links to other African-American materials at the Library.

Going back to the American Memory Home Page, you can click Documents to explore other source material. Some of the items you'll find here include:

- Almost 200 books describing the personal experiences of individuals in and on the way to California during and after the Gold Rush.

- Hundreds of objects dealing with the Women's Suffrage movement.

■ Significant and interesting documents from Americans obscure to famous, as collected in the first 100 years of the Library of Congress Manuscript Division.

■ American Life Histories: Manuscripts from the Federal Writer's Project, 1936 to 1940.

A third area of the American Memory section of the Library for you to explore is the Maps section. Clicking on Maps brings you to a searchable Web page (http://memory.loc.gov/ammem/mapcoll23.html) containing hundreds of digitized maps from 1639 to 1988. You'll find city maps, conservation maps, exploration maps, immigration and settlement maps, military maps, and transportation maps, to name a few. And the amazing thing is that this wealth of maps is only a tiny part of the Library of Congress's full 4.5-million-item Geography and Map Division holdings.

The Research Tools link from the Library of Congress Home Page takes you to a large set of useful databases, as well as to links to other resources of interest for researchers. One such link is Vietnam Era Prisoner of War/Missing in Action and Task Force Russia Databases (http://lcweb2.loc.gov/pow/powhome.html). This takes you to a page (Figure 7-20) that gives you access to a massive database of over 137,000 records pertaining to U.S. military personnel listed as unaccounted for as of December 1991. At the bottom of this page is a link to Task Force Russia (http://lcweb2.loc.gov/frd/tfrquery.html), a set of documents dealing with Americans who are believed to have been held in the former Soviet Union.

Finally, under the Exhibitions heading on the Library of Congress Home Page, check out the American Treasures of the Library of Congress link. You'll find reproductions of dozens of the most treasured objects in the Library's collection. Each one of the objects featured, from the *Whole Booke of Psalmes Faithfully Translated into English Metre* from 1640, to the Dorothea Lange notebooks, shown in Figure 7-21, the 1954 game program of the Kansas City Monarchs vs. The Indianapolis Clowns, has some special historical significance. You may not find any long-lost ancestors when browsing this collection, but there's sure to be something of interest to every genealogist.

Find Your Own Favorites

Throughout this book, I've tried to point you to the best genealogy newsgroups and Web sites. But the rate of change on the Internet is incredi-

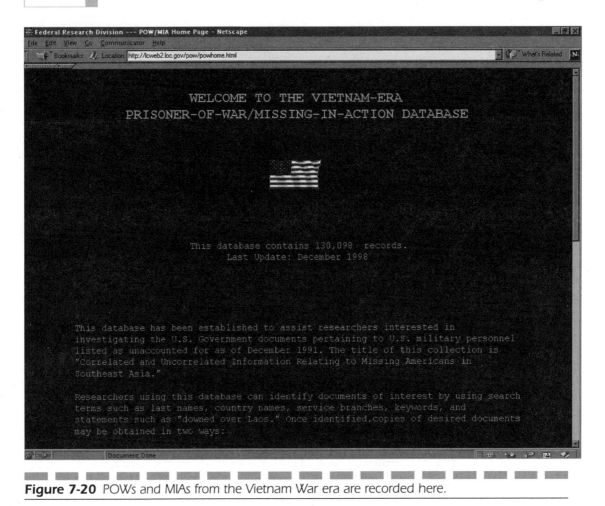

Figure 7-20 POWs and MIAs from the Vietnam War era are recorded here.

ble. Web sites disappear or move to a new server, which changes their URLs. Great new newsgroups and Web sites pop up all the time. Besides, as a genealogist, you know the thrill of discovering things for yourself. It can be quite a kick to find a Web site or newsgroup none of your friends knows about.

So what you need is a way to find genealogical resources on the Internet on your own. You could find sites that link to other sites. But a better way is to search for what you want yourself. That's where search engines and directories come in.

A *search engine* is a program that looks for information on the Internet, creates a database of what it finds, and lets you use a Web browser to search that database for specific information. AOL NetFind

AMERICAN TREASURES OF THE LIBRARY OF CONGRESS

The Exhibition

The *American Treasures* is an unprecedented permanent exhibition of the rarest, most interesting or significant items relating to America's past, drawn from every corner of the world's largest library. On display in the Jefferson Building Treasures Gallery in Washington, D.C., the "Treasures" exhibition presents more than 250 items arranged in the manner of Thomas Jefferson's own library, the seed from which the present collections grew: *Memory* (History); *Reason* (Philosophy, including Law, Science and Geography); and *Imagination* (Fine Arts, including Architecture, Music, Literature and Sports). This World Wide Web version of the exhibition will allow you to see many of the same "Treasures" and read about their significance to this institution and to our country's history.

Treasure-Talks - Enter Exhibition

After visiting the exhibition, please take a few minutes to

Figure 7-21 The American Treasures exhibition contains myriad documents and objects of great historic, if not genealogical, value and interest.

(http://www.aol.com/netfind/home.html) is one example of a powerful search engine that has other features. When a search engine offers chat, news, forums and other services, it becomes a *portal*.

A *directory* is similar to a search engine in that you can search the directory for specific information. But in a directory, the newsgroups and Web sites are sorted, categorized, and sometimes rated. Yahoo! (http://www.yahoo.com) is one example; it is also a good example of a portal, where lots of Internet services are gathered into one site.

The following two sections describe various search engines and directories. While the content in them overlaps a great deal, each one uses slightly different methods to search, and each rates sites slightly differently. This means you may find what you are looking for with one search engine or directory, but not another.

AOL NetFind

AOL NetFind (http://www.aol.com/netfind/home.html) is a powerful general-purpose search engine with some additional capabilities, including a people search engine, covered later in this chapter. To reach AOL NetFind from within America Online, you can go to the Internet window and click the NetFind button, or you can go directly there by entering the keyword NETFIND. In either case, you'll get to the AOL NetFind home page, shown in Figure 7-22.

To do a basic search, all you have to do is enter the word or phrase you want to search for in the text box, and click on Find!. However, in most cases, you'll end up finding too much stuff. For example, a search on the word genealogy returns more than 95,000 matches! This is a general problem with search engines, which have been known to return over a million matches for common terms.

To get around this challenge, search engines give you various ways to narrow your searches. Here are some search tips for AOL NetFind:

- *Use phrases instead of single words in your searches.* Type several words that are relevant to your search. *Spencer genealogy Ohio* will narrow a search well.

- *Enclose phrases in quotes.* Searching with the phrase *Mann family history* will match all pages that have any of those three words included somewhere on the page, in any order, and not necessarily adjacent. Searching with the phrase *Mann family history* will return only those pages that have those three words together, in exactly that order.

- *The more specific you are, the better.* Searching for *Irish genealogy databases* will give you fewer, but closer, matches than searching for *Irish genealogy.*

- *Use + and − in your searches.* A word preceded by a plus sign (+) must appear on the page for there to be a match. A word preceded by a minus sign (-) must not appear on the page for there to be a match. There can be no spaces between the plus or minus signs and the words they apply to. For example, entering cats-dogs monkeys would tell AOL NetFind you wanted pages that definitely used the word *cats*, didn't use the word *dogs*, with *monkeys* optional.

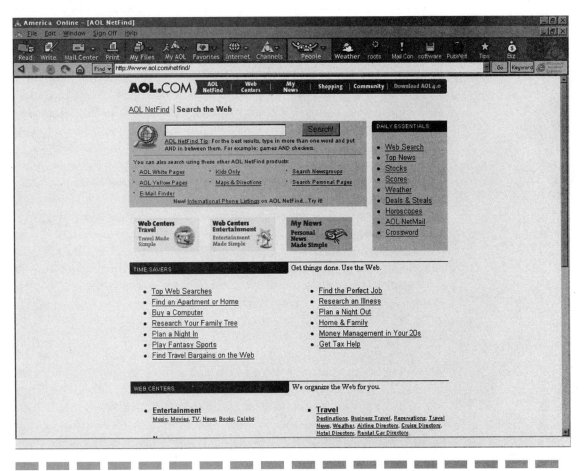

Figure 7-22 The AOL NetFind home page is a good place to start when you want to search the World Wide Web.

■ *Narrow or broaden your searches.* Once AOL NetFind completes a search, you have the chance to narrow or broaden the search. You do this by entering more search terms in the Search box at the end of the search results page if you want to narrow the search, or by removing search terms if you want to broaden the search.

NOTE *If you want more search tips, click* Search Tips. *If you are really stuck, follow the links from that page to some advanced tips.*

Lycos

Lycos is named for a spider that hunts at night and is very, very fast. Lycos uses a program called a "spider" to hunt for new Internet files. Lycos Web Search (http://www.lycos.com/) works very much like AOL NetFind, but may return different results for the same search. Lycos does have some special pluses. The search engine includes separate databases for pictures, sounds, programs, and other categories of information.

Lycos is also a portal: It has chat, news headlines, and other services. Worth a look is the Lycos Top 5% (http://point.lycos.com/categories/), a catalog or directory to what Lycos feels are the best 5 percent of all Web sites. Figure 7-23 shows the results of searching the Top 5% for "genealogy."

Since Lycos reviewers have to hear of a site, visit it, review it, and post it (assuming the site makes the top 5 percent) this isn't a good place to look for a brand-new site. But if you are looking for sites that someone else has reviewed and rated for you, this is a great resource.

Excite

Excite was one of the first search engines; it soon developed the ability to "personalize" the Excite page with your favorite links, news headlines that match your keywords, and local information such as TV and movie schedules. Now a portal like Yahoo! and Infoseek/GO, it offers chats, email, forums, and other services. There is a genealogy section, as a matter of fact, at http://www.excite.com/lifestyle/hobbies_and_recreation/genealogy/. Here you'll find a "Genealogy Book of the Day" reviewed, pointers to new sites, and a browsable index of 50,000 genealogy sites. That should keep you busy for a while!

Excite uses plus and minus signs and quotation marks as noted in AOL NetFind. Excite's search algorithm gets very good results. In fact, many other search sites use Excite's search software, simply tweaking it to look for their specialties.

General Directories

Yahoo! (http://www.yahoo.com)

The first Internet directory worthy of the name, Yahoo! is an edited, sorted catalog of sites. And it is big. It features about half a million sites

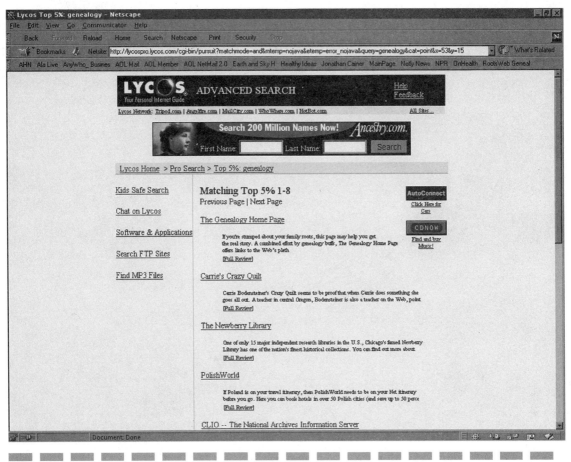

Figure 7-23 The Lycos Top 5% is a collection of Web sites rated among the best on the Internet by Lycos reviewers.

divided into 25,000 categories. Yahoo! (shown in Figure 7-24) is arranged in a hierarchy of categories, so you can browse through it. But with so many sites and categories, it is good to know that Yahoo! has a search engine built in. Mind you, this search engine doesn't search the Web, it searches Yahoo!, looking for sites and categories within the directory. The genealogy page of the catalog was mentioned earlier in this chapter.

Yahoo! gets updated frequently, with users providing most of the new sites. Each site gets visited by a Yahoo! surfer, who decides where each site should appear within the directory. It's also a portal with chat, email, forums, and other services.

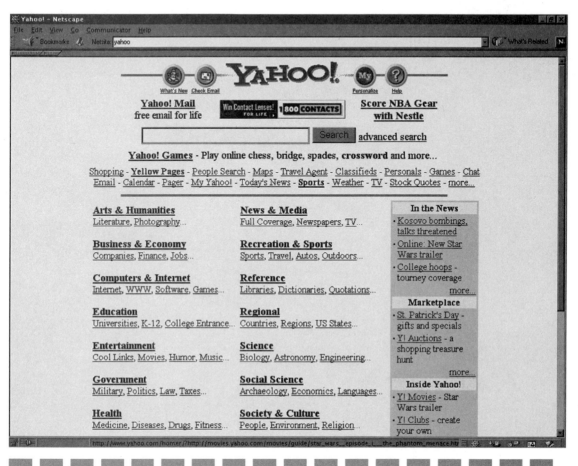

Figure 7-24 Yahoo! is a huge directory containing links and information for over half a million Web sites.

Infoseek/GO (http://www.infoseek.com/)

This is my favorite search engine. Infoseek/GO is an Internet portal similar to Yahoo!. It is run by the folks who created Infoseek in conjunction with Disney/ABC. You can browse the Infoseek channels (categories), or you can run a search on the contents of the Infoseek databases (see Figure 7-25). When doing searches on Infoseek, capitalization counts, so you can search for surnames such as "Weeks" and "Fox," without getting as many irrelevant matches. Like AOL NetFind, Infoseek uses plus and minus signs in its searches. In addition, Infoseek doesn't ignore common words like *the* and *new*, so you can efficiently search for states like New Hampshire.

As you can see in Figure 7-25, four tabs offer links to different services. The search engine input box is at the top of all of them. The Centers tab in the main page shows news headlines, stock quotes, and links to levels of the catalog. The Web Directory tab leads to the browseable catalog. The Community tab takes you to the chat, forum, and other interactive services. The Shop tab, as you'd expect, is a small online mall, with mostly Disney products.

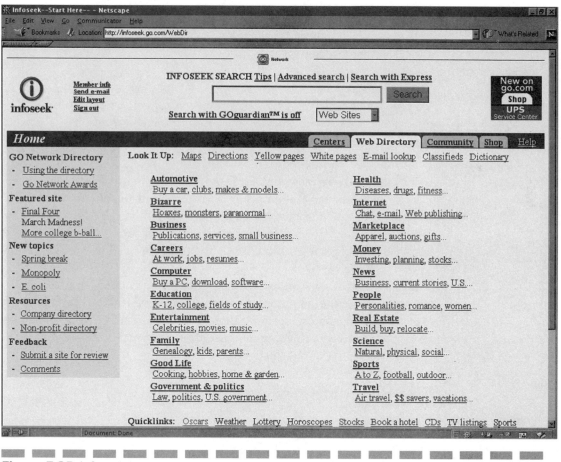

Figure 7-25 Infoseek is another massive directory you can use. This is the Web Directory tab of the main page: Genealogy is under Family.

People Search Engines

The search engines and directories you've looked at so far are for finding a Web site. But what if you need to find lost, living relatives? In that case, you need people search engines. These specialize in finding people, not pages. As with regular search engines, the place to start is at the versatile AOL NetFind.

AOL NetFind, at http://www.aol.com/netfind/person.html and http://www.aol.com/netfind/emailfinder.html, actually has two sections that can help you find people. The first is the Find a Person page. Here you can enter the first and last name of a person, as well as the city (optional) and state the person lives in. A successful search turns up a person's mailing address and phone number. Beside each name returned by the search are three buttons. You can send them personal greetings, flowers, or some other gift.

NOTE *The people you find using the Find a Person window are AOL subscribers. The E-mail Finder lets you find the email address of a person if you know his or her first and last name.*

Switchboard (www.switchboard.com) is one of many White Pages services on the Web. It's free and has the email and telephone numbers of millions of people and businesses taken from public records, as well as a Web site catalog. If you register as a user (registration is also free), you can ensure that your listing is not only accurate but has only the information you wish it to reveal.

Bigfoot (http://www.bigfoot.com) is another such effort to catalog people, with the same general rules: Input your information, and you get searches that are more specific. Bigfoot also has surface mail addresses as well as email and telephone information.

File Search Sites

Sometimes what the online genealogist needs isn't a site or a person—it's a program. To find programs you may hear of, such as new Web browsers or genealogy programs, you can go to several sites that keep track of software and where the latest versions are. Some of these are File Mine, TUCOWS, Shareware.com, and ZDNet Software Library.

File Mine (http://www.filemine.com) is a vast collection of software, most uploaded by the authors and offered as shareware, or rarely, freeware. File Mine catalogs and rates the software. In the category Home & Leisure, you'll find a Genealogy section, but as of this writing, it was empty. However, you can search the database, and *genealogy* comes up with such all-time favorites as Brother's Keeper and Family Matters. When you find a category that has files in it, you can choose to look at their edited catalogs of software. Under the Jewels category, you'll find software judged best in its class. Under Packs, you'll find customized collections of software around a theme (holidays, privacy, etc.). Digs, on the other hand, gives you a list of software that compete head-to-head (Web browsers, etc.). The New category will have the newest files.

The Ultimate Collection of Winsock Software, or TUCOWS (http://www.tucows.com), is a site that tracks more than Windows, despite the name, and has a capsule profile and a rating for each program. TUCOWS has mirror sites all over the world, so you can choose a site close to you for faster downloads.

Shareware.com (http://www.shareware.com) is a premier software search site. Updated weekly, the search engine lets you choose your operating system, choose a keyword, and even choose a date for the newest software *or* the oldest. Shareware.com then lets you see where the file can be found and rates the reliability (how easy it is to get in and get a file) of each site.

ZDNet Software Library (http://www.hotfiles.com/) has the latest software, usually rated by the staff on a five-star system. All the ZD sites are now integrated to some extent, so you can search from the ZDNet Software Library into a bunch of magazines (*PC Magazine*, *Computer Shopper*, and *Yahoo! Internet Life*, to name a few) for site reviews as well as the latest software.

Searching for Information in Newsgroups

I covered this topic in Chapter 5 on Usenet, but for completeness I cover it here as well. While newsgroups can be great source of genealogy information, reading all the messages, or even the headers, can be a lot of work. Fortunately, you don't always have to read the whole newsgroup to find the information you need. There are several places where you can search newsgroups, one, several, or all at a time.

The search engine for the Infoseek directory (http:///www.infoseek.com) can not only search Web sites, but newsgroups, news archives, and company listings as well. With regard to newsgroups, Infoseek has the most recent two weeks of newsgroups stored in a searchable database. To search newsgroups, just enter the text you want to search for, click on Newsgroups, then click on Seek. To do quick and easy genealogical searches, type in the surnames you are interested in and follow them with +genealogy. Infoseek will return a list of the genealogical messages. Each message title is a link; click on it to read it.

Deja.com carries over 50,000 newsgroups, with postings going back as far as two and a half years, and it makes basic searches simple, yet supports more complex ones. You can click on Power Search to get fancy. Create a Query Filter by typing in the first part of the name of a group of newsgroups you want to search. For example, enter soc.genealogy.*. Now type in the surnames you're looking for, and click Find. Within seconds, Deja.com will return a list of messages that are in the soc.genealogy.* group and mention the surnames you gave it. You can also limit the date of those messages to a certain range; when you use this feature, a monthly search will let you know if something interesting is happening in your surname on Usenet.

Moving On

There's more to the Internet than just passively reading. In the next chapter, I'll show you Chat, one of the most popular Internet services.

8

Chat

Hail Thy Fellow on the Net!

Sometimes you need a little chat to get beyond a genealogical problem. The online world can help you there too, with "chat." Chat has two versions: Internet Relay Chat (IRC) and Internet presence chat.

Chat has been around for a long time. From the earliest days of The Source (an early information utility) and CompuServe to the era of AOL and the Web, chat has been a staple of online communications. It's useful whether you're collaborating on a genealogy project, sending digital reunion memos to your extended family, or discussing your hobby with a large crowd.

NOTE *Throughout this chapter you'll find references to newsgroups, mail lists, and Web sites. This is just to illustrate how interconnected the genealogy resources on the Internet can be. You will learn everything you need to know about newsgroups and Web sites in other chapters.*

Internet Relay Chat, better known as IRC, is the most popular group chat. Although it can support one-to-one, one-to-many, and many-to-many messages, usually IRC is a lot of people on a "channel" typing messages back and forth in many-to-many format. IRC uses a system of clients and servers, allowing people all over the world to communicate in real time by typing on their computers. So, people in Australia, France, Hong Kong, Kenya, British Columbia, and Vermont can all sit at their computers at the same time, log in to the same server, connect to the same channel, and type messages interactively, each seeing what all the others are saying.

If you just wander into any old chat room, you may be dismayed at the level and tone of the conversation. Even if you get into a genealogy chat room, the conversations overlap, and it's sometimes hard to keep track of who's saying what. Unmoderated, general chat rooms (sometimes called "drop in" chat rooms) are like going by the corner coffee shop. You don't know who'll you'll find there and whether anyone there will be of any help to you. And, a lot of what's going on will be totally irrelevant to you.

A moderated, or hosted, chat, however, is more like attending a class or a genealogy club meeting. There is usually a specific topic at hand, an expert or two available, and a system for asking and answering questions so that the conversations are at least a little easier to follow.

A one-on-one chat, between yourself and a buddy, can be even more productive. If you can set up a specific time and channel to discuss a problem or a great find, you can get a lot done this way.

Another, more controlled type of chat is called "Internet presence" or "instant message," which is growing in popularity by the day, in large part thanks to America Online's Instant Messenger program. In this form of chat, a select, invited list of people (from two to a whole "room") exchange typed messages in real time. This feature has become so popular that instant messaging is used 180 million times a day, according to AOL. ICQ ("I-seek-you"), a different Internet presence program, gets hundreds of new users a day. Microsoft's standard, Microsoft Chat, works just great, both as an IRC client and a one-to-one client. And there are newer programs to use too, like Ding!, an intranet/Internet collaboration tool.

NOTE *You might ask, why not just use email instead? Live chat can be more efficient, especially if you're collaborating on a project. You can create a channel where the only people allowed to participate are the ones you invite. Internet presence programs can tell you who's online now and hook you up for a conversation on the spot. Best of all, many chat clients I'm covering here are free. And so far, most aren't bombarding you with ads or asking for much demographic data.*

Important Warnings about Chat

I discussed unsolicited bulk email (UBE) in detail in Chapter 2. Those who send UBE, especially the pornographic kind, have special programs that spy on chat rooms and report the email addresses of everyone who logs on, regardless of the topic of the chat room. They are especially vigilant about chat rooms on AOL. Within minutes of participating in an AOL chat on genealogy, you will be bombarded by unsolicited email about porn sites.

How do you prevent this? Simple: You must wear a disguise. On AOL, CompuServe, and Prodigy, you can create screen names under your primary account. You should create one just for chat and encourage everyone in the family to use this one *only* to chat.

Then, on AOL you can block all email to that screen name. On CompuServe and Prodigy, as of this writing, you'll just have to set up mail filters (see Chapter 2) that delete any messages sent to the chat account.

If you use Ding!, AOL Instant Messenger, ICQ, or a similar program, you are hidden from the unsolicited bulk emailers because you don't log on to the open, public chat servers, so you can use your real email address. These programs use their own private, secure servers, and everyone on them has agreed to a terms of service statement that forbids sending unsolicited email to members. Furthermore, they give you the ability to filter out specific people. Thus, you don't have to worry that your chats will result in a flood of UBE.

If you use one of the other chat clients that uses the open, public chat servers (such as Microsoft Chat or mIRC), you could enter false information in the "email address" portion of the setup screens to hide from unsolicited bulk email. You could enter your email address as something like `LIBBIC@nospam.prodigy.net`, and most people will know to take out the `nospam` part to get your real email address, but the unsolicited bulk emailer's automatic programs won't. However, my common practice is to enter this as my email address: `available@polite.request`. If someone wants my address, they have to give me theirs first.

All the clients I mention here have security features. You can block others from adding you to their buddy list until you give permission, you can block people from sending you messages until you give permission, and so forth. Each program has its own way of handling twit filters, and all of them are constantly trying to improve their privacy features. You'll have to try them out to see what's new with them.

Some chat is based on Java (a simplified programming language used on the Web) so you don't need a chat client to use them. Several personal and commercial genealogy sites have Java-based chats that require only a browser and can deal with Java (Microsoft Internet Explorer or Netscape Navigator 4.0 or newer are examples). However, if your email address is recorded in your browser's settings, UBE senders might get hold of it.

How It Works

How do chat services and programs work? You use the client program to log on to a chat server.

But where are the servers? I'll profile some genealogy ones below, but you can also look at the chat sections on Yahoo!, Excite, Microsoft Network (MSN), or any other portal, or just go look for the home page of your IRC client of choice. Most IRC programs also come with a list of public chat servers.

If it's an open, public chat server (IRC), you can use a program like mIRC or Microsoft Chat. You log on and search for a channel to suit your interest. If there isn't one at the moment, you can create one (calling it #genealogy, perhaps) and wait for interested people to come chat with you. Once the chat gets going, it's a lot like citizen's band radio in print.

Other programs, like AOL Instant Messenger, are set up so that only people using the same program can contact you (however, as we'll see, they don't have to be AOL users). With such a program, you can usually indicate your status (gone, accepting calls, connected but away from your desk, and so on) and keep a list of people you want to contact (often called a "buddy list" or "address book") and who are allowed to contact you. (Alas, you can't import a buddy list from your email address book—you usually have to ask permission to add someone to your list.) To find people to add to your list, you usually can look them up by email address, or you can email them an invitation to use the same program as you use and exchange ID names.

When someone hails you, a sound or small message window (or both) will alert you. Chatting typically takes place in two panes of one window: one for your outgoing messages and one for incoming ones.

If you're worried about security or just want to be left alone, fret not. Most of these programs let you shield your presence from specific people or from the world at large, as suits your mood. You can also let yourself be "seen" but not heard with an online "I'm busy now" indicator.

On all these systems you can choose a "handle" or nickname for your login ID. This is the name by which people will know you on IRC; everyone in a channel must have a unique nickname. Remember that there are many hundreds of thousands of people on IRC, so it's possible that someone might already be using the nickname you've chosen. If that's the case, just choose a unique one. Some programs record your preferred nickname in the setup screen and allow you to choose an alternative if someone is using your first choice in a certain channel.

Make use of the help files of any chat program. That's the best way to learn how to get the most out of it.

Security Risks in IRC

When you use the IRC type of chat, you are open to some security risks. For example, while you are logged on to an IRC server, bad guys can look up your dynamic IP settings and bombard you with packets, clogging up your TCP/IP connection until you disconnect and reconnect.

Microsoft's security page at http://www.microsoft.com/security contains information on these security threats, along with links to fixes.

Another important caution: If someone you don't know tells you to type an unfamiliar key sequence, phrase, or command in chat, don't do it! You may be opening the chat room or even your own computer to hackers.

Chat Flavors

The programs in this section can allow you to have one-on-one and multiperson conversations with people. Some require you to sign on to a chat server, where the program you use doesn't matter. Others only let you chat with people using the same program, who have allowed you to put them on their buddy list. The former lets you connect with more people; the latter gives you more security. A few, as noted, will let you do both.

AOL Instant Messenger

www.aol.com/aim/home.html

Free

Internet Presence

Shown in Figure 8-1, the most used Internet presence program is AOL's Instant Messenger (AIM) program (which is separate from the Instant Message facility on the AOL service). The Instant Messenger software gives Internet users the ability to send instant messages and create chat rooms with other AIM users, whether they use AOL or not. While easy to use, it doesn't have all the features of ICQ or Ding! below. The program is available as a Navigator or Eudora plug-in and will be part of the upcoming version of Lotus Notes.

AIM installs quickly and loads by default whenever you connect with the Internet. If you're not an AOL subscriber, you must register with the AOL Instant Messenger service at the above Web site and supply a name and password. Then you can create your own buddy list, which you can organize into various categories. The program has Buddies, Family, and Coworkers folders already in place.

Once online, Instant Messenger tells you who on your lists is online. And when you reach out and buzz someone, you can control what personal information appears and which type size, font, and background

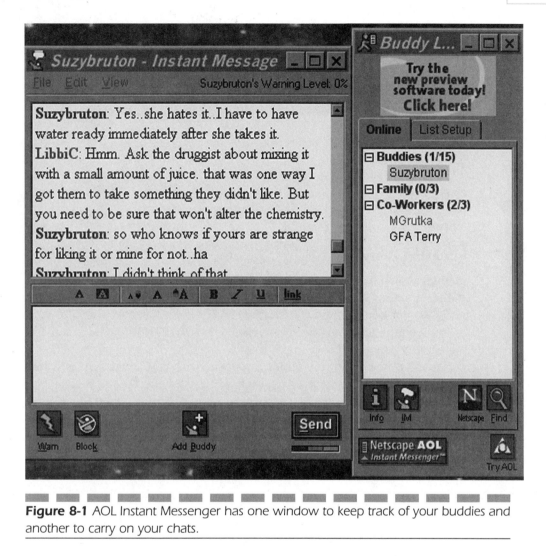

Figure 8-1 AOL Instant Messenger has one window to keep track of your buddies and another to carry on your chats.

color is used in your messages. Type or drag a URL from your browser's bookmark file or a Web page into an instant message, and the program converts it into a live link.

AIM has good privacy features. You can list which people can and can't send you messages, much like AOL's mail controls. If you step away from your PC, you can leave a custom message that's sent to anyone trying to reach you, such as "Gone for a moment. Be back soon."

In short, AIM works just like AOL's built-in Instant Message/Buddy Lists feature, with one notable exception: Now you can communicate with and track people who aren't members of AOL. Note, too, that all

Instant Messenger traffic goes through AOL's servers. Given AOL's history with online traffic jams, don't be surprised if you experience occasional delays and failures.

AOL Chat on the service itself is a whole other kettle of fish. This doesn't require a separate program; it's included in the AOL software.

Ding! 2.5

http://www.activerse.com/ding/dingintro.html

Free

Internet Presence

Ding!, shown in Figure 8-2, is a Java chat program for IBM-type PCs (no Mac version). Shown in Figure 8-2, Ding! installs easily and is versatile; it is free for noncommercial use. You can use it for one-to-one or multiple-person chats, and you can create rooms. It is not an IRC client, and you don't stay connected to a chat server to use it.

You can download, install, and register with the Ding! server in less than 10 minutes. When you register, you get a Ding ID and a password to protect your account so no one can pretend to be you. Ding! has a database of registered users, which you can search and add to your buddy list with a click or two. Go to www.activerse.com/ding/whoson.html to see who's connected. (If you register on Ding!'s private server, your online presence won't be published.) You can also just type in a Ding! address to connect with someone. For example, My Ding! address is whodp://ding.activerse.com/EPCWriter.

Ding! does everything AOL's Instant Messenger does and more. You can look at a list of the folks you want to talk to and check their status message or see who's checking you out. If you don't want certain people to check your connection status, add their names to your Denied Watchers list.

An unlimited number of people can join a chat via Ding!, and if the two people who started the chat leave, the others can carry merrily along. You can organize your buddy list any way you want and change your status from "available" to "busy" just by clicking a little door icon.

There's a key difference between this scheme and AOL's. The Ding! server is only used to establish your presence. Once you start chatting, you're connected PC-to-PC via the Internet, and the server is out of the loop. This setup means fewer traffic jams, less security risk (see sidebar), and more privacy.

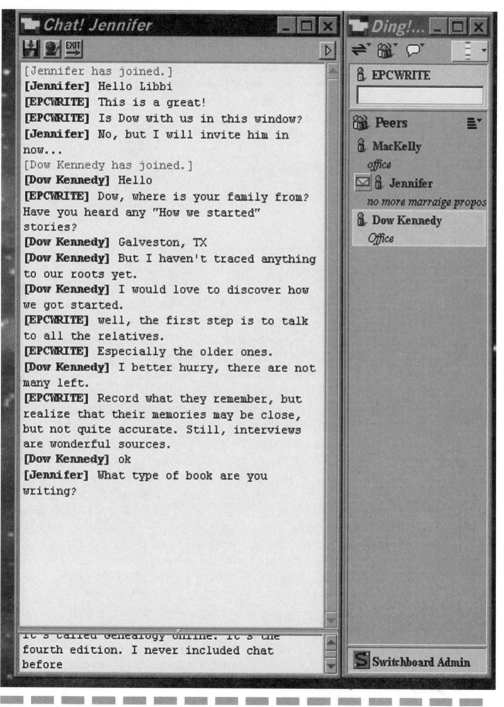

Chat! Jennifer

```
[Jennifer has joined.]
[Jennifer] Hello Libbi
[EPCWRITE] This is a great!
[EPCWRITE] Is Dow with us in this window?
[Jennifer] No, but I will invite him in
now...
[Dow Kennedy has joined.]
[Dow Kennedy] Hello
[EPCWRITE] Dow, where is your family from?
Have you heard any "How we started"
stories?
[Dow Kennedy] Galveston, TX
[Dow Kennedy] But I haven't traced anything
to our roots yet.
[Dow Kennedy] I would love to discover how
we got started.
[EPCWRITE] well, the first step is to talk
to all the relatives.
[EPCWRITE] Especially the older ones.
[Dow Kennedy] I better hurry, there are not
many left.
[EPCWRITE] Record what they remember, but
realize that their memories may be close,
but not quite accurate. Still, interviews
are wonderful sources.
[Dow Kennedy] ok
[Jennifer] What type of book are you
writing?
```

```
it's called Genealogy Online. It's the
fourth edition. I never included chat
before
```

Ding!...

EPCWRITE

Peers

MacKelly
office

Jennifer
no more marraige propos

Dow Kennedy
Office

Switchboard Admin

Figure 8-2 Ding! can be used to carry on chats with just two people or with several, as shown here.

When a message is sent to you (which can include a file, picture, or sound), a little envelope with the sender's name appears on screen, accompanied by a ding sound. When a chat request arrives, a little mouth icon appears. In either case, click the icon to get the messages. You can save transcripts of chats, and the program keeps a history of your communication with others so you can refer to earlier messages. To send a message or file, initiate a chat, or view your online history, simply right-click the name on your list and pick the proper menu option.

ICQ

www.icq.com

Free

Internet Presence

Shown in Figure 8-3, ICQ is a one-to-one or multiple-person chat in the Internet presence model. When you are online, it registers your presence with the secure ICQ server so that other ICQ users can "see" you. You can keep a buddy list and be informed when your buddies log on. You can send messages and files, even talk by voice or send live video. The program runs in the background, taking up a minimum amount of memory and Net resources, so you can continue to surf the Web or run your genealogy program while ICQ runs.

Launching an Internet phone or video call involves just a click of a button, instantly connecting you and a friend (or friends). This can be done with two or more users at a time. All these functions are organized in one easy-to-use interface that sits on the desktop.

ICQ does not connect to IRC servers; it only connects to ICQ servers. Like Ding! and AOL Instant Messenger, you and your chat partners must all be using the same software. ICQ also has a wide range of privacy options.

When you register with ICQ you can include hobbies such as genealogy and choose to be in the ICQ white pages for other ICQ members to find you. While trying the program out, I found about 10 other people who had put "genealogy" in their profile, whom I could have invited to chat with me.

You can also right-click to set ICQ to be "open" to a chat with anyone on a specific subject. Or you can go to the ICQ Guide and look for an open

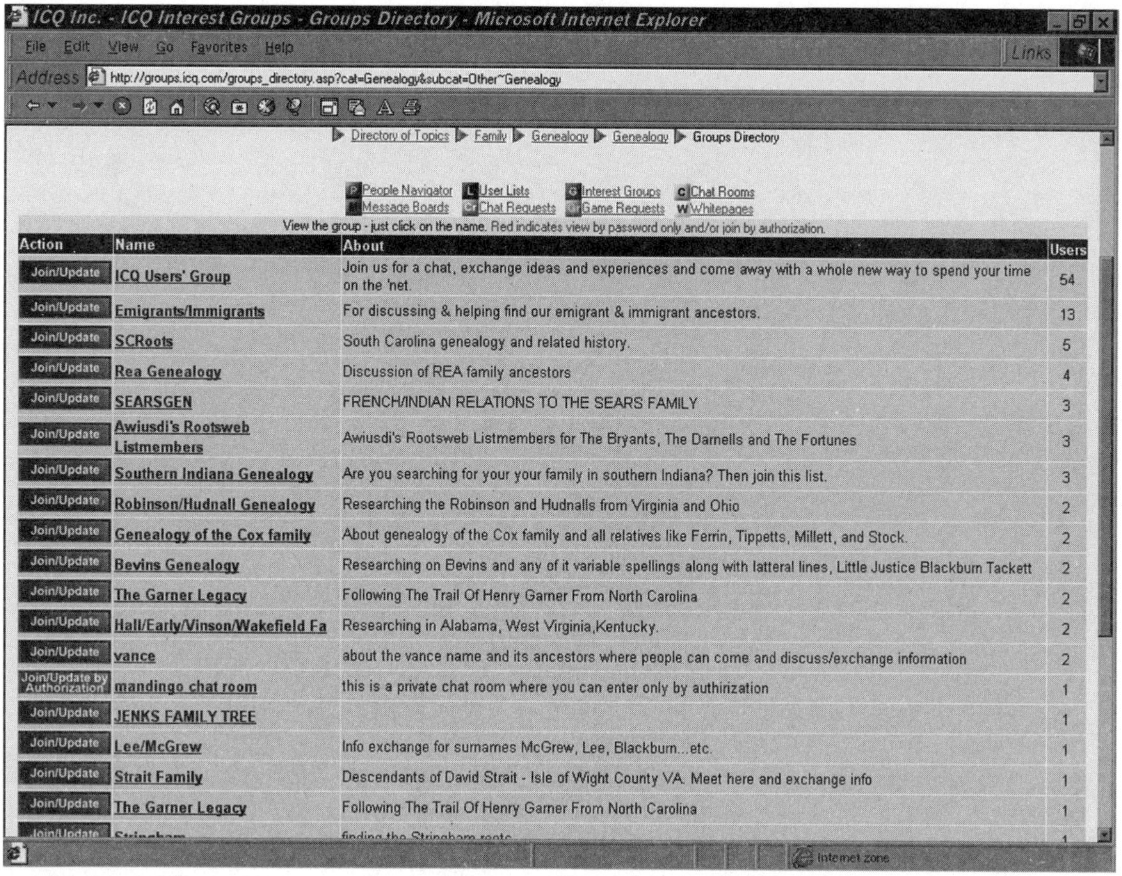

Figure 8-3 To join a genealogy group or chat, visit the ICQ Web page and look for "genealogy."

chat room by topic (look under Family-Genealogy). You can elect to keep a chat room open all the time, just join a user's group on genealogy for occasional chat invitations, or participate in a message forum, where the messages aren't in real time.

Probably the best way to use ICQ, though, is to set up specific times and rooms with your friends who also use ICQ. People have even told me about holding online family reunions this way!

Microsoft Chat

www.windowsupdate.com

Free

IRC

Microsoft Chat is a free IRC client that connects to the open, public chat channels. In Figure 8-4, I've connected to the RootsWeb chat room for site administrators, and we're discussing access to the RootsWeb pages.

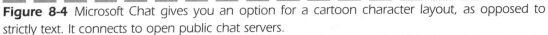

Figure 8-4 Microsoft Chat gives you an option for a cartoon character layout, as opposed to strictly text. It connects to open public chat servers.

In this view I've chosen the option to have the people shown as cartoon characters. You don't have to chat this way: You can have the traditional text interface too, but when you choose a different face for each person, you can more easily track the several conversations going on at once.

There are commands to go to a private chat with someone, to look up their logon information (name, Internet service provider, etc.), and to save the entire conversation to a file. Microsoft Chat has lots of powerful features and a good help file, and it's free. I recommend it as a first chat program until you get used to the way chat works.

Microsoft Chat does not, however, track the online presence of a list of buddies as AOL Instant Messenger, Ding!, and ICQ do.

mIRC

www.mirc.co.uk/get.html

$20

IRC

mIRC, shown in Figure 8-5, doesn't have a cartoon character mode as Microsoft Chat does, but otherwise it has all the same features and more. A very popular IRC program, mIRC is shareware, so you can try it for a while before you send the author $20 for it.

As in Microsoft Chat, you can set your own text and background colors, and send a sound file with a chat message. In addition, you can customize the toolbar for the commands you use most often and change your nickname on the channel on the fly. A really neat feature is the channel filter: If you log on to a public IRC that has 19,000 channels going, you can simply filter the channel names for "genealogy" or "family" and see if there's a chat you want to join. You can also hide or even totally block channels that you dislike.

How to Chat

IRC and Internet presence programs work slightly differently but have many of the same functions. Let me urge you again to read the help file of your program; most of the time the help file is a mini-manual that will tell you how to best use the client.

```
mIRC32 - [#rootsweb-admins]                                    _ □ X
  File  Tools  DCC  Commands  Window  Help                       _ ⊟ X
```

```
                                                              ▲ @Linda
<woosle> gee and he's not around                                @Marceline
<Marceline> It's been so long since I''ve done text manipulation, I can't   @woosle
   remember, and I sitll don't have my books from CA              EC
<Linda> they went to Anaheim I think
<woosle> ok
<Linda> where do you research, EC?
<woosle> I could tell you the code he told me if I could find it, but he left
   some out , you might know what he was talking about though
<woosle> yep Linda
<EC> I'm in Alabama, physcially. We're looking for Spencers in Ohio and
   Powells in SC.
<EC> (Didn't know which "where" you meant)
<Linda> woo.. probably a cousin of yours. <g>
<EC> Spencer???
<Linda> that's what I meant, EC :)
<woosle> hehehe or marce's
<woosle> no we have some ancestors in SC
<woosle> near the NC line
<EC> Powells?
<Linda> woo and Marce research the Carolinas
<woosle> Floyds
<EC> Haven't found one of those yet, but we might.
<woosle> marce have any Powells?
<Marceline> Not yet
<EC> we have a Reason Powell in SC early 1820s.
<EC> Very honest and very poor....can't find much about him in court or tax
   records.
<Marceline> My Lewis/NIchols/Baldwin people intermarried so much, I'll die of
   shock if I ever find another surname!
<Linda> I need to go lay out in the sun. <ducking> It's in the 80's here again
   today.
<EC> It's sunny here, but dadgum cold :-(
<Linda> talk to y'all later. Welcome to IRC, EC
```

Figure 8-5 mIRC has a traditional IRC text display and can connect to all IRC servers.

Many modern IRC chat programs type the commands you need for you; you just choose what you want to do from a menu. Still, you should learn a few of them anyway. See the sidebar in case you want to type commands directly. To enter commands, you just type them directly into the message window. Just type that into the same place you would a message. (Anything preceded by a / is a command in an IRC chat room.)

Some Common IRC commands

IRC servers may vary, but you will generally find these commands available on most IRC channels. (*Note*: These won't work in Internet presence programs; you'll have to use the menu commands to do the same things.)

/ACCEPT   Accepts an invitation to join a chat room.

/ACTION   Sends virtual hugs, etc. For example, you could type `/ACTION ECWriter hands DearMYTRLE the "Best Chatter Award!` It will appear in special type or colors to the rest of the group. **/THOUGHT** is a similar command.

/AWAY   Tells others that you are still connected to the server but had to step away from the computer for a moment. Some servers use **/BUSY**.

/EXIT   Logs off chat.

/GNAME   Changes the group name or inquires about the group.

/JOIN   Puts you in a chat room or leaves the current group and enters another.

/LIST   Shows a list of active channels. You'll usually want to use the menu version of this; some IRC servers have tens of thousands of channels going at once! Most IRC clients can let you filter the list.

/MODE   Can be used to set properties for chat rooms as well as for individuals. Can generally only be used by the moderator(s) of the room.

/NAME   Declares your nickname or handle. Also checks status.

/PAGE   Asks a member to join (use *membername*).

/PASS   Sets password for admittance into password-protected chat rooms.

/RNAME   Shows the "real name" of a member.

/SEND   Sends a one-line private message to any member logged into the chat room, like `/SEND MARY`. Again, this is a *private* message.

/SQUELCH   Ignores another member Other IRC servers may use **/KICK** or **/IGNORE**.

There are other commands for moderators (i.e., the person who started the group, and anyone that person designates with the `/MODE` command).

When you join an IRC chat room, the server will send you the Message of the Day, or MOTD. Some IRC programs show you this in a side window; some in the main window. If it flies by too fast for you to see it, send the command /MOTD.

Most IRC clients will log you into the default channel, usually called Lobby, while you search for a channel or room that you want. Once you find one, lurk for a moment, reading the messages. If this is a room you want to join, send a polite greeting (like "hello, everyone!). You may find some rooms so friendly that the moment you log on, someone sends you a greeting. Politely acknowledge it.

Besides /JOIN and /MOTD, the most important IRC command for you to know is /IGNORE (or whatever the equivalent is for that server). When someone is offending, bothering, or flaming you, typing /IGNORE <badguy's handle> will keep that person's messages from appearing on your screen.

If the chat is a moderated one, you often have to send a line with a question mark, wait for the moderator to recognize you, and then send your question or comment.

Internet presence programs such as AOL Instant Messenger allow you to warn people or block them entirely from paging or chatting with you.

Where to Chat

Okay, let's say you have Microsoft Chat, mIRC, or some other program that uses public, open chat servers. Where do you go to chat?

NOTE *If you want to keep on top of the genealogy IRC scene, subscribe to GEN-IRC-L (or GEN-IRC-D for digest mode). To do this, send an email message to GEN-IRC-L-request@rootsweb.com (or -D if you want digest mode) with just the single word* subscribe *in the body of the message.*

This mailing list covers mainly the IRC genealogy channels on NewNet, but other networks are also discussed. The main purposes of this list are to enable a genealogist to communicate and set times for live discussions on IRC with other genealogists, post problems or ask questions relating to genealogy and IRC, and announce new channels or top-

ics of channels in genealogy and IRC. (See Chapter 6 for a discussion of mailing lists.)

Several genealogy sites have scheduled and impromptu chats. RootsWeb (point your chat client to irc.rootsweb.com, port 6667, alternative 7000) is just about the best place for genealogy chats. The chat server is hosted in conjunction with the International Internet Genealogy Society (IIGS), at http://www.iigs.org/. If you point your IRC chat client to irc.IIGS.org, it will send you on to irc.rootsweb.com in a couple of seconds. There's usually an impromptu open chat going on among the people who manage genealogy Web sites.

Among the most wonderful resources on the whole Net, however, are the moderated RootsWeb/IIGS chats. The scheduled ones are listed at http://www.iigs.org/cgi/ircthemes/ircthemes. (See Figure 8-6.) The topics range from very general, such as the Dear MYRTLE help chat for beginners, to very specific, such as Estill County, Kentucky, genealogy. DearMYRTLE is online many nights for just casual chats, as well. Check out her page at http://members.aol.com/DearMYRTLE/ for scheduled topics.

Besides the wonderful experts and helpful people, the niftiest thing about this IRC server is the translation bot. This is a program on the server that allows you to log on to a chat channel and have the conversations translated to another language for you. DearMYTLE told me of a recent chat where people speaking German, Spanish, and Norwegian were all able to ask her questions (which were translated into English for her) and receive her answers (translated back to their respective languages).

Still in testing as I write this, the translation bot runs a parallel window for the translation so you can follow the conversation in the original window as well as in the translation. It works automatically; all you have to do is join the original chat, and then join the translation channel for your language of choice. I think this is one of the most exciting developments in online genealogy in this decade!

NOTE *Often IRC programs like Microsoft Chat come with a list of chat servers. Just let your IRC client connect to one and look for rooms with* genealogy *in them, trying all those listed under dalnet, undernet, and newnet; another popular server is irc.scscorp.net.*

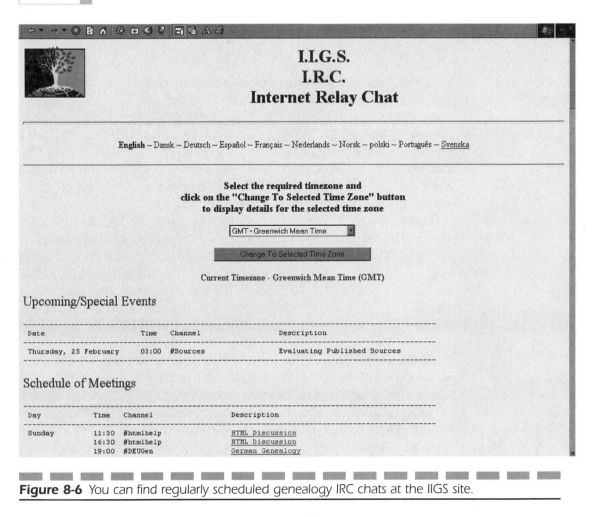

Figure 8-6 You can find regularly scheduled genealogy IRC chats at the IIGS site.

In particular, look for these channels on these servers:

Server	Channels
irc.dal.net	*#Canadian GEN #Fianna (Irish Genealogy), #genealogy-events, #genealogy-help, #Genealogy_IRC, #Gen_Family_Tree, #Gentrace, #lunie-links (Lunenburg Co., NS, Canada)*
irc.afternet.org	*#GenealogyForum, #Genealogy-n-UK, #Genealogy-Native*
irc.rootsweb.com	*#DearMRYTLE, #IIGS-UnivHelp, #htmlhelp*
irc.webmaster.com	*#TMG (the Master Genealogist software discussion)*

Chat without a Chat Program!

Some chat sites don't require you to have any sort of extra program besides your browser. Many surname-specific chat sites set up browser chats. The Georgia Tribe of the Eastern Cherokees has a members-only chat room (http://members.aol.com/Gacher/). The Gen Forum (http://chat.genforum.com/), Celtic Origins (http://www.genealogy.ie/celticorigins/index.html), Jewish Genealogy (http://www.jewishgen.org), and Genealogy Online (http://genealogy.emcee.com/) Web sites all have brower-based chat as well.

In addition, many portal sites have developed communities where people exchange messages. Many of these sites have browser-based chats, and the genealogy ones are often the most popular. The following table shows how to go about entering various chat sites.

Site	URL	Click On	You'll Need
Excite	http://www.excite.com/communities/	Lifestyle>Hobbies>Genealogy>Chat About Lifestyles. Page through the rooms to see if a room is discussing genealogy.	Java-enabled browser; go through the member sign-up procedure.
Yahoo!	http://chat.yahoo.com	Sign in. When chat starts, you'll see Tools in the bottom frame. Click `Change Room`, choose `Hobbies and Interests`, then choose `Genealogy`	Go through the member sign-up procedure. Has Java and HTML chat.

Site	URL	Click On	You'll Need
Infoseek/GO	http://www.go.com/Community/Good_Life/Hobbies/Genealogy	Click on `Chat`. In next screen, click on `Chat Now!`	Go through the member sign-up procedure. Has Java and HTML chat.
Snap	http://www.snap.com	Click on `Chat`, and sign in. In side frame, click on `Change Room`. If there are no genealogy rooms going, click on `Create Room` and start one.	Go through the member sign-up procedure. Get the Ichat plug-in (free) for Netscape, allow ActiveX control for Microsoft Internet Explorer

Chat Etiquette

Generally, you are going to find helpful, polite people in genealogy chat rooms in IRC. Of course, if you have one of the Internet presence programs, you will be chatting with people you have at least contacted before. Nevertheless, in both scenarios, there are certain etiquette standards to meet in chat.

All the etiquette tips covered in Chapter 3 apply to chat: Capital letters, except to mention the surnames you are researching, will be considered shouting. Flames are useless and annoying; show respect for everyone. IRC servers and the Internet presence programs track your connection; many require you to input an email address. Therefore, don't believe that you can hide behind the modem.

When you choose a nickname or "handle" to join a chat, or to use the Internet presence program, as a security measure, you may want to avoid using one that reveals your real name or gender, where you live, and so on. Of course, never use offensive handles or nicknames. Chat is very public, so be careful about what you reveal in chat rooms.

Stay on topic, or if you get sidetracked, create a separate room to follow your tangent. In addition, lurk before you leap into sending messages: Check out the room and see if the topic is what you are looking for.

Obscenity, cursing, and the like are forbidden on such systems as AOL; you can report people for using them. You can also use the `/IGNORE` command in IRC to block all messages from someone who is annoying you. If it's persistent, read the Message of the Day to find out the name of the system administrator and report that person's handle.

You can send your email address by private message, but don't post it in the IRC channel. If someone refuses to give you theirs, don't be insulted; it's probably just a security measure.

If you want a particular person's attention (for example, to ask or answer a question), precede your message with his or her handle or an abbreviation of it. Someone with the handle RootsNewbie might send: `ECWriter: where can I buy your book?` I could reply, `RN: it's a mass-market paperback, so it should be in most bookstores! :-)`

Smileys will be common, as will all sorts of acronyms; see the sidebar for some of the more common ones.

Many IRC servers, and most of the Internet presence programs, allow you to send sound files, pictures, even programs over the chat room. Be wary of this feature for two reasons: First, it obviously represents a secu-

Chat Shorthand

If you see:	*The chatter meant*:
Y	Why
U	You
C	See
BRB	Be right back.
\<g\>	Grin
\<bg\>	Big grin
\<vbg\>	Very big grin
BTW	By the way
CWYL	Chat with you later.
FWIW	For what it's worth
GIWIST	Gee, I wish I'd said that!
HHOK	Ha, ha! Only kidding!
HTH	Hope this helps.
HTHBE	Hope this has been enlightening.
IMHO	In my humble opinion
IMNSHO	In my not so humble opinion
IOW	In other words
IRL	In real life
ITRW	In the real world
LOL	Laughing out loud
OTP	On the phone
OTF	On the floor
OIC	Oh! I see!
OTOH	On the other hand
POV	Point of view
RL	Real life

ROTFL	Rolling on the floor laughing
RTFM	Read the fine manual [or help file]
TTFN	Ta ta for now
TTYL	Talk to you later
WRT	With regard to

rity risk to receive files from someone you don't know very well; second, it adds to the traffic on the server and will slow down everyone's interaction, not just the sender and receiver.

Chat programs have some limit to the number of characters that can be sent in one chunk. If you find your thoughts running longer, type the message in parts, each ending in an ellipsis (...) until you are done. Don't be surprised to find that as you do this, other messages are "walking on your lines," so to speak. Those paying attention will be able to better follow your train of thought if you have taken advantage of a feature of many of the programs: the ability to send your text in a specific color and/or typeface.

Don't ignore people who are asking polite questions (such as "how are you?"). If someone is being rude, you can use the command /IGNORE<person's nickname>.

NOTE *Several Web sites have tons of information about chat. Check the Cyndi's List page at http://www.CyndisList.com/chat.html for the latest.*

Chat can be a very useful Internet tool, especially moderated ones with specific subject. But it can also be addictive, and if you're not careful, you may find yourself doing more chatting than researching. Just remember I warned you!

3

Specific Online Resources

Though we looked at some interesting Web sites in Chapter 7, there are some places that deserve even closer inspection. These sources have actual data on them—sometimes secondary sources, sometimes transcriptions of primary sources, but a lot closer to cold hard facts than most of the pages in Chapter 7. However, some of these sites, unlike most in Chapter 7, may charge a fee for their services.

In Chapter 9, I'll show you online genealogy heaven: RootsWeb. The services here are free; but if you make a contribution, you get some special privileges. Either way, you'll find the RootsWeb site one of your favorites, I'm sure.

Chapter 10 will explore online library card catalogs. It's a way to go to the library from home; the search costs only your time and may save you a trip.

Chapter 11 shows you the most exciting online genealogy event of the decade: The Church of Jesus Christ of Latter-day Saints has launched Ancestral File, the result of research by Mormons around the world, on the Web. The International Genealogical Index (IGI), a CD-ROM set of temple work by members, is not on the Web, nor are other important Mormon CD-ROM sets, so this chapter will also explore how to use a Family History Center.

In Chapter 12, I'll show you the sites of some of the most important genealogy publishers, such as Everton and Ancestry. Many of these services charge a fee.

RootsWeb

The Hub of What's Happening in Online Genealogy

How would you like a place where you can search dozens of databases of genealogical material and hundreds of genealogical Web pages, as well as subscribe to thousands of mail lists? Or perhaps publish your own page, upload your own data, and create your own mail list? Welcome to online genealogy heaven: It's called RootsWeb, http://www.rootsweb.org. It started out as a site for a group of people who work at RAND who happened to like genealogy. They had a little mailing list hosted at the University of Minnesota and a little database on the RAND server. That was 11 years ago. Now it is the major volunteer genealogy site on the Web.

NOTE   *The main page of RootsWeb has this statement:*

"The RootsWeb project has two missions:

1. *To make large volumes of data available to the online genealogical community at minimal cost.*
2. *To provide support services to online genealogical activities such as USENET newsgroup moderation, mailing list maintenance, surname list generation, etc."*

A quick guided tour of the site will only scratch the surface of all the wonderful things at RootsWeb. Still, let's give it a try.

RSL—RootsWeb Surname List

One of the first areas you'll definitely want to look at is the RSL, or the RootsWeb Surname List. Open the page http://rsl.rootsweb.com/cgi-bin/rslsql.cgi. In the input boxes, type in the surname you want to search for. If you want, also input a location, using the abbreviations you'll find at the link below the location box. Use the radio buttons to choose whether your search is "surname" (exactly as you spelled it) or "Soundex" or "Metaphone" (sounds like it, even if spelled differently). In future searches, you can limit the search to new submissions within the last week, month, or two months.

In the blink of an eye, you'll get a chart that shows the surname, date range, and locations that match, and a link to the person who submitted the data, showing how to contact him or her (see Figure 9-1). The Migration field shows you the path the family took. SC>GA, for example, shows migration from South Carolina to Georgia.

You can use the information to email that person what you have and what you need.

Other Search Engines

The RSL will be very helpful in your research, but there are other databases at RootsWeb that you can do searches in too. You'll find the search engines for the RSL and the other databases at http://www.rootsweb.com/rootsweb/searches/ (see Figure 9-2).

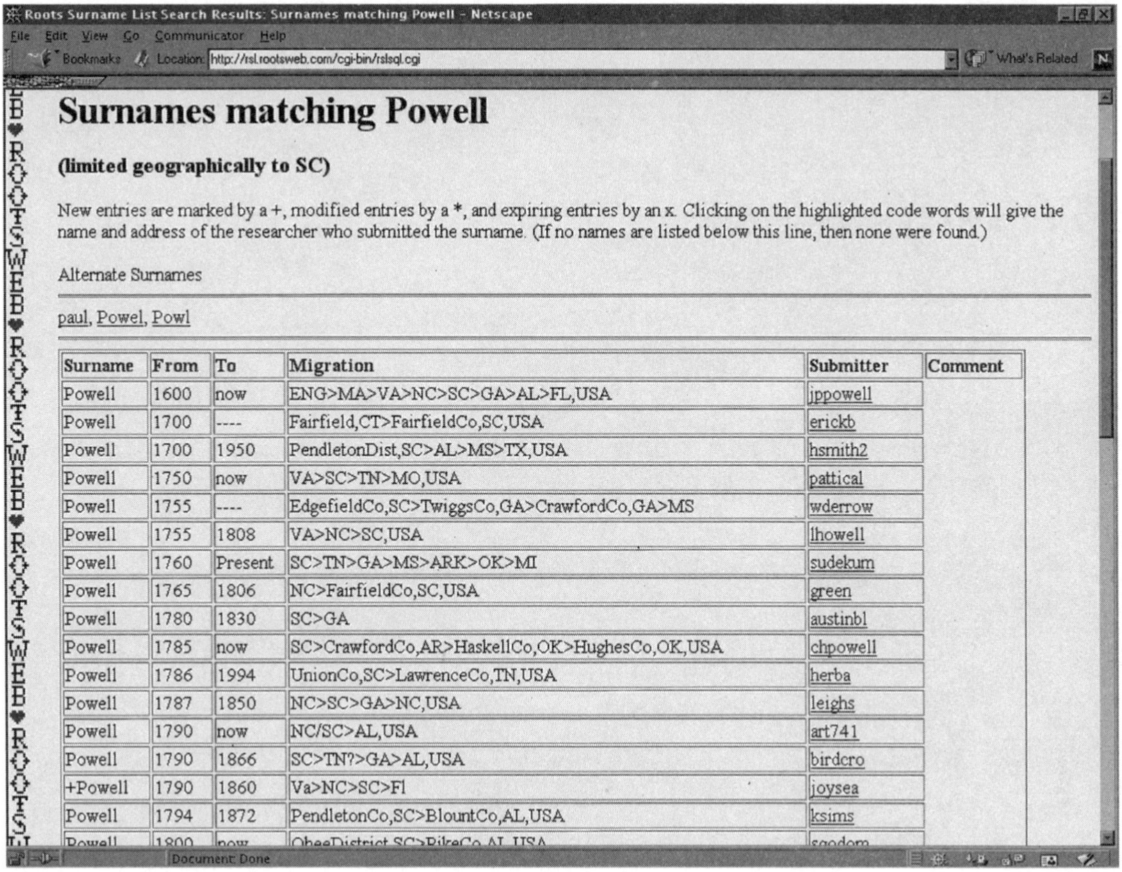

Roots Surname List Search Results: Surnames matching Powell - Netscape

http://rsl.rootsweb.com/cgi-bin/rslsql.cgi

Surnames matching Powell

(limited geographically to SC)

New entries are marked by a +, modified entries by a *, and expiring entries by an x. Clicking on the highlighted code words will give the name and address of the researcher who submitted the surname. (If no names are listed below this line, then none were found.)

Alternate Surnames

paul, Powel, Powl

Surname	From	To	Migration	Submitter	Comment
Powell	1600	now	ENG>MA>VA>NC>SC>GA>AL>FL,USA	jppowell	
Powell	1700	----	Fairfield,CT>FairfieldCo,SC,USA	erickb	
Powell	1700	1950	PendletonDist,SC>AL>MS>TX,USA	hsmith2	
Powell	1750	now	VA>SC>TN>MO,USA	pattical	
Powell	1755	----	EdgefieldCo,SC>TwiggsCo,GA>CrawfordCo,GA>MS	wderrow	
Powell	1755	1808	VA>NC>SC,USA	lhowell	
Powell	1760	Present	SC>TN>GA>MS>ARK>OK>MI	sudekum	
Powell	1765	1806	NC>FairfieldCo,SC,USA	green	
Powell	1780	1830	SC>GA	austinbl	
Powell	1785	now	SC>CrawfordCo,AR>HaskellCo,OK>HughesCo,OK,USA	chpowell	
Powell	1786	1994	UnionCo,SC>LawrenceCo,TN,USA	herba	
Powell	1787	1850	NC>SC>GA>NC,USA	leighs	
Powell	1790	now	NC/SC>AL,USA	art741	
Powell	1790	1866	SC>TN?>GA>AL,USA	birdcro	
+Powell	1790	1860	Va>NC>SC>Fl	joysea	
Powell	1794	1872	PendletonCo,SC>BlountCo,AL,USA	ksims	

Figure 9-1 The RootsWeb Surname List tells you who else among the RootsWeb users is looking for your surnames and how to reach them. You can submit your own entry too!

The top of the page has the table of contents, which will probably have been updated by the time you read this. As you can see, you can search the Roots Location List (like the surname list, but it concentrates on geography); databases of information from Arkansas, California, and other states; archives of Usenet newsgroups; and archives of mail lists hosted by RootsWeb. They all work pretty much the way the surname search does.

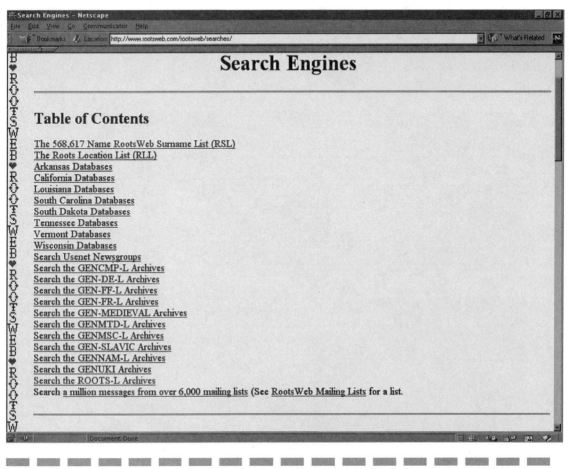

Figure 9-2 From this page you can reach dozens of searchable databases on RootsWeb.

Automatic Surname Notification Program

All this searching can be fun at first, but if you find you're forgetting to check the monthly update of RSL, then give the Automatic Surname Notification program a try. You can enter your surnames in this program, and the RootsWeb computer will generate a baseline report that shows you all the places within RootsWeb that the surname appears. After that, you'll receive email notices anytime a file or database is added that contains your surnames—or if an update or modified file has added your surnames.

This is one of the few areas that is restricted to Sponsors ($24 a year), Donors ($50 a year), and Patrons ($100 a year), who help support RootsWeb. Details on becoming a supporter are at the end of this chapter.

Once you have received the confirmation letter from RootsWeb thanking you for becoming a Sponsor (or higher), you can submit your surnames into the program from http://sponsors.rootsweb.com/cgi-bin/notify/notify.pl.

GenConnect

The GenConnect meeting places on RootsWeb are like forums on the commercial online services. They are message boards, somewhat like a mailing list, in that researchers share messages with each other on a specific surname or topic. However, a mailing list message is sent by email to all the subscribers of that list. GenConnect boards require more effort, because you post your message, and then you come back to the site to see if anyone answered it. You will also see "suites" of GenConnect boards. A surname may have a variety of boards, for queries, obituaries, wills, and so on. A query board for the name Spencer is shown in Figure 9-3.

Perhaps the easiest way to understand GenConnect boards is to visit their site at http://genconnect.rootsweb.com/. Someday you may want to administer a GenConnect board, or a suite of boards. If so, you'll find information on how to request a board or boards on the GenConnect pages.

Web Sites

RootsWeb hosts thousands of genealogy Web Sites. Some, like Cyndi's List at http://cyndislist.com/ or the USGenWeb Project's main site at http://www.usgenweb.com/, you have already read about in this book. RootsWeb also hosts the WorldGenWeb Project, at http://www.worldgenweb.org/, and most of the country sites. Most of the RootsWeb-hosted boards can be found on the index at http://www.rootsweb.com/~websites/

Chapter 9

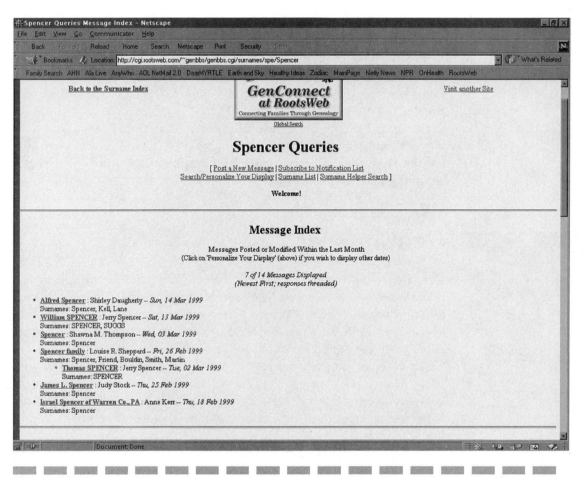

Figure 9-3 On a GenConnect board, you leave a message and come back later to see if someone has answered it.

It won't include all the Web sites at RootsWeb because listing is voluntary, and because there are always more Web sites coming online. Announcements of the newest ones are in the email newsletter RootsWeb Review (see below).

ROOTS-L and State Resource Pages

As discussed extensively in Chapter 6, one of the best resources on this site is ROOTS-L, at http://www.rootsweb.com/roots-l/. You will literally spend hours at a time on that portion of RootsWeb.

One of its main areas is the state resource pages, for those researching in the United States. The state pages (http://www.rootsweb.com/roots-l/usa.html) offer you a wealth of information. Just the top part of it is in Figure 9-4.

The HelpDesk

The HelpDesk maintains a page at http://helpdesk.rootsweb.com/, where you will find an FAQ (frequently asked questions) file about RootsWeb and its services. Check there first if you have a question or problem; if

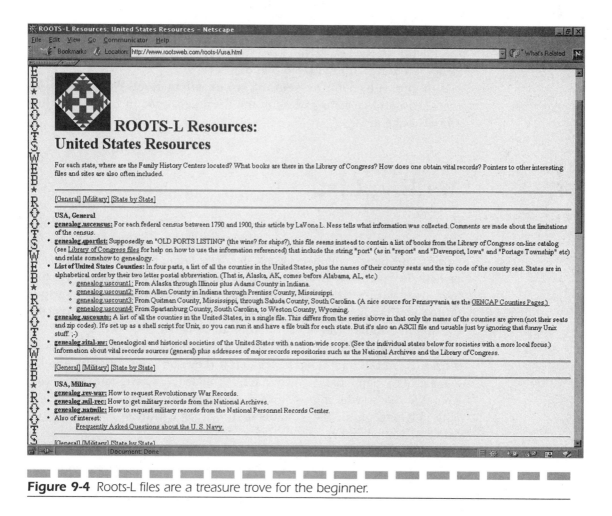

Figure 9-4 Roots-L files are a treasure trove for the beginner.

you can't find an answer there, you can follow the links from that site to the message board, where you can post a question for the HelpDesk team to answer.

RootsWeb Review

RootsWeb is always growing, and you can't depend on luck to find out about the latest and greatest. The RootsWeb Review is a free weekly newsletter sent to contributors and users via email. You'll find announcements of programs and services for RootsWeb users, new mailing lists, GenConnect boards, and Web sites, plus success stories of other telegenealogists.

If you are a new contributor, you will automatically begin to receive the RootsWeb Review. If you are interested in reading through previous issues, go to ftp://ftp.rootsweb.com/pub/review/.

You can subscribe by sending an email to RootsWeb-Review-L-request@rootsweb.com, with only the word *subscribe* in the subject line and message area.

Mailing Lists

Besides Roots-L and RootsWeb Review, RootsWeb hosts literally thousands of mailing lists. As mentioned in Chapter 6, you can find lists for surname or family names, regions, or topics being researched. The index at http://www.rootsweb.com/~maillist/ lists thousands of lists you may join, along with instructions explaining how to subscribe. It won't include all the mailing lists at RootsWeb, however, because it's a voluntary listing and not all listowners have chosen to be listed.

A good rule of thumb: Be choosy in joining lists. Take on just a few at a time. Read them for a while, sign off if they don't prove useful, and try some others. Some lists are very active, indeed, overwhelmingly so. One RootsWeb user who signed up for every possible mailing list for the United Kingdom had 9000 emails in his in-box within 24 hours! Be careful what you wish for...

And remember that some lists are archived, so you don't have to subscribe to see if that list is talking about subjects that interest you. Just search the archive for your keywords, and save those messages that are important.

Someday you may even want to start a mailing list of your own, which contributors can do. You can learn more about what is required of a listowner by following the link titled Information for Listowners and Potential Listowners at the main page for mailing lists.

How RootsWeb Is Different

So, let's finally talk about money. RootsWeb has an all-volunteer staff, but they have to come up with the money for hardware and software somehow. The somehow is at http://www.rootsweb.com/rootsweb/how-to-subscribe.html.

RootsWeb is committed to keeping genealogical data free on the Internet. You can access any (and every) file at RootsWeb right now. But if you can afford as little as $1 a month, you can help keep the quantity and quality of information and services available to everyone.

RootsWeb's support levels start at $12 (U.S.) a year, figured to be the average cost for keeping the files online for each of the users. At that rate, you could sponsor one mail list and one message board.

For $24, you get access to several RootsWeb databases, two mail lists, and two message boards, and you are a Sponsor. Sponsor Plus at $50 and Donor at $100 a year get more boards and lists, plus disk space to store databases of family history or Web pages.

While your financial support is very important, there are other ways you can play a role too. You can contribute your time—perhaps helping transcribe records so the entire genealogical world will benefit. If you would like more information on how you can help, write to the staff at webspinner@rootsweb.com. You can also contribute by being an active researcher and telling others about RootsWeb and the programs and services they offer.

RootsWeb is often describe as the "genealogical cooperative." But I just think of it as online genealogy heaven.

Online Library Card Catalogs

Despite all the wonderful things appearing online, many of your genealogical expeditions will still be in libraries. But you can use the Internet to search some libraries too.

One of the wonderful things about the online world is the plethora of libraries going to electronic card catalogs. This speeds up the search when you are physically present in the library, of course. With an online catalog and many terminals scattered throughout the building, you don't have to look up your subject, author, or title on one floor, then run to another to actually find the referenced material. If your local library hasn't computerized its card catalog yet, it probably will soon.

But, oh, the joys of looking in the card catalog before you actually visit the library. You know immediately whether that library owns the title. With a few more keystrokes, you can find out whether the title is on the shelf, on reserve, on loan to someone, or lost without a trace. If the title in question isn't at that library or branch, you can find out whether the book is available by interlibrary loan. Some libraries are part of an online system, like the Greater Manchester Integrated Library Cooperative System (Figure 10-1). These systems link groups of libraries, allowing you to search for titles across most or all of the libraries in the area. Some more advanced systems will even let you enter your library card number, in effect checking the book out to yourself, without leaving home.

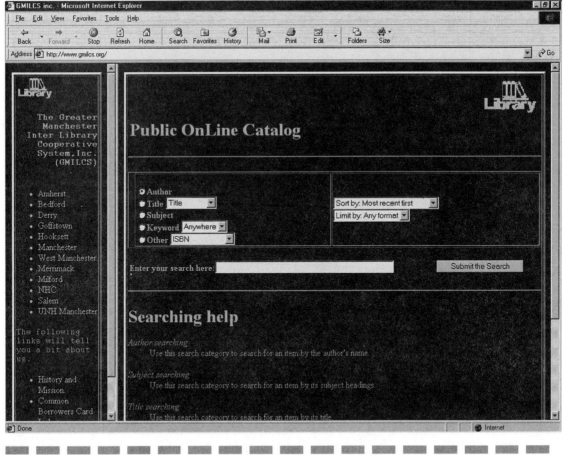

Figure 10-1 Sometimes a group of libraries shares a Web site, making it easy to search all of them at once.

There are two main ways to connect to online card catalogs. The newest and easiest way is through the World Wide Web. The card catalog appears to be like any of the Web-based databases you've encountered in this book.

Or the connection could be by Telnet. Here you use a separate program to send commands to and receive information from the database. More on this later in the chapter.

A third way to connect to an online card catalog is with a hybrid Web/Telnet connection. In this case, the library maintains a Web site with all the relevant information on how to use the card catalog, Then, when it is time to actually look at the card catalog database, your browser starts a Telnet program to actually work with the database.

Connecting to Card Catalogs by Web Browser

The easiest and most visually appealing way to connect to online card catalogs is via the World Wide Web. The mechanics of how this works is irrelevant. What's important is that a Web-based interface lets you use the card catalog without having to install and load a Telnet program.

A wonderful example is the University of Texas at Austin's UTNetCAT (http://dpweb1.dp.utexas.edu/lib/utnetcat/). You can use the forms that appear at this Web site to search by author, title, subject, or any combination (see Figure 10-2). The results of the search are links to the card catalog.

Another, slightly more complicated example is at the University of Alabama in Huntsville Web site. By going directly to the Complex Search page for the card catalog at (http://libsirsi.uah.edu/uhtbin/cgisirsi/33/60/30034), you can choose any of several ways to enter search terms (see Figure 10-3). You can find items that contain certain words or phrases in any field. Using Boolean options (AND, NOT, OR, etc.), you can specify that words, author names, title words, or subject terms must have a particular relationship to each other. If you want something written by a specific person, searching by author makes sense. If you know most of the words in the title, a title search can tell you if the library has the item and where it is located. If you don't know an author or title, you can search by subject.

You'll have better luck with your searches if you narrow them down as much as possible. Search on Author and Title, Subject, and Word or

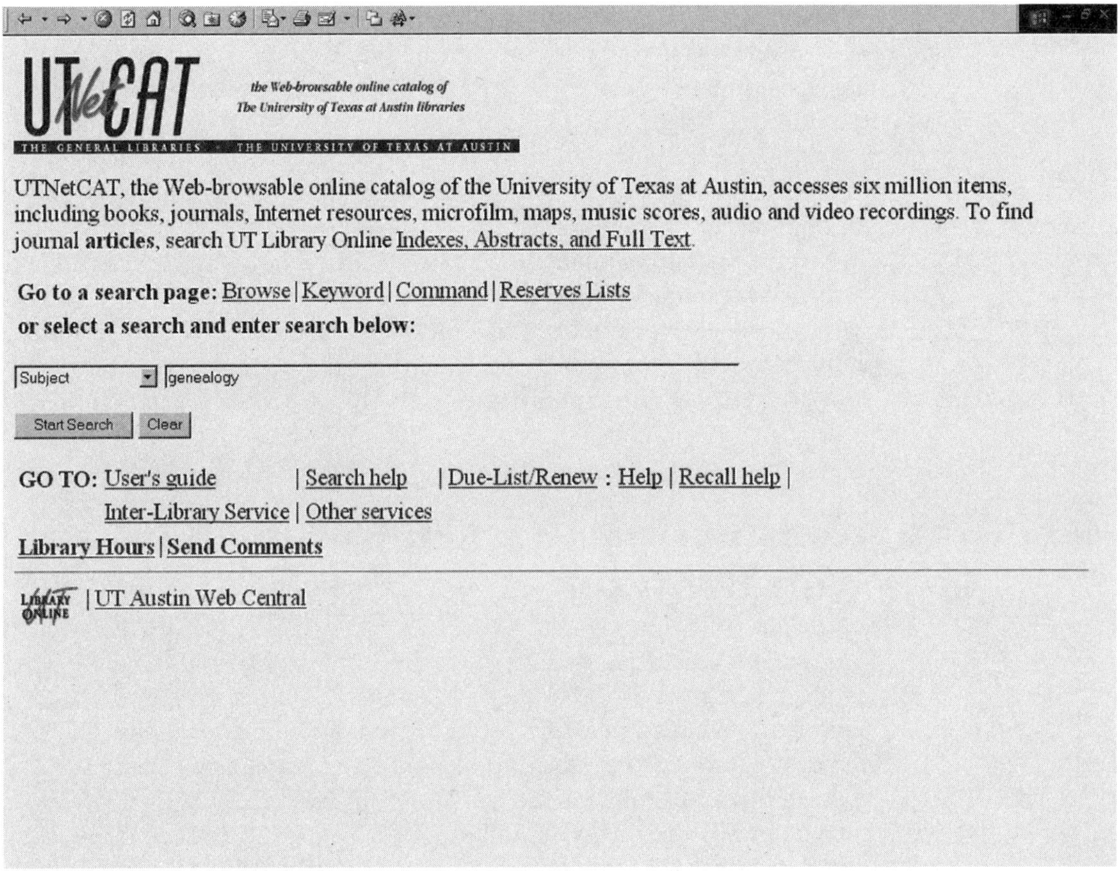

Figure 10-2 The University of Texas provides a wonderful example of a Web-based card catalog.

Phrase. Optionally, you can search recent issues of magazines with the periodical title option.

To show you how this works, I chose a search with *genealogy* in the general keyword field and *Alabama* in the subject field. Figure 10-4 shows the results of that search. The search turned up seven cards that matched my search criteria. Each matching card has a short synopsis that appears on the Results page. By clicking the View button next to a synopsis, you can get additional detail about the card. Do this, and you will see information like the publication date, author, and cross-links to other relevant cards in the catalog. You can print the results or have a copy of them emailed to you.

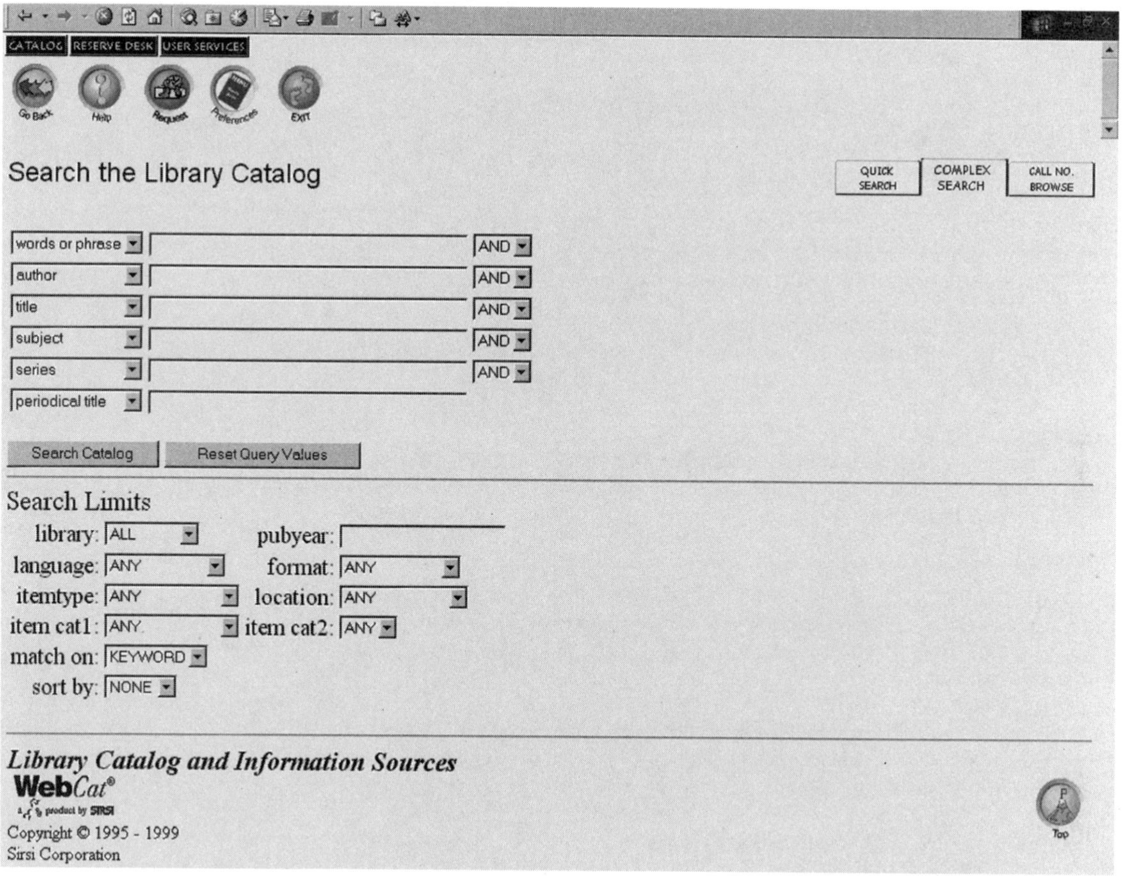

Figure 10-3 The University of Alabama's card catalog lets you construct complicated queries if you select Complex Search.

Another nice Web site to see is the card catalog for the University of Virginia (http://eagle.vsla.edu/catalog/). The wonderful thing about this system is the library's collection of Bible records. Go to the page shown in Figure 10-5 to test out this system yourself.

I ran a test with *genealogy* as the general keyword and *Powell* as the subject keyword. The results (see Figure 10-6) consist of links directly to the catalog's cards. This card catalog also allows you to use Boolean terms (AND, NOT, OR, etc.) to further refine your searches. This card catalog presentation is very easy to understand and read, a real pleasure to work with.

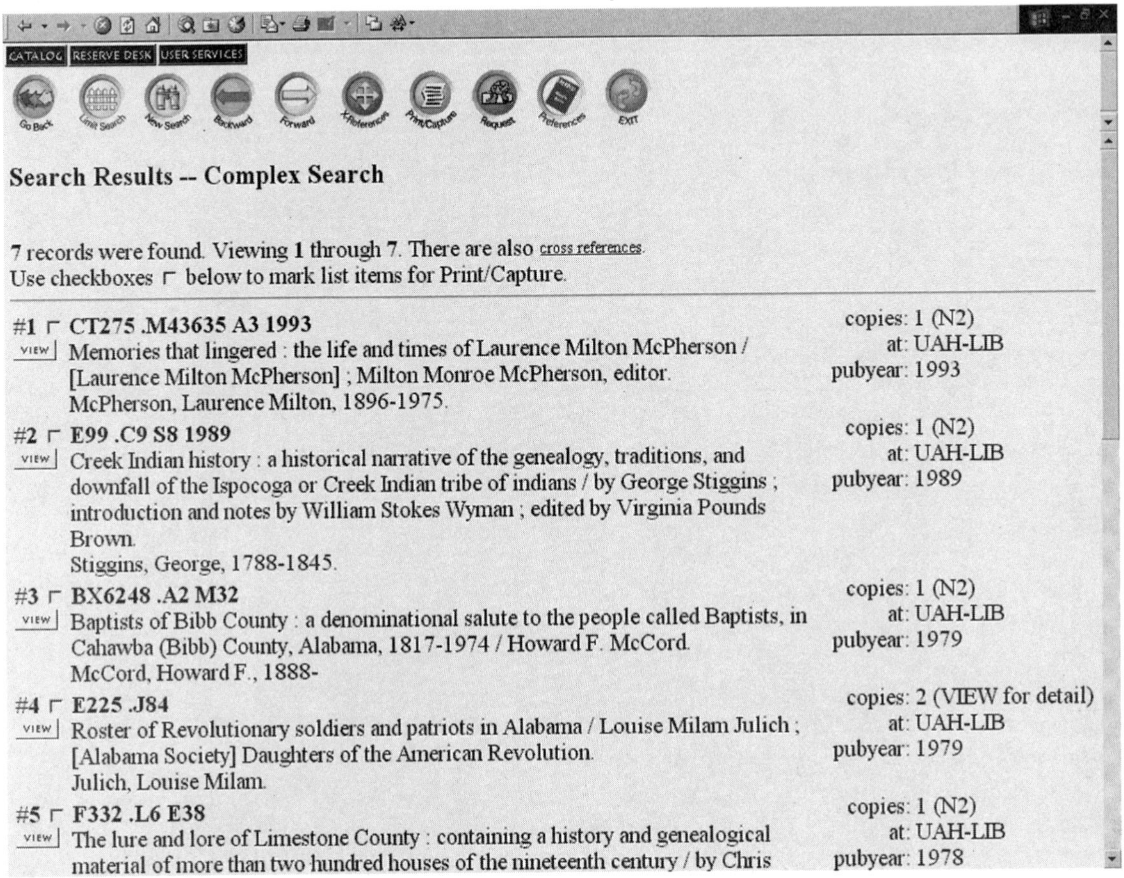
CATALOG
RESERVE DESK
USER SERVICES
Go Back
Limit Search
New Search
Backward
Forward
X-References
Print/Capture
Request
Preferences
EXIT
Search Results -- Complex Search
7 records were found. Viewing 1 through 7. There are also cross references.
Use checkboxes below to mark list items for Print/Capture.
#1 CT275 .M43635 A3 1993
VIEW
Memories that lingered : the life and times of Laurence Milton McPherson / [Laurence Milton McPherson] ; Milton Monroe McPherson, editor.
McPherson, Laurence Milton, 1896-1975.
copies: 1 (N2)
at: UAH-LIB
pubyear: 1993
#2 E99 .C9 S8 1989
VIEW
Creek Indian history : a historical narrative of the genealogy, traditions, and downfall of the Ispocoga or Creek Indian tribe of indians / by George Stiggins ; introduction and notes by William Stokes Wyman ; edited by Virginia Pounds Brown.
Stiggins, George, 1788-1845.
copies: 1 (N2)
at: UAH-LIB
pubyear: 1989
#3 BX6248 .A2 M32
VIEW
Baptists of Bibb County : a denominational salute to the people called Baptists, in Cahawba (Bibb) County, Alabama, 1817-1974 / Howard F. McCord.
McCord, Howard F., 1888-
copies: 1 (N2)
at: UAH-LIB
pubyear: 1979
#4 E225 .J84
VIEW
Roster of Revolutionary soldiers and patriots in Alabama / Louise Milam Julich ; [Alabama Society] Daughters of the American Revolution.
Julich, Louise Milam.
copies: 2 (VIEW for detail)
at: UAH-LIB
pubyear: 1979
#5 F332 .L6 E38
VIEW
The lure and lore of Limestone County : containing a history and genealogical material of more than two hundred houses of the nineteenth century / by Chris
copies: 1 (N2)
at: UAH-LIB
pubyear: 1978

Figure 10-4 The results of a search at this site include a short synopsis.

Connecting to Card Catalogs by Telnet

Some card catalogs, while online, haven't been put in Web format. You have to get at them another way. That way is with Telnet. *Telnet* is a system that lets you connect to another computer as if your PC were a terminal on that computer, regardless of where each computer actually is. Telnet is an older Internet service, but it is still in fairly widespread use for online card catalogs.

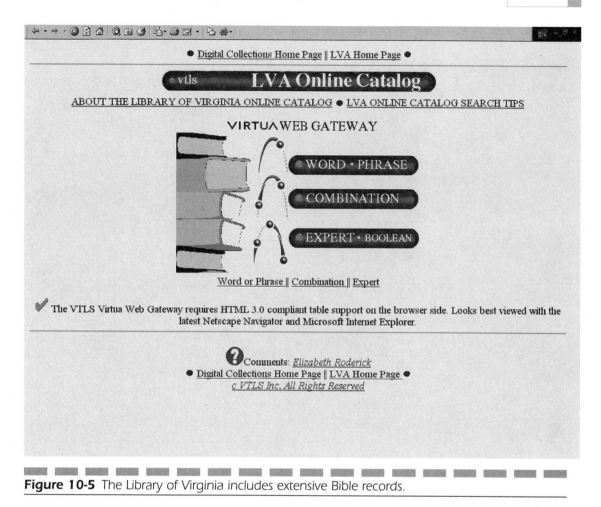

Figure 10-5 The Library of Virginia includes extensive Bible records.

Windows 95 comes with a basic Telnet program. Internet Explorer or Netscape Navigator will activate that Telnet program whenever it tries to connect to a Telnet address. Just enter the Telnet address on the browser's address line, and a Telnet window will pop up, ready to go.

A typical example of an online card catalog you can reach using Telnet and the Internet is the South Carolina State Library card catalog (telnet://leo.scsl.state.sc.us). Enter this address, and the Web browser will start the Telnet program with a connection to the library. Enter the password (LION) listed in the first window (just type it in where the cursor appears) and press Enter. You'll see the library's main menu (Figure 10-7).

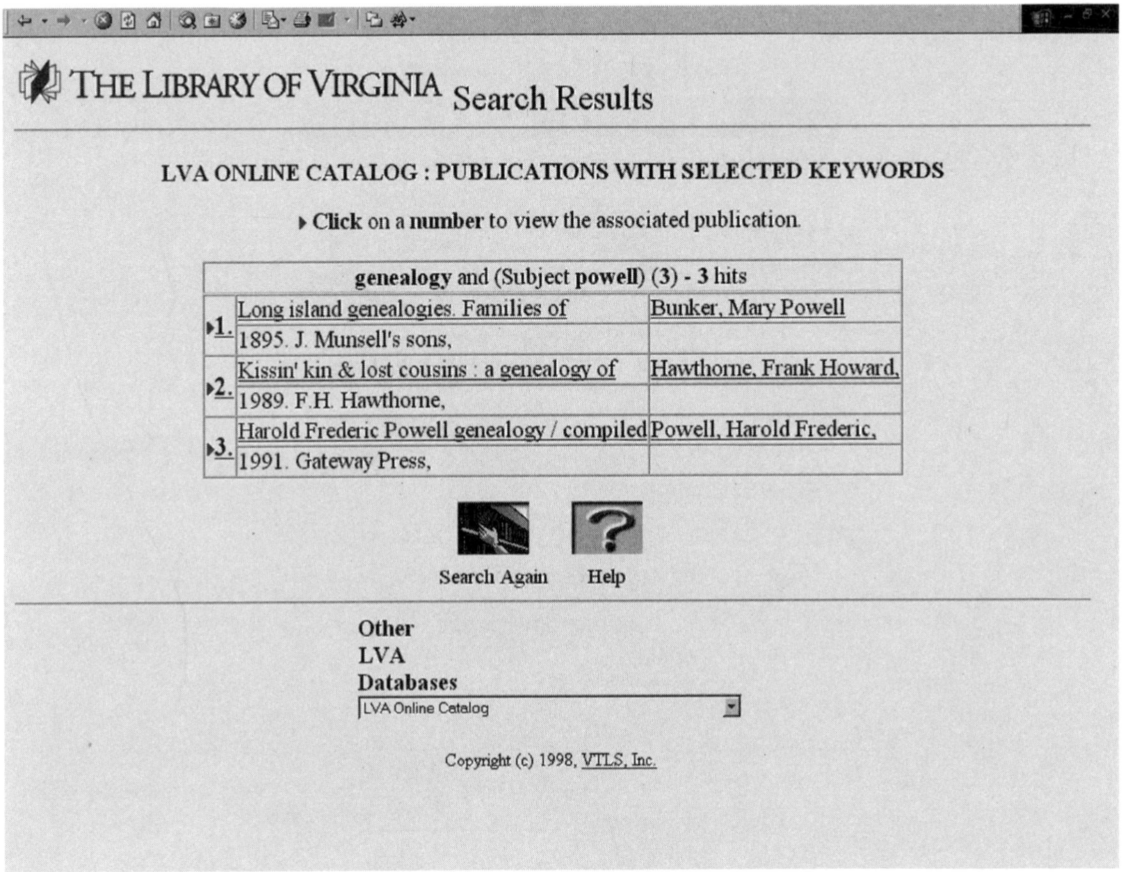

THE LIBRARY OF VIRGINIA Search Results

LVA ONLINE CATALOG : PUBLICATIONS WITH SELECTED KEYWORDS

▶ **Click** on a **number** to view the associated publication.

genealogy and (Subject powell) (3) - 3 hits	
▶1. Long island genealogies. Families of 1895. J. Munsell's sons,	Bunker, Mary Powell
▶2. Kissin' kin & lost cousins : a genealogy of 1989. F.H. Hawthorne,	Hawthorne, Frank Howard,
▶3. Harold Frederic Powell genealogy / compiled 1991. Gateway Press,	Powell, Harold Frederic,

Search Again   Help

**Other
LVA
Databases**

LVA Online Catalog

Copyright (c) 1998, VTLS, Inc.

Figure 10-6 The results of a search here are links to the actual cards in the catalog.

I started by typing a 1 to get into the LION card catalog and began my research with a subject search. I searched for the term *genealogy,* and the catalog returned a list of cards that had the term *genealogy* on them. I also got a number of references to other sections of the card catalog (see Figure 10-8).

If you've ever used the electronic card catalog at your local library, this should all look pretty familiar to you. By following the onscreen instructions, you can find out what titles are available and where they are located. In short, you can get all the information you would get if you were physically in the library looking at the card catalog.

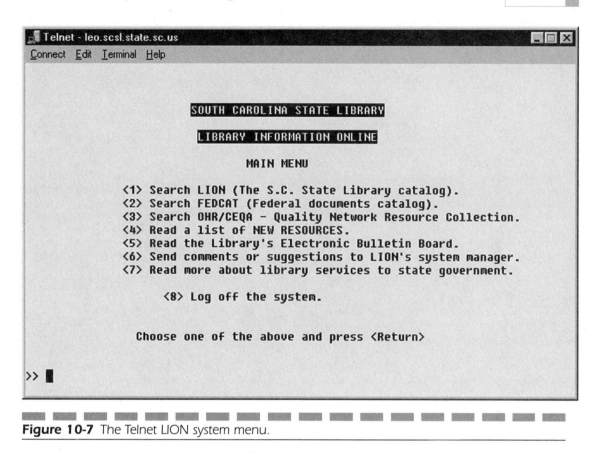

Figure 10-7 The Telnet LION system menu.

Where to Find More Online Card Catalogs

Once you've explored the online card catalogs shown in this chapter, it's likely you'll want to find some more. One place to look for both the Web and Telnet kinds is the Genealogy Resources page at the University of Minnesota. Browse down to the Libraries and Archives section (http://www.tc.umn.edu/~pmg/genealogy.html#libraries). As Figure 10-9 shows, this section of the page includes links to both types of online card catalog.

Learn to use these systems. Who knows what treasures you will find!

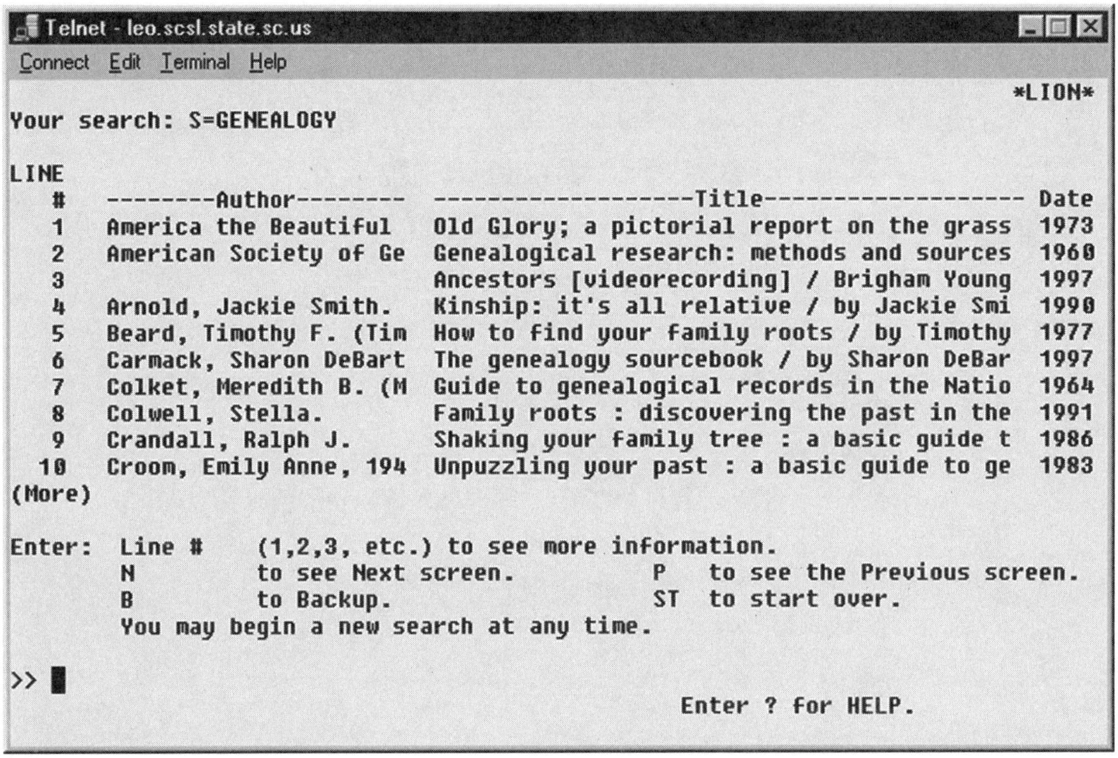

```
 Telnet - leo.scsl.state.sc.us                                    _ □ ×
 Connect  Edit  Terminal  Help
                                                              *LION*
Your search: S=GENEALOGY

LINE
  #      --------Author--------   -------------------Title------------------ Date
  1   America the Beautiful    Old Glory; a pictorial report on the grass  1973
  2   American Society of Ge   Genealogical research: methods and sources  1960
  3                            Ancestors [videorecording] / Brigham Young  1997
  4   Arnold, Jackie Smith.    Kinship: it's all relative / by Jackie Smi  1990
  5   Beard, Timothy F. (Tim   How to find your family roots / by Timothy  1977
  6   Carmack, Sharon DeBart   The genealogy sourcebook / by Sharon DeBar  1997
  7   Colket, Meredith B. (M   Guide to genealogical records in the Natio  1964
  8   Colwell, Stella.         Family roots : discovering the past in the  1991
  9   Crandall, Ralph J.       Shaking your family tree : a basic guide t  1986
 10   Croom, Emily Anne, 194   Unpuzzling your past : a basic guide to ge  1983
(More)

Enter:  Line #    (1,2,3, etc.) to see more information.
        N         to see Next screen.       P    to see the Previous screen.
        B         to Backup.                ST   to start over.
        You may begin a new search at any time.

>> ▮
                                            Enter ? for HELP.
```

Figure 10-8 The results of a search of the South Carolina State Library card catalog.

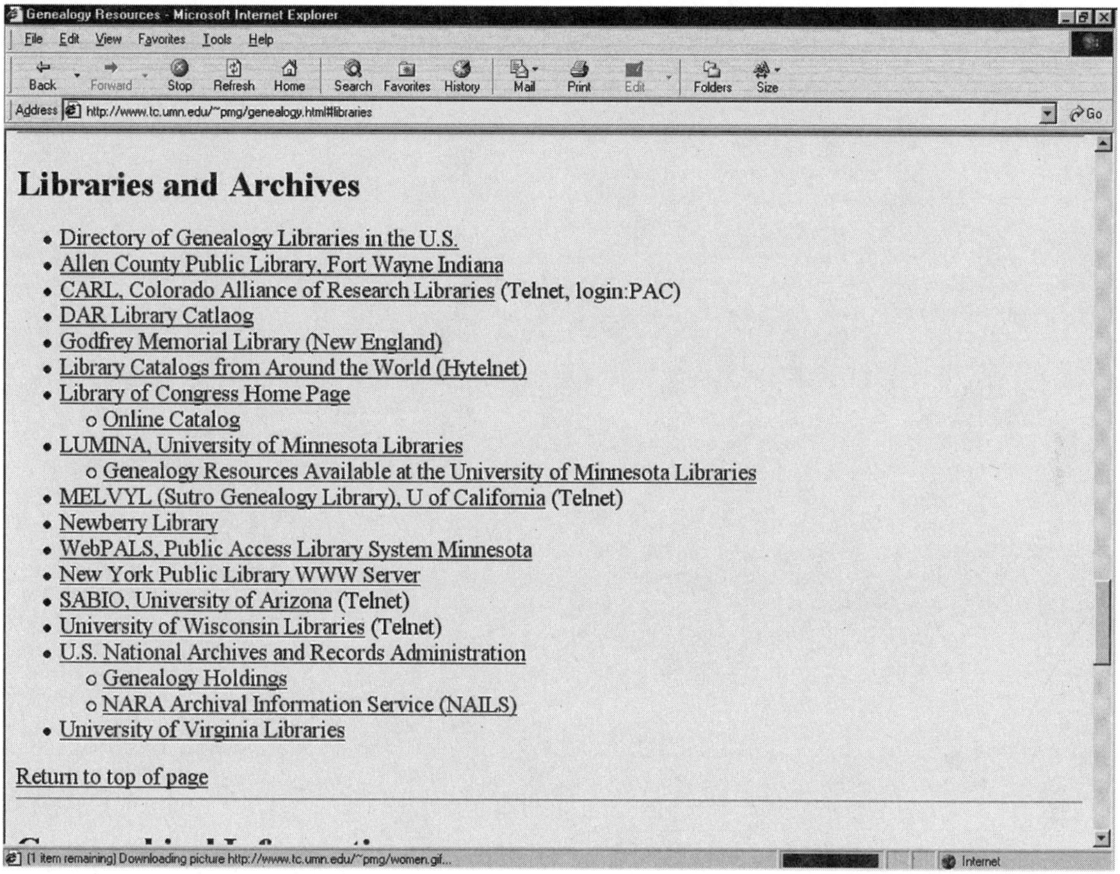

Genealogy Resources - Microsoft Internet Explorer

File   Edit   View   Favorites   Tools   Help

Back   Forward   Stop   Refresh   Home   Search   Favorites   History   Mail   Print   Edit   Folders   Size

Address http://www.tc.umn.edu/~pmg/genealogy.html#libraries

Libraries and Archives

- Directory of Genealogy Libraries in the U.S.
- Allen County Public Library, Fort Wayne Indiana
- CARL, Colorado Alliance of Research Libraries (Telnet, login:PAC)
- DAR Library Catlaog
- Godfrey Memorial Library (New England)
- Library Catalogs from Around the World (Hytelnet)
- Library of Congress Home Page
    o Online Catalog
- LUMINA, University of Minnesota Libraries
    o Genealogy Resources Available at the University of Minnesota Libraries
- MELVYL (Sutro Genealogy Library), U of California (Telnet)
- Newberry Library
- WebPALS, Public Access Library System Minnesota
- New York Public Library WWW Server
- SABIO, University of Arizona (Telnet)
- University of Wisconsin Libraries (Telnet)
- U.S. National Archives and Records Administration
    o Genealogy Holdings
    o NARA Archival Information Service (NAILS)
- University of Virginia Libraries

Return to top of page

[1 item remaining] Downloading picture http://www.tc.umn.edu/~pmg/women.gif...   Internet

Figure 10-9 Here's a collection of online card catalogs you can browse through the Web or Telnet.

11

The Church of Jesus Christ of Latter-day Saints

What we've all been hoping and praying for finally came true in 1999: The Church of Jesus Christ of Latter-day Saints (often abbreviated as LDS) put up a searchable Web site of their millions of names in May 1999. At this writing, access to the Web site is free, though some sort of fee in the future is possible.

NOTE *The information in this chapter is based on the May 1999 version of FamilySearch Internet. Refinements, additions, and deletions are sure to be introduced as users give the Webmasters feedback. Consider this a general guide to the site.*

FamilySearch Internet

FamilySearch Internet (www.familysearch.org) searches these records:

- Ancestral File (AF)
- International Genealogical Index (IGI)
- FamilySearch Internet Pedigree Resource File
- Family History Centers (FHCs)
- Family History Library Catalog
- Family History SourceGuide
- Non-LDS genealogical Web sites from a list compiled by LDS editors, some of which have original source records.

All except the last are from LDS records. FamilySearch Internet is designed to be a first step in searching for family history information. When you are searching LDS proprietary sources, the first screen doesn't give you the information itself. The search results simply tell you if the information you need is available, along with links to the Web site, Family History Library Catalog citation, International Genealogical Index or Ancestral File reference, or citation in one of the CD-ROMs the LDS has for sale.

However, that is more help than it sounds. Just finding a match in the Family History Library Catalog can save you hours of research. Some Family History Centers (FHCs), discussed below, are so busy that patrons are only allowed 1 hour per week at the computer! Searching the catalog before you venture out to these centers can make your trip much more productive. Finding a reference in the CD-ROMs might tell you if it's worth the price to order it. Finding a reference in the IGI or AF will tell you if someone else has already found the primary record or source you're looking for, and sometimes how to contact the person who found it. In short, this can save you a lot of time and travel. However, only rarely will you be able to use this resource to get to primary (original record) sources.

Most of the records in FamilySearch Internet are abstracts of original records. If you find a reference to a record you want in the LDS sources, you usually can get a complete copy of it from a Family History Center. Family History Centers are located throughout the world, and they have many of the records found in FamilySearch Internet. We'll explore more about FHCs later in the chapter.

Another big advantage to this site is that it has more international data than most online sources. While the greatest part of the data is from English-speaking countries, you'll find some information from every continent. Asian sources are the scarcest; North American and European the most abundant.

A Run-Through

Many days the site was so popular that I found it hard to get through to the server. The record so far is 11 million hits in one day, according to some newspaper reports. Even after I got on, I found it hard to maintain contact with the server. Don't give up, just keep pressing Enter once you have www.familysearch.org entered in the address box (see Chapter 2).

The opening page of FamilySearch is shown in Figure 11-1. To the left is a navigation menu of the types of information that can be searched. By clicking on one of those links, you can narrow your search to just one of those sources. However, by using the form on the opening page, you can search them all for mention of a particular name.

In Ancestor Search, by using a pedigree chart form on the main screen, you can input just a last name, or first and last names, or even spouse and parents if you know them. Of course, the more information you put in, the fewer matches you will get. The less specific you are, the more matches you will get.

I searched on our family's most elusive ancestor, Abraham Spencer. After 20 years of searching, Mother and I still cannot find his parents. We know he was born in 1792 and was in Ohio with his wife and children by 1832. So, I put those dates as limits in the search. I also put in his spouse. The results are shown in Figure 11-2.

There were five hits, some in LDS records and some on the Web. The LDS hit was in the IGI (see Figure 11-3) and contains the information my mother submitted years ago in hopes someone would see it and supply the missing information.

There were no matches in the other databases (Ancestral File, Family History Library Catalog, FamilySearch Internet Pedigrees). I checked

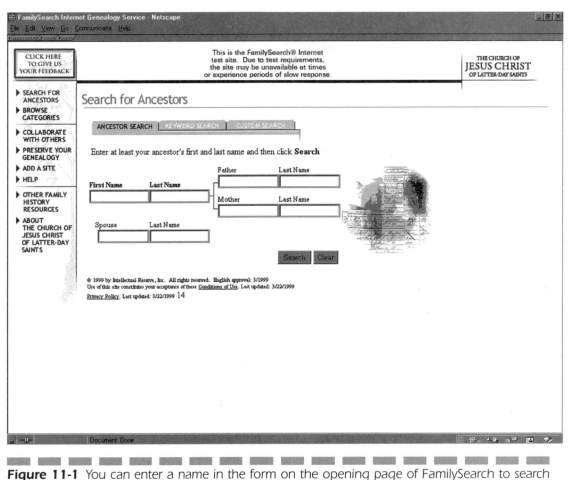

Figure 11-1 You can enter a name in the form on the opening page of FamilySearch to search all available databases.

out the Web sites, but none had both Spencer *and* Crippen on them, just one or the other and none of them mine.

Clicking the Keyword tab on this page allows you to search by keyword, such as *wills* or *birth records*. Clicking the Custom Search tab allows you to search specific parts of the site: Ancestral File, International Genealogical Index, Family History Library Catalog, a list of Family History Centers, SourceGuide (a list of good sources of information), and Web sites.

Your search may be more productive than mine, though.

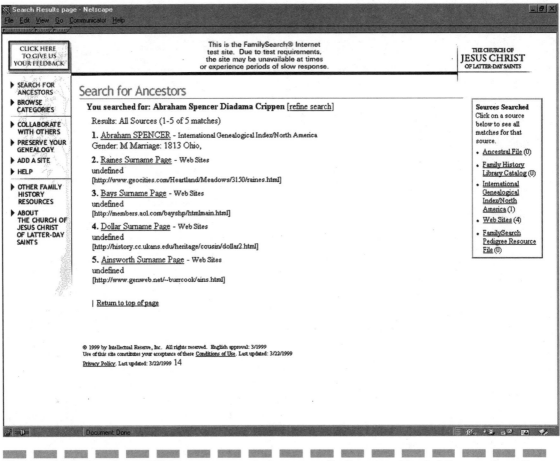

Figure 11-2 As of yet, IGI has not recorded anyone finding Abraham's father and mother. However, some Web sites mentioned at least one of the names I put in.

Alternative Methods

Searching from the main page is not your only option. By choosing `Browse Categories` from the main page, you can look at each category of sources (see Figure 11-4). Browsing the categories gives you a chance to peruse several different kinds of records, some of which are at FHCs, and some of which are only on the Internet.

Looking under Vital Records gave me the screen in Figure 11-5. The page presented 45 different links to sites that have at least something to do with vital records information. Sometimes all you'll find at the site is the correct address to write for vital records for specific places. Other

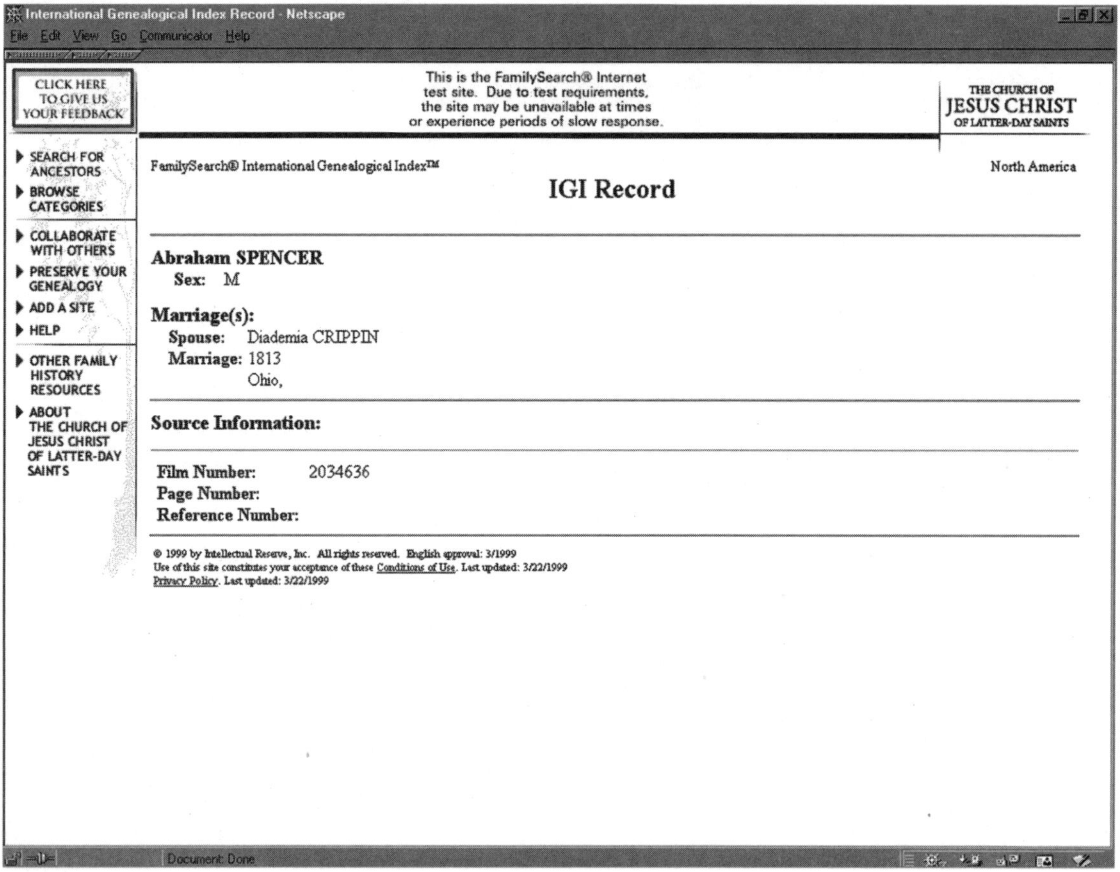

Figure 11-3 The IGI record that has Abraham and Diademia in it.

times you'll find a database of transcribed records. The list changes each day as the editors of FamilySearch Internet add more sites.

Other Cool Stuff

Just as with any Web site worth its salt, FamilySearch Internet has interactive elements. You find this under Collaborate with Others. Before you can enter this area, you need to register as a user. Enter your name and street address, along with your email address, and choose a username and password. (Keep in mind that Microsoft Internet Explorer 5.0 will store and remember passwords for you.) When I registered as a

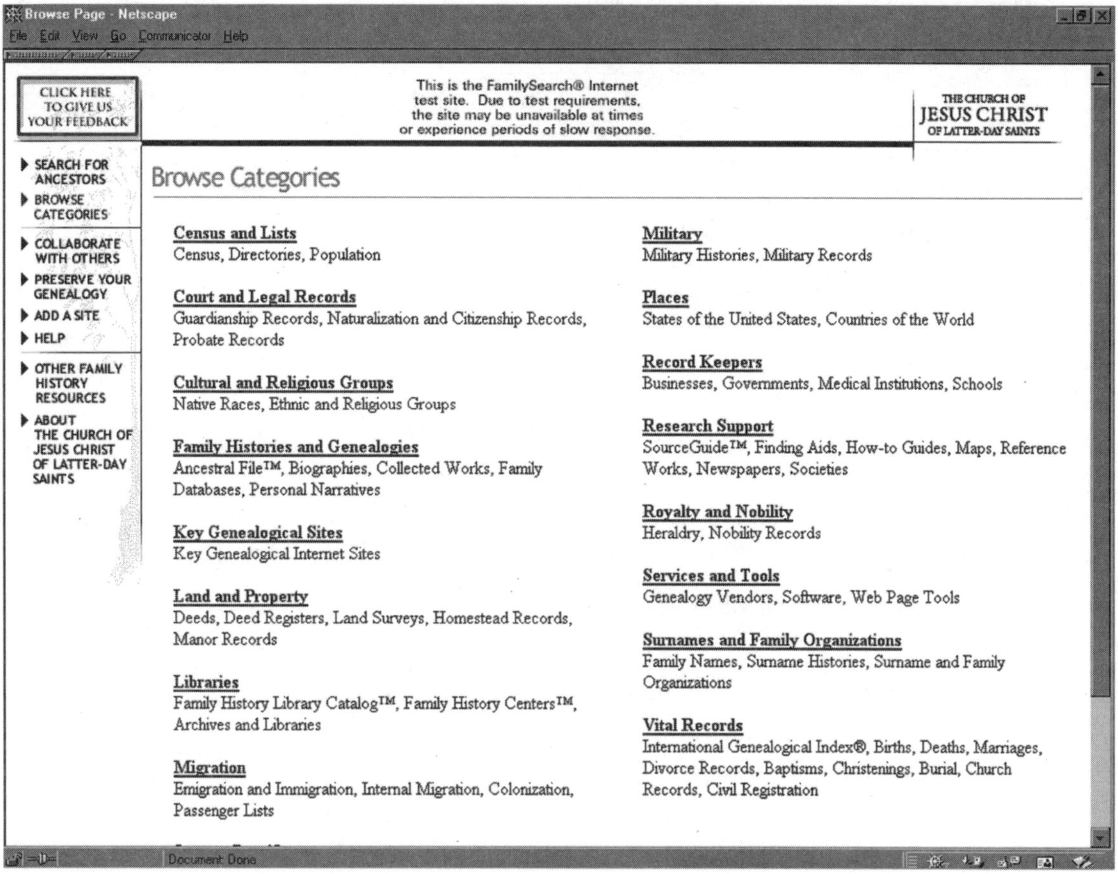

Figure 11-4 By choosing `Browse`, you can look at specific kinds of records, such as vital records.

user under Collaborate with Others, I was able to look at the complete list of mailing lists, which you can search or browse alphabetically. (See Figure 11-6.)

On this list of mailing lists, I came across one for Spencer and one for Powell. One click on `Join` and I was a member of the lists. The lists were started on the FamilySearch site on April 02, 1999. Clicking on `Powell`, my mail program opened up: the link is a mail to: link. So I sent in a query to the list. I started receiving messages from these lists within a day. When the site was so new, it was not surprising that each list often had only one message per day. As of this writing, both lists are getting 10 to 20 messages a day.

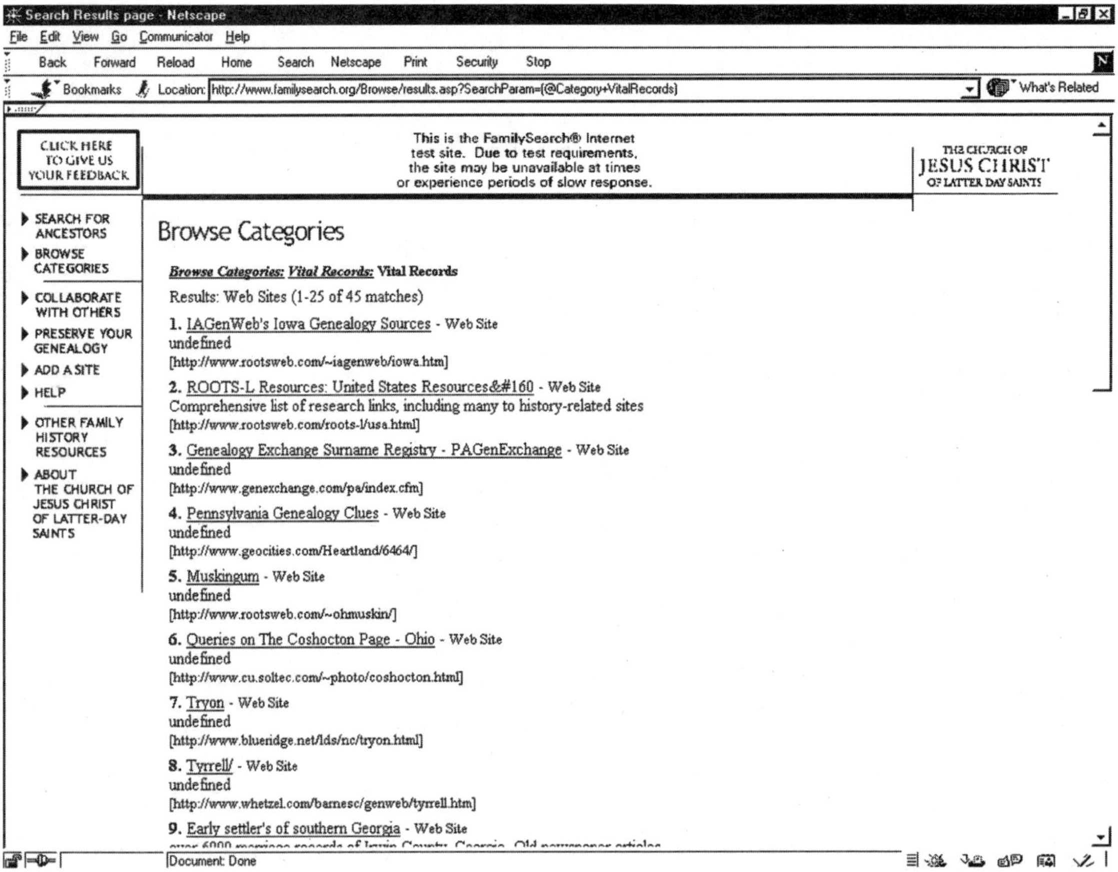

Figure 11-5 The Vital Records category includes links to Web sites both broad and specific.

Another interactive area allows you to share your research with others on FamilySearch Internet. By clicking on Preserve Your Genealogy, you get instructions on how to upload a GEDCOM for the LDS church to store in its granite vaults in Utah. (See Appendix C for Information on GEDCOMs.)

NOTE *Be sure of the accuracy before submitting your data. It would be a shame to preserve for all time some mistakes and miscalculations. Also be aware that when you submit, you must verify that you have the right to submit the information and allow it to be used. You also accept*

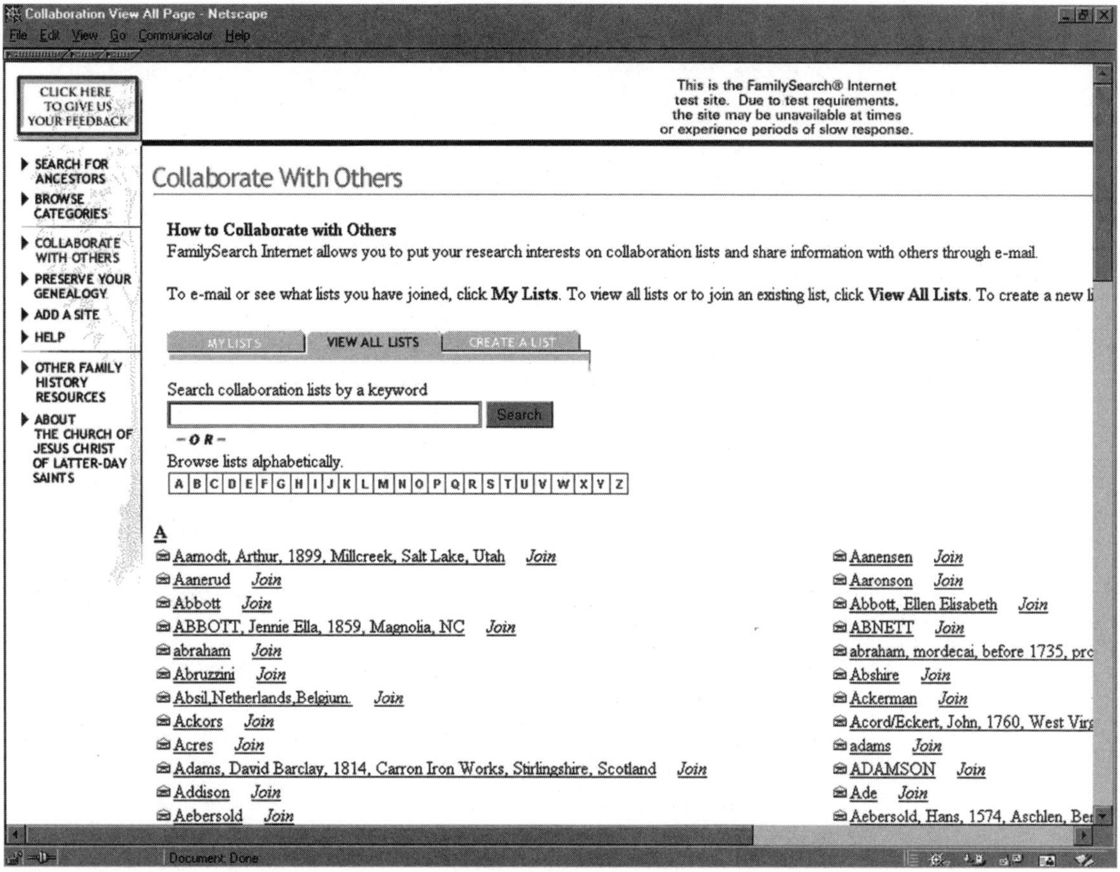

Figure 11-6 The Collaborate page under FamilySearch has several mailing lists, like those on Roots-L.

legal responsibility for any permitted use made of the information by LDS or anyone using the site.

GEDCOMs submitted to FamilySearch Internet will be preserved at the Granite Mountain Records Vault near Salt Lake City, Utah. They also will become part of the FamilySearch Internet databases. The information will become publicly available on compact disc or at FamilySearch Internet site. Although your genealogy may later be added to the Ancestral File, if you want to be sure it is, you should follow the normal process for contributing information to it.

NOTE Carefully read the conditions before you upload. For example, you must get permission from all living persons named in your GED-COM to send their information to FamilySearch Internet. By uploading, you give the LDS permission to publish your name and address as the contributor of the information you submitted. Uploading your GEDCOM gives the LDS permission to use, copy, modify, and distribute any of the information included in your submission without compensation and permission in order to create new databases.

Even though you give LDS certain rights to your information, uploading it to FamilySearch Internet does not limit your right to publish, sell, or give the information you submit to others.

To upload your GEDCOM, have your genealogy program create the file. Go to Preserve Your Genealogy and fill out the form. Microsoft Internet Explorer 4.0 or better and Netscape Navigator 4.0 or better can upload the file when you click on the Submit button.

In Add A Site (Figure 11-7), you can register your genealogy site with FamilySearch Internet. The editors of the site will review it and decide if it will be included in the database of Web pages to be searched from the opening page of the site.

Other Resources lists CD-ROMs that you can buy from the LDS store. Some of these CD-ROMs are included in the search from the first page of the site. However, only the indexes to the CD-ROMs are searched. If you get a hit from, say, the vital records index of the British Isles, then that will tell you whether it's worth buying for you. Other family history products (CD-ROM only) include the 1851 British Census SourceGuide 1.0; Personal Ancestral File Companion 2.0; Personal Ancestral File 3.0; British Isles Vital Records Index; North American Vital Records Index; and Australian Vital Records Index

How to Use Information from LDS

The LDS has scores of computerized resources. They willingly share much of the data as a public service through their Family History Centers. Their microfilms, computer programs, and other sources are slowly becoming available to libraries, archives, societies, and the general public. Modern genealogical research owes a great deal to the Mormons, and it seems natural to include their publicly available resources, whether available online or not.

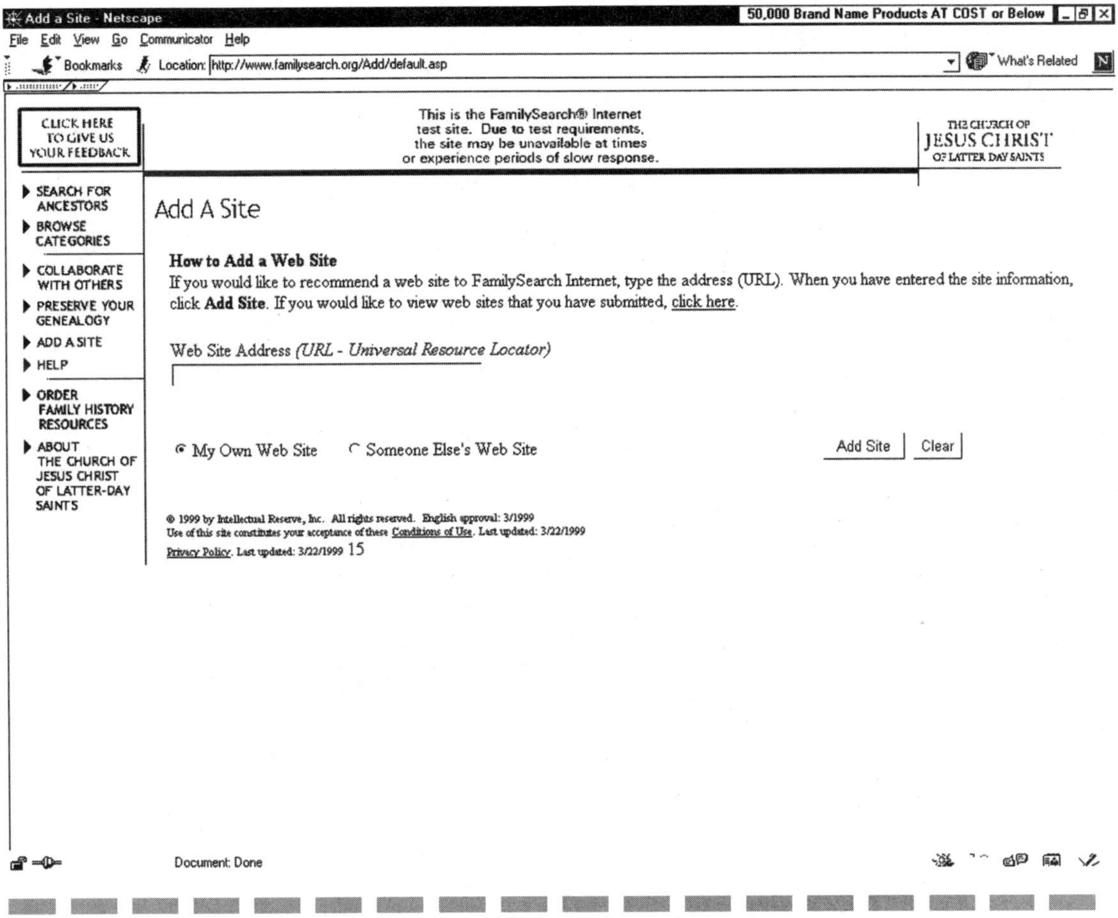

Figure 11-7 You can add your genealogy Web site for consideration.

. Information is collected from temple work that goes into the IGI from both submissions and extractions, and other submissions that may or may not have temple work go to the Ancestral File. If you have not submitted your ancestors to one of these files, and they have not been extracted as part of some other activity, they will not be in there. Also remember if they are in there, you should check out the original documents to make certain they are your ancestors and that the submissions are correct. Remember that these files, like the books and CDs you can purchase, are only as good as the work of the submitter or author. All of these are wonderful, helpful guides to finding your ancestors, but you still have to do the work to determine if they are yours, as well as if they are correct. And much is in error in all published work, whether in paper or on CD-ROM or on the Web.

Some Background

Without trying to explain the theology involved, I'll simply say that Mormons consider it a religious duty to research their family history. A detailed explanation can be found at the LDS home site, http://www.lds.org/ (Figure 11-8).

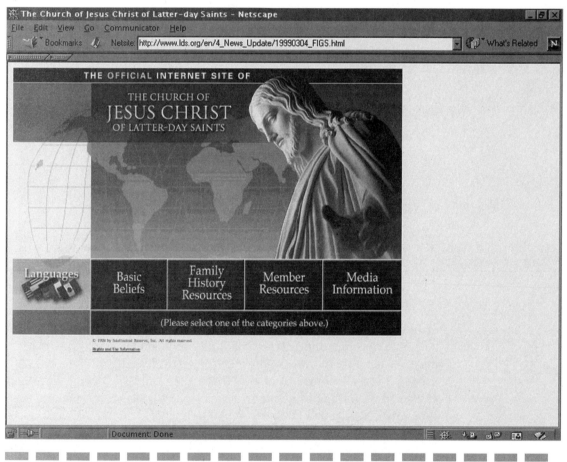

Figure 11-8 Figure 11-8. The LDS home site has tips on family history searches, explanations about the church, news, and more.

The results are archived at the church's headquarters in Salt Lake City and are distributed in microfilm, microfiche, and CD-ROM to their many Family History Centers throughout the world. The data is in several forms, but the most important to the online genealogist are the Ancestral File and the International Genealogical Index. Both of these were updated in early 1999: New data were inserted in the databases, but new compression techniques kept the set to seven CD-ROMs.

One of the LDS church's objectives is to build their copyrighted databases, known as the Ancestral File and the International Genealogical Index, and continually improve their accuracy and the software used to search them. The IGI is a record of the temple work; the AF offers pedigrees that the IGI doesn't.

NOTE *According to LDS, the IGI contains "several million names of deceased persons from throughout the world." However, this refers to "entries," not distinct individuals. Different people descended from the same family duplicate many entries. Furthermore, many individuals are listed with both a birth and a marriage entry.*

The IGI contains two basic kinds of entries: (1) submissions by individual LDS members of data on their ancestors (which may or may not be accurate) and (2) submissions from the extraction program. This is a systematic and well-controlled volunteer program of the church. Members all over the world extract birth or christening dates, as well as marriage dates and locations, from microfilms of original parish and civil records.

The source of the data from information provided for each entry is on the CD-ROM version of the IGI. But always remember, the IGI is only an index. You should go to the source document to verify the information.

The IGI and the AF are really unrelated, as data entered in one file don't necessarily show up in the other file. Each has a value of its own, and both files are worth searching. The advantage of the AF is that you can get pedigrees from it; the advantage of the IGI is that there's more detailed information.

Most non-LDS genealogists see the IGI as the more valuable of the two. While errors turn up in both, the IGI is closer to the original records (data is normally entered into the IGI first), and it has excellent bits and pieces of information, especially its references as to where the information came from. Many non-LDS genealogists will always go to the IGI first, but the Ancestral File with the new 5.5 GEDCOM format allows you to find out what documentation supports the entry. Considering you can get the submitter's name and address, as well as pedigree or descendancy charts, Ancestral File is a very valuable resource too.

While errors do exist, the percentage seems low; plenty of genealogy books printed in the past 100 years have more errors than these databases. The fact that the data are computerized and compiled by a religious organization is irrelevant.

Treat the AF and IGI the same way as you treat a printed book about a surname—with great caution. Use it as an excellent source of clues, but always cross-check it with primary records. While the computer increases the amount of data you can scan and makes things much easier, it doesn't necessarily improve accuracy. Human beings are still the source of the data.

The LDS apparently wants to make the AF and IGI available to more people. Originally, you had to visit the Family History Library in Salt Lake City, Utah, to use these databases. Today, that library has these CD-ROMs on a LAN that's connected to the Joseph Smith Memorial Building next door and about 200 access terminals scattered about the buildings. But there's still no remote access.

About 15 years ago, the church set up local Family History Centers around the world. In 1988 they started selling the databases on microfiche. In 1991 the church released them on CD-ROM to their local centers, and later to societies and libraries. The New England Historic Genealogical Society has a copy at their library in Boston, as does the California State Sutro Library in San Francisco. More are certain to follow suit. In 1994 the LDS began testing in-home use of the CD-ROMs, but as of yet they are still not available to individuals. Discussion continues about future online access.

The pattern here is more and more access via more and more means. However, the Mormons are very cautious, and they take very small steps, one at a time. The church has not worked out all the legalities of online access and is very concerned about presenting a useful, viable program and database for its members and the rest of the world. Their main concern is in not turning out a bad product.

A Visit to an FHC

Terry Morgan, Genealogy Forum staff member on America Online (terryann2@aol.com), is also a volunteer at the two Family History Centers in Huntsville, Alabama. The setups there are very typical, she says, and she gave me a personal tour of the one closest to our homes.

"The best way to find one near you is to look in the White Pages of the phone book for the nearest LDS church," Morgan says. "Call them and find out where the nearest FHC is, and the hours. Honestly, since the hours vary so much from place to place, the best time to call is Sunday morning around 10; everyone's at church then!" If you call any other time, she says, give the staffers lots of rings to answer the phones, which might be on the other side of the church from the FHC. Or, she says, you could write to the LDS main library at the address listed in the last section and ask for the latest list of FHCs. You also can find a list of FHCs at the LDS web site at http://www.lds.org/Family_History/Where_is.html and on the Family Search site by clicking Browse Categories from the home page, then Libraries, then Family History Centers.

All Family History Centers are branches of the main LDS Family History Library in Salt Lake City. The typical FHC is a couple of rooms at the local Mormon church, with anywhere from 1 to 10 computers, a similar number of microfilm and microfiche readers, and a collection of books, including atlases, manuals, and how-to genealogy books.

The FHC I visited had two IBM compatibles that shared a printer in a room with a small library of about 25 reference books. A room away, there were two film readers and two fiche readers. Users are asked to sign in and out, and a cork bulletin board holds the latest genealogical technique brochures from the Salt Lake City Family History Library.

In some FHCs, Terry told me, the computers are networked so that patrons can use the CD-ROMs in a shared environment. In the future, perhaps before the year 2000, FHC might have a direct satellite hookup to the main FHL and the latest version of the CD-ROMs there, cutting distribution time of the member data. However, this is still in the development stage. Meanwhile, FamilySearch Internet and IGI are available at most FHCs, and usually only one person at a time can use them.

"Some centers offer training on the programs, some insist they train you before you start using the computers, and some just help if you ask," she says. "We offer help if you ask. We've not had much trouble installing ours here. The only tricks were it has to have expanded memory, and you can have some TSRs [terminate-and-stay resident programs, which sometimes cause conflicts] running, but few enough to have low memory and expanded memory as well." The programs as of this writing won't run under Windows, but Morgan said that could be in the future.

In the typical FHC setup, you must reserve a computer and you get a certain block of time to use it. Printouts to paper of what you find are usually a nickel a page. Some centers allow you to bring your own disk to record the information, but others insist you buy certified virus-free disks from the FHC at a nominal fee.

The Future

As I write this, the FamilySearch Internet site is being refined and polished. By the time you read this, it should be a wonderful additional tool to use in conjunction with Family History Centers. In addition, more and more information is being gathered, extracted, and submitted, so you can expect a steady flow of CD-ROMs in the future. And, finally, look for more access to Mormon library catalogs.

12

Commercial Web Sites

A lot of the information on the Internet is free, except for your connect time. However, some places charge for their databases of information. This has led to some controversy on the mailing lists and Usenet groups over whether information is being sucked up for commercial purposes, leaving researchers with no choice but to shell out money for what should be public record. This debate is ongoing; check out the archives of Roots-L to follow the discussion (see Chapter 6).

This has led to some satire, as in Buy an Ancestor (http://wavecom.net/~fulker/special.html), a site that claims to give you bogus information to enter into your database so you can declare yourself to be descended from anyone you like. I personally think this site was an early April Fool's joke, but others took it seriously. Nevertheless, it serves as a reminder that there are scam artists on the Web, just as there are in the real world. Before you send off any money for a book or document, unless it's to a state or federal government office, a library, or a reputable publisher, check out the list of Myths, Hoaxes, and Scams at Cyndi's List (http://www.CyndisList.com/myths.htm).

Having said that, let me point you to some commercial online services that offer genealogical services. These are from some of the most respected names in genealogy and may have resources you need. You can decide for yourself if their offerings are worth the money.

Ancestry (www.ancestry.com)

Ancestry, a 15-year-old company, publishes books, magazines, and other materials. The online service is less than three years old, but it has grown rapidly. Their online services include:

■ One of the world's largest online genealogy libraries, searchable from the Web. The library includes such records as land, birth, marriage, death, census, and immigration records; the Periodical Source Index (PERSI); Daughters of the American Revolution Lineage Books; the 1790 Census Collection and the Early American Marriages Collection; and hundreds more.

■ Name databases, which are updated frequently, so future searches may turn up what today's did not.

■ And, of course, it's available 24 hours a day, 7 days a week, just as your Internet connection is. You can also get email support on using the site from their customer service department. Mail in your question and get an answer within a couple of days.

The cost is about 30¢ a day: $60 for a year or $20 a quarter.

Even if you don't sign up for a subscription, you can find lots of useful information in the free areas on Ancestry. Every workday, Ancestry adds a new database, such as Andersonville Prisoners of War or New York City Wills.

Without a doubt, the most popular part of the site is their searchable database of the Social Security Death Index (SSDI). If you are looking for someone who died after the 1930s, this is a good place to start. Be aware, however, that errors do sneak in. My recent search failed to turn up my father, who died in 1992; he was in earlier versions of the database.

Another popular free area is the Ancestry World Tree database. Visitors to the site are welcomed to submit what data they have for this database, the largest collection of its kind on the Internet. It's all volunteer, and Ancestry has pledged to keep the searches free. Be aware, however, that Ancestry doesn't check the data submitted, and it all must be considered secondary material at best. Nevertheless, it can give you some good clues.

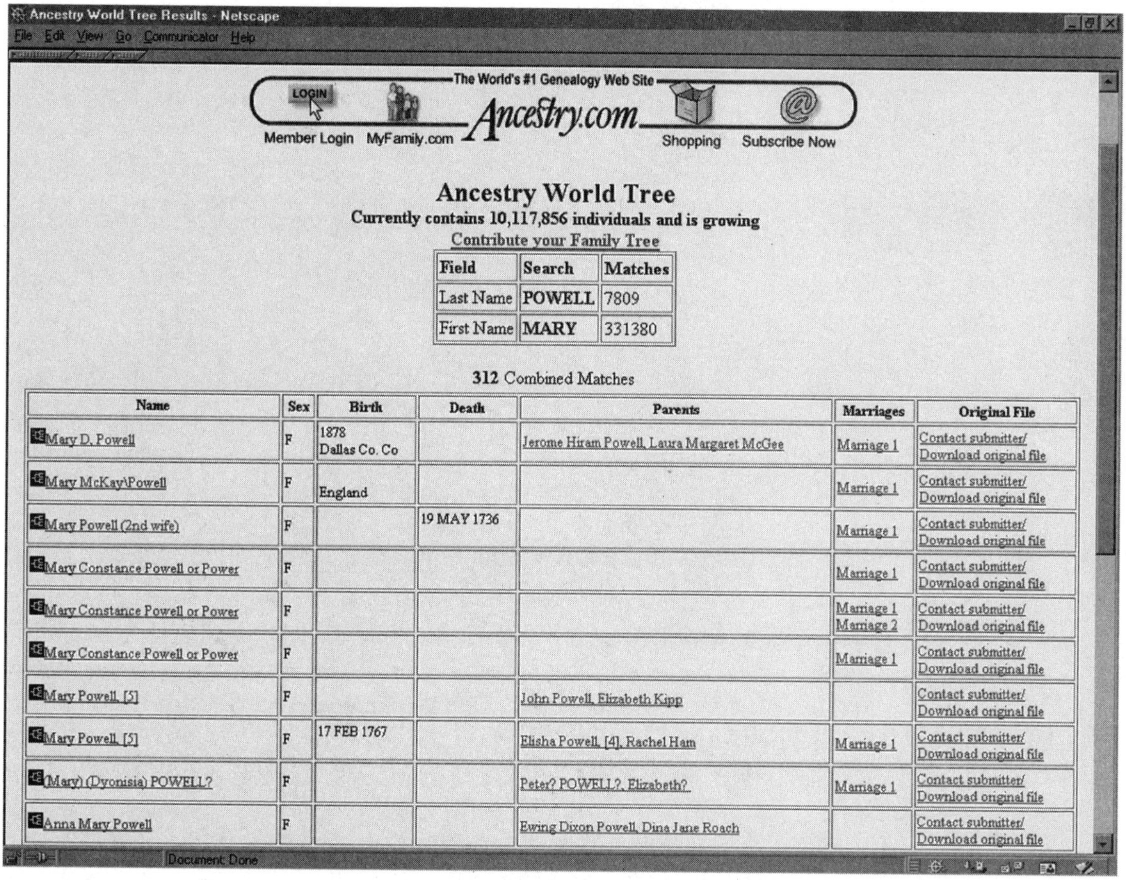

Figure 12-1 In the Ancestry World Tree, you can find information from other genealogists. You can download the GEDCOM or contact the submitter.

To use it, you simply enter a name, along with birth and death dates if you have them. The results are presented in a table, as in Figure 12-1. You can click on the links in the far right to download the GEDCOM as submitted or contact the person who uploaded it.

Other good links in the free area include the regular columnists (Dick Eastman, DearMYRTLE, and others), genealogy lessons, phone and address searches, Juliana's Links, a searchable database of Web sites, and maps and gazetteers.

It's worth looking at the What's New page (http://www.ancestry.com/whatsnew.htm) and its link to Ancestry Daily News (www.ancestry.com/dailynews/<xx_xx_xx.htm>), where the X's are replaced by the month, date, and year. Here you'll find announcements of new databases and Web sites, news flashes, essays on historical and genealogical events, and more.

The site also features a chat area, bookstore, and sample articles from *Ancestry Magazine*, print version.

Everton's (www.everton.com)

One of the venerable publishers in genealogy, Everton Publishers produces books, CD-ROMs, *Everton's Genealogical Helper*, and this excellent Web site. Like Ancestry, Everton's accepts GEDCOM files from genealogists; unlike Ancestry, theirs is available for free searching only on a limited basis. Submitting your GEDCOM files gets you one month free searching on their database of such files. For $50 a year (which includes a subscription to *The Genealogical Helper*), you can have access to that database and their many others as well.

Everton's also has a searchable database of the SSDI included in the free guest databases. Other guest privileges include a searchable catalog of genealogical CDs, a photo database, and a relationship chart, shown in Figure 12-2.

Their resource page (http://www.everton.com/genealogy/ols/resource-index.htm) is worth a bookmark: Here you'll find links to queries, online classes, blank charts you can print out for your research, and even links to RV-n-Genealogists, folks who camp and trace!

In the Download Area, you'll find Everton's Ancestor Research Tool program. This software is designed to help you sort and store your information, including where you got it. A very simple genealogy program, it is shareware and costs $15, which gets you a printed manual and free, unlimited technical support.

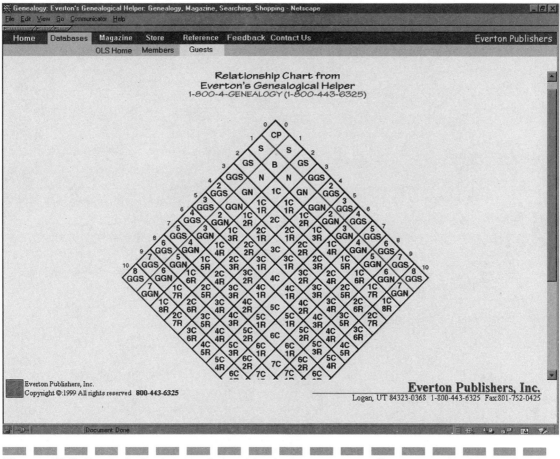

Figure 12-2 Everton's site has a relationship chart, so you can figure out who is your fourth cousin!

Kindred Konnections (www.kindredkonnections.com)

Another subscription site with searchable databases, Kindred Konnections offers several free services:

- A database of voluntarily submitted GEDCOMs
- U.S. SSDI
- A searchable census of Cornwall, UK, 1871
- A message board on research interests

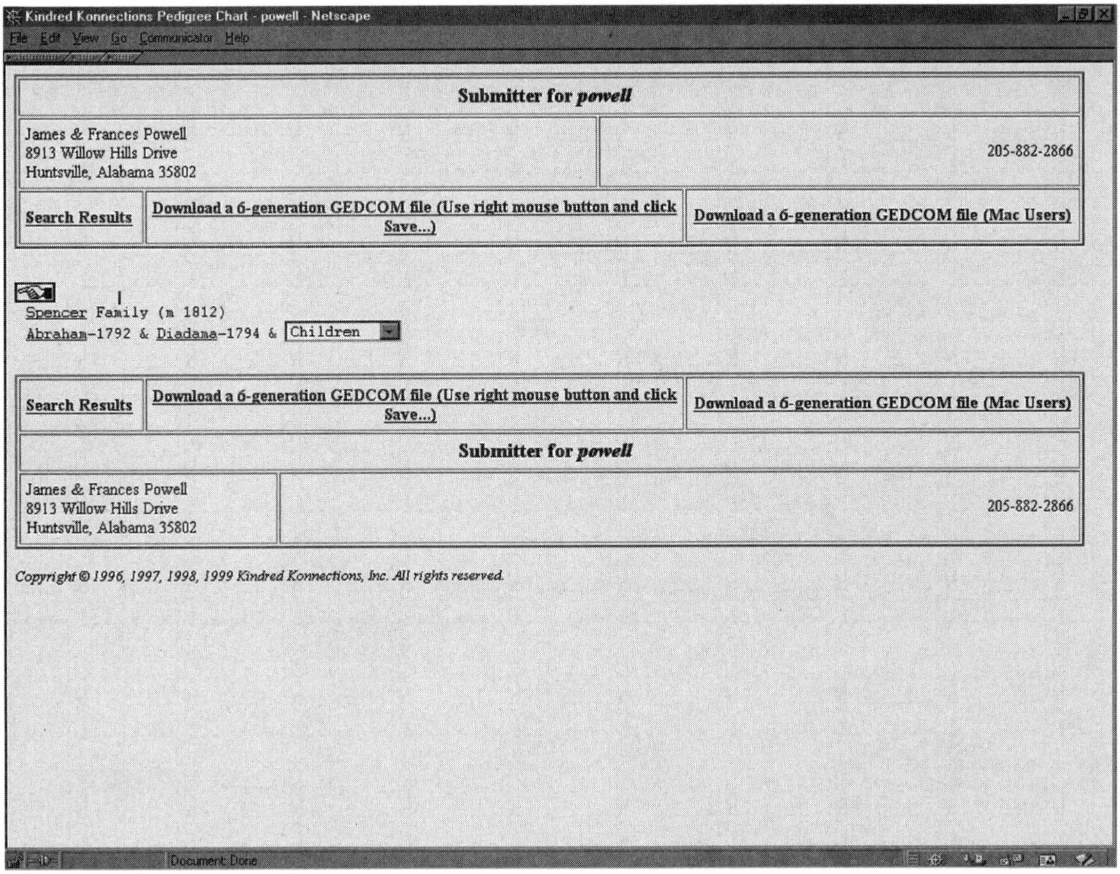

Figure 12-3 Kindred Konnections offers free time on their fee areas in exchange for your data.

- A list of professional genealogists
- A list of genealogy libraries
- Family reunion sites

You can get a free hour or month of subscription services. You simply register as a free member, then help them with their indexing. From a Web page, you type in the names from a record image, submit it to their site, and you get an immediate hour of subscription services. You can do this often to save up subscription credits; the more you work, the less you pay; it's possible never to pay at all if you extract enough documents.

By submitting your own family history as a GEDCOM file (must be at least 15 families and 60 individuals) or into My-Tree On-Line, you get a one-time free month of subscription services (see Figure 12-3). These services include:

- Ancestral Archive; search 30 million names, with results in pedigree views plus submitter information.

- Complete name matching against the Ancestral Archive.

- Special Collections Archive of cemetery records, birth, death and marriage records, and more.

- Scanned-in document collections (family group records, pedigree charts, census records, etc.).

- Census records selections from the 1851 UK census and the 1871 Canadian census.

- Soundex search for surname spelling variations.

Kindred Connections' Web site isn't as old and established as Ancestry and Everton's, but there are a lot of good resources here, and the chance to get the services for free in return for some typing is unique.

Genealogy.com (www.genealogy.com)

Message boards, online genealogy lessons, free genealogy Web posting, genealogy how-to, and online books are at this site from The Learning Company, publishers of Family Tree Maker (FTM). On this site you can post your genealogy using the FTM program. You can also search the entire Web for your ancestor names or look for citations in the CD-ROMs the company sells. As far as I can tell, all the services on this site are free, but he accepts donations.

Family Search is the service you will probably use most often. You type the name you are looking for into a form on the Web site. If it is found on a CD-ROM or book that they sell, you'll just get confirmation of citation in the book or CD, and a link to get information on how to buy it. If the search hit is on the Internet, you'll get a link to the site.

Other features of the site are a message board for queries and help, along with several how-to files about learning to do genealogy. (See Figure 12-4).

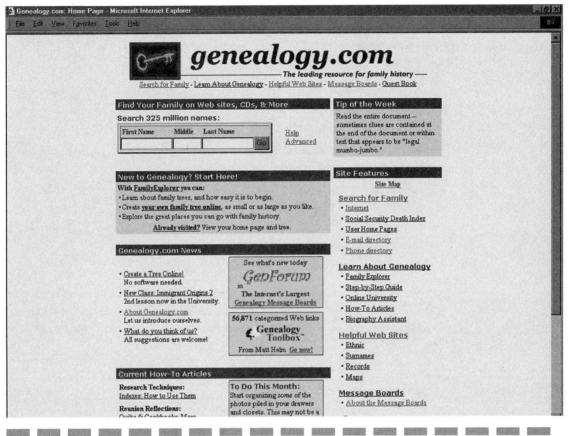

Figure 12-4 Genealogy.com is where users of Family Tree Maker post their results for others to search.

Yourfamily.com

This site, shown in Figure 12-5, seems to be a sort of genealogy cooperative, although on a much smaller scale than RootsWeb. The features on the site are as follows:

- *Long Lost Family.* A listing of resources for families that have been separated.

- *Making a Family Home Page.* A how-to of Web publishing with genealogists in mind.

- *Videos, Albums, and Taped Oral Histories.* A listing of resources for pursuing these topics.

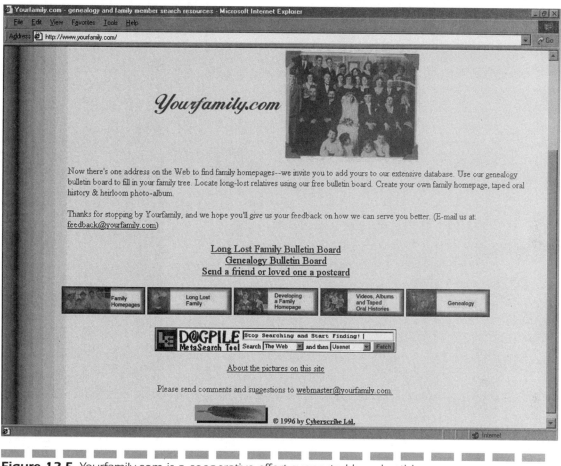

Figure 12-5 Yourfamily.com is a cooperative effort supported by advertising.

- *Bulletin Board.* A message forum for queries, research problems, etc.
- *Family Home Pages.* Fill out a simple form and have your family become part of the database. Search through the files of those that have already signed up. Update your page as you find new data.
- *Genealogy.* A list of helpful links in genealogy.

Commercial Online Services

Long before general public access to the Internet existed, most of us got our online jollies from the major commercial online services: America Online (AOL), CompuServe, and Prodigy among them. While each online service has something that distinguishes it from the others, they have several things in common: proprietary content, mail, Usenet, and files.

Proprietary Content

The commercial online services offer you content you can't get on the Internet, such as special connections to news and research services. For example, on CompuServe and AOL, you can search databases of magazine articles and databases of genealogy submitted by members.

Because access to the commercial online services comes at a premium, you get a smaller group sometimes than you get on an Internet site; this can be a good thing, if it's a group of knowledgeable people. You also have someone to enforce the rules should someone get out of line on an online service. You can usually search online services for other members who share the same interests you do, and with whom you can exchange chat, email, and forum messages. On the Internet, it's sometimes hit and miss.

Internet sites called *portals* are trying to compete with the commercial online services in content with news, Usenet searches, chat rooms and message boards. Time will tell whether they make it.

Front-End Software

Commercial online services offer you a graphical interface, complete with a Web browser, to help you connect to the service and use it. Often, after you get used to online life, you find the front end more trouble than it's worth. In all the major online services right now, the front end consists of some form of Microsoft Internet Explorer wrapped in a specialized software that has other functions besides just browsing. The deal between AOL and Netscape may change this setup in the near future.

Quick Jumps

All the commercial online services have their proprietary content divided into sections, often called "channels." You can browse through them, clicking perhaps `Lifestyles`, then `Hobbies`, then `Genealogy`. However, after you get used to where the genealogy section is, you'll want a short cut. On AOL, these are called "keywords"; on CompuServe, "GO words." It means you can type in a single word, such as `Roots`, and skip the three or four clicks it would take you to get to the genealogy area the normal way.

Forums

Forums are message exchanges. You leave a message, as if tacking a 3×5 card to a bulletin board. On a later visit, you'll find others have replied to your message with comments and questions of their own. Like a mailing list, the conversation does not occur in real time. Like Usenet, you have to remember to go get the new messages at some point. Unlike either of them, you have to join a specific service in order to participate in forums.

Mail

All commercial online services offer you email. They often offer you a way to download your mail, sign off the service, and then read and answer the messages while offline. Sometimes they offer a way to do this with Usenet and forums as well.

Usenet

All the commercial online services have a Usenet newsreader as part of the front-end software. AOL and CompuServe allow you to filter out the porn, unsolicited advertising posts, and get-rich-quick messages, as discussed in Chapter 2. Both also allow you to download Usenet messages to read offline.

Files

The claim to fame of commercial online services has always been access to files, especially patches and fixes to commercial programs. All the major software vendors have a presence on the commercial online services where you can post questions and problems and find the latest versions. Genealogy software companies are no exception.

In this section, I'll show you the commercial online services with genealogy sections. Others, such as Microsoft Network (MSN),

MindSpring, and others, have small genealogy sections without much happening on them. However, should you decide to go with a service that is not profiled here and you think it's worthwhile, email me at libbi_ powell_crowe@bigfoot.com. I could include it in future editions of this book.

13

America Online's Golden Gate Genealogy Forum

If you live in North America, you have probably received a free trial membership from America Online in the mail or with your modem. But just in case you didn't, here's how to contact the company:

8619 Westwood Center Drive
Vienna VA 22182-2285
cs@aol.com
1-800-227-6364

The history of America Online is nothing short of amazing. Just seven years ago, AOL wanted to be as big as CompuServe and Prodigy. Now it's bigger than those two services combined. In fact, it now owns CompuServe and Netscape, as well as other software companies, such as ICQ. And the genealogy forum is one of the best offerings on all of AOL.

AOL is "open" 24 hours a day, 7 days a week. Their basic rate is unlimited use for $29.95 a month; that includes AOL's own content as well as surfing the Internet with their browser, Usenet reader, and FTP programs.

A warning though: AOL sends out software with a free month's membership about three times a year. Whenever they do, getting connected to AOL and staying connected is problematic, because AOL's hardware gets overloaded. And even if you get on and stay on, the response from the system can sometimes slow to a frustrating crawl. This has caused some people to deride the service as "Almost Online."

In such a case, your best bet is to sign off the system and log back on at a time when things are less busy. Mornings are usually good, the earlier the better, as well as late afternoons. And the offerings in the AOL genealogy forum are worth trying at those times of day.

Like most commercial online services, AOL is available only through their proprietary front-end software. AOL's network has local access numbers throughout the world, but not necessarily in rural areas. The software package will find the phone number closest to you during the setup procedure; but every now and then, go to the list of local access numbers (Keyword: ACCESS) to see whether you are using the best and closest connection.

During the sign-up process, you choose a main screen name for your account. Choose this carefully; you cannot change it without closing the old account and starting a new one. However, you may have up to five screen names assigned to the main account, so each family member can have a mailbox, a set of favorites, and a place to file messages and downloads. To add and delete additional screen names, use the keyword NAMES.

The Genealogy Forum (Keyword: ROOTS or GENEALOGY) is the center of genealogical activity on America Online. From the Beginners' Center to the genealogy chat rooms and the Resource Center, this forum is an incredibly rich resource. The Forum's tens of thousands of members make it the largest genealogical society in the world, online or off. Figure 13-1 shows the Golden Gate Genealogy Forum's main window.

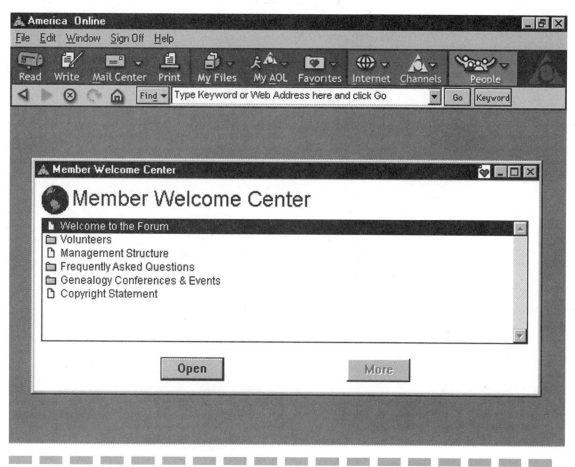

Figure 13-1 The Golden Gate Genealogy Forum. Details will change from time to time, but the basic choices will remain the same.

NOTE   In 1998, the AOL Genealogy Forum became the Golden Gate Genealogy Forum. The Golden Gate Genealogy Forum on America Online is a production of Golden Gate Services, Inc. of Franklin, Massachusetts. The president of Golden Gate Services is George Ferguson, who has been the forum leader for years (screen name: GFL George). For simplicity, we'll refer to the forum throughout this chapter as the Genealogy Forum.

Don't forget to add the Genealogy Forum to your list of Favorite Places. To do this, just click the heart on the top right side of the forum main window.

Member Welcome Center

On your first visit to the Genealogy Forum, plan to spend some time in the Member Welcome Center (Figure 13-2). You get there by double-clicking the folder labeled Member Welcome Center in the Genealogy Forum main menu.

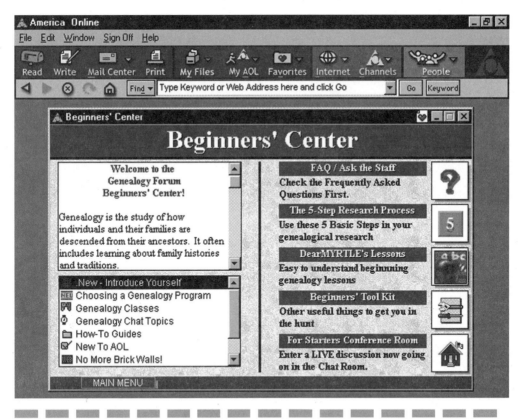

Figure 13-2 You'll be spending a lot of time in the Genealogy Forum, so visit the Member Welcome Center for background information on the forum and its staff.

In the center, you'll be able to read about the people who keep the Genealogy Forum running, see how the forum is managed, and find out about upcoming genealogy conferences and events. Most important, you'll be able to read the Genealogy Forum's frequently asked questions (FAQ) files.

As I've noted before, FAQ files are indispensable reading, not only in forums but also in electronic mailing lists, newsgroups, and at Web sites. The FAQ files are collections of the most commonly asked questions pertaining to the forum, list, newsgroup, or site. Read these files before you start asking questions or posting messages. Online areas like the Genealogy Forum are similar to real-world communities in that they have their own rules of behavior. The FAQ files will give you a basic understanding of the forum from the start.

Once you finish with the Member Welcome Center, you have two paths you can follow. One is to head to the Beginners' Center, which is designed for people who are new to genealogy. Or, if you are already a genealogist, you can skip the Beginners' Center and begin with the Quick Start Guide, which tells you how to start researching your roots with the Genealogy Forum.

Beginners' Center

To reach the Beginners' Center, you click the big `Beginners Start Here` button on the Genealogy Forum main window. This takes you to the Genealogy Quick Start window. At the bottom of the window is the `Beginners' Center` button. Click this button and you'll see a window similar to the one in Figure 13-3. As you can see in the figure, the Beginners' Center has lots of interesting content. Each major section of the center is described in the sections that follow.

FAQ/Ask the Staff

Click the `FAQ/Ask the Staff` button to see a list of frequently asked questions (Figure 13-4). This list is identical to the one you'll find in the Member Welcome Center, except for the last item in the list. The last item is Ask the Staff. Click it and you'll get to send email directly to one of the Genealogy Forum staff members.

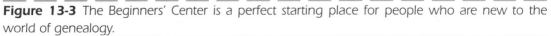

Figure 13-3 The Beginners' Center is a perfect starting place for people who are new to the world of genealogy.

The 5-Step Research Process

The 5-step Research Process is a systematic approach to doing any genealogical research. This is an excellent tutorial on how to get started in genealogy. According to the process, family history research includes asking yourself the same questions, in order, in cycles:

1. What do I already know?
2. What specific question needs to be answered?
3. What records might answer my question?

4. What do the records actually tell me?

5. What conclusions can I reach now?

Click the `5-Step Research Process` button to open the window, shown in Figure 13-5) and start applying the process to your research today.

DearMYRTLE's Beginner Lessons

Begun in January 1997, DearMYRTLE's Beginning Genealogy Lessons (Figure 13-6) are weekly text files on aspects of genealogical research for the beginner. They are well worth saving for future reference.

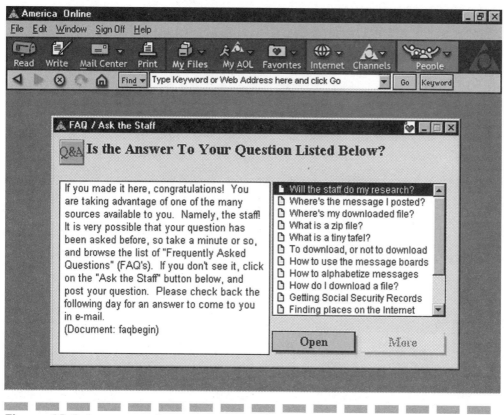

Figure 13-4 Answers to the most common beginner questions are gathered in the FAQ/Ask the Staff area.

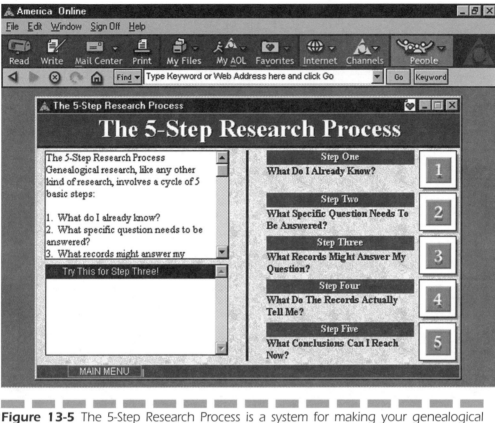

Figure 13-5 The 5-Step Research Process is a system for making your genealogical research fast and efficient.

Beginners' Tool Kit

The Beginners' Tool Kit (Figure 13-7) is a grab bag of information files, from how to get addresses to what different forms you can use to display your research. There are all sorts of gems in the tool kit. Do you want to learn about colonial diseases and cures? Can't figure out a genealogical abbreviation? If so, this is the part of the Genealogy Forum for you. Here you'll find guides on getting started in genealogy, organizing your data as you get more experienced, tips on how to get information (who to write, how to ask), and links to related services on America Online.

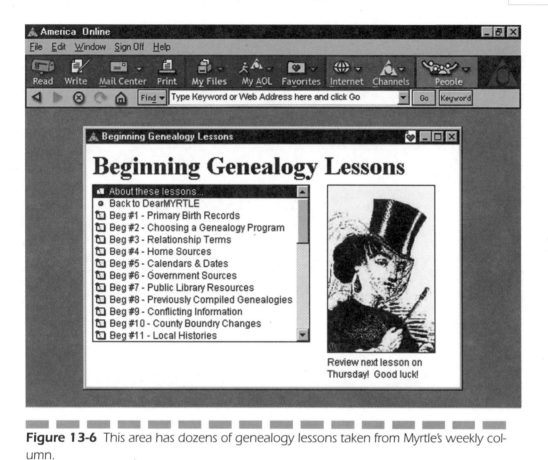

Figure 13-6 This area has dozens of genealogy lessons taken from Myrtle's weekly column.

For Starters Conference Room

If you want to talk to other beginners exploring genealogy on AOL, click the button for the For Starters Conference Room. Here you'll find beginners asking questions and generally chatting back and forth on genealogy.

Other Resources

Still more genealogy resources for beginners are found in the menu on the bottom left side of the Beginners' Center window. There is an assortment of information here, including such valuable items as a suggested reading list, list of genealogy supply companies, and a guide to choosing a genealogy program (Figure 13-8).

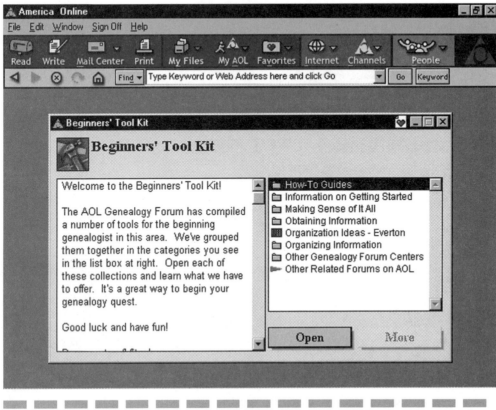

Figure 13-7 The Beginners' Tool Kit contains links to all sorts of resources and information, both on AOL and off.

Quick Start Guide

If you're already a practicing genealogist, you can skip the Beginners' Center and start with the Genealogy Quick Start Guide. The guide tells you how to put the resources of the Genealogy Forum to work for you immediately. To reach it, you click on `Beginners Start Here` on the Genealogy Forum main window.

The Quick Start Guide has four sections, each describing specific resources within the forum and telling you how to use them. The four sections are as follows:

1. *Search by topic.* The fastest way to search in the Genealogy Forum. Most people begin by typing in one surname to see what

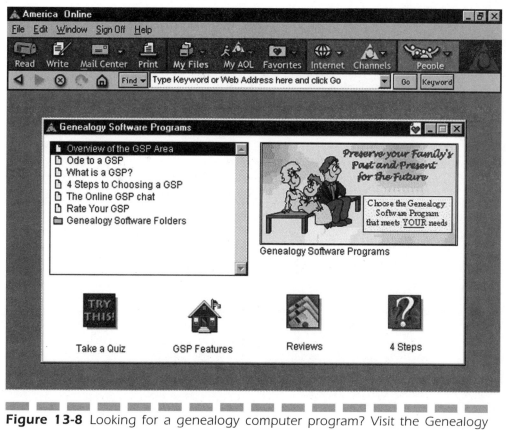

Figure 13-8 Looking for a genealogy computer program? Visit the Genealogy Software Program area for information and advice.

pops up. You can also put in a geographical term (Ohio, France) and see what files and articles there might be.

2. *Surname message boards.* Use these to look up a surname directly.

3. *Files library center.* Look in this area to see if other forum members have already uploaded useful material like GEDCOM files that are helpful to your research.

4. *Special centers provide additional resources.* This is a quick introduction to some of the other useful resources in the Genealogy Forum, some of which are described below, such as the genealogy column DearMYRTLE.

Message Boards

The message boards in the Genealogy Forum are the place to post messages when you need information you can't find elsewhere in the forum. The boards operate on a volunteer basis; you're invited to post any questions you might have and are encouraged to post a reply to anybody else's question that you have information about. Also, don't forget to post the family names you're looking for in the message board under the Surname category.

To reach the message boards, click the large `Messages` button in the Genealogy Forum main window. Using the Message Board Center (Figure 13-9), you can post messages in any of five major subject areas:

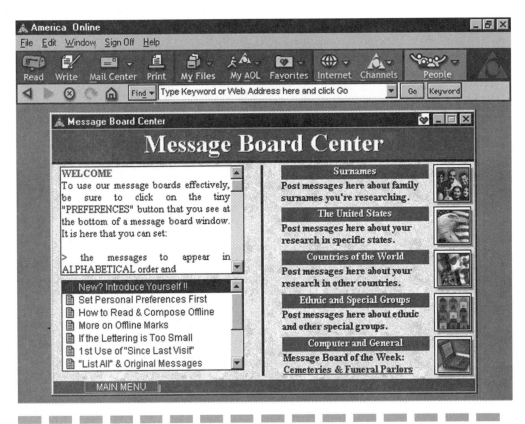

Figure 13-9 The Message Board Center is the place to read and post messages about a wide range of genealogy topics.

1. *Surnames.* Post messages asking about specific family names you are researching.

2. *The United States.* Post messages about research within specific states or regions of the United States.

3. *Countries of the World.* Post messages about research in countries other than the United States.

4. *Ethnic and special groups.* Post messages about your research into ethnic or other special groups.

5. *Computer and General.* Post messages about topics that don't fit into the other message boards.

Before you start exploring the message boards, it's a good idea to read the messages that appear in the menu on the lower left side of the Message Board Center main window. They explain how the center and the message boards work. In particular, pay attention to the Set Personal Preferences First and How to Read & Compose Offline messages. They can make the Message Board Center much easier to use. Once you've read these messages, you should set your preferences, then start exploring the message boards.

Within each of these message board topic areas, you may find dozens of specific boards. For example, within Surnames there are areas for surnames that begin with each letter of the alphabet. Within those areas are boards for surnames that begin with specific combinations of letters. These finally lead to the actual message boards.

Searching for the surname Mann, you begin with the Surnames topic. Under Surnames, select the M Surnames folder, then the MAN-MBZ message board. You'll know when you've reached an actual message board because the icon for it is a green piece of paper with a pushpin through it.

Continuing this example, the MAN-MBZ message board (Figure 13-10) is an example of a specific message board. The large list in the window lists the subject of each posted message and the number of postings to each subject. When someone replies to a message that has been posted, it creates a message thread, which is sort of a conversation on that particular subject. The Postings column tells how many messages are in the thread.

Each board also has a set of controls that make it easy to use and customize. Here is a rundown of the controls and what they do:

■ *Read Post.* Displays the contents of the message (or message thread) that is selected in the message list.

File   Edit   Window   Sign Off   Help

Read   Write   Mail Center   Print   My Files   My AOL   Favorites   Internet   Channels   People

Find ▼   Type Keyword or Web Address here and click Go   Go   Keyword

Post last names beginning with Man through Mbz here. Please do not start messages with symbols such as *** or {{.

Subjects	Postings
"Marley" "Marley" HELP!	1
Re: ***MAYNARD***of W.Mass. connected to Canada	1
Alonzo Matthews - Minnesota	1
CALVIN MARTIN/VERMONT	1
catherine martin	1
Chief Justice John Marshall	4
Re: Desperately seeking Maynards....	6
James Massey , came to MD in 1657	2
John Anthony Maher	1
JOHNSON, William	1
Re: Joseph MAY 1838 Kentucky	1
LOOKING FOR FAMILIES OF MAUST, GEORGE SAMUEL,	1
Looking for father	1
Looking for Manes from pa. near Pittsburgh	1
LOOKING FOR MAULDEN"S	2
Looking for the family of Angelo Marre.	1
M. C. MAYBERRY & AMELIA J. BELCHER	1

Read Post   List Posts   More   Find Since   Create Subject

PREFERENCES | MARK READ | MARK ALL READ | HELP

Figure 13-10 Each message board has a set of controls that make it easy to use and customize.

■ *List Posts.* Displays a list of relevant information about the message (or message thread) that is selected in the message list.

■ *More.* If you selected More in your preferences, and more messages are available than the message list holds, you can click this button to load more messages into the message list.

■ *Find Since.* Click this if you want to do a search of the message list.

■ *Create Subject.* Click this to create a new subject in the message board.

■ *Preferences.* This button allows you to control how messages appear in the message list.

■ *Mark Read.* Click this to mark the selected messages and threads in this list as read. The list will then treat them according to your preferences, as if you actually read them.

■ *Mark All Read.* Click this to mark all the messages and threads in this list as read. The list will then treat them according to your preferences, as if you actually read all of them.

Reading online isn't bad, but I find it much more efficient to read offline, using Automatic AOL and the File Cabinet's Search function. You can only do this with message boards that have been converted to Usenet format, and even at the rate of 4000 boards a day, not all of them have been converted. But for those that have, this can be a real time-saver.

Here's how to go about it. Let's say the topic of interest is messages about Powells. First, click on Message Board Center. In the top left scroll-down box, move down until you see the link All Genealogy Forum Message Boards. Click on this link.

When the All Genealogy Forum Message Boards window appears (*Tip*: Remember that you can use the heart icon to put this window in your Favorites or on the toolbar), click on the topic Genealogy Message Boards. For this example, you would click TOP SURNAMES IN THE US. When you have that window, keep clicking MORE until you get to the POWELL message board. Then highlight it, and click the button Read Offline. You'll get a message that the board has been added, and to view your list, go to keyword MY BOARDS. (*Tip*: Remember, you can add the keyword MY BOARDS to your shortcuts list.) At the keyword MY BOARDS you can delete message boards from your list, set the maximum number to be downloaded, toggle the read offline setting, and set other preferences for each board on your list.

Now when you run an Automatic AOL session, the new messages are retrieved with your email and placed in the Personal Filing Cabinet. Once a session is done, click on My Files, and then Personal Filing Cabinet. Your message board will be a folder under Newsgroups. To read all the messages, just as you would email or newsgroups, simply open the folder and click on each message. However, you don't really have to look at every one.

To save time, you can use the Find button in the Personal Filing Cabinet and look for messages that interest you. Say I want to know about Powells in South Carolina. Now, the Find button gives you a choice of searching all folders or only open folders, and either full text or only the subject lines. To make the search faster, open the Powell folder, closing all others, and choose Open Folders. Then choose either Full Text or Titles Only, whichever you feel is most likely to get a hit. Then enter the term South Carolina in the text box and click Find Next. If no messages match the search, you can delete all that day's messages, compact the Filing Cabinet, and try another day.

Chapter 13

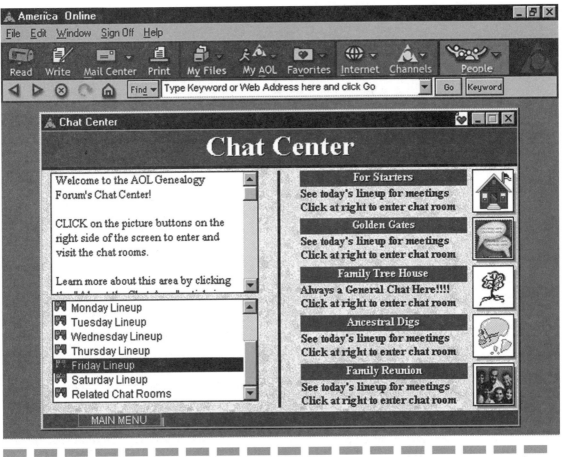

Figure 13-11 Go to the Chat Center for real-time, live chat sessions with other genealogists from around the world.

Genealogy Chat Center

The Chat Center (Figure 13-11) is where you go to hold online, real-time conversations with other genealogists. To get to the Chat Center, click the Chats button on the forum's main window. There are chat rooms for many different topics: Beginning Genealogy Chat, Southern Chat, and War Between the States Chat are three examples. Some chats are continuous, some are active at specific times; schedules and lineups appear in the list on the left of the Chat Center main window.

As with the Message Board Center, the first order of business is to read the messages in the menu on the lower left of the Chat Center window. Pay particular attention to the Lineup lists. Since chat is a real-time activity, many sessions are scheduled in advance. If you just want to drop in, one of the five main chat rooms usually has someone in it.

Figure 13-12 shows a chat room. I've used an empty room here to avoid reproducing anyone's chat without their permission.

The large window on the left is where the chat messages appear. As new ones arrive, they all shift up the screen, so the newest messages are at the bottom.

Below the chat window is a box where you enter the text of the message you want to send. Click Send to transmit the message to the other participants in the chat.

To the right of the chat window is a list of the people present in the chat room. Right now, Bill is the only one there, but the chat rooms can hold dozens of people. To find out more about someone in the chat room, double-click that person's screen name in this list.

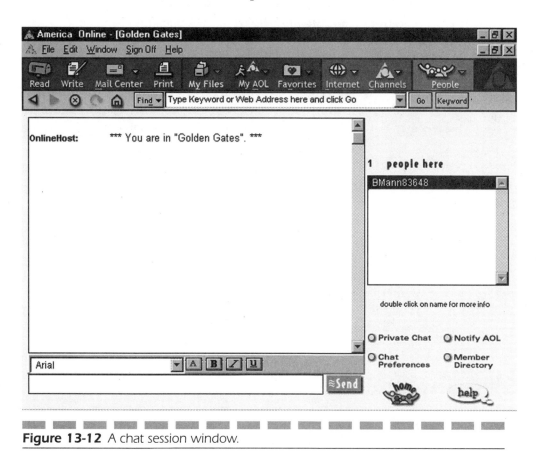

Figure 13-12 A chat session window.

Other controls in the chat window are as follows:

- *Private Chat.*   This allows you to invite someone in the chat room to chat with you privately.

- *Chat Preferences.*   Click on this to set the five chat options available.

- *Notify AOL.*   If someone is misbehaving in the chat, you can click on this to report the infraction to AOL.

- *Member Directory.*   This lets you request the profile of a person, whether they are present in the chat room or not.

File Libraries Center

The File Libraries Center (Figure 13-13) is a central location for all sorts of computer files of interest to genealogists. Divided into five sections, each containing multiple libraries, the center has thousands of files you can download.

You'll find files here ranging from trial versions of popular genealogy software to GEDCOMs and other genealogy information from members. You can use the new Library Sort feature to make it easier to find specific files in the libraries, or you can click on `Search the Forum` on the main Genealogy Forum window to use the Search Genealogy Forum feature.

Resource Center

The Resource Center is chock-full of information to save you lots of trial and error. This area has articles, helps, and tips in the subjects of Regions of the World Addresses, Ethnic Resources, Vital Records/Other Records, and Other Resources. Here you'll find guides and tips to making your research more productive.

To visit the Resource Center, you click on `Resources` on the main Genealogy Forum window.

Internet Center

The Internet Center in the Genealogy Forum is where you'll find Web sites, FTP and Gopher sites, newsgroups, and mailing lists that specifi-

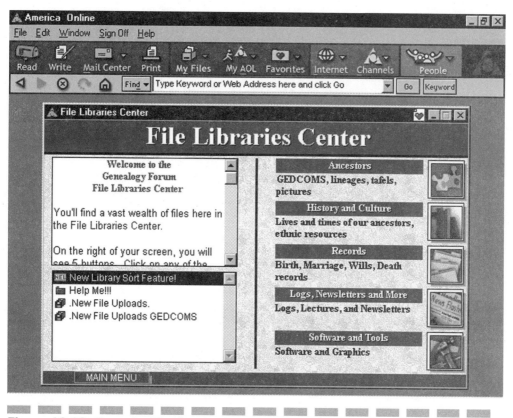

Figure 13-13 Go to the File Libraries Center to find virtually any genealogy-related file you can think of.

cally have to do with genealogy. This can save you a lot of time as compared to randomly searching the Internet for specific genealogy items. However, if you want to go farther afield, be sure to check out Net Help-the Answer Man, where tips, tricks, and FAQs about the Internet in general and AOL's connection in particular are stored. You can subscribe to newsgroups here or at Keyword: USENET. Click on Expert Add and type in the soc.genealogy newsgroups you want.

NOTE *Section 2 of this book covers using the Internet for genealogical research.*

Here's a newsgroups tip: In your Automatic AOL windows (also called Flashsessions), check the box Retrieve unread NewsGroup messages and the box Send outgoing NewsGroup messages. Then, when online, go to Keyword: USENET. Click on the Read offline button. Your subscribed newsgroups will be listed on the left. Any you add to the box on the right will be put in your filing cabinet during Automatic AOL. This will increase the time of your Automatic AOL with very busy newsgroups, but your online time will still be greatly reduced. You'll just have to remember to erase the old messages regularly to save disk space.

To visit the Internet Center, click on Internet in the main Genealogy Forum window.

Surname Center

The Surname Center (Figure 13-14) is another collection of message boards that's organized by surname. But here individual surnames have their own boards, as opposed to the surname boards you can reach from the Quick Start Guide, which group surnames alphabetically.

The same rules and suggestions discussed earlier apply to these message boards. The only difference is that these message boards are each focused on a single surname, so you will likely find the messages to be more useful than on another board, even though there will be fewer of them.

Search the Forum

Clicking Search the Forum on the Genealogy Forum main window opens the Genealogy Search window. When you enter a search term in this window, the program will search the file libraries in the forum. The program does not search the messages. The result is a list of files that contain the search term.

Other Resources

You've now learned about the main areas of the Genealogy Forum. But beyond those areas are all sorts of other useful resources. The following sections are short descriptions of some of these resources.

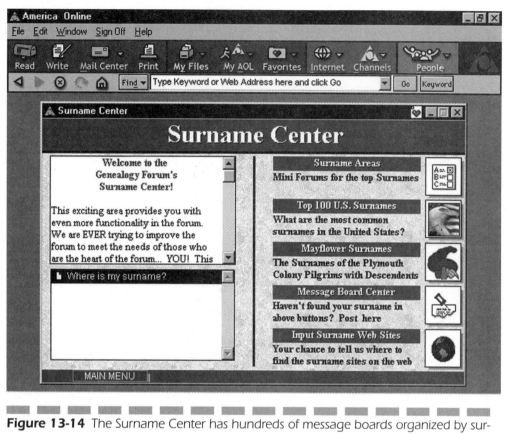

Figure 13-14 The Surname Center has hundreds of message boards organized by surname.

Genealogy Forum News

In the Genealogy Forum News window, you'll find various announcements, the monthly forum newsletter, schedules for chats and classes, and all the other fast-changing information in the forum. Several genealogy special-interest groups (SIGs), like the U.S. Civil War SIG, also post monthly newsletters here.

DearMYRTLE Daily Column

A daily column on genealogy topics, DearMYRTLE Daily is always helpful and informative. Use Keyword: DEARMYRTLE to come here directly.

The DearMYRTLE Daily Column area (Figure 13-15) not only contains Myrtle's columns but also a message board, a collection of how-to guides, and much more.

Telephone Search Facilities

The Telephone Search Facilities window gives you access to nine World Wide Web sites that you can use to track down the phone numbers and addresses of people. If you discover the existence of a long lost cousin, use this section to help you track down that cousin's address and phone number.

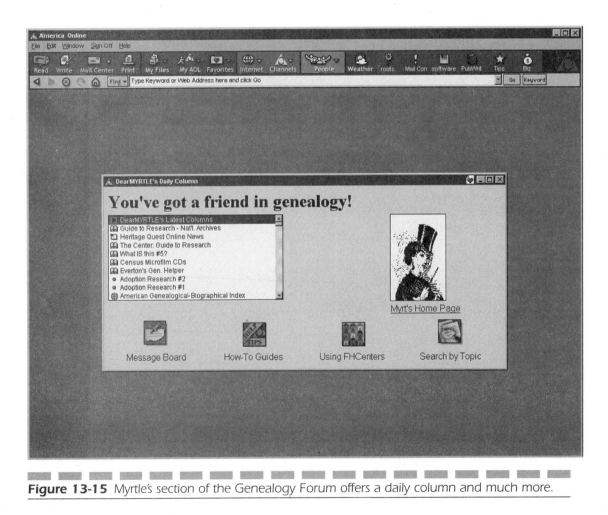

Figure 13-15 Myrtle's section of the Genealogy Forum offers a daily column and much more.

The best place to start your search is with AOL's own Switchboard (http://www.switchboard.com/). Switchboard lets you find people, businesses, Web sites, and email addresses.

Software Search

Start with AOL's Software Center (Keyword: FIND SOFTWARE). Here you have four choices: search for shareware (try-before-you-buy programs such as Brother's Keeper), search for commercial software (such as Family Tree Maker), check out the recommended Daily Download (usually a general purpose program), or browse the Computing Superstore.

To search for shareware, click the link. You'll get the Software Search window (Keyword: FILESEARCH). You can limit your search by time (all dates, past month, past week) the file was uploaded and by categories: applications, operating system, and so on. Then type your keywords (genealogy programs, for example). In a few seconds you have a list of matches. You can select one, read its description, and decide whether to add it to your Download Manager list of files to be downloaded. When you have your list complete, you can just choose Download Manager from the window that pops up when you choose Download Later, and tell it to start.

Golden Gate Store

The Golden Gate store offers books and CD-ROMs on genealogy at good prices. There are different delivery and payment options, and they guarantee prompt service.

Ancestral Seasonings Cookbook

It's time for a tasty finale to your visit to the Genealogy Forum. From the forum's main window, click Resources to go to the Resource Center. Now look in the menu on the left side of the window, and double-click Ancestral Seasonings to open the Ancestral Seasonings Cookbook (Figure 13-16).

In the cookbook, you'll find favorite recipes from other AOL genealogists, many passed down from generation to generation. Like most other

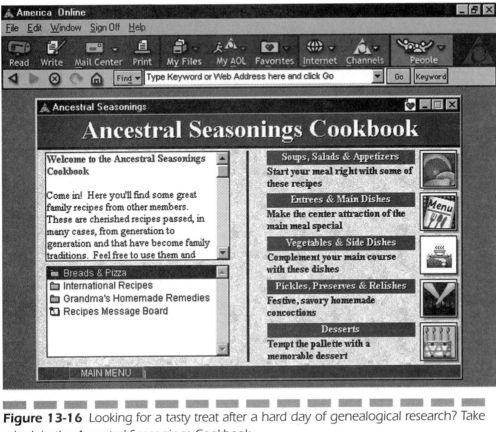

Figure 13-16 Looking for a tasty treat after a hard day of genealogical research? Take a look in the Ancestral Seasonings Cookbook.

areas of the forum, this cookbook has five main sections. But there's a difference. These main sections are as follows:

- Soups, Salads & Appetizers
- Entrees & Main Dishes
- Vegetables & Side Dishes
- Pickles, Preserves & Relishes
- Desserts

The menu on the left also has some interesting headings. How about these: Breads & Pizza, International Recipes, or Grandma's Homemade Remedies. Whether any particular recipe has been handed down through the ages or not, you are sure to find something to please your palate.

The Staff of the Genealogy Forum

While the Genealogy Forum is full of interesting and useful treasures, by far the most valuable treasure in the forum is the people who staff it. One of the system operators, or "sysops," GFS Judy, said:

> The Genealogy Forum provides a sense of family. Not only the "real" relatives you are searching for, but the sense of family you get entering a chat room and being recognized, the information that total strangers go out of their way to type up and email you, the forwarding of problems to others so that everyone can offer a suggestion or just encouragement to keep on going. I am constantly amazed that people who have spent 20 years of their lives, and countless dollars researching their family lines, will freely give out information just to help another researcher and perhaps get a tidbit in return. The materials people upload into the genealogy libraries save me hours of time traveling around the country, as does the Internet access. Computers truly make genealogy a realistic, global project that anyone can join in on regardless of age or income.

The Genealogy Forum is full of wonderful resources for the beginner, intermediate, and advanced genealogist. One of the best features about this forum is the excellent staff of experienced genealogists to help you.

GFL George is the forum leader. GFA Robin, GFA Terry, GFA Beth, and GFA Drew are some of the sysops. There are over 100 staff members in the forum—anyone with *GFS* at the beginning of their screen name is a Genealogy Forum staff member. A list of the staff, with short bios, can be found in the Welcome Center folder named Volunteers.

GFA Terry is one example. Director of a Mormon Family History center (FHC), she's the Genealogy Forum expert on FHCs and the Family History Library in Salt Lake City. As she says:

> I have been working in the Genealogy Club for years. It started in about 1986 when I joined Q-Link (the first network from the owners of AOL, it was designed for Commodore computers). I worked in the genealogy area of Q-Link as a staff member. When AOL came about and when my husband and I upgraded to an IBM, we joined this network. I was already a staff member on Q-Link (owned by the same company), so it was possible to become one here too.
>
> My duties cover many things—I greet the new members, answer some of the questions on the message boards, do some librarian duties as I help make files go live, archive message boards, host meetings, and well, there's a lot to do, but I enjoy it very much.

The network has helped her with her genealogy as well, and she says:

I have made contact with several folks by posting the surnames I was looking for. I even found a distant cousin! This all works on a volunteer princi-
ple—folks helping other folks. One of them lived in Connecticut where I
had ancestors and looked up some information for me. In turn I looked up
some information for her from Georgia. And the genealogy libraries have
helpful text files too.

Another person you should introduce yourself to is GFL George, the
forum leader. A professional genealogist, George Ferguson has over a
decade's experience with online genealogy and is willing to share, help,
and inform. As he says:

The Genealogy Forum on AOL has been my love and my passion since its
inception in 1988. With the help of many wonderful and dedicated volunteers, we have guided it to the place it is today. My Great Aunt Gertrude
Durham started me on my genealogy work when I was a boy by presenting
me with a 10-generation pedigree chart that was partially filled. I knew
right then my life's work was to fill in the spaces.

George started doing online genealogy research the day after he got
his first modem. George told me:

The best feature of the America Online Genealogy Forum would have to be
the ability to get 48 people from all over the country together in one online
room and talk about genealogy. It's great because you don't have to leave
the comfort of your own home, but you can get all kinds of questions
answered. We also have an outstanding collection of downloadable files. We
have programs and utilities for IBM-compatible systems, Macintosh systems, as well as Apple II systems. We have hundreds of lineage files, GED-
COM database files, genealogical records files, tiny tafel files, alphabetic
surname files, as well as logs of past meetings. We have a surnames area
where anyone can post a message about someone they are looking for. We
also have message boards that are designed to exchange information about
computer and non-computer genealogical subjects.

We have started several special-interest groups (SIGs), which are becoming quite popular. On different nights we have beginners' classes, an
African-American genealogy SIG, a Southern SIG, and a Scot-Irish SIG. In
the near future we hope to expand these offerings with expanded beginner
services, a New England research SIG, and a reunion software users group.

He points out that the online real-time conversations are a valuable
resource. There have been many meetings where somebody finds a

cousin or a possible link. It is also an opportunity to chat with people who have similar interests to you. And you don't have to go out at night or drive into a big city to do it. Also, unlike the big genealogy groups that get together only once every month or so, AOL members can get out and talk almost any night of the week. As George said:

> We expect people to come and share the passion for genealogy. We expect nothing but hope that everyone will share what they have with the rest of us and have fun doing it. What we find is that people freely give of themselves and that we can have a good time while learning different ways of investigating the past.

Another Forum host, GFH Ranch, said:

> Long before I assisted with a chat or had any formal involvement with AOL, I was a regular. For me, personally, the chats and message boards have been very instrumental in meeting cousins, which in turn leads to more sources, more information, and more options for research.
>
> I had used the genealogy newsgroups but prefer working the breakdown of topics that AOL offers. Messages boards are broken into portions of the alphabet and geographic locations, which dramatically reduces the amount you have to look through to find a possible connection. Chat sessions are narrowed to geographic areas (as well as offering general and beginner chats) and historical time periods.

Like many others on AOL, she has had good luck finding real information there:

> It is especially fun the first time you find a cousin. One time I helped a lady find a missing link because I had an editor's note in a book. And another contact sent me an ancestor's photograph, giving me a rare opportunity to share it with my family. I now have trouble remembering all the cousins I've met. Chats focus on families and heritage with a strong sense of "helping our brother out." We have folks in Tennessee offering to assist someone in Texas by calling the court house or photographing a tombstone.

For a beginning genealogist, AOL's Genealogy Forum is a wonderful tool.

14

CompuServe's Genealogy Forums

CompuServe is one of the oldest, and best, online services. For years it was based on a text interface: You typed in a command such as GO ROOTS and a text menu would appear for looking at messages, files, and announcements. A graphics interface was introduced in the early 1990s. CompuServe still uses GO words; the list of them is at GO WORD LIST; but other than that, little remains of the CompuServe interface of 20 years ago.

After CompuServe was bought by America Online in 1998, the service's software got a major overhaul. Underneath, it's still our beloved CompuServe. Despite sporting quite a few AOL-like features in the new interface, it's still the premier service for serious users ("adult" in the good sense). CompuServe users tend to be those who work for a living and use CompuServe to do their work and their hobbies faster, better, and cheaper. Following is the contact information for CompuServe:

5000 Arlington Centre Blvd.
P.O. Box 20212
Columbus, OH 43220
ph: 800-848-8199

The genealogy forums are still very active and have expanded to several different groups:

- *Genealogy Techniques Forum.* The place for beginners to share successes and to ask about how to get beyond a brick wall in their research. Here you can learn how to use your computer for genealogy, how to use the World Wide Web, and where to find professional genealogists. You can also learn about coats of arms, adoption searches, and more. This is the forum you get when you use the GO word ROOTS.

- *Genealogy Support Forum.* Major genealogy software vendors and major genealogy societies supply staff to answer questions, resolve problems, and make announcements about new events, software, patches, and updates. GO word: GENSUP.

- *North American Genealogy Forum.* For queries about ancestors in Canada, the U.S., and Mexico. GO word: NAROOTS.

- *World Wide Genealogy Forum.* For queries about ancestors anywhere but North America. GO word: WWROOTS.

CompuServe 2000, as the service is now called, has over two million subscribers; of those over 10,000 a week visit the Roots Forum, according to system operator Dick Eastman. However, true to form for most CompuServe forums, only about 5 percent of those who visit actually leave messages. That's a lot of lurkers! Yet the forum sees plenty of action, and the files and messages are valuable and worthwhile.

CompuServe's online genealogy resources have much to offer:

- Social Security Death Records online (link to ancestry.com)

- Nearly 2000 genealogy book reviews available online in the Roots forum

- More than 8000 genealogy-related files available online, including shareware and free genealogy programs for Windows, MS-DOS, Macintosh, Amiga, UNIX, and even older computers

The members of the forum are varied. There are online assistant system operatops ("sysops") and some recognized professional genealogists who drop in; other members are rank beginners. Many are in between.

The members are just as cooperative, outgoing, and friendly as anywhere online; in my opinion, this is one of the best hangouts for the online genealogist.

The newest software is based on the Microsoft Internet Explorer browser. However, not all the commands that work in Microsoft Internet Explorer work in CompuServe. For example, you can click the back arrow on the toolbar to go back a page, but ALT-LEFT ARROW won't work.

The software will be very familiar if you've ever used AOL. There's a check mark to add a forum or other service to your list of "favorites" instead of a heart, but the process is the same. Click the check mark, and choose from Add to Favorites, Add to an Instant Message, or Add to an Email Message (the latter two as links).

Getting to via the Internet and getting to the Internet via is wonderfully easy with 2000, and the software's interface hardly changes a whit when you do. You can either have a local ISP account and use that TCP/IP connection to get to CompuServe, or you can use the dial-up network connection and surf from CompuServe. Microsoft Internet Explorer is so masterfully integrated into the software you don't realize that's what you're using should you want to jump from the Genealogy Techniques Forum straight to the Library of Congress site. The only way you can tell the difference: The page box in the top of the screen is a URL with CompuServe somewhere in the name if you're still on the service. On installation, the software does a good job of installing the proper dial-up connection, complete with logon script. It worked the first time I used it.

Something that's missing from the new software as of this writing is the ability to download forum messages that interest you to read and answer offline. This has been available on CompuServe since the beginning up to the 1999 version of the software, but the new CompuServe 2000 requires you to be online to read and answer messages. This is a grave error, in my estimation, and makes the software much less usable. For this reason, many people are choosing to stay with the CompuServe Classic software, which allows you to download forum messages and file them in your filing cabinet.

However, many useful features have been added in CompuServe 2000:

■ Instant messaging, with buddy lists. It works only with other CompuServe members logged on at the same time you are. It is integrated into the Contact List, where you keep email addresses of people you write to often. It also works with AOL Instant Messenger (see Chapter 8).

- Spell check, special fonts, pictures, and attachments in email. In short, fully multimedia email. It's also POP3-compliant, so you can use Eudora, Outlook, or any other POP3 email reader. (POP stands for Post Office Protocol.)

- 56K/V.90 access with many access points in the U.S. and around the world, making it easy to use CompuServe when you travel.

- The ability to have several member names under your main account.

- Ability to download Usenet and email messages, and upload them at specified times. Unfortunately, this does not include messages in forums at this writing; for this, you have to stick with CompuServe Classic.

Forum Decorum

Regardless of the version of CompuServe you use, with the genealogy forums on CompuServe, you can exchange information with thousands of other members around the world, from experts and professionals to beginners. Everyone has something to contribute.

The goal of the three main forums is to create an atmosphere that encourages intelligent interaction and lively debate. They are very insistent on members using common sense and courtesy. If you have questions about how to proceed, you can contact the forum managers by posting a message addressed "To: SYSOP" on the message board of any forum.

This is a place that values free expression; you'll often find lively discussions and spirited debates. The membership is international; members are from diverse ethnic backgrounds and from backgrounds widely varied in education—something to keep in mind when you are reading and answering messages. The give-and-take can get quite energetic!

Dick Eastman, the sysop, encourages people of all backgrounds to participate. He is especially eager for members of ethnic minorities to become active in genealogy in order to ensure preservation of both their heritage and the records of importance to their genealogy.

There are a few rules:

- Keep it clean. No obscenities, slurs, or dirty jokes.
- No flames.
- Use smileys (emoticons; see Chapter 3 and Glossary) if your words could be taken the wrong way. Regardless, choose your words carefully.

- Use the spell checker. Also, avoid jargon, because the newbies need to understand your messages too.

- There are specific sections of the forum for posting on different subjects; be sure to post yours to the right one. If you simply place all your messages in the New to Genealogy...section, the people who can help you might miss them.

- Advertising is allowed under specific restrictions, as discussed immediately below.

Advertising on the Forums

Online advertising is a touchy subject. On the one hand, new products and services are a legitimate discussion topic among genealogists. On the other hand, some people feel they are already paying for CompuServe, and having to endure advertisements on top of that is insupportable.

In an attempt at compromise, the Genealogy Techniques Forum (GO word: ROOTS) has specific sections dedicated to announcements and discussions of commercial genealogy services and products. That way, if you want to see such information, you can find these messages and files quickly and easily. If you don't, just ignore those sections.

In the File Libraries, you can look at (and post to) Products/Services for advertising and announcements. The message board has two sections: Professional Genealogists and Services and Products. Now, Professional Genealogists is also a place for professional genealogists to gather and ask questions or discuss the latest issues in their business, so it is not a strictly advertising section. Still, you will find a fair number of ads there.

The catch to this permissible advertising: You are allowed to post only one message and only one text file per product. The file stays there until you ask a sysop to delete it; the message may scroll off as all messages eventually do. (You may answer any questions posted by others about your services or products at any time.) The text file should be in a "press release" format, ending with "For further information, contact..." or something similar. You can encourage the reader to contact you online or by conventional means, as appropriate.

On any genealogy forum's message board, do not post a message about goods or services that you produce or sell without clearly stating your connection. Avoid jumping into threads to recommend products you create or sell. So-called "bombing runs" (when you post many messages in different forum sections or by CompuServe Mail to promote your products or services) is rude, as is responding to forum messages by sending private email "advertisements."

In general, don't clutter the genealogy forums with nongenealogy, nonhistory or nonadoption traffic without the express permission of the managers (sysops). An exception is the sale of personal items, which is allowed; but even then it should be genealogy related.

All that said, you are nevertheless encouraged to provide technical support of your customers on the Genealogy Techniques Forum. There is a major difference between providing support and "advertising, soliciting, or promoting the purchase of goods or services."

If you see anyone breaking these general rules, you should contact the Genealogy Techniques Forum managers. Just post a message "To: SYSOP" on the forum, and it will be read by the next manager who enters the forum.

Sysops: The Forum Managers

Forum sysops manage the activities of the forums. This involves duties such as checking files and messages for appropriateness, chastising those who break the rules, and sometimes kicking off habitual offenders. The sysops will answer your questions about how to use the forum or general questions about genealogy; just address your message to "SYSOP." Remember, though, that addressing your message to "ALL" will get the attention of everyone; and that will let you tap into the know-how of thousands of Genealogy Forum members.

Sysops are not employees of the service; they are CompuServe users just like you. They just have more familiarity in genealogy and in the use of home computers for genealogy uses.

A Tour

I'm going to take you on a tour of the Genealogy Techniques Forum (GO word: ROOTS). You'll find that the North American Genealogy Forum (GO word: NAROOTS) and the World Wide Genealogy Forum (GO word: WWROOTS) work in much the same way. The Genealogy Vendors' Support Forum (GO word: GENSUP) is a bit different; it is operated by a number of genealogy societies and companies and used to support their customers.

Sign onto CompuServe, and use the GO word ROOTS. That is, type ROOTS in the white box at the top of the screen and click GO or press ENTER. As you can see in Figure 14-1, the opening screen has a lot on it. Let's take it bit by bit.

My username is at the bottom ("Welcome, EPCrowe/AL"). The first time you sign on, you are asked to choose a name to use in the forum; often people put the state they live in as part of the forum name. All genealogy forums ask that you use your real name, not a handle or your CompuServe sign-on ID. At the same time, I filled out a profile to tell

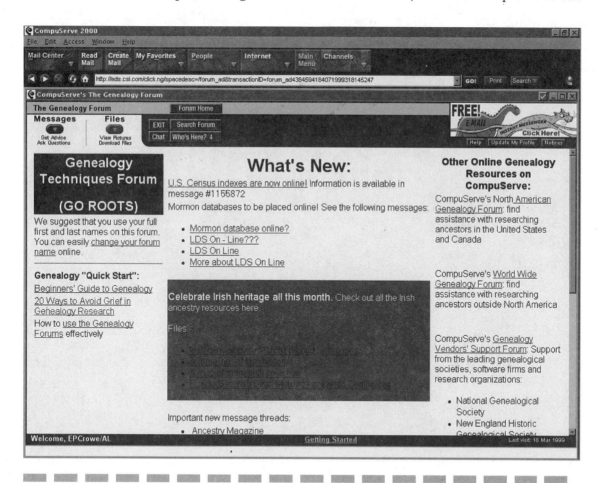

Figure 14-1 The opening screen of the Genealogy Techniques Forum has links to all the things you can do on the forum.

other users in the forum my interests. The tradition in the genealogy forums is to start with the surnames you are searching, perhaps with geographical locations and other items of interest. My profile is shown in Figure 14-2; you get to this screen by clicking on `Update My Profile` in the upper right corner of the screen. You can search the forum's member database for surnames.

At the very top of the screen is the menu bar, where you find the usual commands: `File`, `Edit`, `Window`, and `Help` behave as you'd expect them to. `Access` allows you to change things like what number is dialed to log

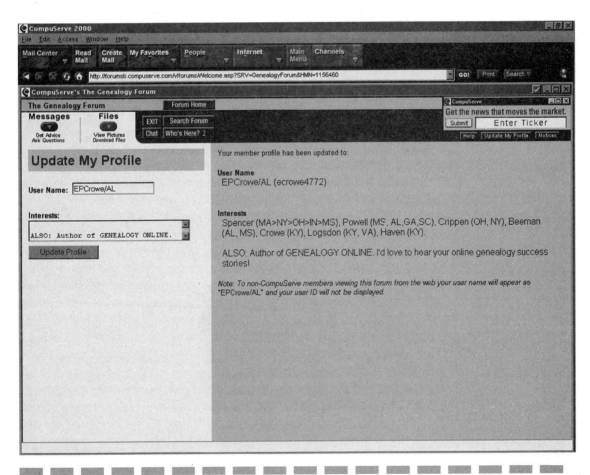

Figure 14-2 List the surnames you are searching for in your profile; you can also search member profiles for the surnames you are interested in.

on, passwords, and parental controls. You can also check on how long you've been on.

Under the menu bar is the CompuServe toolbar. You can customize it by choosing to have it large or compact, and you can drag the check mark of any window to create a toolbar button.

Under the CompuServe toolbar is the standard Microsoft Internet Explorer toolbar: The round buttons are for forward and back, stop, reload, and home. The URL box is where you type in GO words or WWW URLs. Click the `GO` button to activate the GO word; the `Print` and `Search` buttons do what you'd expect.

Just below that you have a window within a window; this is the forum's opening page. The bar across the top has the name of the forum; the `Forum Home` button brings you back here from the other screens in the forum. This bar remains constant no matter what you're doing in the forum.

The screen in Forum Home has links, news, and announcements pertinent to the specific forum. The details on this page will change often; you'll notice that this screen capture was made in March 1999, so the highlights have to do with Irish genealogy and history.

The two buttons, `Messages` and `Files`, have similar functions. They will both change the window to show the sections of the forum and let you search or browse through them. When I searched for *online* in messages, I got four message threads with *online* in the subject. By clicking on `Census Indexes Online`, I got the results in Figure 14-3.

In this view, you can see four topics that matched my search in the upper left, the names of those who posted messages on the selected topic in the lower left, and the text of the first message in the right. By clicking on any message, I can read it in the right-hand pane. Searching Files looks much the same.

So, now I'll click on the `Files` button and browse instead of search. By clicking on the topic `Internet Genealogy` in the Files section, I get the screen in Figure 14-4.

One thing I don't like about the version of the software available in 1999: In the older versions you could sort this list of files by date, title, author, or how many times it's been downloaded by members. You could also mark several files for batch download. Neither option remains in the software as of this writing. It's something I hope they fix soon.

Browsing Messages looks much the same as Browsing Files: click on the section, look at the topics, read specific messages. You can also right-click and save messages to your file cabinet on disk for later reference.

Figure 14-3 Topics, authors, and messages are read in this window.

This is a good idea, since messages tend to "scroll off"—that is, the oldest get deleted to make room for the newest.

To contribute a file, click the `Contribute` button. Choose the appropriate file section, and then click the `Contribute File` button. Do not upload anything unless you have the rights (under copyright law, for example) to the files you contribute.

The first time you visit this page, CompuServe will attempt to automatically download and install software (an ActiveX control) on your computer. You may be asked for permission to download this control, depending on your security settings. Go ahead and allow it.

As mentioned in Chapter 8, CompuServe has regularly scheduled chats on genealogy in all the forums. Anytime you are on, you can click

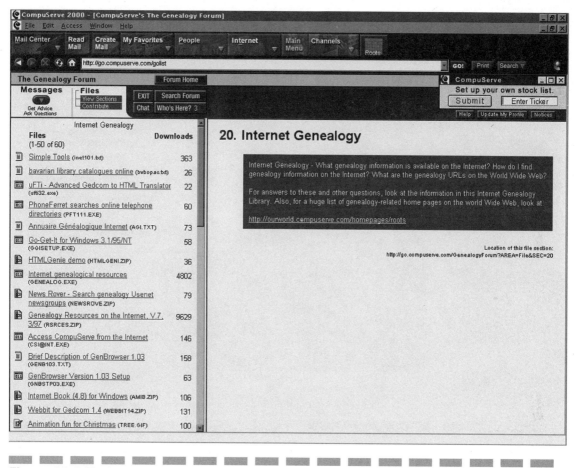

Figure 14-4 To download a file on CompuServe, simply right-click the title and save it to your disk.

the `Chat` button to see whether any chats are going on. Or you can click the `Who's Here?` button and invite someone to an impromptu chat. Figure 14-5 shows you the windows that pop up when you click those buttons. They are separate from the main CompuServe window, so you can click on the main window and send them to the back, or cascade or tile them all.

The hosted conferences (chats) on CompuServe are excellent. In one famous case, sysop Dick Eastman saved the life of a member who was having a stroke during a live chat by noticing that something was wrong and getting help to the member's home. Usually, however, chats are exciting only for the fun and interesting people who participate. You are free to host one whenever you like. Just announce it in the messages.

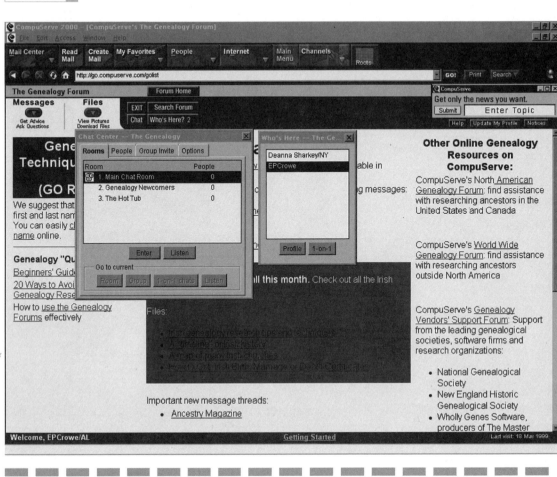

Figure 14-5 Find someone to chat with on CompuServe's genealogy forums.

The schedule as of this writing is as follows:

- The traditional, weekly "free-for-all conference" is held every Tuesday evening at 10:00 P.M. EST, 7:00 P.M. PST (02:00 A.M. Wednesday GMT). Join everyone in the Main Conference Room on this forum. (Sign on, go to ROOTS at that time, click on CHAT, then click on Main Conference Room.) The subjects discussed in this chat are wide-open. Genealogy-related conversations and nongenealogy chats mingle together in the Tuesday evening online chats.

- A New England conference is held on the first Thursday of each month at 9:00 P.M. EST in the New England Conference Room of NAROOTS. Watch the message board for topics to be covered at each conference.

- Monthly online conferences discussing the excellent genealogy resources of the Daughters of the American Revolution are held on the fourth Sunday of the month at 7:00 P.M. EST.

- Online chats for birth mothers are held every Monday evening at 9:00 P.M. EST, 6:00 P.M. PST in the North American Genealogy Forum at GO word: NAROOTS. These online conferences are held in the Adoption Searches Conference Room.

- Check out all the new conference rooms in the North American Genealogy Forum (GO word: NAROOTS) and the World Wide Genealogy Forum (GO word: WWROOTS). You probably will find a conference room devoted to one of your favorite topics.

The final button for you to notice is the `Notices` button (just beyond the `Help` button). Here is where you'll find text files with the latest information about the workings of the forum. News Flash, Messages, General, and so forth all have information the sysops want you to know. See Figure 14-6.

The Genealogy Vendors' Support Forum

The genealogy-related forum that is different, as I indicated, is the Genealogy Vendors' Support Forum (GENSUP). It is slightly misnamed, because besides the strictly commercial groups such as Wholly Genes Software and Brother's Keeper, you'll also find the New England Historic Genealogical Society and the National Genealogical Society. The opening page (Figure 14-7) gives links to each area.

How it works: Each group gets a section in the files and messages; the topics must stick to the section subject; and all notices, members, and profiles are shared among them. Conferences are not scheduled within GENSUP; you can hold them whenever you wish. Just be sure to use the appropriate room for the product, service, or organization that you want to discuss. The conference rooms are as follows:

- *Room 1* New England Historic Genealogical Society
- *Room 2* Wholly Genes Software (The Master Genealogist)
- *Room 4* Brothers Keeper
- *Room 5* CommSoft, Inc. (Roots IV)
- *Room 7* Everton Publishers
- *Room 8* National Genealogical Society

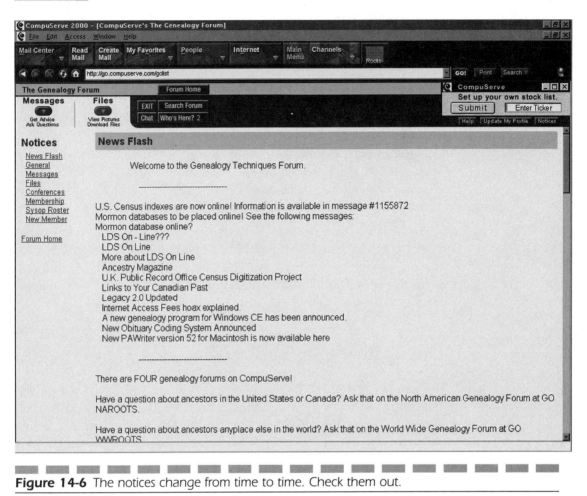

Figure 14-6 The notices change from time to time. Check them out.

■ *Room 9*   Schröder and Fülling GbR (German-speaking genealogy research service)

Genealogy Sysop Dick Eastman

Of being a sysop, Dick Eastman says: "It's lots of fun, but no money." Along with several other Roots Forum members, he attends all GEN-TECH conferences to help promote the forum. That's just one of his many functions as sysop. He also manages the files, checks for viruses, keeps the messages where they should be, and offers advice to new genealogists. Eastman recruits assistant sysops as well. He's the buffer between

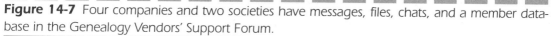

Figure 14-7 Four companies and two societies have messages, files, chats, and a member database in the Genealogy Vendors' Support Forum.

the technical people at CompuServe headquarters and the CompuServe user. The goal is to keep problems to a minimum, both in using the service and in doing genealogy.

"We're very much a referral service," Eastman says. "Like a football coach, we won't play the game for you, but we'll help you learn the best game plans." He likes to do that on the forums, but, amazing as it is to him, he says that many people are too shy to post a public message; they send him private email with their questions instead. He'd prefer to answer questions where all can benefit from the answers, though.

"We're a social group," he says, "and we have a lot of fun. We get together at conferences like this [GENTECH] and meet face-to-face when we can. But I love the online environment. I'm a die-hard techie, and I think it's so much fun!"

Over and over, he says, people have found relatives on the Roots Forum, or because of it. One of the most affecting, he says, was once when he was demonstrating Roots and the Phone*File system at a National Genealogical Society meeting. A woman found a name and number she thought might be her long-lost father, though she didn't dare hope. Still, she went to the pay phone, and sure enough, was on the phone to him in minutes, arranging a reunion after 30 years. "She had tears running down her cheeks because she was flying to Philadelphia to see her father that next week. I could hardly talk the rest of the day, I was so choked up," he says.

Gaye Spencer, another sysop, had a mysterious Amirilla Eastman in her lineage, whose parents she just couldn't place. One day, though, a long message was posted on the Roots Forum about an Eastman family of the right period and all the siblings of that family—and there was Amirilla!

Dick Eastman himself found a relative he was able to help online. His French-Canadian Dubay line was hard to find, partly because of variant spellings. But he knew of a history professor of that name, and using Phone*File, Eastman discovered that the fellow lived within 25 miles of where Eastman knew his ancestors to be from.

Calling the gentleman, he found out that the professor had just self-published 1200 copies of a genealogy of the family and was having trouble selling them. Eastman sent the professor gummed labels with every Dubay (and variant spelling) he could find on Phone*File. The professor mailed each one a notice of the book. The result was a wonderful Dubay reunion, and a sold-out printing of the genealogy!

Dick Eastman is typical of the sort of person you'll find on CompuServe. The CompuServe genealogy forums were the first online genealogy resource I found, nearly 20 years ago. I still find them among the best of online resources.

APPENDIX A

The GenServ Project

The Original GEDCOM exchange

GenServ, which stands for Genealogical GEDCOM Server, is an idea that was unique at its beginning (see Appendix C) but has been copied by several commercial Web sites since. People upload their GEDCOMs, and for a fee of $1 a month, they are free to search the thousands of uploaded GEDCOMs, finding other researchers to correspond with. Two differences with GenServ: (1) the searches can be done by email; send in your query, go shopping, then come home and get your answers, and (2) the cost is minimal (in fact, you can do a trial search for free!). GenServe is more of a cooperative effort than similar commercial Web sites.

The GenServ System contains an international collection of GEDCOM files submitted by the subscribers. The system is based on the idea of sharing your family history information with others by using your GEDCOM data. To become a member, you must send in a GEDCOM file; the money is only to help support the people who are using their computers, hard drives, and Internet service provider accounts to run GenServ.

You don't download GEDCOMs from GenServ; instead, you search them for specific data, and then get reports on the data, including the name and address of the person who contributed it. Then you can start corresponding with the people whose data matches your family.

NOTE *Do not send in a check without sending your data.*

Loading your data to the system is key. Although you can find out if you have matches in GenServ without contributing either money or data, to get the names and addresses of submitters on the system, you must be a contributing member of GenServ—and that means you must provide data.

Let me remind you: The information in GEDCOMs should always be considered secondary source information. Even if the GEDCOM has cited sources, you should verify the information yourself in case of inadvertent errors.

NOTE *If you need to write to a real live person about all this, Cliff Manis is the guy. You can contact him at:*

Cliff Manis
Gen Serv System
P.O. Box 33937
San Antonio, TX 78265-3937
U.S.A.
or at:
Cmanis@genserv.com

How to Subscribe

Here are four easy steps to join GenServ:

1. *Create a GEDCOM file.* Every commercial genealogy program can do this. Usually, it's under File or Export on the commands menu. An example is shown in the upcoming sidebar. GenServ has a very helpful file on how to make sure your GEDCOM comes out well. To get it, send email to gedmake@genserv.com. The instructions will be sent back to you via email.

    GenServ's site also has a list of genealogy software programs on this system showing links to many different programs that have been used by the subscribers to send in GEDCOM data.

Exporting a GEDCOM is usually easy. For example, the GenServ site shows you how to do it in Family Tree Maker:
1. Open the family file you'd like to use to make the GEDCOM.
2. Select `File`, then `Copy/Export Family File`.
3. Click on the `Save as Type` drop-down list and select `GEDCOM (*.GED)`.
4. In the File Name field, type a name for the GEDCOM file. It must have the extension .GED.
5. In the Save in fields, select the drive and folder where you want to place your file.

6. Click on Save, and the File Type dialog box will be displayed. In the Destination field, if available, choose FTW. This offers the most complete selection. If the program you are exporting to is not listed, choose FTM. In the GEDCOM field, select Version 5.5. In the Character Set field, select ANSI.

NOTE Be sure to leave the Indent Tabs checkbox unselected. The Abbreviate Tags checkbox should be selected.

7. Click on OK, and Family Tree Maker creates the GEDCOM file.

NOTE Protect the privacy of living persons in your database. You can do this in two ways. You can copy the original Family Tree Maker file and remove the vital statistics for your living relatives from this copy, or you can use a utility program to delete that information for you. Please remember to use the utility on the copy of your original Family Tree Maker file.

8. There is a very easy GEDCOM utility available for free to remove living people's vital statistics from your GEDCOM file. This utility should be run after you've created your GEDCOM file. It's available for download from http://www.rootsweb.com/~gumby/ ged.html.

9. Run the GEDCOM utility. In the From field, click on Browse and select your new GEDCOM file. In the To field, save this new GEDCOM file (with living people's data removed) with a new name. Select Remove Details in the Processing Options field and select the cutoff year. Then click on Process.

10. Now you're ready to send your GEDCOM file to GenServ. Open your email program and create a new email document, addressing it to gedcom@genserv.com

11. Attach the GEDCOM file to this email, and click on Send.

2. Go to http://www.genserv.com/gs3/ inforeq.html. Here, you'll find the GenServ Information Request Form (see Figure A-1). This form gives them your name and address, and allows them to collect some profile data of their users, helping them fine-tune the site for better features. Fill out and submit the form.

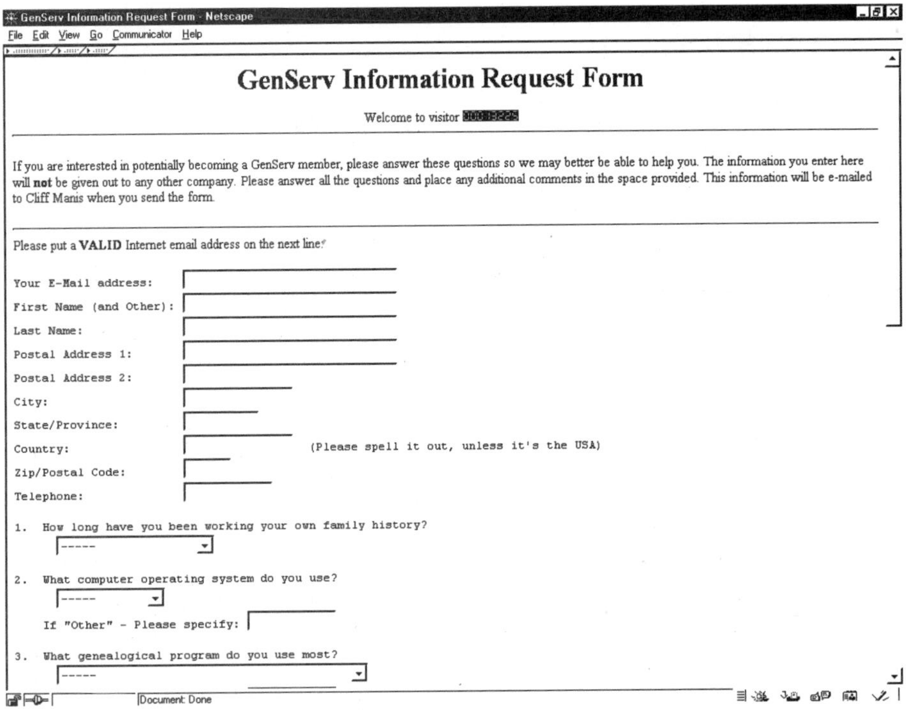

Figure A-1 The registration form on GenServ is part of the sign-up process.

3. Send your GEDCOM file to GenServ. You will receive confirmation within 24 hours that your file was received. For information on the different ways to send the file, send for one of these explanations:
   - How to send a GEDCOM email; send email to genem@genserv.com
   - How to send a GEDCOM FTP; send email to genftp@genserv.com
   - How to postal mail a GEDCOM; send email to genpostal@genserv.com

4. Choose your type of membership:
   - *Trial Subscription.* You can try GenServ for free for two months after submitting your GEDCOM. You get 12 requests per hour to the system. Trial subscriptions do not include access to the Web pages or submitter information with the reports from the data-

bases. One trial access per person/email address regardless of the number of GEDCOM files submitted. Also, members over the age of 80 are given complimentary memberships!

- *Regular Subscription.* For $12 (£8 UK), you get a one-year membership, with a maximum 12 requests per hour.
- *Senior or Student Subscription.* If you're over 60 or a student, a one-year subscription costs $6 (£4 UK), with a maximum of 12 requests per hour.
- *Sponsor Subscription.* A sponsor account costs $20 or more per year (£14 UK) and allows you up to 25 requests per hour.
- *Prime Sponsor Subscription.* A Prime Sponsor account costs $35 or more per year (£20 UK) and allows you up to 60 request per hour.

NOTE *Use only this address for postal mail to GenServ or Cliff Manis: Cliff Manis, GenServ System, P.O. Box 33937, San Antonio, TX 78265-3937, U.S.A. Or for those living in Europe only: Jon Rees, Church Cottage, Ringsfield, Beccles, Suffolk, NR34 8JU, UK. email: J.M.Rees@cefas.co.uk.*

How soon you hear back depends on how you sent in your GEDCOM, from 24 hours for FTP to a couple of weeks for surface mail. As soon as your GEDCOM file is tested and successfully uploaded to GenServ, you will be sent an ID and instructions on how to use email to access GenServ.

NOTE *If you have questions or problems, send them to ADMIN@genserv.com with the following information:*

Your name

Your email address

How, when, and where you sent your GEDCOM file and what you named it.

Please remember that the staff members at GenServ are all volunteers. Most of them also have full-time jobs and family. They are all addicted to genealogy and do the best they can to get your files uploaded as fast as possible and to help you learn the system.

How Does GenServ Work?

The simple answer: You send an email message with your GenServ ID number and a search command, with or without limiters. Within minutes, you will get back a formatted reply with the information you asked for. (See Figure A-2.)

The detailed explanation, of course, is a little more involved. The details are in the file GenHow2. The latest version of this file may be obtained anytime by sending any message (even a blank one) to genhow2@GenServ.COM.

The file as of this writing includes these topics:

1) RULES FOR SUBSCRIBERS
   1. For best results in using this system, read these instructions all the way through before trying them.
   2. Subscribers in REGULAR, SENIOR, or STUDENT GenServ Subscription Categories may send up to 12 commands per any one hour. You may upgrade your category at anytime by sending the difference in subscription amounts. Subscribers over age 80 get access free; email cmanis@genserv.com for details.
   3. Subscribers in the PRIME SPONSOR category may send up to 60 requests to the server per any one hour. (Please note: This was only 50 per hour but has been changed to 60 requests per hour.)
   4. For your own benefit, read the GenServ DISCLAIMER page.
   5. Do not forget that New Info will be seen first by Subscribers in the "fileset" file.

2) SEARCHCOUNT
   SearchCount tells you how many hits you have in all the databases. It's a quick way to see what's there. All SearchCount commands go to: SEARCHCOUNT@GenServ.com.

```
ID: CM12345
```

(Instead of `CM12345`, use your own ID#.)

```
SEARCH NAME: manis
```

Instead of `manis`, you may put any surname.)

Note: The options listed under 4) SEARCH NAME COMMAND EXPANDED can be used with SearchCount.

```
☑ Search: spencer, abraham (Part:001) - Message (Plain Text)                              _ 🗗 ✕
 File  Edit  View  Insert  Format  Tools  Actions  Help
 ✉Reply  ✉Reply to All  ✉Forward   🖨  ✂ 🖹  ▼  ⬚ ✕  ▲ ▾ ▾  ⬚ 🖼 ⓘ ✇  ⬚ Options...
From:     GenServ - Genealogical Server [gendaemon@GenServ.COM]           Sent:  Tue 4/13/99 7:42 AM
To:       Crowe, Elizabeth Powell
Cc:
Subject:  Search: spencer, abraham (Part:001)

Please DO NOT REPLY to this message. Requests for HUMAN INTERVENTION          ▲
should be addressed to <ADMIN@GenServ.COM>.

*-Cut-----> Cut on this line and at the end of this message <------Cut-*
This is request number 1 of 12 allowed for this hour.
Your account expires on 31 December, 2001.

                   INDEX OF SURNAMES FOUND
===============================================================================
(SNDX=Soundex, S=Sex, P=Parents known, F=# families, Chi=# children)

Last, First Name     INDI#  Spouse Name      SNDX Birthdate   Deathdate    Dbase
------------------   -----  ---------------- ---- ----------- -----------  -------
Spencer, Abraham     10037  , Patty          S152                          THOC8JR

Spencer, Abraham     12729  Comer, Mary      S152      1827         1880 STEC7NF

Spencer, Abraham     12958  , Christena      S152      1811              STEC7NF

Spencer, Abraham     13170                   S152                         STEC7NF

Spencer, Abraham     2089   ?, Nancy L. (W\O S152      1808         1850 SMIN8DA

Spencer, Abraham     2369   Donaldson, Grazi S152      1801         1861 STEC7NF

Spencer, Abraham     2771                    S152 04 Jul 1753 26 Jan 1766 WILQ7NA

Spencer, Abraham     5050                    S152      1616         1655 STEC7NF

SPENCER, Abraham     5404   CROSS, Mary A.   S152 23 Jun 1786              EAGB6EA

Spencer, Abraham     589                     S152 17 Oct 1738         1741 STOC8CM

Spencer, Abraham     6066   Bush, Tabatha    S152      1779              SMIN8DA

Spencer, Abraham     638                     S152                         FORCE1

Spencer, Abraham     9236   Dickerson, Lucy  S152                         SMIN8DA
                                                                              ⬚
```

Figure A-2 This list of Abraham Spencers came back to me within five minutes of my request.

3) *SEARCH NAME COMMAND BASICS*

All search name commands go to: SEARCH@GenServ.com. ID and SEARCH NAME are the *only* required fields, everything else is optional. Names with apostrophes (like "O'Brian") will be found with SEARCH NAME.

You may send the command:

```
ID: CM12345
```

(Instead of CM12345, use your own ID#.) Only those subscribers who have sent in a GEDCOM datafile will have access to this system.

```
SEARCH NAME: manis
```

(Instead of manis, you may put ANY SURNAME).
or

```
ID: CM12345
SEARCH NAME: Spencer, A
```

or

```
ID: CM12345
SEARCH NAME: Spencer, Abraham
```

You then will get something like this:

```
Please DO NOT REPLY to this message. Requests for HUMAN INTERVENTION

should be addressed to <ADMIN@GenServ.COM>.

*-Cut—> Cut on this line and at the end of this message <—Cut-*

This is request number 1 of 12 allowed for this hour.

Your account expires on 31 December, 2001.

                INDEX OF SURNAMES FOUND


======================================================================

(SNDX=Soundex, S=Sex, P=Parents known, F=# families, Chi=# children)

Last, First Name INDI# Spouse Name SNDX Birthdate Deathdate Dbase

_____  ___  _____  __  ____  ____  ___


Spencer, Abraham 10037 , Patty    S152           THOC8JR

Spencer, Abraham 12729 Comer, Mary  S152  1827   1880 STEC7NF

Spencer, Abraham 12958 , Christena S152  1811       STEC7NF
```

```
Spencer, Abraham 13170          S152        STEC7NF

Spencer, Abraham 2089 ?, Nancy L. (W\O S152 1808    1850 SMIN8DA

Spencer, Abraham 2369 Donaldson, Grazi S152 1801    1861 STEC7NF

Spencer, Abraham 2771 S152 04 Jul 1753 26 Jan 1766 WILQ7NA

Spencer, Abraham 5050 S152     1616        1655 STEC7NF

SPENCER, Abraham 5404 CROSS, Mary A. S152 23 Jun 1786   EAGB6EA

Spencer, Abraham          589 S152 17 Oct 1738    1741 STOC8CM

Spencer, Abraham 6066 Bush, Tabatha S152     1779       SMIN8DA

Spencer, Abraham 638          S152          FORCE1

Spencer, Abraham 9236 Dickerson, Lucy S152       SMIN8DA

Spencer, Abraham D 13164      S152    1837       STEC7NF

Spencer, Abraham H 12749 Fisher, Rebecca S152 19 Jul 1851 1934 STEC7NF

Spencer, Abraham M 13181        S152 07 Oct 1871 06 Nov 1894
STEC7NF

***** 16 entries found for name: "spencer, abraham" *****
```

Our supply of data is constantly growing. If these search results do not include the person(s) you are particularly hunting, you should try again later. When you do, you can make things easier for yourself by looking only at new data by excluding all data submitted before today. (See the documentation for a description of how to do that by using the "LOADED SINCE" phrase.)

4) SEARCH COMMAND EXPANDED

ID and SEARCH NAME are the *only* required fields; everything else is optional. Say you want to exclude your own database or your cousin's, or ones you know from past searches just don't have what you want. Then you use the EXCLUDE command with the database name (the last column in the example).

```
ID: AA12345
EXCLUDE: smittd1, bruq6na
```

You can put in up to 10 EXCLUDEs, separated by commas, spaces, or commas and spaces. If you want to be sure to search a particular database:

```
INCLUDE: mb5
```

This command has the same limitations as EXCLUDE. However, you cannot have both INCLUDE and EXCLUDE in the same message.

To search for specific names:

```
SEARCH NAME: Abbott
```

     or

```
SEARCH NAME: Abbott, J
```

     or

```
SEARCH NAME: Abbott, John
```

This has some optional commands:

```
BORN BEFORE: 01 Jan 1960
BORN AFTER: 01 Jan 1940
DIED BEFORE: 01 Jan 1960
DIED AFTER: 01 Jan 1940
LOADED SINCE: 10 Feb 1996
```

Of course, you would put in your wanted date after the colon in each example.

LIST FIELDS Command

With this command, you can have only specific fields of a match sent back to you. The field numbers and their associated data are as follows:

1. Name
2. INDI#

3. Spouse Name

4. Soundex

5. Birth Date

6. Death Date

7. Database Name

8. S = Sex (M or F)

9. P = Parents (Y or N)

10. F = Family (# of generations)

11. Chi = Children (# of)

12. Birthplace

13. Death Place

14. Last Update of this Database

If you use LIST FIELDS : All, then you will get all this information on a certain name. If you omit it, you get the results shown in the example, 1 through 8 above. So, the command:

```
LIST FIELDS: 1 2 3 4 5 8
```

will give you those fields, and the records will be sorted by the first field. The command:

```
LIST FIELDS: 5 1 2 3 7
```

would show *only* the birth date, name, INDI, spouse name, and database, in that order, sorted by the first field (birth date).

You can also control the look of the output. Using the LIST WIDTH command tells GenServ where to put the right margin on your reports. There is a minimum of 60, a maximum of 200, and a default of 80.

If your email account has limits on the size of a message, you can use the SPLIT command to control the length of reports. It can be set as high as 5000 KB or as small as 16 KB.

NOTE *Before using any split size over 100 KB, ask your Internet provider if they have any limitations on email message size. Omitting SPLIT leaves your messages at the default limit of 50 KB.*

By default your original request is appended to the end of the message sent from GenServ. If you want to disable this feature, add the following line to any request you send:

```
SHOW REQUEST: NO
```

SEND COMMAND

To get files from GenServ, send a message with your ID on one line and SEND: <fileid> in the next.

NOTE *All SEND commands go to SEND@GenServ.com.*

```
SEND: datadate - Current listing and time each database was loaded.
SEND: datatot - Name and date/time/size of last few databases loaded.
SEND: genhow2 - The How-To file
SEND: geninfo - The latest current documentation for the GenServ
       system
SEND: genrpts - Samples of all available reports. Get this and print
       it out. It's very handy.
SEND: idinfo - You will receive back your own name/address info.
SEND: fileset - Current listing of files, plus late-breaking news.
Some older files are also listed in the fileset file.
```

Send a blank message to the addresses below to request these files:

geninfo@GenServ.com—Latest information about GenServ

genhow2@GenServ.com—How to format requests

genrpts@GenServ.com—Sample reports; a must have!

gedmake@GenServ.com—How to make a GEDCOM file

genem@GenServ.com—How to send a GEDCOM email

genftp@GenServ.com—How to send a GEDCOM FTP

genpostal@GenServ.com—How to send a GEDCOM postal mail

disclaimer@GenServ.com—GenServ disclaimer

There are many more, detailed searches you can do with GenServ; be sure to get the file GENRPTS, mentioned above, to see a good selection of them.

GenServ is not the only GEDCOM exchange, but it's the most reasonably priced, and it's a cooperative venture. Furthermore, updating your GEDCOM twice a year on GenServ is a good plan to back up your data.

You should at least give the one free search a try at http:/
www.genserv.com/gs3/samplesearch.html. (See Figure A-3.)

Report Command

When you get back your results of a name search, you can get more information on individuals listed in the reply to your search query. The
reports you can get are vitals, family, Ahnentafel (see Appendix C), four
generations, two kinds of descendant trees, and any special report you
design. The two important things to use are the INIV number (column 2)
and database name (column 7).

To get a report, you send an email message to REPORT@genserv.com
formatted like this:

```
ID: Your ID number here
REPORT: The name of the report you want here.
DATABASE: The database name from column 7 of the search response.
INDI: The number of the person you want information on, from column 2
of the search response.
```

For example, if you want the vital statistics on someone, you would
send a message such as:

```
ID: xx12345 <your number here>
REPORT: vitals
DATABASE: MB5
INDI: 171
```

You would get this:

```
GenServ Report Output: vitals                    11 Jan 1997
        Alda Clifford MANIS (171), born 11 Mar 1939, Knoxville,
        Knox Co, TN (Twin), son of Fuller Ruben MANES (76) and
        Edith Alberta MANIS (169). SOURCE NOTES: RESEARCH NOTES:
        Clifford only lived at two different locations before he
graduat                                    .
        (cut short to show here and on the web)
            Children of Alda Clifford MANIS and Joyce Fern
OWENS:
    1 Gregory Scott MANIS (429), born 15 Sep 1963, Warren-
      ton, Fauquier Co, VA. SOURCE NOTES: RESEARCH NOTES: Scott
      attended school in Mexico City, Mexico, where he started
            (cut short to show here and on the web)
    2 Sheila Ann MANIS (430), born 7 Apr 1968, Mexico City,
      Mexico DF.
        Alda Clifford MANIS and Marianne Florence KRAMER had no
children
```

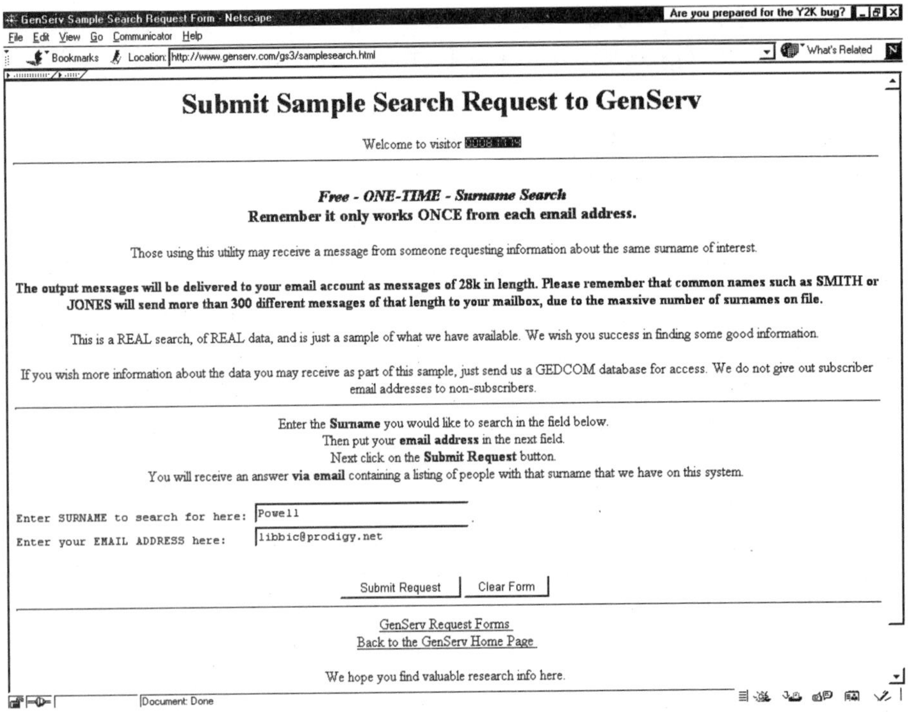

Figure A-3 You can have one free sample search of the GenServ GEDCOM database by filling out this Web form.

```
                        listed in the database.

=======================================================================

Information is from the MB5 database belonging to:
  submitter: Manis, Cliff
  email: ADMIN@genserv.com
  street_1: PO Box 33937
  street_2:
  city: San Antonio
  state: TX
  zip: 78265
  country: USA
```

The FAMILY report is a basic family group sheet: the individual, spouse, and children with known dates and locations. The AHNENTAFEL gives you a complete, direct ancestry of the individual you requested, with brief information, in Ahnentafel format. The 4GEN report gives you the individual's parents, grandparents, and great-grandparents, each generation indented another space. DESCENDANTS, as you'd expect, gives you direct descendants of the individual. The other reports are simply the same information in different formatting.

APPENDIX B

Genealogy Online Books

Title	Publisher	Author	Price	ISBN
Genealogy Via the Internet: Tracing Your Family Roots Quickly and Easily	Alexander Books	Ralph Roberts	$12.95	1570900094
Genealogy Online for Dummies	IDG Books Worldwide	Matthew L. Helm April Helm	$24.99	0764503774
Netting Your Ancestors	Genealogical Publishing Co.	Cyndi Howells	$19.95	0806315466
Virtual Roots	Scholarly Resources	Thomas J. Kemp	$24.95	0842027203
Cyber Roots	Ancestry, Inc.	Laurie Bonner Steve Bonner	$16.95	0916489787
The Genealogy Forum on America Online: The Official User's Guide	Ancestry, Inc.	George G. Morgan	$19.95	0916489876

APPENDIX C

Forms of Genealogical Data

Ahnentafels, Tiny Tafels, and GEDCOMs

One of the reasons to get involved in the online genealogy world is to share the information you have, as well as to find information you don't have. To do that, standards have been set up for transmitting that information: Ahnentafels, tiny tafels, and GEDCOMs. They are all designed to put information in a standard format. The last two are readable by many different genealogical database programs, and many utilities have been written to translate information from one to another.

Ahnentafels

Ahnentafels are not big tiny tafels. The word means "ancestor table" in German, and the format is more than a century old. It lists all known ancestors of an individual and includes the full name of each ancestor, as well as dates and places of birth, marriage, and death. It organizes this information along a strict numbering scheme.

Once you get used to Ahnentafels, reading them becomes very easy as you move up and down from parent to child and back again. The numbering scheme is the key to it all. Consider this typical pedigree chart:

```
                              8. great grandfather
            4. paternal grandfather, |
            |                 9. great grandmother
      2. Father, |
      |     |                 10. great grandfather
      |     5. paternal grandmother, |
      |                       11. great grandmother
1. Person, |
      |
      |                       12. great grandfather
      |     6. maternal grandfather, |
      |     |                 13. great grandmother
      3. Mother, |
            |                 14. great grandfather
            7. maternal grandmother, |
                              15. great grandfather
```

Study the numbers in the above chart. Every person listed has a number, with a mathematical relationship between parents and children. The number of a father is always double that of his child's. The number of the mother is always double that of her child's plus one. The number of a child is always one-half that of its parent (ignoring any remainder).

In this example, the father of person #6 is #12, the mother of #6 is #13, and the child of #13 is #6. In Ahnentafel format, the chart reads like this:

1. person
2. father
3. mother
4. paternal grandfather
5. paternal grandmother
6. maternal grandfather
7. maternal grandmother
8. great grandfather
9. great grandmother
10. great grandfather
11. great grandmother
12. great grandfather
13. great grandmother
14. great grandfather
15. great grandmother

Notice that the numbers are exactly the same as in the pedigree chart. The rules of father = 2 × child, mother = 2 × child + 1, child = parent / 2, ignore remainder, and so on remain the same. This is an Ahnentafel chart.

In practice, Ahnentafels are rarely uploaded as text files, but it's one way to show what you do know about your tree quickly and in few characters. Just clearly state that it's an Ahnentafel. Some Web sites list genealogies as Ahnentafels.

Tiny Tafels

Despite the similar name, a tiny tafel (TT) is a different animal. It provides a standard way of describing a family database so that the information can be scanned visually or by computer. It was described in an article entitled "Tiny-Tafel for Database Scope Indexing" by Paul Andereck in the April-May-June 1986 issue (vol. 5, no. 4) of *Genealogical Computing*.

The concept of TTs was adopted by COMMSOFT first in their popular program, Roots II, and later in Roots III. It has since been adapted by other genealogical programs, such as Brother's Keeper and GED2TT.

A TT makes no attempt to include the details that are contained in an Ahentafel. All data fields are of fixed length, with the obvious exceptions of the surnames and optional places. A TT lists only surnames of interest (with Soundex) plus the locations and dates of the beginning and end of that surname. Tiny tafels make no provision for first names, births, marriages, deaths, or multiple locations.

The format of the tiny tafel is rigidly controlled. Here's the specification as released by COMMSOFT:

```
Header:
Column       Description
1     Header type
2     Space delimiter
3 - n Text (n < 38) (n + 1) Carriage Return
Defined types:
Header
Type         Description                  Remarks
N Name of person having custody of data    Mandatory first record
A Address data                    0 to 5 address lines
                            Optional
T Telephone number including area code    Optional
S Communication Service/telephone number  0 to 5 service lines
  (MCI, ITT, ONT, RCA, ESL, CIS, SOU, etc, Optional
e.g., CIS/77123,512)
B Bulletin Board/telephone number       Optional
C Communications nnnn/X/P               Optional
    nnnn = maximum baud rate
    X = O(riginate only), A(nswer only), B(oth)
    P = Protocol (Xmodem, Kermit, etc.)
D Diskette format d/f/c           Optional
    d = diameter (3, 5, 8)
    f = format MS-DOS, Apple II, etc.
    c = capacity, KB
F File format                 Free-form, optional
    ROOTS II, ROOTS/M, PAF Version 1, etc.
R Remark                      Free-form, optional
Z Number of data items with optional text Required last item
```

In the COMMSOFT tiny tafel, the name of the database, the version of the database, and any special switches used when the tiny tafel was generated are shown on the Z line. The definitions of the special switches are as follows:

D—DATEFILLDISABLED. Tiny tafel normally suppresses the output of data for which the birth dates necessary to establish each line of output are missing. When this switch is on, the tiny tafel generator has estimated missing dates. The tiny tafel program applies a 30-year-per generation offset wherever it needs to reconstruct missing dates.

N—NOGROUPING. Tiny tafel normally "groups" output lines that have a common ancestor into a single line containing the most recent birth date. Descendants marked with an interest level greater than zero, however, will have their own line of output. Alternatively, when this switch is enabled, one line of output is created for every ultimate descendant (individual without children).

M—MULTIPLENAMES. Tiny tafel format normally lists a surname derived from the descendant end of each line. Specifying this option lists all unique spellings of each surname (up to five), separated by commas.

P—PLACENAMES. Tiny tafel format will include place names for family lines when this switch is enabled. Place names will be the most significant 14 to 16 characters of the birth field. When this option is enabled, the place of birth of the ultimate ancestor and the place of birth of the ultimate descendant of a line of output, respectively, are added to the end of the line.

S—SINGLEITEMS. Tiny tafel format normally suppresses lines of output that correspond to a single individual (that is, in which the ancestry and descendant dates are the same). This switch includes single-person items in the output.

#I—INTERESTLEVEL. Tiny tafel format normally includes all family lines meeting the above conditions no matter what its interest level. An interest level may be specified to limit the lines included to those having an interest level equal to or greater than the number specified. For example, with the interest level set to 1, all lines that have an ancestor or descendant interest level of 1 or higher will be listed.

Tiny tafel data is divided this way:

Column	Description
1 through 4	Soundex code (note 1)
5	Space delimiter

Column	Description
6 through 9	Earliest ancestor birth year
10	Interest flag for the ancestor end of the family line
11 through 14	Latest descendant's birth year
15	Interest flag for the descendant end of the family line
16 through 16+	SL—Surname string area (SL = Total surname length) above + PL—Place name area (PL = Total place name length) above + 1—Carriage return

The Soundex code for any given line is obtained from the end of the line that has the highest interest level. If the interest level is the same at each end, however, the name at the ancestor end will be used. If the application of these rules yields a surname that cannot be converted to Soundex, however, the program will attempt to obtain a Soundex code from the other end of the line.

Interest flags are one character each. The codes for interest level are as follows:

[space] No interest (level 0)

. Low interest (level 1)

: Moderate interest (level 2)

* Highest interest (level 3)

Up to five surnames can be on one line where the surname has changed in that line. If more than five surnames are found in a line, only the latest five will be shown. The inclusion of additional surnames is enabled by the M switch.

Place names for the birth of the earliest ancestor and the latest descendant may be included by using the P switch. If a place name is not provided for the individual whose birth year is shown, the field will be blank. The place for the ancestor is preceded by a backslash (\) and for the descendant by a slash (/).

The Terminator field looks like this:

W Date Tiny Tafel file was generated, DD MMM YYYY format.

That's how you build one manually. Most genealogical software packages now have a function to create and accept either a TT or GEDCOM, or both, from your information in the database. Always be certain a downloaded GEDCOM or TT has verified information before you load it into your database, because taking it back out isn't fun.

The best way to use computers is to take some of the drudgery out of life, and the best way to use tiny tafels is to compare and contrast them with as many others as you can. Thus the Tiny Tafel Matching System (TTMS) was born. It's a copyrighted software program from COMMSOFT, Inc., and is on many BBSs, which have to be on The National Genealogy conference (FidoNet) to carry the program. You have to be a qualified user of a BBS and submit your own TT file to be allowed to use TTMS to the fullest. Your file can have more than one tafel in it.

To find a TTMS near you, call the COMMSOFT BBS at 707-838-6373, register as a user, and look at the Files section under genealogy-related files. You can also get a description of the system there. Or call Brian Mavrogeorge's board named Roots(SF!) at 415-584-0697. He also has an eight-page article about the system. Send him an email message at brian.mavrogeorge@p0.f30.n125.z1.fidonet.org to ask for a copy.

The TTMS system has three main functions:

- Collecting and maintaining a local database of TTs
- Presenting "instant" matches on the local database
- Allowing "batch" searches of all other databases on the National Genealogical Society (NGS) BBS

In this context, "instant" means while you sit waiting at your keyboard, hooked onto the BBS. This process could take some time, tying up you and your line. For this reason, some BBSs will limit the time of day you can try this. A "batch" search means that your query is sent out on the NGS and, in a few hours or days, you'll receive messages about other TTs that match yours. Then you can contact the persons who submitted the data.

Anyone who can sign on to a BBS can look for instant matches, but you have to submit a TT file of your own to do a batch search. The searches can be limited by dates, Soundex, interest level, and so on to make the hits more meaningful.

Your TTs should be machine-generated (by Brother's Keeper, for example) to avoid formatting errors. Keep the TT as concise as possible, and submit to only one board; for the batch system to be most efficient, redundancies have to be minimal. And be sure to experiment with the date overlap features to keep the reports short. As you find new information, you can replace your old TT file with new information; this is especially important if your address changes.

GEDCOMs

In February 1987, the Church of Jesus Christ of Latter-day Saints (Mormon church) approved a standard way of setting data for transfer between various types of genealogy software, including its own Personal Ancestral File, or PAF. The standard has been adopted into most major genealogical database programs, including MacGene, Roots, Family Roots, Family Ties, Brother's Keeper, and so on. The standard is a combination of tags for data and pointers to related data.

If data from one database don't fit exactly into the new one even with GEDCOM's format, the program will often save the extraneous data to a special file. A good program can use this data to help you sort and search for whether it has what you're looking for. This is why so many people upload GEDCOMs to BBSs; perhaps someone somewhere can use the data. However, because GEDCOMs tend to be large, many BBSs have a policy against uploading them. Instead, you upload a message that you're willing to exchange your GEDCOM for the price of the disk, or some other arrangement.

As a practical matter, it's often easier to turn a GEDCOM into a TT for uploading, although some details won't go through. Then you can exchange GEDCOMs when someone's TT matches yours at some point.

APPENDIX D

Internet Error Messages

The Information Superhighway is full of potholes, dead ends, and wrong turns. You know you've hit one of these when you are met with something that says "404 Not Found" or "Failed DSN Lookup." Scratching your head, you wonder, "40 what? Failed who? What do those cryptic messages mean anyway?"

They mean the Internet is trying to tell you something. Here's a short guide to some of the most common error messages, their probable cause, and what you can do about it.

Browser Error Messages

403 Forbidden The Web site you're trying to access requires special permission—a password at the very least. No password? You'll probably have to give up or find out how to register for the site. Your browser has made it as far as the remote host computer, but it can't find the page or document you want.

404 Not Found Your browser found the host computer but not the specific Web page or document you requested. Check your typing, make sure you have the address (URL) right, and try again. If this doesn't work, shorten the address, erasing from right to left to the first slash you encounter. For example, if http://www.benchley/pub/dottie isn't working, try http://www.benchley/pub/. If that doesn't work, keep erasing the address back to the first single slash.

Bad File Request You're trying to fill out an on-screen form, and you get this message. This error means that either your browser doesn't support forms or the function isn't turned on. Another possibility is that the form you filled out or the HTML coding at that Web site has an error in it. If you are sure your browser isn't the problem, send an email to the site administrator and surf on.

Cannot Add Form Submission Result to Bookmark List A script—say, from a WebCrawler search—returns variables, such as the results from a query. You can't save the results as a bookmark because it's not a permanent file on the Internet. It's just a temporary display on your computer at this moment. You can save only the address of a page or document that's stored on some computer on the Internet. You can, however, save the results of a search to your own hard disk and create a bookmark that points to that.

Connection Refused by Host   *See* **403 Forbidden**.

Failed DNS Lookup   The Web site's address couldn't be translated into a valid IP address—the site's officially assigned number. Either that, or the domain name server (DNS) was too busy to handle your request. What does this all mean? Well, the vespucci.iquest.com site I visit is also known as 199.170.120.42. The computer that translates the site's name into that number is called a *domain name server*. If I see this message, it means that the DNS couldn't take the word-based URL and translate it into an IP address (numbers). First, check your spelling and punctuation. If you still get the message, run a ping program. Most ISPs have such programs on their server, and Windows 95 and 98 comes with one. Just type `ping <site name>`. The ping program will tell you if the target site is working. If this doesn't work, assume the DNS was busy, and try again later.

File Contains No Data   The browser found the site but found nothing in the specific file. If you typed in a URL and got this message, check your spelling and punctuation. If you got this message after using an interactive page, perhaps you didn't finish the form, or the script on the page is faulty. Try again at least once.

Helper Application Not Found   Your browser downloaded a file that needs a viewer (like a video clip), and your it can't find the program to display it. Go to your browser's Option menu (or similar menu) and make sure you've properly specified the necessary helper program, along with its correct directory and executable filename. Then try again. *Note*: You can usually ignore this error and download the file to view it later.

NNTP Server Error   You tried to connect to your Internet service provider's newsgroup server, the computer that handles messages going to and from all newsgroups supported by your ISP. The problem is that your browser couldn't find it. This could be because the server is down or because you typed in the wrong server. Be sure you entered the news server correctly in the Preferences or Options dialog box and try connecting again.

　　Another cause could be that you have tried to access one Internet service provider's news server from your account on another Internet service provider. You can't use CompuServe's network to read Usenet off Prodigy Internet, and vice versa.

Not Found   The link to a page or document or some other site no longer exists. Shorten the URL back to the first single slash and try again. If you still can't find the site, access a Web search program like WebCrawler or Lycos and see if you can find the site's new address.

TCP Error Encountered While Sending Request to Server   Some kind of erroneous data got in the pipes and are confusing the easily confused Internet. This could be due to a faulty phone jack, line noise, sunspots, or gremlins. Try again later, and if the problem persists, report it to your system administrator.

Too Many Users   Many servers, especially FTP servers, have a limit on the number of users that can connect at one time. Wait for the traffic to die down and try again.

Unable to Locate Host   Your browser couldn't find anything at the URL you specified. The address could have a typo, the site may be unavailable (perhaps temporarily), or you didn't notice that your connection to the Internet service provider has dropped.

FTP Error Messages

There are probably hundreds of FTP programs for the PC and Mac, and the error messages will vary. Nevertheless, here are some errors, along with their causes and resolutions.

Invalid Host, or Unable to Resolve Host   This is FTP's equivalent to "404 Not Found." It doesn't mean the site isn't there; it just means your FTP program couldn't find it. First, check your syntax and try again. If you still run into a brick wall, run a ping program and see what's going on. Most ISPs have a ping program on their server; Windows 95 and 98 come with one. Just type `ping <sitename>`. If the site exists, ping will tell you how long it took a signal to travel there and back. If ping couldn't get through, then assume the site is down, at least temporarily. Try another day.

Another way to find out if a site exists is to run nslookup, a program available from many ISPs. It looks up a server's IP address in a master Internet directory. When you are logged onto your ISP, just type `nslookup <hostname>`.

Too Many Consecutive Transmit Errors   This means line noise has confused your FTP program and it can't continue. This could be caused by your modem. If you got a bargain 28.8-Kbps modem for $99, it's possible that modem has fewer configurable options and cheaper interface circuits between the modem's real guts, the chipset, and the phone line. Modem connections above 9600 bps require real care in these circuits, and cheaper modems cut corners. Call your manufacturer to see if they have some workarounds.

Another possibility is you're choking Windows, the communication program, or the modem by setting the COM port's speed to higher than 38.4 or 57.6 Kbps. Even though most 28.8-Kbps modems claim to handle communications at speeds up to 115 Kbps, something in the link may not be able to. Reset the COM port speed and try again.

This could also be a problem with the command string sent to your modem before dialing. Check with your vendor and be prepared to supply the model number; the current initialization string sent to the modem; and settings for hardware flow control, error correction, and so on.

> **NOTE:**   *If your FTP program connects then suddenly freezes shortly after you log in, try using a hyphen (-) as the first character of your password. This will turn off the site's informational messages, which may be confusing your FTP program.*

Usenet Error Messages

Reading and participating in newsgroups is one of the Internet's oldest and most enjoyable pastimes. But to avoid glitches and online faux pas, read some FAQ files first. You can find a good set at http://www.cs.ruu.nl/wais/html/nadir/usenet/faq/part1.html.

Usenet error messages are usually specific to your newsreader, but there are some common traps:

Invalid Newsgroup   This jarring note can appear for various reasons. You may have spelled the newsgroup name wrong; it's easy to put periods in the wrong place. Or maybe the newsgroup no longer exists. This is very common with the alt.* groups. Search your provider's list of all newsgroups. You can also find a list of active newsgroups at http://www.cis.ohio-state.edu/hypertext/faq/usenet/active-news-groups/top.html.

Also, if you try to add a newsgroup but get the address wrong, you'll get this message. Finally, your news server may not carry this group. Talk to the sysop about adding it, or find the archived messages of the group via FTP at rtfm.mit.edu in the /pub/usenet, /pub/usenet-by-group, or /pub/usenet-by-hierarchy directories. If all else fails, search for the newsgroup (or its archives) with DejaNews (http://www.deja.com) or the Excite searcher (http://www.excite.com/).

No Such Message Sometimes, especially if you are using a browser, you'll get a list of messages that is out-of-date. The message you wanted to read is still listed in the index, but it has "scrolled off" the server. This means it has been erased to make room for newer messages. Go to Deja.com or one of the archive sites to search for that message. Some archives are as follows:

ftp.uu.net/usenet/news.answers

ftp.seas.gwu.edu/pub/rtfm

Could Not Connect to Server Either the news server is busy (you can try again later) or down (you should notify your ISP), or you are not allowed access to the news server. Another possible cause is you have set up your browser or newsreader client incorrectly. Check your typing in your configuration screen.

NOTE: *If a Usenet message looks like gibberish, it means that it is a binary file, such as a picture, sound, movie, or program, that has been uuencoded into ASCII characters. You can copy that message to a file and use a uudecoding program to restore it; however, the newest and best newsreaders come with automatic decoding. Read the instructions for getting coded messages for your newsreader.*

Email Error Messages

Email is what the Internet was originally designed for, and it's very dependable. Most mail errors are user syntax errors. When addressing a message, you must get the syntax exactly right. Commas and spaces are never allowed in email addresses. The first thing to do when an email you've sent is bounced back is to check your typing. Following are some common error messages:

Unknown User   Usually you have typed the name wrong. Sometimes you have the wrong address. Call the person and ask for the correct email address.

NOTE: If mail from a mailing list suddenly stops, it could be caused by a temporary glitch in that site or the Internet. If you are not getting mail from anywhere else, the latter is probably the case. If you are, you may have been involuntarily "unsubscribed" by the mailing list program at the site. (The usual reason is because mail it sent you was bounced back with an error.) The solution is to resubscribe.

Another possibility is the list may have been discontinued and you weren't reading the messages closely. If you suspect this, send an email to the site with just review <listname> *in the body of the message, with* <listname> *being the name of the list. You should get back the list's current status including the address of the owner, whom you may query.*

Message Undeliverable Mailer Daemon   You've just met the mail program that parses all messages. If something is wrong, the header will try to tell you what. Read the whole header and you'll probably find the problem. Usually, it's spelling.

WARNING: Message Still Undelivered After *xx* Hours   Sometimes the Internet is kind enough to warn your when you mail isn't getting through. This message is typically followed by one saying the mailer will keep trying for so many hours or days to deliver the message. You don't have to do anything about this message, but you might want to call the recipient and tell him or her the email will be delayed.

Glossary of Terms

Ahnentafel   The word means "ancestor table" in German, and the format is a more than a century old. An Ahnentafel lists all known ancestors of an individual and includes the full name of each ancestor, as well as dates and places of birth, marriage, and death. It organizes this information along a strict numbering scheme.

anonymous FTP   The procedure of connecting to a remote computer as an anonymous or guest user, in order to transfer public files back to your local computer. Anonymous FTP is usually read-only access; you often cannot contribute files by anonymous FTP. *See also* **File Transfer Protocol** and **protocol**.

Archie   An Internet program for finding files available by anonymous FTP to the general public. *See also* **Jughead** and **Veronica**.

backbone   A set of connections that make up the main channels of communication across a network.

baud   A measure of speed for data transmission across a wire. It is not equivalent to bits per second, but to changes of state per second. Several bits may go across the wire with each change of state, so bits per second can be higher than the baud rate.

BBS   *See* **Bulletin Board System**.

Bitnet   Originally a cooperative computer network interconnecting over 2300 academic and research institutions in 32 countries. Originally based on IBM's RSCS networking protocol, Bitnet supports mail, mailing lists, and file transfer. It eventually became part of the Internet, but some colleges restrict access to the original Bitnet collection of computers.

browser   An internet client for viewing the World Wide Web.

Bulletin Board System (BBS)   A set of hardware and software you can use to enter information for other users to read or download. In this book, a BBS is usually a stand-alone system that you dial up with the phone, but many are now reachable by Telnet. Most bulletin boards are set up according to general topics.

catalog   A search page for the Web where only an edited list is covered, not the "whole Internet."

chat   When people type messages to each other across a host or network, live and in real time. On some commercial online services this is called "conference."

client A computer or program that provides an interface to remote Internet services, such as mail, Usenet, Telnet, and so on. In general, the clients act on behalf of a human end user (perhaps indirectly).

compress A method of making a file, whether text or code, smaller by various methods. This is so that it will take up less disk space and/or less time to transmit. Sometimes the compression is completed by the modem. Sometimes the file is stored that way. The various methods to do this go by names (followed by the system that used it) such as: PKZIP (DOS), ARC (DOS), TAR (UNIX), StuffIt (Macintosh), and so on.

Computer Research and Education Network (CREN) The new name for the merged computer networks, Bitnet, and Computer Science Network (CSNET). It supports electronic mail and file transfer.

conference **1.** Live, online chat. **2.** a forum or echo of email mes-sages.

CREN *See* **Computer Research and Education Network**.

database A set of information organized for computer storage, search, retrieval, and insertion.

directory **1.** A level in a hierarchical filing system. Other directories branch down from the root directory. **2.** A type of search site where editors choose the Web sites and services in the catalog, instead of a robot collecting them indiscriminately.

domain name The Internet naming scheme. A machine on the Internet is identified by a series of words from more specific to more general (left to right), separated by dots: microsoft.com is an example *See also* **IP address**.

Domain Name Server (DNS) A machine with software to translate a domain name into the corresponding number (IP address).

door A program on a BBS that allows you to perform specific functions, for instance, download mail, play a game, scan the files, and so on. The BBS software shuts down while you are in a door and while the door's commands are in effect.

download To copy information, such as files, email, and programs, from a remote computer to your own.

echo A set of messages on a specific subject sent to specific BBS, which have requested those messages.

electronic mail An electronic message, text, or data, sent from one machine or person to another machine or person. Usually called *email*.

email *See* **electronic mail**.

File Transfer Protocol   File Transfer Protocol allows an Internet user to transfer files electronically from remote computers back to the user's computer.

flame   A message or series of messages containing an argument or insults. Not allowed on most systems. If you receive a flame, ignore the message and all other messages from that person in the future.

flash ROM   A chip in a modem that can be used to upgrade the unit if new technology comes along after you bought it. The upgrade comes in the form of a program that, when run, rewrites the read-only memory in the modem with the new standard, protocol, or whatever else has been improved.

forum   A set of messages on a subject, usually with a corresponding set of files. Can be on an open network such as I-Link, or restricted to a commercial system such as CompuServe.

FTP   *See* **File Transfer Protocol**

gateway   Used in different senses (e.g., mail gateway, IP gateway), but most generally, a computer that forwards and routes data between two or more networks of any size or origin. It is never, however, as straightforward as going through a gate; it's more like a labyrinth to get the proper addresses in the proper sequence.

GEDCOM   The standard for computerized genealogical information that is a combination of tags for data and pointers to related data. Stands for Genealogical Data Communication.

GENDEX   A WWW server which indexes hundreds of World Wide Web genealogical databases, and allows a user to locate and view data from any of these databases, without having to go and visit each database separately. It is located at http://www.gendex.com.

Gopher   An Internet program to search for resources, present them to you in a menu, and perform what ever Internet program (Telnet, FTP, etc) is necessary to get the resource. *See* **Jughead** and **Veronica**; all three are read-only access.

host computer   In the context of networks, a computer that directly provides service to a user. Contrasts with a network server, which provides services to a user through an intermediary host computer.

hot key   In a BBS system, a hot key is a command that is completed with a single keystroke, without the need for pressing Enter. Some BBS software enables hot key with no option to turn it off; others let you set your user configuration to choose this option. Without hot key, some systems let you string together several commands on one line.

HTML   *See* **Hypertext Markup Language**.

hub   A BBS that collects email regionally and distributes it up to the next level; it also collects the email from that level to distribute it back down the chain.

Hypertext Markup Language   A coding system to format and link documents on the World Wide Web and intranets.

Internet   The backbone of a series of interconnected networks that includes local area, regional, and national backbone networks. Networks in the Internet use the same telecommunications protocol (TCP/IP) and provide electronic mail, remote login, and file transfer services.

Internet Relay Chat (IRC)   Real-time messages typed over an open, public server.

Internet presence   A type of chat program that requires users to register with a server. Users build "buddy lists" of others using the same program and are notified when people on their buddy list are available for chat and messages.

Internet service provider (ISP)   A company that has a continuous, fast, and reliable connection to the Internet and sells subscriptions to the public to use that connection. The connections may use TCP/IP, shell accounts, or other methods.

INTERNIC   The company that has contracted to administer certain functions of the Internet, such as maintaining domain names and assigning IP addresses. Its home page is at http://rs1.internic.net/.

intranet   A local network that is set up to look like the World Wide Web, with clients such as browsers, but that is self-contained and not necessarily connected to the Internet.

Internet Protocol (IP)   The Internet standard protocol that provides a common layer over dissimilar networks; used to move packets among host computers and through gateways if necessary.

IP   *See* **Internet Protocol**.

IP address   The alpha or numeric address of a computer connected to the Internet; also called *Internet address*. Usually, the format is user@someplace.domain but is also seen as ###.##.##.##.

ISP   *See* **Internet service provider**.

Jughead   An Internet program that helps Gopher build menus of resources by limiting the search to one computer and a text string.

list (internet)   Also called **mailing list**. These are electronically transmitted discussions of technical and nontechnical issues. They come to you by electronic mail over the Internet and are sent via LISTSERV commands. Participants subscribe via a central service, and lists often have a moderator who supervises the information flow and content.

lurk   To read a list or echo without posting messages yourself. It's sort of like sitting in the corner at a party without introducing yourself, except it's not considered rude online. In fact, in some places you are expected to lurk until you get the feel of the place.

mail list   *See* **list**.

MNP   Data compression standard for modems. Stands for Microcom Network Protocol.

modem   A device to modulate computer data into sound signals and to demodulate those signals to computer data. Short for modulator-demodulator, these devices are the most common way people connect to the Internet.

moderator   The person who takes care of an echo, list, or forum. This person removes messages that are off topic or inappropriate, chastises flamers, sometimes maintains a database of old messages, and sometimes handles the mechanics of distributing the messages.

The National Research and Education Network (NREN)   A proposed national computer network to be built upon the foundation of the National Service Foundation (NSF) backbone network, NSFnet. NREN would provide high-speed interconnection between other national and regional networks. SB 1067 is the legislative bill proposing NREN.

Network Information Center (NIC)   A facility that provides administrative support, user support, and information services for a network.

NIC   *See* **Network Information Center**.

NREN   *See* **National Research and Education Network**.

offline   The state of not being connected to a remote host.

online   To be connected to a remote host.

Online Public Access Catalog (OPAC)   A term used to describe any type of computerized library catalog.

OPAC   *See* **Online Public Access Catalog**.

Open Systems Interconnection (OSI)   This is the evolving international standard under development at International Standards

Organization (ISO) for the interconnection of cooperative computer systems. An open system is one that conforms to OSI standards in its communications with other systems. As more and more genealogical data become available online, this standard will become increasingly important.

OSI *See* **Open Systems Interconnection**.

Point-to-Point Protocol (PPP)   A type of Internet connection. An improvement on Serial Line IP (SLIP), it allows any computer to use the Internet protocols and become a full-fledged member of the Internet with a high-speed modem. The advantage of SLIP and PPP accounts is that you can usually achieve faster connections this way than a shell account. *See also* **Serial Line IP (SLIP)** and **shell account**.

PPP *See* **Point-to-Point Protocol**.

protocol   A mutually determined set of formats and procedures governing the exchange of information between systems.

remote access   The ability to access a computer from outside another location. Remote access requires communications hardware, software, and actual physical links, although this can be as simple as common carrier (telephone) lines or as complex as Telnet login to another computer across the Internet. *See also* **Telnet**.

RAM *See* **Random Access Memory**.

Random Access Memory (RAM)   The working memory of a computer. RAM is the memory used for storing data temporarily while working on it, running application programs, and so on. "Random access" refers to the fact that any area of RAM can be accessed directly and immediately; in contrast to other media such as a magnetic tape, when data is accessed sequentially. RAM is called *volatile memory*; information in RAM will disappear if the power is switched off before it is saved to disk.

Read-Only Memory (ROM)   A chip in a computer or a peripheral that contains some programs to run the unit; under normal circumstances, the memory can be read but not changed. Unlike RAM, it retains its information even when the unit is turned off.

ROM *See* **Read-Only Memory**.

search engine   A program on the World Wide Web that searches parts of the Internet for text strings. It may search for programs, for Web pages, or for other items. Many claim to cover "the whole Internet," but that's physically impossible. Getting more than 20 percent of it is a good amount.

Serial Line IP (SLIP)   A system allowing a computer to use the Internet protocol (IP) with a standard telephone line and a high-speed modem. Most ISPs now offer Point-to-Point Protocol (PPP) or SLIP accounts for a monthly or yearly fee.

server   A computer that allows other computers to log on and use its resources. A client program is often used for this. *See also* **client**.

shareware   Try-before-you-buy concept in microcomputer software, where the program is distributed through public domain channels and the author expects to receive compensation after a trial period. Brother's Keeper, for example, is shareware.

shell account   A method of connecting to the Internet. You dial an Internet service provider with regular modem software and connect to a computer there that is connected to the Internet. Using a text interface, usually with a menu, you use the Internet with this shell, using commands such as Telnet. In this system, the Internet clients do not reside on your computer, but on the ISP's. *See also* **Internet service provider** or **Telnet**.

signature   A stored text file with your name and some information, such as names you are searching or your mailing address, that is appended to the end of your messages. Should contain only ASCII characters, no graphics.

SLIP   *See* **Serial Line IP**.

Soundex   A code for surnames based on phonetics rather than spelling. It was developed during the FDR administration as part of a WPA program to index US Censuses. Surnames that sound the same, but are spelled differently, like SPENCER and SPENSER, have the same code. The SOUNDEX coding system can help you find a surname even though it may have been recorded under diverse spellings. It can be used to search many genealogy databases, such as The SOUNDEX Machine at the National Archives and Records Administration site. http://www.nara.gov/genealogy/soundex/soundex.html.

spider   A program that gathers information on Web pages for a database, usually for a search engine.

sysop   The system operator of a BBS, forum, or echo. The sysop sets the rules, maintains the peace and operability of the system, and sometimes moderates the messages.

tagline A short, pithy statement tagged onto the end of a BBS email message. Example: "It's only a hobby, only a hobby, only a...". Taglines are rarely seen on commercial networks such as America Online, Microsoft Network, and CompuServe.

TCP/IP *See* **Transmission Control Protocol/Internet Protocol**.

Transmission Control Protocol/Internet Protocol (TCP/IP) A combined set of protocols that performs the transfer of data between two computers. TCP monitors and ensures correct transfer of data. IP receives the data from TCP, breaks them up into packets, and ships them off to a network within the Internet. TCP/IP is also used as a name for a protocol suite that incorporates these functions and others. *See also* **protocol**.

telnet An Internet client that connects to other computers, making yours a virtual terminal of the remote computer. Among other functions, it allows a user to log in to a remote computer from the user's local computer. On many commercial systems, you use it as a command, for instance, `telnet ftp.cac.psu.edu`. Once there, you are using programs and, therefore, commands from that remote computer.

terminal emulation Most communications software packages will permit your personal computer or workstation to communicate with another computer or network as if it were a specific type of terminal directly connected to that computer or network. For example, your terminal emulation should be set to VT100 for most online card catalog programs.

terminal server A machine that connects terminals to a network by providing host Telnet service.

thread A discussion made up of a set of messages in answer to a certain message and to each other. Sometimes very worthwhile threads are saved into a text file, as on CompuServe's Roots Forum. Some offline mail readers will "sort by thread"—that is, according to subject line. Also called a *message thread*.

tiny tafel (TT) A TT provides a standard way of describing a family database so that the information can be scanned visually or by computer. All data fields are of fixed length, with the obvious exceptions of the surnames and optional places. Many TTs are extracted from GEDCOMs. *See also* **GEDCOM**.

TN3270 A version of Telnet providing IBM full-screen support, as opposed to VT100 or some other emulation.

upload   To send a file or message from one computer to another. *See also* **download**.

Usenet   A set of messages and the software for sending and receiving them on the Internet. The difference between Usenet and a mailing list lies in the software and the way you connect to them.

V.32   A data compression standard for modems.

Veronica   A search program for Gopher. *See also* **Archie** and **Jughead**.

World Wide Web (WWW or the Web)   A system to pull various Internet services together into one interface called a *browser*. Most sites on the WWW are written as pages in HTML (Hypertext Markup Language).

Z39.50 Protocol   Name of the national standard developed by the National Information Standards Organization (NISO) that defines an applications-level protocol by which one computer can query another computer and transfer result records, using a canonical format. This protocol provides the framework for OPAC users to search remote catalogs on the Internet using the commands of their own local systems. Projects are now in development to provide Z39.50 support for catalogs on the Internet. SR (Search and Retrieval), ISO Draft International Standard 10162/10163 is the international version of Z39.50. protocol.

Smiley (Emoticon) Glossary

Because we can't hear voice inflection over email, a code for imparting emotion has sprung up. These punctuation marks that are used to take the place of facial expressions are called *smileys* or *emoticons*. Different systems will have variations of these symbols. Two versions of this unofficial smiley dictionary were sent to me by Cliff Manis (Internet: cmanis@csf.com; ROOTS-L Mailing List Administrator), and I have edited and combined them. Several versions are floating around, but I think this one sums up the ones you are most likely to see.

:-)	Your basic smiley. This smiley is used to show pleasure, or a sarcastic or joking statement
;-)	Winky smiley. User just made a flirtatious and/or sarcastic remark. Somewhat of a "don't hit me for what I just said" smiley.
:-(	Frowning smiley. User did not like that last statement or is upset or depressed about something.
:-I	Indifferent smiley. Better than a frowning smiley but not quite as good as a happy smiley.
:->	User just made a biting sarcastic remark.
>:->	User just made a really devilish remark.
>;->	Winky and devil combined.

Those are the basic smileys. Here are some somewhat less common ones. *Note:* A lot of these can be typed without noses to make midget smilies.

- -:-)	Smiley is a punk rocker.
- -:-(	Real punk rockers don't smile.
;-)	Wink.
,-}	Wry and winking.
:,(	Crying.
:-:	mutant Smiley.
.-)	Smiley only has one eye.
,-)	Ditto...but he's winking.
:-?	Smiley smoking a pipe.
:-/	Skepticism, consternation, or puzzlement.
:-\	Ditto.

:-`	Smiley spitting out its chewing tobacco.
:-~)	Smiley has a cold.
:-)~	Smiley drools.
:-[	Unsmiley blockhead.
:-[	Smiley is a vampire.
:-]	Smiley blockhead.
:-{	Mustache.
:-}	Wry smile or beard.
:-@	Smiley face screaming.
:-$	Smiley face with its mouth wired shut.
:-*	Smiley after eating something bitter or sour.
:-&	Smiley is tongue-tied.
:-#	Smiley with braces.
:-#|	Smiley face with bushy mustache.
:-%	Smiley banker.
:-<	Mad or really sad smiley.
:-=)	Older smiley with mustache.
:->	Hey, hey.
:-|	"Have an ordinary day" smiley.
:-0	Smiley orator.
:-0	No yelling! (quiet lab).
:-1	Smiley bland face.
:-!	Another smiley bland face.
:-6	Smiley after eating something sour.
:-7	Smiley after a wry statement.
:-8(	condescending stare.
:-9	Smiley is licking his/her lips.
:-a	Lefty smiley touching tongue to nose.
:-b	Left-pointing tongue smiley.
:-c	Bummed out smiley.
:-C	Smiley is really bummed.
:-d	Lefty smiley razzing you.
:-D	Smiley is laughing.

:-e	Disappointed smiley.
:-E	Bucktoothed vampire.
:-F	Bucktoothed vampire with one tooth missing.
:-I	Hmm...
:-i	Semi-smiley.
:-j	Left smiling smiley.
:-o	Smiley singing national anthem.
:-O	Uh oh.
:-o	Uh oh!
:-P	Disgusted or nyah-nyah.
:-p	Smiley sticking its tongue out (at you!).
:-q	Smiley trying to touch its tongue to its nose.
:-Q	Smoker smiley.
:-s	Smiley after a *bizarre* comment.
:-S	Smiley just made an incoherent statement.
:-t	Cross smiley.
:-v	Talking head smiley.
:-x	"My lips are sealed" smiley.
:-X	Smiley with bow tie.
:-X	Smiley's lips are sealed.
::-)	Smiley wears normal glasses.
:'-(	Smiley is crying.
:'-)	Smiley is so happy, s/he is crying.
:^)	Smiley with pointy nose (righty). Sometimes used to denote a lie, myth, or misconception.
:^)	Smiley has a broken nose.
:(	Sad midget smiley.
:)	Midget smiley.
:[	Real downer.
:]	Midget smiley.
:*	Kisses.
:*)	Smiley is drunk.
:<	Midget unsmiley.

:<)	Smiley is from an Ivy League school.
:=)	Smiley has two noses.
:>	Midget smiley.
:D	Laughter.
:I	Hmmm...
:n)	Smiley with funny-looking right nose.
:O	Yelling smiley.
:u)	Smiley with funny-looking left nose.
:v)	Left-pointing nose smiley.
:v)	Smiley has a broken nose.
`:-)	Smiley shaved one of his eyebrows off this morning.
,:-)	Same thing, other side.
~~:-(	Net flame.
(-:	Smiley is left-handed.
(:-(	Unsmiley frowning.
(:-)	Smiley big-face.
):-)	Another smiley big-face.
(:I	Egghead.
(8-o	It's Mr. Bill!
):-(	Unsmiley big-face.
)8-)	Scuba smiley big-face.
[:-)	Smiley is wearing a Walkman.
[:]	Smiley is a robot.
[]-	Hugs.
{:-)	Smiley with its hair parted in the middle.
{:-)	Smiley wears a toupee.
{:-(	Toupee in an updraft.
@:-)	Smiley is wearing a turban.
@:I	Turban variation.
@=	Smiley is pro-nuclear war.
*:o)	Bozo the Clown!
%-)	Smiley has been staring at a green screen for 15 hours straight.

%-6	Smiley is brain-dead.
+-:-)	Smiley is the Pope or holds some other religious office.
+:-)	Smiley priest.
<:-I	Smiley is a dunce.
<:I	Midget dunce.
<I-(	Smiley is Chinese and doesn't like these kind of jokes.
<I-)	Smiley is Chinese.
=)	Variation on a theme.
>:-I	net.startrek.
I-)	Hee hee.
I-D	Ho ho.
I-I	Smiley is asleep.
I-O	Smiley is yawning/snoring.
I-P	Yuck.
I^o	Snoring smiley.
II	Asleep smiley.
0-)	Smiley cyclops (scuba diver?).
3:[	Mean pet smiley.
3:]	Pet smiley.
3:o[	net.pets.
8 :-)	Smiley is a wizard.
8 :-I	net.unix-wizards.
8-)	Smiley with glasses.
8-)	Smiley swimmer.
8-)	Smiley is wearing sunglasses.
8:-)	Smiley with glasses on forehead.
8:-)	Smiley is a little girl.
B-)	Smiley with horn rims.
B:-)	Smiley with sunglasses on head.
C=:-)	Smiley is a chef.
C=}>;*{))	Mega-smiley. A drunk, devilish chef with a toupee in an updraft, a mustache, and a double chin.
E-:-)	Smiley is a ham radio operator.

E-:-I	net.ham-radio.
g-)	Smiley with pince-nez glasses.
K:P	Smiley is a little kid with a propeller beanie.
O :-)	Smiley is an angel (at heart, at least).
O I-)	net.religion.
O-)	Megaton man on patrol! (or else user is a scuba diver).
X-(	Smiley just died.

INDEX

A

Acadian Genealogy Homepage, 114
/ACCEPT (IRC command), 169
Access, Internet:
   methods, access, 20
   to servers, 60–61
   speed, access, 13
   from television, 11
ActifFTP, 24
/ACTION (IRC command), 169
Addresses:
   email, 87, 95
   entering, 110
   site, 61
Adoptees:
   mailing lists for, 96, 97
   Web sites for, 115
Adoption issues:
   mailing lists for, 96
   newsgroups for, 78
ADSL (see Asymmetric DSL)
Advertising:
   on CompuServe genealogy forums, 263–264
   email, 27
   on ROOTS-L, 90
   on Usenet, 71
African genealogy, newsgroups for, 79
African-American records site, 114
AfriGeneas, 99, 114, 131–134
AfroAm-L mailing list, 99
Ahnentafels, 293–294
Alabama:
   mailing list, 103
   Web sites, 128
Alaska, mailing list for, 103
Allen County (Indiana) Public Library
   Historical Genealogy Department site,
   114

America Online (AOL), 232, 259
   FileGrabber utility of, 81–82
   reading Usenet with, 75–76
   and spam control, 28
   Web browser on, 110
   See also Golden Gate Genealogy Forum
American Civil War Home Page, 114
American Standard Code for Information
   Interchange (ASCII), 32, 61
Analog phone lines, 7, 8
Ancestral File (LDS), 213–214
Ancestral Seasonings cookbook (Golden Gate
   Genealogy Forum), 253–255
Ancestry, 218–220
Ancestry Inc., 114
Andereck, Paul, 295
"Anonymous," 60
Antivirus programs, 36–37
AOL (see America Online)
AOL Genealogy Forum (see Golden Gate
   Genealogy Forum)
AOL Instant Messenger, 156, 160–162
AOL NetFind, 146–148, 152
.arc files, 61
Archaic Words & Phrases, 115
Ariadne, 21
Arizona:
   mailing list, 103
   Web sites, 126
.arj files, 61
Arkansas-Roots-L mailing list, 102
ASCII (see American Standard Code for
   Information Interchange)
Asymmetric DSL (ADSL), 10–11
Attachments, file, 32–33
Australian genealogy:
   newsgroups on, 79
   Web site on, 115
Automated mailing lists, 87

Automatic Surname Notification Program
  (RootsWeb), 182–183
/AWAY (IRC command), 169

Bulletin boards, Internet (*see* Usenet)
/BUSY (IRC command), 169
Buy an Ancestor, 218

B

Bad File Request error message, 301
Belgian genealogy, 79
Bell companies, 11
<bg> (chat shorthand), 175
Bigfoot, 152–153
Binaries for Beginners, 33
Binary encoding, 81
Binary files, 32, 81–82
Binary Info-Page FAQ, 33
Binary mode, 61
BINHEX (.HQX, .HEX files), 32, 33
.biz groups, 71
BK-L mailing list, 104
Blocking, binary file, 81
Bookmarks, 21, 23
Books:
  online genealogy, 291
  of ROOTS-L subscribers, 92
Boolean operators, 191, 193
Branching Out Online, 115
Brazil mailing list, 99
BRB<f$> (chat shorthand), 175
British genealogy, 120
The British Heraldic Archive, 115
Brother's Keeper discussion list, 104
Browser(s), 19–24
  changing opening page of, 111–112
  choosing, 20–21
  connecting to card catalogs via, 191–196
  error messages, 301–303
  History folder in, 112, 113
  of ISPs, 110
  mail readers in, 26
  menu bar of, 21–22
  reading newsgroups with, 75
  searching newsgroups with, 85–86
  terminology, 19–20
  title bar of, 21
  toolbars in, 22, 23
  using, 21–24
BTW (chat shorthand), 175

C

C (chat shorthand), 174
Cable modems, 11
Cajun genealogy, newsgroups for, 78
Calendars Web site, 115
California, mailing list for, 103
Canadian genealogy, 120
Canadian Genealogy made Easy!, 115
Canadian Heritage Information Network, 115,
  116
Cannot Add Form Submission Result
  to Bookmark List error message,
  301–302
Card catalogs, 189–199
  connecting to, 191
  features of, 190
  finding, 197
  Telnet, connecting via, 194–199
  Web browser, connecting via, 191–196
Caribbean genealogy, 81
Carpenter, Rick, 90
Carrie's Adoptee & Genealogy Page, 115
Cemetery transcriptions Web site, 115
Census Bureau Home Page, 115
Census records, 126–127
  in RootsWeb, 63
  at U.S. government site, 65
  Web site for links to, 115
Central American genealogy, newsgroups for,
  79
Channels, 228–229
  chat, 170–173
  IRC, 170–173
Chase, Dan, 89
Chat, 155–176
  caution when using, 157–158
  commands, 169
  on CompuServe genealogy forums, 268–271
  email vs., 157
  etiquette for, 173–174
  finding channels for, 170–173
  on Golden Gate Genealogy Forum, 246–248

Chat (*Cont.*):
 programs for, 160–168
  AOL Instant Messenger, 160–162
  Ding!, 162–164
  ICQ, 164–165
  Microsoft Chat, 166–167
  mIRC, 167, 168
 security risks with, 159–160
 shorthand with, 174–175
 using, 158–159, 167–170
 without chat program, 172–173
 See also Internet presence chat; Internet
  Relay Chat
Christophersen, Alf, 89
Church of Jesus Christ of Latter-day Saints
  (LDS) (*See also* FamilySearch Internet)
 Ancestral File of, 213–214
 computerized resources of, 210–212
 Elijah-L mailing list for, 96–97
 Family History Centers of, 214–216
 genealogical objectives of, 212–213
 International Genealogical Index of,
  213–214
Church records Web site, 115
CIS (CompuServe Information Service), 28
CIVIL-WAR mailing list, 101
Clients, 34
CLIO-The National Archives Information
  Server-Genealogy, 116
"Coats of arms" scams, 52
Coded files, 32–33
Codes, tag line, 49
.com files, 61
Commands:
 for chat, 169
 for IRC, 169
Commercial online services, 227–230
 email with, 229
 file access with, 229–230
 proprietary content of, 228–229
 Usenet with, 229
 See also specific online services
COMP newsgroups, 69
CompuServe, 232
 reading Usenet with, 76
 and spam control, 28
 Web browser on, 110
CompuServe 2000, 261

CompuServe genealogy forums, 259–274
 advertising on, 263–264
 chat on, 268–271
 Genealogy Vendor's Support Forum, 271
 rules for using, 262–263
 sysops, 264, 272–274
 Techniques Forum, 260, 264–271, 264–272
CompuServe Information Service (CIS), 28
Computer viruses, 36–37
COMSOFT, 295–298
Congressional Medal of Honor, 123
Connecting to Internet, 12–15
 card catalogs, 191
 charges for, 14–15
 by DSL, 9–11
 by ISDN, 7–9
 methods, access, 20
 by modem, 4–6
 precautions for, 4
 servers, access to, 60–61
 speed, access, 13
 from television, 11
Conventions, FTP, 61
Copyrights, 52
Corporate Investigative Services Searchable
  Databases on the Internet, 116
Could Not Connect to Server error mes-
  sage, 305
Crispen, Patrick Douglas, 120
CuteFTP, 24
CWYL (chat shorthand), 175
Cyndi's List of Genealogy Sites on the Internet,
  107, 117, 183
Czarnik, Tom, 69

D

Data communications cards, 7
Databases:
 of overland trails graffiti, 102
 on ROOTS-L, 91–92
 Thousand Genealogy Links Web site, links in,
  115
David Eppstein's home page, 117
Dead Person's Society, 117
DearMYRTLE, 105, 134–138, 170, 251–252
Decode Windows 95 Shell Extension, 33

Decoding, 32–33
Deep-South-Roots-L mailing list, 103
DejaNews, 85–86, 154
Delaware, mailing list for, 103
Demodulation, 4
Dictionaries, genealogical, 119
Digest mode (ROOTS-L), 92–93
Digital data services, 4
Digital Subscriber Line (DSL, xDSL), 4, 9–11
    hardware for, 9, 11
    types of, 10–11
Ding! 2.5, 162–164
Directories, 20, 146
Directory of Royal Genealogical Data, 117
Discovering Your Heritage, 114
District of Columbia, mailing list for, 103
DMP Net, 12
Dott's Genealogy Home Page, 119
Downloading files, 24
DSL (*see* Digital subscriber line)
Duke University, 70

E

Eastman, Dick, 260, 262, 269, 272–274
Eastman's Online Genealogy Newsletter, 105,
    117
Editing, 50
Electronic mailing lists (*see* Mailing lists)
Elijah-L mailing list, 96–97
Email, 26–36
    accounts, public vs. private, 27
    boxes, email, 14
    chat vs., 157
    with commercial online services, 229
    error messages, 305–306
    filters for, 26
    and spam, 26–32
Emoticons, 50–51, 83, 262
Encoding, 32–33, 81
English genealogy, newsgroups for, 81
Error messages, 301–306
    browser, 301–303
    email, 305–306
    FTP, 60, 303–304
    Usenet, 304–305
Errors, 54

Ethnic group mailing lists, 99–100
Etiquette, online, 47–52
    answering messages, 49–50
    for chat, 173–174
    on CompuServe, 262–263
    sending messages, 48–49
    for Usenet, 82–85
Eudora, 28
Eudora Light, 34–35
Eudora Pro, 34
Europe (Northern) genealogy, newsgroups for,
    80
European genealogy, newsgroups for, 78
Evaluation of resources, 54–55
Everton's, 117, 220–221
Excite, 148, 149, 172
.exe files, 61
/EXIT (IRC command), 169
External modems, 5, 6

F

Failed DNS Lookup error message, 302
Family Chronicle, 117
Family History Centers (LDS), 202, 214–216
Family History-How Do I Begin?, 117
Family name mailing lists, 100–101
Family Origins 7.0, 38–40
Family Tree Maker (FTM), 40–41, 223
Family Tree Maker Online, 117
Family-Origins-Users mailing list, 104
FamilySearch Internet, 202–211, 216
FAQs (*see* Frequently asked questions)
Fax capabilities, 5
Fetch, 60
FidoNet, 78
File Contains No Data error message,
    302
File Mine, 153
File Transfer Protocol (FTP), 24–25, 59–65
    conventions for, 61
    error messages, 303–304
    Genealogy Anonymous, 63–64
    Genealogy Online, 64–65
    RootsWeb, 61–63
    U.S. Government Census, 65
    using, 60–61

File(s), 20
    attachments to, 32–33
    binary, 34, 81–82
    commercial online services, accessing via, 229–230
    decoding, 33
    deleting stored, 112
    downloading/uploading, 24
    encoding schemes for, 32–33
    multipart, 33
    pornographic, 81
    for ROOTS-L, 91–92
    search sites, 153
    transferring, 36–37 (*See also* File Transfer Protocol)
Filters, email, 26, 28
Flames/flaming, 48, 82
Flash upgrade programs, 5
Florida, mailing list for, 103
Follow-ups, 50
Forte Agent, 72, 74
Forte software, 71
Forums, 229
Free Agent, 14, 71–74
FreeBMD (Free Births, Marriages, and Deaths), 118
French Acadian/French Canadian genealogy, 114
French genealogy, 79
Frequently asked questions (FAQs):
    Golden Gate Genealogy Forum, 235
    for newsgroups, 95
    Usenet, 68, 82
FTM (*see* Family Tree Maker)
FTP (*see* File Transfer Protocol)
"Ftp" (as login name), 60
FWIW (chat shorthand), 175

G

<g> (chat shorthand), 175
GAQ files, 82, 85
Gateways, 6
Gathering of the Clans Home Page, 118
GEDCOM-L mailing list, 104
GEDCOMs, 208–210, 213–214, 275–280 (*See also* GenServ)

GedPage 2.0, 41, 42
GenCmp-L mailing list, 104
GenConnect meeting places (RootsWeb), 183, 184
Gen-DE-L mailing list, 100
GENDEX, 119
Gene (shareware), 117
Genealogical Dictionaries, 119
Genealogy Dictionary, 119
Genealogy for Teachers, 119
Genealogy Forum (*see* Golden Gate Genealogy Forum)
Genealogy Gateway to the Web, 119
Genealogy Home Page, 111, 119, 129–130
Genealogy Listservers, Newsgroups, and Special Home Pages, 101
Genealogy of the Royal Family of the Netherlands, 119
Genealogy on the Web Ring, 119
Genealogy Online, 64–65, 119
Genealogy Resources on the Internet (AOL), 119–120
    Mailing Lists, 101
    Surnames, 101
Genealogy Support Forum (CompuServe), 260
Genealogy Techniques Forum (CompuServe), 260, 264–272
Genealogy Today, 105, 120
Genealogy Vendor's Support Forum (CompuServe), 264–265, 271
Genealogy.com, 223–224
Generations Easy Tree (GET), 44–45
Gen-FF-L mailing list, 100
GEN-MEDIEVAL-L mailing list, 101–102
GenMsc-L mailing list, 97
GenMtd mailing list, 98
Gen-Newbie-L mailing list, 98
GenServ, 120, 275–289
    LIST FIELDS command of, 285–286
    REPORT command of, 287–289
    SEND command of, 286–287
    subscribing to, 276–280
    using, 280–284
GENUKI, 120
GenWeb Database Index, 120
GenWeb mailing list, 104
Georgia, mailing list for, 103

German genealogy:
  newsgroups for, 79
  Web sites for, 115
German Genealogy Home Page, 120
GET (*see* Generations Easy Tree)
GIWIST (chat shorthand), 175
Global: Everything for the Family Historian, 120
Global Gazette, 120
/GNAME (IRC command), 169
Golden Gate Genealogy Forum, 231–257
  Ancestral Seasonings cookbook of, 253–255
  Beginners' Center of, 235–241
  Chat Center of, 246–248
  DearMYRTLE Daily Column in, 251–252
  File Libraries Center of, 248, 249
  Golden Gate store, 253
  Internet Center of, 248–250
  Member Welcome Center of, 234–235
  message boards of, 242–245
  News window of, 251
  Resource Center of, 248
  Search window of, 250
  Software Search window fo, 253
  staff of, 255–257
  Surname Center of, 250, 251
  Telephone Search Facilities window of, 252–253
Greater Manchester Integrated Library Cooperative System, 190
.gz files, 61

H

HAHAHA, 50
Hardware:
  for browsers, 21
  for DSL, 9
  with ISDN liens, 8
  for modems, 6
  protection of, 4
Hauser-Hooser-Hoosier Theory: The Truth about Hoosier, 120
Hawaii, mailing list for, 103
HDSL (high bit rate DSL), 10
Helper Application Not Found error message, 302

.HEX files, 32
HHOK (chat shorthand), 175
High bit rate DSL (HDSL), 10
HIR Genealogy Page, 120
Hispanic genealogy:
  newsgroups for, 79
  Web site for, 126
Hispanic Genealogy Special Interest Group (AOL), 115
Historical group mailing lists, 101–102
History folder, 112
HMS Bounty, descendants of, 124, 125
House of Orange-Nassau genealogy, Web site for, 119
How to Get Past Genealogy Road Blocks, 120
Howells, Cyndi, 215
.HQX files, 32
HTH (chat shorthand), 175
HTHBE (chat shorthand), 175
HTML (Hypertext Markup Language), 20
HUMANITIES newsgroups, 69
Humor, use of, 50–51, 83
Hungarian genealogy, Web site for, 120
Hypertext, 20
Hypertext Markup Language (HTML), 20

I

IA-NEB-Roots-L mailing list, 103
ICQ, 164–165
Idaho, mailing list for, 103
IGI (*see* International Genealogical Index)
/IGNORE (IRC command), 169
IIGS (International Internet Genealogy Society), 121
IMHO (chat shorthand), 51, 175
IMNSHO (chat shorthand), 175
Index mode (ROOTS-L), 93
Indiana, mailing list for, 103
Indian-Roots-L mailing list, 100
Infoseek, 85, 150–152, 154
Infoseek/GO, 172
IN-Roots-L mailing list, 103
Inscriptions-L mailing list, 103
Instant Messenger (AOL), 156, 160–162
Insulting messages, 48

Integrated Services Digital Network (ISDN), 4, 7–9
 costs of, 8
 features of, 7–8
 power sources for, 8
Intelligent phones, 7–8
Internal modems, 5, 6
International Genealogical Index (IGI), 213–214
International Internet Genealogy Society (IIGS), 121
International Research, 121
International Telecommunications Union (ITU), 5
Internet Black List, 28
Internet bulletin boards (*see* Usenet)
Internet presence chat, 155, 156
 AOL Instant Messenger, 160–162
 Ding!, 162–164
 etiquette for, 173–174
 ICQ, 164–165
Internet Relay Chat (IRC), 155, 156
 commands, 169
 etiquette for, 173–174
 finding channels for, 170–173
 Microsoft Chat, 166–167
 mIRC, 167, 168
 security risks with, 159–160
 using, 158–159, 167–170
Internet service providers (ISPs):
 browsers used by, 110
 choosing, 12–15
 software provided by, 17–19
 and spam control, 28–29
The Internet Sleuth: Surnames, 101
Internet Tourbus, 120
Introductions, online, 47
Invalid Host error message, 303
Invalid Newsgroup error message, 304–305
IOW (chat shorthand), 175
Iowa, mailing list for, 103
IRC (*see* Internet Relay Chat)
Irish genealogy:
 newsgroups for, 81
 Web sites for, 120, 124
The Irish/Canadian List, 92
IRL (chat shorthand), 175
Isaacson, Karen, 89
ISDN (*see* Integrated Services Digital Network)

Isleuth-Arts & Humanities-Genealogy, 121–122
ISPs (*see* Internet service providers)
Italian genealogy, mailing list for, 100
Italian Genealogy Home Page, 122
ITRW (chat shorthand), 175
ITU (International Telecommunications Union), 5

J

Janyce's Root Digging' Dept., 122
Jewish genealogy, newsgroups for, 79
JewishGen, 122
JewishGen mailing list, 100
JOG newsletter, 105
John Norstad's NewsWatcher, 74–75
/JOIN (IRC command), 169
Journal of Online Genealogy, 105, 122, 123
Junk email (*see* Spam)

K

Kentucky, mailing list for, 103
Keywords (AOL), 228–229
/KICK (IRC command), 169
Kindred Konnections, 221–223
KYRoots mailing list, 103

L

LDS (*see* Church of Jesus Christ of Latter-day Saints)
The Learning Company, 223
LeechFTP, 24
Libbi's Spammer Twit List, 29–32
Library card catalogs (*see* Card catalogs)
Library of Congress, 122, 140–145
Library of Virginia Digital Collections, 122
Licenses, 52
Lindsay, Vicki, 90
Lineages, Inc., 122
Links, 20
LIST FIELDS command (GenServ), 285–286
/LIST (IRC command), 169

LISTSERV at Indiana University, 102–103
Login names, 60
LOL (chat shorthand), 51, 175
Louisiana-Roots-L mailing list, 103
Lurking, 47
Luxembourg genealogy, newsgroups for, 79
Lycos, 148, 149
.lzh files, 61

M

Machine names, 20
Maggie_Ohio mailing list, 103
Mail (*see* Email)
MAIL CONTROLS (AOL keyword), 28
Mail mode (ROOTS-L), 93
Mailboxes, 14
Mailing lists, 87–107
  addresses, 95
  Adoptees, 96, 97
  adoption, 96
  automated, 87
  Cyndi's List for, 107
  Elijah-L, 96–97
  ethnic group lists, 99–100
  family name lists, 100–101
  finding, 107
  GenMsc-L, 97
  GenMtd, 98
  Gen-Newbie-L, 98
  historical group lists, 101–102
  hosted by RootsWeb, 186–187
  management of, 95
  moderated, 87
  multiple email addresses with, 88
  newsletters, email, 105–106
  regional group lists, 102–103
  software lists, 103–104
  subscribing to, 88
  welcome messages on, 95
  See also ROOTS-L
Manis, Cliff, 90
Maps, Web site for, 127
Marston Manor, 122
Maryland, mailing list for, 103
The Master Genealogist (TMG), 41–43
MAYFLOWER mailing list, 102

Mayflower Passenger List, 53
Mayflower Web Pages, 123
Meckler Media, 12
Medal of Honor Citations, 123
Medieval times genealogy, newsgroups for, 79
MegaHome residential service, 11
Message of the Day (MOTD), 170
Message readers, 14
Message Undeliverable Mailer Daemon
  error message, 306
Messages:
  answering, 49–50, 83
  appropriate, 82–85
  error, 60
  Golden Gate Genealogy Forum, 242–245
  insulting/offensive, 48
  length of, 90
  on mailing lists, 87
  Meta Genealogy FAQ (for newsgroups), 82
  to people vs. software at ROOTS-L, 91
  in ROOTS-L, 92–93
  sending, 48–49
  spot-checks of, 52
  subject line of, 84
  targeting, 48
  UNSUBSCRIBE (ROOTS-L), 90
  on Usenet, 67
Meta Genealogy FAQ message (for newsgroups), 82
Mexican genealogy, Web sites for, 124
Microsoft Chat, 156, 166–167
Microsoft Internet Explorer, 14, 21, 23, 110, 111–112, 261
Microsoft Network (MSN), 76, 232
Microsoft Outlook 98, 36, 37
Microsoft System Diagnostics (MSD.EXE), 6–7
Mid-Atlantic-Roots-L mailing list, 103
MIME (.MME, .MM files), 33
MindSpring, 230
mIRC, 167, 168
MISC newsgroups, 69
Missing Links newsletter, 105
Mississippi, mailing list for, 103
Missouri-Roots-L mailing list, 103
.MM files, 33
.MME files, 33
/MODE (IRC command), 169

Modem(s):
  cable, 11
  determining type of, 6–7
  DSl, 9
  selecting, 4–6
Moderated mailing lists, 87
Moderated newsgroups, 69
Modulation, 4
Montana, mailing list for, 103
Monty Python, 27
Morgan, Terry, 214–215
Mormons (*see* Church of Jesus Christ of Latter-day Saints)
Mosaic, 21
MOTD (Message of the Day), 170
MSD.EXE (*see* Microsoft System Diagnostics)
MSN (*see* Microsoft Network)
Multipart files, 33
Multiple attachments, 33
Multiple email addresses, 88
Multipurpose Internet Mail Extensions encoding scheme, 33
Myers, Sandy, 89

N

/NAME (IRC command), 169
Names:
  in Census Bureau Home Page, 115
  family, mailing lists for, 100–101
  login, 60
National Genealogical Society Web site, 123–124
Native American Genealogy, 124
Native American records site, 114
NC-SC-Roots-L mailing list, 103
Nebraska, mailing list for, 103
NetFind (AOL), 85
Netherlands genealogy:
  newsgroups for, 79
  Web sites for, 119
Netscape Navigator, 14, 19, 21, 110–112
  Genealogy Home Page in, 21–24
  icons in, 22–24
  Location box in, 23
  newsreader window in, 75, 76
Nevada, mailing list for, 103

New England, mailing list for, 103
New England Historic Genealogical Society, 124
New Jersey, mailing list for, 103
New Mexico, mailing list for, 103
New Zealand genealogy:
  newsgroups on, 79
  Web site on, 117
NEWS newsgroups, 69
News servers, 72
Newsgroups, 69
  error messages with, 304–305
  FAQs for, 95
  genealogy-related, 77–81
  and Golden Gate Genealogy Forum, 249–250
  searching, 154
  subscribing to, 70
Newsletters, email, 105–107
Newsreaders, 71–75
NewYork-Roots-L mailing list, 103
NNTP Server Error, 302–303
No Such Message error message, 305
North American Genealogy Forum (CompuServe), 260
North Carolina, mailing list for, 103
Northeast-Roots-L mailing list, 103
Northern European genealogy, newsgroups for, 79
Not Found error message, 303

O

Offensive messages, 48
Office 97 Professional Edition, 36
OfficeConnect 56K LAN modem, 6
Ohio-Roots-L mailing list, 103
OIC (chat shorthand), 175
Oklahoma, mailing list for, 103
Online Genealogy Classes (Web site), 124
Opera, 21, 110
Oregon, mailing list for, 103
Oregon History & Genealogy Resources, 124
OTF (chat shorthand), 175
OTOH (chat shorthand), 175
OTP (chat shorthand), 175
Our Spanish Heritage: History and Genealogy of South Texas and Northeast Mexico, 124
OVERLAND-TRAILS mailing list, 102

P

PAF mailing list, 104
/PAGE (IRC command), 169
Pages, 20
PARENTAL CONTROLS (AOL keyword),
    81
/PASS (IRC command), 169
Passenger lists, 115, 123
PC Magazine, 6
Pegasus Mail, 336
Pennsylvania-Roots-L mailing list, 103
People search engines, 152–153
Personal Ancestral File, mailing list for,
    104
Pie mailing list, 100
Pitcairn Island Web Site, 124
Plagiarism, 52
Points of presence (POPs), 14
Point-to-Point Protocol (PPP), 14
Poland Worldgenweb, 124
POPs (points of presence), 14
Pornographic files, 81
Portals, 228
Posting queries, 48
POV (chat shorthand), 175
PPP (Point-to-Point Protocol), 14
PREFERRED MAIL (AOL keyword), 28
Prodigy, 110, 232
Protocols, modem, 4–5
Publishing online, 38, 52, 54–55

Q

Queries, posting, 48
Questions (in message subject lines), 84
Quick Guide to Genealogy in Ireland, 124
Quotations:
    altered, across networks, 52
    in messages, 50

R

RADSL (rate-adaptive DSL), 10
RAND, 179

Rate-adaptive DSL (RADSL), 10
Read-only memory (ROM), 5
REC newsgroups, 69
References, citing, 52
Regional group mailing lists, 102–103
REPORT command (GenServ), 287–289
Repositories of Primary Sources,
    124–125
Resources, evaluation of, 54–55
RL (chat shorthand), 175
RLL (*see* The Roots Location List)
/RNAME (IRC command), 169
ROM (read-only memory), 5
Roots Location List (RLL), 92, 181
Roots Surname List (RSL), 91–92
    on RootsWeb, 180, 181
ROOTSBOOK, mailing list for, 104
RootsComputing, 124, 125
ROOTS-L, 184, 185
    Home Page for, 125
    mailing list for, 88–95, 99
        communicating on, 91
        losing contact with, 94–95
        rules for, 90–91
        using, 92–94
    messages to people vs. software in, 91
    modes/messages in, 92–93
    subscribing/unsubscribing to, 90
RootsWeb, 61–63, 179–187
    Automatic Surname Notification Program of,
        182–183
    GenConnect meeting places on, 183, 184
    HelpDesk of, 185, 186
    mailing lists hosted by, 107, 186–187
    Review, RootsWeb, 186
    RSL on, 180, 181
    searching from, 180–182
    state resource pages on, 185
    uniqueness of, 187
    Web sites hosted by, 183–184
    See also ROOTS-L
RootsWeb Newsletter, 105
RootsWeb Review, 186
RootsWeb Surname List (RSL), 180, 181
ROTF (chat shorthand), 51
ROTFL (chat shorthand), 175
RSL (*see* RootsWeb Surname List)
RTFM (chat shorthand), 175

S

Salter, John, 90
Sarcasm, use of, 50–51, 83
Scams, 52, 218
SCI newsgroups, 69
Scottish genealogy:
  newsgroups for, 81
  Web site for, 118
SDSL (single-line DSL), 10
Search engines, 145–146, 152–153
Searching:
  with Free Agent, 73–74
  ROOTS-L files/databases, 91–92
  from RootsWeb, 180–182
  on Usenet, 85–86
Secondary materials, 54
Security:
  and antivirus programs, 36–37
  with chat, 159–160
  indicators of, 23
  with IRC, 159–160
  and tag line codes, 49
SEND command (GenServ), 286–287
/SEND (IRC command), 169
Sending files, 24
Serial communications programs, 18
Serial Line Internet Protocol (SLIP), 14
Servers, accessing, 60–61
Shareware programs, 63
Shareware.com, 153
Shorthand, chat, 174–175
Signatures, email, 48–49
Signatures, surname, 91
Single-line DSL (SDSL), 10
Site addresses, 61
Slavic genealogy, newsgroups for, 80
SLIP (Serial Line Internet Protocol), 14
Smileys, 50–51, 83, 262
Snap, 172
SOC newsgroups, 69
Social Security Death Index (SSDI), 125,
  218–220
Software, 18–45
  antivirus, 36–37
  browser, 19–24
    choosing, 20–21
    terminology, 19–20

Software, browser (*Cont.*):
    using, 21–24
  FTP, 24–25
  at Genealogy Anonymous site, 64
  mailing lists for, 103–104
  mail-reading, 26–36
    Eudora Light, 34–35
    file attachments/formats with, 32–33
    filters for, 26
    Microsoft Outlook 98, 36, 37
    Pegasus, 35–36
    and spam protection, 26–32
  for modems, 6
  online-ready genealogy, 38–45
    Family Origins, 38–40
    Family Tree Maker, 40–41
    GedPage, 41, 42
    Generations Easy Tree, 44–45
    The Master Genealogist, 41–43
    Ultimate Family Tree, 38
  posting licensed, 52
  for uncompressing files, 61
  for Usenet, 71–78
    browsers, 75–77
    commercial online services, 75–76, 78
    newsreaders, 71–75
Sources:
  primary, 52–55
  secondary, 54
South American genealogy, newsgroups for, 79
South Carolina, mailing list for, 103
South Carolina State Library, 126, 195–198
Spam, 26–32
  deleting/filtering out, 27–28
  Libbi's Spammer Twit List for, 29–32
  sources of, 27
  tracking senders of, 28–29
Spanish Heritage home page, 126
Spencer, Gaye, 274
/SQUELCH (IRC command), 169
SSDI (*see* Social Security Death Index)
State resource pages, 185
Subdirectories, 60
Subject lines, 48, 84
Subscriptions:
  for Free Agent, 74
  to GenServ, 276–280
  to mailing lists, 88

Subscriptions (*Cont.*):
  to newsgroups, 70
  See also specific mailing list names
Surge protectors, 4
Surname signatures, 91
Surnames: What's in a Name?, 126, 127
Surnames (in message subject lines), 84
Surnames-Canada-L mailing list, 100
Surnames.com, 126
Swiss Genealogy Project, 126
Switchboard, 152
Sysops, 260–261, 272–274

T

TAFN, 51
Tag lines, 49
TALK newsgroups, 69
Targeting messages, 48
TCP Error Encountered While Sending Request to Server error message, 303
TCP/IP (*see* Transmission Control Protocol/Internet Protocol)
Techniques Forum (CompuServe), 264–271
Telephone lines:
  ISDN, 7–9
  and thunderstorms, 4
Television, Internet access from, 11
Telnet, 15, 194–199
Tennessee, mailing list for, 103
Texahoma-Roots-L mailing list, 103
Texas, mailing list for, 103
Texas genealogy, Web sites for, 124
Text files, 63
/THOUGHT (IRC command), 169
A Thousand Genealogy Links, 115
Thunderstorms, 4
Tiny tafels (TTs), 82, 294–299
Titles, of queries, 48
TMG (*see* The Master Genealogist)
TNRoots-L mailing list, 103
Tolerance, on Usenet, 83
Tombstones, mailing list for, 103
Too Many Consecutive Transmit Errors error message, 304
Too Many Users error message, 303
TOSSPAM (AOL keyword), 28
Tracking Your Roots, 126

Transmission Control Protocol/Internet Protocol (TCP/IP), 18–19
Traveller Southern Families, 126
Treasure Maps: The How-To Genealogy Site, 126
Treasure Maps Newsletter, 105
TTFN (chat shorthand), 175
TTs (*see* Tiny tafels)
TTYL (chat shorthand), 51, 175
TUCOWS, 153

U

UART (*see* Universal Asynchronous Transmitter and Receiver)
UBE (*see* Unsolicited bulk email)
UDSL (*see* Universal DSL)
Ultimate Family Tree, 38
Unable to Locate Host error message, 303
Unable to Resolve Host error message, 303
Unarj.exe, 61
Uniform Resource Locators (URLs), 20–23
  clipboard, copying to, 111
  entering, 23
  retrieving, 112
"Uninspected" files, 62
Universal Asynchronous Transmitter and Receiver (UART), 6–7
Universal DSL (UDSL), 10–11
University of Minnesota, 179, 197
University of Texas at Austin, 191, 192
UNIX, 13, 14
UNIX-to-UNIX encoding, 32
Unknown User error message, 306
Unmoderated newsgroups, 69
Unsolicited bulk email (UBE), 27, 157 (*See also* Spam)
UNSUBSCRIBE message (ROOTS-L), 90
Unsubscribing:
  to ROOTS-L, 90
  unintentional, to mail lists, 94
URLs (*see* Uniform Resource Locators)
U.S. Civil War Units file, 92
U.S. Gazetteer, 126–127
U.S. West, 11
Usenet, 14, 67–86
  access to, 71
  binary files on, 81–82
  with commercial online services, 229

Usenet (*Cont.*):
  error messages, 304–305
  etiquette for, 82–85
  GAQ files on, 82, 85
  genealogy-related newsgroups on, 77–81
  and Golden Gate Genealogy Forum, 249–250
  history of, 70
  Internet vs., 69
  searching for information on, 85–86
  software for, 71–78
    browsers, 75–77
    commercial online services, 75–76, 78
    newsreaders, 71–75
  tolerance for others on, 83
USGenWeb, 127, 137–141
Utah, mailing list for, 103
Utah State Archives, 127
Utilities, general-purpose, 64
UTNetCAT, 191, 192
UUENCODE files, 32, 33
Uuencoding, 81

V

Value Added NewsWatcher, 75
VA-Roots mailing list, 103
VA-WVA-Roots-L mailing list, 103
<vbg> (chat shorthand), 175
Very high bit rate DSL (VDSL), 10
Virginia, mailing list for, 103
Virginia genealogy, Web site for, 122
"Virus-checked" files, 62
Viruses, 36–37, 62–63

W

WARNING: Message Still Undelivered
  After x hours error message, 306
Washington, mailing list for, 103
Web (*see* World Wide Web)
Welcome messages, 95
West Virginia, mailing list for, 103
Western-Roots-L mailing list, 103
WinCode 2.7.3c, 33
Windows 95, 5, 18, 23
Windows 98, 5, 6, 18, 23

Windows Fax, 5
World Wide Genealogy Forum (CompuServe),
  260, 264
World Wide Web (WWW), 109–154, 217–220
  browsing, 110–112
  development of, 19
  finding information on, 145–154
    with AOL NetFind, 146–148
    with Excite, 148, 149
    with file search sites, 153
    with Infoseek, 150–152
    with Lycos, 148, 149
    newsgroups, searching, 154
    with people search engines, 152–153
    with Yahoo!, 149–150
  list of genealogy-related sites on, 112–128
  publishing on, 38–45
  sites hosted by RootsWeb, 183–184
  terminology for, 19–20
  See also specific Web sites
WorldGen Web Project, 183
WRT (chat shorthand), 175
WS_FTP, 24–25
WS_FTP32, 60
WWW (*see* World Wide Web)
Wyoming, mailing list for, 103

X

xDSL (*see* Digital subscriber line)
Xerox Map Server, 127
XXENCODE (.XXE files), 32, 33

Y

Y (chat shorthand), 174
Yahoo!, 149–150, 172
Yourfamily.com, 224–225

Z

.Z files, 61
ZDNet Software Library, 153
.zip files, 61
ZIP format, 61

ABOUT THE AUTHOR

Elizabeth Powell Crowe is the author of three books, including *Genealogy Online AOL Edition*. Besides previous best-selling editions of that book, she also wrote *Information for Sale* with John Everett, and *The Electronic Traveller*, both published by McGraw-Hill. She is contributing editor for *Computer Currents* magazine and author of numerous articles in both popular and technical publications. She lives in Huntsville, Alabama, with her husband and two children.